THE ARDEN SHAKESPEARE

GENERAL EDITORS: HAROLD F. BROOKS AND HAROLD JENKINS

KING LEAR

THE ARDEN EDITION OF THE
WORKS OF WILLIAM SHAKESPEARE

KING LEAR

Edited by
KENNETH MUIR

ARDEN SHAKESPEARE PAPERBACKS

METHUEN & CO. LTD
I I NEW FETTER LANE, LONDON EC4

The general editors of the Arden Shakespeare have been
W. J. Craig (1899–1906), succeeded by R. H. Case (1909–44),
and Una Ellis-Fermor (1946–58).

Present general editors: Harold F. Brooks and Harold Jenkins.
W. J. Craig's edition of *King Lear* first published 1901
It was reprinted six times

Eighth edition (Kenneth Muir), revised and reset, 1952
Reprinted with minor corrections, 1955
Reprinted with further corrections 1957, 1959
Reprinted 1961
Reprinted with corrections, 1963
First published in this series 1964
Reprinted 1965 and 1966
1.3

Printed and bound in Great Britain by
Richard Clay (The Chaucer Press), Ltd, Bungay, Suffolk.

A hardbound, library edition is available
from Methuen & Co, Ltd, London

CONTENTS

GENERAL EDITOR'S PREFACE

WHEN it was proposed, in 1946, to re-issue the Arden Shakespeare, little more was intended than a limited revision, bringing introductions and collations into line with the work of recent years and modifying appendices whenever additions were necessary or the material had been accepted into the common body of knowledge. In the main part of each volume the form of the original page was to be undisturbed, in order that the stereotype plates of those originals might still be used. This meant that practically no alterations could be made in the text, which was based on the Cambridge edition of 1863–6 (revised, 1891–3), and that any alterations in the commentary must be so arranged as to occupy the same space as the notes which they replaced.

It had been recognized from the first that in the case of a few plays it might be necessary to modify this restriction and it soon became clear that the first two volumes, *Macbeth* and *Love's Labour's Lost*, would prove more costly to produce if the stereotypes were retained than if they were abandoned. The two editors, therefore, who had gallantly endeavoured to preserve the original lay-out of the pages, found themselves freed from this necessity when their work was done or partly done, so that much of it had to be done again. As conditions became more stable, it became possible also to consider sparing their successors what they had experienced and at last to allow all editors to start afresh without tying them to the Cambridge text or to the lay-out of the original pages.

Thus a major change of policy came about by degrees, as the conditions of the years immediately after the war began to allow of it, and what had begun as a revision became a new edition.

This meant that publishers, editors, and general editor were faced with an entirely new responsibility: that of establishing the text of each play in place of a text which had hitherto been prescribed. Since we were unwilling to suspend activities until textual critics should be agreed that a text had been established as nearly authoritative for our day as that of the 1891–3 edition was held to be for its own, we decided to continue the work begun, in full awareness of the difficulties involved in publishing an edition such as this at a moment when there is not yet full agreement on a generally acceptable text. Each individual editor would thus be responsible for the text of his play, as well as for the introductions, collations, commentary and appendices.

The policy of the original edition in respect of introductions, commentary and appendices remains what it has always been; the lines laid down by those scholars who first designed its form have proved their worth throughout the past half-century. The introductions, though the emphasis must vary with the nature of the given play, include, together with the results of the editor's own thought and investigation, a survey of as many as possible of those studies which throw light upon the nature of the play or the problems surrounding it. The general commentary, which we have kept in its original position, at the foot of the page, provides such brief notes as may be required for the elucidation of specific passages or textual problems or for general comment and comparison; these often, therefore, serve to illustrate the general account given in the introduction.

The policy in respect of text is of necessity neither so simple nor so consistent as that of the editors of the original series, who were enjoined to use as their base the Cambridge text of 1891–3, and in most cases did so willingly, believing it to be as nearly authoritative as could be. Much has happened in the last fifty years, through the great extension of palæographical, bibliographical and textual scholarship;

and our better understanding of (among other things) the nature and relations of Folio and Quarto texts has led us not always into more certainty, but sometimes rather into wholesome and chastened uncertainty. Each editor's text must now be his individual concern, since each play presents its own group of problems. Some of us may prove to have solved these in a way which posterity will repudiate. But an attempt will be made in every case to present the evidence for the editor's decisions fairly and to give at the same time representation to solutions other than that editor's own.

UNA ELLIS-FERMOR

LONDON, 1952

PREFACE

THIS revision of W. J. Craig's edition has been rendered simpler than it would otherwise have been by the publication of the Shakespeare Association Facsimile of the First Quarto, Dr. J. Dover Wilson's facsimile of the Folio text, Sir Walter Greg's *The Variants of the First Quarto of " King Lear "* (1939–40), and Professor G. I. Duthie's splendid edition (1949). I have used all these; and I have consulted the works listed in Tannenbaum's useful *Bibliography*, besides many more books and articles since published.

It has recently been suggested that a study of all the extant copies of the First Folio would reveal variants comparable in importance with those in the extant copies of the First Folio. As no evidence has yet been produced that the text of *King Lear* contains any substantial variants, I am sceptical of this theory; but I have consulted facsimiles of two different copies of the Folio as well as the two originals accessible in Leeds, without discovering any variants. To have collated all extant copies of the Folio would have involved several years work and the expenditure of several thousand pounds.

I prepared a text of the play some fifteen years ago for an amateur production; but that text has been extensively revised in the light of recent textual study. The Introduction and Appendices are entirely new; Craig's collations have been thoroughly revised; and though many of the notes have been adapted from his, few of them have been left unchanged.

I am indebted to Professor H. Kökeritz, Mr. J. C. Maxwell, Mr. J. M. Nosworthy, and Professor Harold Orton for some valuable suggestions; and to Mr. A. C. Cawley, Mr. H. H. Huxley, Mr. Harold Fisch, Professor P. Alexander, and Mr. J. M. Cameron for help of various kinds.

THE UNIVERSITY OF LEEDS   KENNETH MUIR
Christmas, 1950

During the past year there has been a notable addition to the criticism of the play—*The Dream of Learning* by D. G. James. I am further indebted to Mr. Arthur Creedy, Mr. R. T. Davies, Professor C. O. Brink and Professor Simeon Potter for their assistance.

K. M.

The University of Liverpool
February, 1952

Since the above was written, Miss Alice Walker has twice defended the Quarto text (*M.L.R.* xlvii, pp. 376 ff. and *Textual Problems of the First Folio*, 1953). She suggests that the copy for the First Quarto was provided by the actors who played the parts of Goneril and Regan, and that in those scenes in which they do not appear, where they would have to rely only on the manuscript, their text is better than recent editors have supposed. Although I doubt whether we need assume that two actors were involved, Miss Walker's theory seems to be more plausible than Duthie's. It might therefore be desirable to alter the present text in a few places, but I have preferred to wait until the defenders of the Folio have had their say. I have been criticised, with some asperity, for quoting and rejecting a number of absurd interpretations. Perhaps I have been unduly hospitable, but it may be worth pointing out that I have also been criticised for rejecting the very interpretations which others regard as absurd.

I have taken this opportunity of adding a few notes and making some corrections. I am indebted to Mr. Arnold Davenport, Mr. J. C. Maxwell, and Mr. G. K. Hunter for valuable suggestions.

K. M.

December, 1953

ABBREVIATIONS

Abbott	E. A. Abbott, *Shakespeare Grammar*, 1869.
Bradley	A. C. Bradley, *Shakespearean Tragedy*, ed. 1922.
E. K. Chambers	E. K. Chambers, *William Shakespeare*, 1930.
R. W. Chambers	R. W. Chambers, *King Lear*, 1940.
Coleridge	S. T. Coleridge, *Shakespearian Criticism*, ed. T. M. Raysor, 1930.
Danby	J. F. Danby, *Shakespeare's Doctrine of Nature*, 1949.
Duthie	G. I. Duthie, *King Lear*, 1949.
Furness	H. H. Furness, *King Lear* (Variorum), 1908.
Granville-Barker	H. Granville-Barker, *Prefaces to Shakespeare*, 1, 1927.
Greg	W. W. Greg, *The Variants in the First Quarto of "King Lear,"* 1940.
Heilman	R. B. Heilman, *This Great Stage*, 1948.
Kittredge	G. L. Kittredge, *Sixteen Plays of Shakespeare*, 1946.
Knight	G. Wilson Knight, *The Wheel of Fire*, 1949.
Florio	J. Florio's translation of Montaigne's *Essays* (Temple ed.).
Onions	C. T. Onions, *Shakespeare Glossary*, 1911
Perrett	W. Perrett, *The Story of King Lear*, 1904
Taylor	G. C. Taylor, *Shakespeare's Debt to Montaigne*, 1925.

E.L.H.	*English Literary History.*
E.S.	*English Studies.*
M.L.N.	*Modern Language Notes.*
M.L.Q.	*Modern Language Quarterly.*
M.L.R.	*Modern Language Review.*
N.Q.	*Notes and Queries.*
P.M.L.A.	*Publications of the Modern Language Association of America.*
P.Q.	*Philological Quarterly.*
R.E.S.	*Review of English Studies.*
S.A.B.	*Shakespeare Association Bulletin.*
S.P.	*Studies in Philology.*
T.L.S.	*Times Literary Supplement.*
Q 1, Q 2, Q 3	Quartos published 1608, 1619, 1655.
F 1, F 2, F 3, F 4	Folios published 1623, 1632, 1663, 1685.

The usual abbreviations are used for the books of the Bible and for the titles of Shakespeare's plays. (*T.A.* = *Titus Andronicus; Tim.* = *Timon of Athens.*)

INTRODUCTION

1. Text

King Lear was first printed in 1608, the imprint of the
First Quarto (Q 1) being—

LONDON, / Printed for *Nathaniel Butter,* and are to be sold at his
shop in *Pauls* / Church-yard at the signe of the Pide Bull neere /
St. *Austins* Gate. 1608.

This is often known as the " Pied Bull " Quarto. Twelve
copies exist of it, but these are in ten different states because
proof-reading was carried on simultaneously with the
printing. Corrections were made in the formes after the
printing had begun, and corrected sheets were subsequently
bound up with uncorrected sheets. The total number of
variants in the twelve extant copies is 167, though some of
the emendations were incorrect.[1]

The Second Quarto (Q 2), in spite of the evidence of the
title-page (" Printed for Nathaniel Butter. / 1608 "), was
actually printed [2] in 1619 from a copy of Q 1 in which

" sheets D, F, G, H were in the original, and sheets C (probably),
E, K in the corrected state."

The third appearance of the play was in the First Folio
of Shakespeare's plays (1623), where it occupies pages 283-
309 of the section devoted to Tragedies. The Folio text
was printed from a copy of Q 1 in which sheet D was in
the corrected state, sheets H and K in the uncorrected
state, and sheets E and G probably in the uncorrected

---

[1] W. W. Greg, *The Variants in the First Quarto of " King Lear."* Sir Walter
Greg shows that sheets B, I and L exist in only one state; the outer forme of
C exists in one state, the inner forme in three; both the outer and inner formes
of K exist in two states; the outer formes of D, E and G, and the inner formes
of F and H exist in two states.

[2] W. W. Greg, *op. cit.* p. 189. Cf. A. W. Pollard, *Shakespeare's Fight with
the Pirates,* 1920, pp. viii ff. and E. K. Chambers, *William Shakespeare,* 1930,
1. 133 ff.

state. The state of the other sheets is not known.[1] This copy of Q1 had been substantially altered, probably to bring it into line with the prompt-book used by Shakespeare's company. This involved the deletion of some 300 lines of the Quarto text, the addition of some 100 lines which had been omitted from the Quarto, and a very large number of verbal alterations.

A modern editor will, of course, restore these omitted lines, whether his text is based mainly on the Quarto or on the Folio. There is now fairly general agreement that the Folio text is not only more accurately printed, but also much nearer to what Shakespeare wrote, than that of the Quarto. Miss M. Doran, indeed, in her *Text of " King Lear "* (1931), argued that Q was printed from Shakespeare's own autograph MS., and F from a transcript of the same MS. in a later state; but in a later article she seems to withdraw from this position.[2] Mr. M. R. Ridley, in the Preface to his edition (1935), guessed that

" F was set from a better transcript of a common original than that which was available for Q."

His edition follows Q wherever it makes tolerable sense, and sometimes where it does not. He could not have given a more convincing demonstration of the relative badness of the Q text. A third critic, Mr. Van Dam, goes even further.[3] He thinks that Q

" belongs to the class of printed plays nearest to Shakespeare's originals,"

and that F was printed from

" the revised prompt-book, one remove farther from Shakespeare's original than the prompt-book text which served as copy for the Q."

Apart from these three critics, it is generally accepted that Q is substantially inferior to F, and that the latter must therefore serve as the basis of a modern text.

There is less agreement about the reasons for the peculiar nature of the Q text. Sir Edmund Chambers and Sir

---

[1] Greg, *op. cit.* pp. 144-9. [2] *R.E.S.*, 1941, p. 474.
[3] *Materials for the Study of the Old English Drama*, x. (1935), p. 79.

Walter Greg thought that the text was obtained by the use of shorthand during an actual performance. Dr. J. Quincy Adams points to readings in Q which could be explained by the use of Timothy Bright's system of shorthand, *Characterie;* [1] but Miss Doran, Mr. W. Matthews, and Professor G. I. Duthie,[2] who has made a study of the three possible systems of shorthand,[3] believe that they were all too primitive and clumsy to have provided such a text as the Quarto of *King Lear*. Professor Leo Kirschbaum has propounded the theory [4]

" that a bad quarto was created by a reporter's memorizing from a theatrical MS. Mnemonic phenomena which adumbrate a single memory; stage-directions which are like those of the prompt-books; patches of correctly lined blank verse; small patches of perfect reproduction in the midst of wild confusion; isolated bibliographical links of spelling, punctuation, capitalization between the good and bad texts . . . these shew us a reporter imperfectly remembering what he has seen on the written page."

This does not seem to me to be very credible. A man who perused the prompt-book for any length of time would have aroused suspicions unless he were the " book-keeper " himself who is ruled out by other considerations. If, on the other hand, he took the prompt-book away from the theatre, he could have made a copy of it in a shorter time than he would have taken to learn it; and such a surreptitious borrowing would presuppose great carelessness on the part of the book-keeper. Yet *King Lear* does not have quite the same characteristics as known piratical texts, such as the First Quarto of *Hamlet*, where certain parts are more accurately reported than others—presumably because the actors who took those parts were guilty of reconstructing

---

[1] E. K. Chambers, *op. cit.* i. 465-6; Greg, *op. cit.* p. 187. Cf. *Neophilologus,* xviii. (1933), 252-7; *The Library,* xvii (1936-7), 172-183; Greg, *The Editorial Problem in Shakespeare,* 1942, pp. 88-101; Adams, *Modern Philology,* xxxi. 135-63.

[2] Doran, *Modern Philology,* xxxiii. (1935-6), 139 ff.; W. Matthews, *Modern Language Review,* xxvii (1932), 243 ff.; Duthie, *King Lear,* 1949, pp. 73-5; *Elizabethan Shorthand and the First Quarto of King Lear,* 1949.

[3] Bright's *Characterie,* Bales's *Brachygraphie,* Willis's *Stenographie.*

[4] *Modern Language Notes,* 1944, pp. 197-8. Cf. Kirschbaum's *True Text of* " *King Lear* " (1945), where the theory is applied to this play; and *P.M.L.A.,* 1945, pp. 697-715.

the text from memory. In the Quarto of *King Lear*, as Duthie points out,[1]

" there is no consistent variation in the standard of the reporting of the speeches of different characters."

It was left to Duthie to put forward a plausible theory about the Q text. He suggests that it is " a memorial reconstruction made by the entire company," perhaps made

" during a provincial tour, the company having left the prompt-book (and the author's manuscript also, if the prompt-book was a transcript) in London."

There are various difficulties about this theory: some speeches are assigned to the wrong characters in Q, but for this the printer may be to blame; and the stage-directions are so bad that Duthie is constrained to admit that the copy for Q " could not have served conveniently as a prompt-book," and that therefore a transcription was made of the rough copy scribbled at dictation speed.[2] Kirschbaum argues against the theory that bad quartos were stenographic reports by protesting that it is a libel on Elizabethan actors: [3]

" Did the Elizabethan actor customarily jumble his own lines, borrow phrases and lines from other actors, anticipate and recollect his own and other actors' lines, jump ten or more lines because of similar phraseology in two passages, sometimes with the consequent omission of other actors' speeches? "

If, however, we assume that some of the bad quartos were based on memorial reconstructions by actors in the provinces, months or even years after they had last performed the play, it is easy to imagine that their version would be very inaccurate. The comparative accuracy of the Q of *King Lear*—compared, for example, with *Hamlet* Q 1— suggests that the company was at full strength, and that there was no long interval between the last performance and the reconstruction of the prompt-book.

Duthie emphasizes that this is only a working hypothesis; and Kirschbaum has forcibly outlined his objections to it: [4]

---

[1] *Op. cit.* p. 75.   [2] Duthie, *op. cit.* pp. 75-116 (esp. pp. 76-7, 115).
[3] Kirschbaum, *True Text*, p. 6.   [4] *R.E.S.*, April, 1951, p. 169.

" A supposed tour by the King's men in which they did not possess their prompt-book . . . sets up a second hypothesis to bulwark a first hypothesis, that of plural memorial transmission . . . this second hypothesis demands a third to account for the missing prompt-book. And a fourth . . . to explain why actors on a provincial tour should make not an abridged version but one considerably longer than the prompt-book used around 1620 in the city. Furthermore, that Burbadge and his co-actors ' habitually ' delivered their lines as Q gives these lines is an extremely dubious hypothetical corollary to any complex of hypotheses. . . Time after time, for particular Q corruptions Professor Duthie has to give involved explanations in which actor, scribe, and compositor play an unbelievably complex game of simultaneous error."

We may recognize the force of these objections, without necessarily adopting Kirschbaum's own theory of a single reporter.

The present text of the play, therefore, is based on F; but since the F texts of other plays contain numerous errors and " sophistications " (i.e. unauthorized " improvements "), we shall accept Q readings not only where the F readings are manifestly corrupt, but also where Q seems palpably superior. It is not impossible that true readings were preserved by the memories of actors, and so reproduced in Q, though by some accident they have not been preserved in F. Q appeared only three years after Shakespeare wrote the play; and in the fourteen years that elapsed before the Quarto, corrected by the prompt-book, was sent to the printers, errors and deliberate changes would have been made. Moreover, as Greg points out,[1] since the F copy was an altered copy of Q, some mistakes in the latter are certain to have been left uncorrected—

" Thus it is only when the readings of the two differ that there is any strong ground for supposing that the Folio preserves that of the prompt-book; the negative inference, that where the two agree the prompt-book had the same reading, is much weaker. And so we reach the remarkable conclusion that the testimony of the Quarto and Folio together is appreciably less authority than that of the Folio alone."

[1] *Neophilologus*, 1933, pp. 261-2.

We ought therefore to be more prepared to introduce emendations in the text of F where it agrees with Q, than where it differs.

It should be added that Q is punctuated mostly with commas, and that it contains a large amount of mislineation.[1] Even F prints passages as prose which modern editors invariably print as verse.

2. DATE

On 16 March 1603 Samuel Harsnett's *Declaration of Egregious Popishe Impostures* was entered in the Stationers' Register; and as Shakespeare makes considerable use of this book throughout the play we can be certain that it was not written until after that date. From the evidence of the title-page of Q1 and of the Stationers' Register we know that the play was performed on 26 December 1606. The title-page runs as follows—

" M. William Shak-speare: / *HIS* / True Chronicle Historie of the life and / death of King LEAR and his three / Daughters. *With the vnfortunate life of* Edgar, *sonne* / and heire to the Earle of Gloster, and his / sullen and assumed humor of / TOM of Bedlam: / *As it was played before the Kings Maiestie at Whitehall vpon* / *S*. Stephans *night in Christmas Hollidayes.* / By his Maiesties seruants playing vsually at the Gloabe / on the Bancke-side."

Although this Quarto was dated 1608 we know that the Court performance was in 1606, and not 1607, because the entry in the Stationers' Register on 26 November 1607 reads as follows—

" Na. Butter. Io. Busby. Entred for their copie vnder thandes of Sir Geo. Buck knight & Thwardens A booke called. Mr William Shakespeare his historye of Kynge Lear as yt was played before the kings maiestie at Whitehall vppon St Stephans night at Christmas Last by his maiesties servantes playing usually at the globe on the Banksyde   vjd."

---

[1] Duthie, *op. cit.* p. 90, cites Edward Hubler who, in *The Parrot Presentation Volume*, ed. H. Craig, estimates that the verse-lines which Q prints as verse, 650 are divided incorrectly, 1,580 correctly; that 500 lines of verse are printed as prose; and that 61 lines of prose are printed as verse. In an unpublished paper P. Alexander argues that the punctuation of Q resembles that of good quartos.

The play was therefore written between March 1603 and
Christmas 1606.

It is usually assumed that " these late eclipses in the
sun and moon " (I. ii. 107) must have been suggested by
the eclipse of the sun of October 1605, preceded by an
eclipse of the moon in the previous month. Professor
G. B. Harrison, indeed, quotes from a pamphlet entitled
*Strange fearful & true newes which happened at Carlstadt, in the
Kingdome of Croatia*, which was published in February 1606,
and argues that there is a similarity of phrase, sentiment
and rhythm between this passage and the remarks of
Gloucester and Edmund [1]—

" If these mundane & moueable bodies be mutually impressiue
& impressible, nature constant in her Periodes, & reason experience & Iugment in man, be of any power or credit. The
great coniunction of the two superior bodies *Saturne* & *Iupiter*,
constipated with so many seuerall coniunctions and radiations
of other planets, and in the same place very neare, in parle
together as it were for some strange decree of great consequence.
The Earth's and Moone's late and horrible obscurations, the
frequent Ecclipsations of the fixed bodyes; by the wandring,
the [vn-] fixed stars, I meane the planets, within these fewe
yeares more then ordinary, shall without doubt (salued diuine
inhibition) haue their effects no lesse admirable, then the positiues
vnusuall.   Which PEVCER with many more too long to re-
hearse out of continuall obseruation and the consent of all
Authors noted to be, new Leagues, Traytrous Designements,
Catching at Kingdomes, translation of Empyre, downefall of
menn in Authoritye, æmulations, Ambition, Innouations,
Factious Sects, Schisms and much disturbance and trobles in
religion and matters of the Church, with many other thinges
infallible in sequent such orbicall positions and Phænomenes."

If we accepted Harrison's theory we should have to
suppose that *King Lear* was written in the last ten months of
1606.   But astrological jargon inevitably varies little; and
there are closer parallels with Gloucester's remarks in Florio's
Montaigne.   There were several earlier eclipses that would
still be remembered by the audience.   In 1601, for example,
there was an eclipse of the sun on 24 December, preceded

[1] *T.L.S.*, 30 November 1933, p. 856.

by two eclipses of the moon on 15 June and 9 December. But Shakespeare may not have been referring to any particular pair of eclipses; and even supposing a reference was intended to the eclipses of 1605, he might have cunningly inserted the reference because he knew these eclipses were expected later in the year. It is therefore possible that the play was begun before September 1605; or, indeed, that the reference to the eclipses was a later addition. But the most usual hypothesis is that Shakespeare wrote *King Lear* in the winter of 1605-6, and that he used the 1605 edition of *The True Chronicle History of King Leir* which was published after 8 May 1605, when it was entered in the Stationers' Register.

There are three obstacles in the way of this dating. First, the entry for *King Leir* in S.R., referred to the play as a "Tragecall historie." Originally it was called a "Tragedie," but the word has been altered in the Register. This suggests that the story of the play was already known as a tragedy. The title-page of *King Leir* calls it *The True Chronicle History;* and this might seem to show that the mistake in the Register was not due to the publisher.

Secondly, the title-page of the source play proclaims that the text is "as it hath bene diuers and sundry times lately acted." Greg pertinently remarks that he finds

"it very difficult to believe that this respectable but old-fashioned play, dating back in all probability to about 1590 had been 'diuers and sundry times lately acted' in 1605, especially if the playhouse manuscript had been for years in the hands of stationers."

But if the play had not been recently acted it looks very much as though the publishers resurrected the play after a lapse of eleven years, in the hope that it would be mistaken for Shakespeare's new play, or at least derive some reflected glory from it.[1]

W. W. Greg, *The Library*, xx. 381-4. It has been suggested that Scene xxvi of *King Leir* was written not long after the Armada year, or perhaps when the Armada was expected. Another indication of the date is afforded by Daniel's sonnet (*Delia*, 1594) "At the Author's going into Italie." The opening line, "O whither, poore forsaken, shall I goe," resembles *Leir*, 329, "Now whither, poore forsaken, shall I goe." Daniel is thought to have gone to Italy before 1590. There is a similar line in *Mucedorus*. There are close parallels with *Edward II* and *Richard III;* but it is impossible to tell in what order *King Leir* and these two plays were written.

Thirdly, there is not much doubt that *Macbeth* was written by the summer of 1606; and if *King Lear* has to be dated early in 1606, Shakespeare must have been working overtime. Metrical tests, for what they are worth, tend to show that *King Lear* was written before *Macbeth*. It would be easier in some ways, therefore, if we could push back *King Lear* into the winter of 1604-5. The relationship of Shakespeare's play to *King Leir* is discussed on a later page; it need only be said here that this is not an insuperable objection to dating the play before the publication of *King Leir*.

It has recently been argued [1] that Shakespeare was influenced by William Strachey's sonnet "On Sejanus," published with Jonson's play after 6 August 1605—

" How high a Poore man showes in low estate
  Whose Base is firme, and whole Frame competent,
That sees this *Cedar*, made the Shrub of Fate,
  Th'on's little, lasting; Th'others confluence spent.
And as the Lightning comes behind the Thunder
  From the torne Cloud, yet first inuades our Sense,
So euery violent Fortune, that to wonder
  Hoists men aloft, is a cleere euidence
Of a vaunt-curring blow the *Fates* have giuen
  To his forst state; swift Lightning blindes his eyes,
While Thunder, from comparison-hating Heauen,
  Dischargeth on his height, and there it lyes:
If men will shun swolne *Fortunes* ruinous blastes,
Let them vse Temperance. Nothing violent lastes."

The idea of the lightning as a vaunt-courier is used by Lear in his address to the storm; and he uses *invades* in the same metaphorical sense (III. iv. 7). It may be added that the phrases " poor man . . . in low estate," " fortune's ruinous blasts," and " violent fortune " may be compared with Desdemona's " downright violence and storm of fortunes " as well as with the opening lines of Act IV of *King Lear*. Here Edgar mentions " the lowest and most dejected thing of Fortune," and he proceeds virtually to identify fortune and the wind—

" The wretch that thou hast blown unto the worst
  Owes nothing to thy blasts."

[1] Cf. G. Ashe, *N.Q.*, 25 November 1950.

But it would appear that Strachey, not Shakespeare, was
the debtor; and this means that the storm-scenes of *King
Lear*, and possibly the opening lines of Act IV, must have
been written by 2 November 1604, when *Sejanus* was first
registered, unless we assume that the sonnet could have
been added to the copy for the play after it had been licensed.
In any case, there is good reason to believe that *King Lear*
was partly written by 6 August 1605; and, taken in con-
junction with other evidence, the connection of the play
with Strachey's sonnet establishes the winter of 1604-5
as the most probable date.[1]

If *King Lear* was written in the winter of 1604-5 the date
would fit in with the political situation, for between 1604
and 1607 King James was trying to get Parliament to approve of the union of England and Scotland and referring
in speech after speech to the misfortunes that division brought
to early Britain.[2]   Professor Draper thinks that Shakespeare
intended his play to illustrate the evils of disunion.[3]

This dating receives some support from the verbal
affiliations of *King Lear* with *Othello*, *Measure for Measure*,
and *Timon of Athens*, which appear to be more substantial
than those with *Macbeth* and *Antony and Cleopatra*.   *Othello*
was probably written before the publication of the First
Quarto of *Hamlet;* [4] and Bradley has pointed out a number
of striking parallels between *Othello* and *King Lear*.[5]   They
include words which are not used by Shakespeare except

---

[1] Mr. Ashe thinks that Strachey collaborated with Jonson in the first
version of *Sejanus*, and with Shakespeare in the writing of *King Lear* and *Timon
of Athens*.   There is no direct evidence that Strachey was a dramatist, though
he is known to have been a poet.   He was a Cambridge graduate, and the
word *sizes* is used in *King Lear* (II. iv. 177) in a specifically Cambridge sense;
but even if this use was confined to Cambridge men, Shakespeare might have
picked it up from Strachey or another.   The references to fortune in Strachey's
sonnet do not particularly resemble the allegory of fortune in *Timon*.   The
word *confluence*, used once in *Timon*, is also to be found in Florio's translation
of Montaigne, from which Shakespeare may have taken it.   As he uses the
word *estate* nearly sixty times at all periods of his career, we can deduce nothing
from the eight appearances of the word in *Timon*. Cf. *N.Q.* 6 Jan. 1951.

[2] J. W. Draper, *Studies in Philology*, 1937, pp. 178-85.

[3] Shakespeare's company visited Dover on 4 October 1605; but as there
had been a previous visit in September 1597, we need not suppose that the
description of Dover Cliff was inspired by the 1605 visit.

[4] Cf. A. Hart, *T.L.S.*, 10 October 1935.

[5] *Shakespearean Tragedy*, ed. 1922, pp. 441-3.

in these two plays,[1] several words which are used in a sense peculiar to the two plays,[2] and two or three phrases.[3]

There are fewer verbal echoes of *Measure for Measure* in *King Lear*, but we may notice the phrase " furred gown " which appears in both plays,[4] " unaccommodated " which is linked with " accommodations," [5] " warped " used only in these plays and in *All's Well that Ends Well*,[6] and " evasion " used only in these plays and in *Troilus and Cressida*.[7] More significant, perhaps, is the fact that themes dealt with in *Measure for Measure* recur in *King Lear*: the truancy of the Duke may be compared with Lear's abdication from responsibility; the debate on justice and authority which runs all through *Measure for Measure* reappears in the mad scenes of *King Lear*; the idea of " the oddest frame of sense " in madness is repeated in the " reason in madness " of the King; [8] the Duke's advice to Claudio in prison and his later comfort to Isabella [9]—

" That life is better life, past fearing death,
     Than that which lives to fear."—

look forward to several of Edgar's speeches; and his words [10]
     " O our lives' sweetness,
     That we the pains of death would hourly die
     Rather than die at once."—

recall Claudio's fight for life. The sentence " Keep me in patience " occurs in both plays; [11] and the next words in *Measure for Measure*—
          " and with ripen'd time
          Unfold the evil which is here wrapt up
          In countenance! "—

[1] E.g. waterish, besort, potential, unbonetted, deficient.

[2] E.g. decline (I. ii. 73; *O.* III. iii. 265), slack (II. iv. 247; *O.* IV. iii. 88), poise (II. i. 120; *O.* III. iii. 82), commit (III. iv. 81; *O.* IV. ii. 72), secure (IV. i. 20; *O.* I. iii. 10).

[3] E.g. fortune's alms (I. i. 278; *O.* III. iv. 122), stand in hard cure (III. vi. 103; stand in bold cure, *O.* II. i. 51), safer sense (IV. vi. 81; my safer guides, *O.* II. iii. 205), perforce must wither (IV. ii. 35; needs must wither, *O.* v. ii. 15). Cf. note on v. iii. 276.

[4] IV. vi. 167; *M.M.* III. ii. 8. Also used by Florio. Cf. Appendix.

[5] III. iv. 109; *M.M.* III. i. 14.

[6] III. vi. 53; *M.M.* III. i. 142; *A.W.* v. iii. 49.

[7] I. ii. 132; *M.M.* I. i. 51; *T.C.* II. i. 75, II. ii. 67, II. iii. 123.

[8] *M.M.* v. i. 61.   [9] *M.M.* v. i. 402.   [10] v. iii. 184.

[11] *M.M.* v. i. 116.

seem to be echoed in two passages in *King Lear* [1]—

> " Time shall unfold what plighted cunning hides; "
> " in the mature time "

and Isabella's lines about Angelo [2]—

> " His filth within being cast, he would appear
> A pond as deep as hell."—

have been used by Dr. Edith Sitwell as a commentary on
Edgar's words: " Nero is an angler in the lake of darkness."

There are many resemblances between *King Lear* and
Timon of Athens.   The theme of ingratitude is prominent
in both; both have many references to the lower animals;
both stress the natural goodness of the poor in contrast to
the viciousness of the rich; and their versification is similar.
Bradley also draws attention to a number of verbal parallels,[3]
and to a resemblance between the Fool's words and song in
II. iv. and the Poet's allegory of Fortune in the opening
scene of *Timon of Athens*.[4]   But if there is structural weakness
in *Timon of Athens*, few critics would now agree with Bradley
when he finds it in *King Lear* also.

These links with other plays suggest that *King Lear*
may well have been written soon after *Measure for Measure*
and *Othello*, and not long before *Timon of Athens*.[5]

3. SOURCES

One of the sources of *King Lear* was an old chronicle
play which had been published in 1605, *The True Chronicle
History of King Leir*.   From its nature this play would seem
to belong to the sixteenth century; and it so happens that
a *kinge leare* was performed at the Rose Theatre by the
combined Queen's and Sussex's men during an unsuccessful
season early in April 1594.   It was not then a new play
and it probably belonged to the Queen's men.   On 14 May
of the same year the play was entered in the Stationers'
Register, though no edition is known to have appeared for

---

[1] I. i. 280.   IV. vi. 277.   [2] III. i. 93-4.   Cf. note *loc. cit.*
[3] I. iv. 157 (*T.* II. ii. 122); IV. i. 20 (*T.* IV. iii. 76); II. iv. 175 (*T.* v. i. 134).
[4] II. iv. 67 ff.
[5] This date would also fit in with the possibility that Shakespeare was influenced by the madness of Bryan Annesley.   See note on p. xliii *post.*

eleven years.[1]   No one knows who wrote the play, though
H. Dugdale Sykes argued strongly for Peele's authorship.[2]
It is by no means a good play, and few people will see any
substance in the perverse view of Tolstoy:

" However strange this opinion may seem to worshippers of
Shakespeare, yet the whole of this old drama is incomparably
and in every respect superior to Shakespeare's adaptation.   It
is so, firstly, because it has not got the utterly superfluous
characters of the villain Edmund and the unlifelike Gloucester
and Edgar, who only distract one's attention; secondly, because
it has not got the completely false effects of Lear running about
the heath, his conversations with the fool and all these impossible
disguises, failures to recognize, and accumulated deaths; and
above all, because in this drama there is the simple, natural,
and deeply touching character of Leir and the yet more touching
and clearly defined character of Cordella, both absent in Shakespeare.   Therefore there is in the older drama—instead of
Shakespeare's long drawn scene of Lear's interview with
Cordelia and of Cordelia's unnecessary murder—the exquisite
scene of the interview between Leir and Cordella, unequalled
by any in all Shakespeare's dramas." [3]

A brief summary of the plot of *King Leir* will show the
extent to which Shakespeare deviated from it.   In the first
scene, Leir plans a sudden strategem to trick Cordella
into marriage:

> " fayre *Cordella* vowes
> No liking to a Monarch, vnlesse loue allowes . . .
> Yet, if my policy may her beguyle,
> Ile match her to some King within this Ile . . .
> I am resolu'd, and euen now my mind
> Doth meditate a sudden stratagem,

[1] Cf. W. W. Greg, *The Library*, xx. 378-9; E. K. Chambers, *William
Shakespeare*, i. 469; S. Lee, *Leir*, 1909, pp. x-xvi.

[2] H. D. Sykes, *Sidelights on Shakespeare*, 1919, pp. 126-42.   He mentions a
number of words and phrases which appear in Peele's known works and also
in *King Leir*.   Some of these are too common to tell us anything about the
authorship, e.g. " To be enrolled in chronicles of fame "; " The truest friend
that ever "; " good fellows."   Even " heir indubitate " (*Leir*, 42) is to be found
not in Peele's acknowledged works, but in two plays Sykes has elsewhere
argued to be his, *The Troublesome Raigne* and *Alphonsus*: and it is to be found in
Warner, *Albion's England*, viii. 38.   Lee, *op. cit.*, p. xxi, argues against Peele's
authorship because his plays were not published anonymously.   He suggests
that it may have been written by the author of *Locrine* or by William Rankins.

[3] *Tolstoy on Shakespeare*, 1907, pp. 43-4.

> To try which of my daughters loues me best:
> Which till I know, I cannot be in rest.
> This graunted, when they ioyntly shall contend,
> Each to exceed the other in their loue:
> Then at the vantage will I take *Cordella*,
> Euen as she doth protest she loues me best,
> Ile say, then, daughter, graunt me one request,
> To shew thou louest me as thy sisters doe,
> Accept a husband, whom my selfe will woo.
> This sayd, she cannot well deny my sute . . .
> Then will I tryumph in my policy,
> And match her with a King of Brittany."

The honest Perillus (Kent) comments on this scheme:

> " Thus fathers think their children to beguile,
>   And oftentimes themselues do first repent,
>   When heauenly powers do frustrate their intent."

Leir's plan is betrayed to Gonorill and Ragan by the time-serving Skalliger (Sc. 2). The wicked sisters, who are jealous of Cordella, flatter their father and promise to marry anyone he may appoint. Cordella refuses to flatter and Leir, though not banishing her, determines to divide the kingdom between her sisters (Sc. 3). The Gallian King decides to visit Brittayne in disguise to see whether Leir's three daughters are as beautiful as they are reputed to be (Sc. 4). Accompanied by the bluff Lord Mumford he woos and weds Cordella, whom he meets bewailing her lot (Sc. 7). Meanwhile Cornwall and Cambria draw lots for their shares of the kingdom, and Perillus makes an ineffectual attempt to prevent Cordella from losing her share (Sc. 6). These seven scenes of the old play Shakespeare condenses into one; and some critics have argued that his first scene is a failure. Professor Allardyce Nicoll, for example, declares that the author of the old play [1]

" At least provided his main characters with normal and appreciable motives, whereas Shakespeare has left us with something which simply cannot be tolerated on the stage, for to find an explanation of Lear's decisions and demeanour in this first scene we need to know the subsequent development of the plot; by themselves they are perfectly unintelligible."

[1] *Studies in Shakespeare*, 1927, pp. 154-5.

Yet it is perfectly possible to perform the first scene of *King Lear* in such a way as to make the motives of the three sisters intelligible; and the irrationality of Lear is ultimately more credible, and certainly more tragic, than the futile cunning of his prototype. The scene is a kind of prologue; and by making it as short as possible Shakespeare was able to concentrate on the tragic results of the King's foolishness.

The old play continues with a scene in which Perillus laments Leir's stupidity, though he decides not to desert him (Sc. 8). Leir is ill-treated by his favoured daughters, and the Gallian King decides to send ambassadors to invite him to visit Gallia (Sc. 9-16). The man bribed by Ragan to murder Leir is stricken with remorse just as he is about to do the deed (Sc. 17-19). Cordella and her husband decide to go in disguise to Brittayne, accompanied by Mumford (Sc. 20-1). But Leir and Perillus escape to Gallia and there encounter the Gallian King, Cordella and Mumford, disguised as countryfolk. Leir is reconciled to his daughter (Sc. 22-4). The Gallian King invades Brittayne on Leir's behalf, defeats the army of Cornwall and Cambria, and reinstates Leir who, we assume, lives happily for the rest of his life (Sc. 25-32). There is nothing about Cordella's death, whether by murder or suicide. It will be noticed that there is no equivalent here for the story of Gloucester. Leir is not so old as Shakespeare's hero—nor is he in any of Shakespeare's sources—and he is lachrymose and pathetic, without the rage, the energy, or the tragic grandeur of Lear. He is driven out, but not into a storm; and he never loses his sanity. Shakespeare omits Ragan's direct attempt on her father's life; he adds the Fool; and he substitutes the banished Kent for the unbanished Perillus.

There are some resemblances between the two plays in thought and expression, though the extent of Shakespeare's echoes has been variously estimated. Sir Walter Greg details some forty parallels, but some of these might easily be accidental.[1] The " single-line asides in which Cordella comments on the protestations of her hypocritical sisters," and the scene in which Leir and Cordella kneel to each

---

[1] *The Library*, xx. 386-97.

other were clearly remembered by Shakespeare, the latter
both in the reconciliation scene and in the scene where Lear
and Cordella are led away to prison [1]—

> " O, look upon me, sir,
> And hold your hand in benediction o'er me;
> No, sir, you must not kneel."

> " When thou dost ask me blessing, I'll kneel down
> And ask of thee forgiveness."

In the old play Leir and Cordella keep on kneeling and rising
until the scene topples over into absurdity; and before they
have finished the Gallian King and Mumford also join in.
But Shakespeare realized the inherent pathos of the scene,
and transmuted it for his own purposes.

The following verbal parallels are mostly taken from
Greg's list, though a few have been added.   Ragan's words
to Leir (269-70)—

> " I haue right noble Suters to my loue,
> No worse than kings, and happely I loue one . . ."

may be echoed in Cordelia's lines (i. i. 100)—

> " Happily when I shall wed,
> That lord whose hand must take my plight shall carry
> Half my love with him."

Leir's words (512)—

> " I am as kind as is the Pellican "—

may have suggested (iii. iv. 76)—

> " Judicious punishment! 'twas this flesh begot
> Those pelican daughters."

Perillus's description of Leir (755)—

> " But he, the myrrour of mild patience,
> Puts vp all wrongs, and neuer giues reply."

certainly resembles Lear's words (iii. ii. 37)—

> " No, I will be the pattern of all patience;
> I will say nothing."

Leir's remark to Gonorill (844)—

> " poore soule, she breeds yong bones."—

---

[1] Cf. *Leir* (Malone Society), 254, 274, 2295 ff.   Three scenes are given in
the Appendix, pp. 221-34.

and her reply, in which she uses the same phrase, may have suggested Lear's curse (II. iv. 164)—

> " Strike her young bones,
> You taking airs, with lameness! "

Leir remarks to Perillus (1111)—

> " think me but the shadow of my selfe."—

and the phrase may have suggested the Fool's retort (I. iv. 239), " Lear's shadow." Cambria declares (1909) that

> " The heauens are iust, and hate impiety ";

Edgar tells his brother that

> " The Gods are just,[1] and of our pleasant vices
> Make instruments to plague us."

Leir's words, not spoken in Ragan's presence (2144)—

> " Ah, cruell *Ragan*, did I giue thee all."—

are echoed in Lear's words to Regan (II. iv. 252)—

> " I gave you all."

But perhaps the most significant parallel is the last. Perillus upbraids Gonorill with the words (2581)—

> " Nay, peace thou monster, shame vnto thy sexe,
> Thou fiend in likenesse of a human creature."

Four lines later, Leir asks Ragan " Knowest thou these letters? "—letters which she snatches and tears. In *King Lear*, Albany urges Goneril (IV. ii. 59)—

> " See thyself, devil!
> Proper deformity shows not in the fiend
> So horrid as in woman; "

and in the last scene he says to her (v. iii. 154)—

> " Shut your mouth, dame,
> Or with this paper shall I stople it . . .
> Thou worse than any name, read thine own evil!
> No tearing, lady; I perceive you know it.
> *Gon.* Say, if I do! the laws are mine, not thine;
> Who can arraign me for't?
> *Alb.* Most monstrous! Oh!
> Know'st thou this paper? "

[1] Cf. III. iv. 36, " show the heavens more just."

" Shame," " fiend," and " know'st thou " are common to
both passages; " monster," " sex " and " these letters "
are echoed in " monstrous," " woman " and " this paper ";
and the stage direction in the old play was remembered in
Shakespeare's " no tearing."   This last parallel can hardly
be put down to coincidence; and Greg thinks [1] that cumu-
latively the parallels show that as Shakespeare wrote—

" ideas, phrases, cadences from the old play still floated in his
memory below the level of conscious thought, and that now and
again one or another helped to fashion the words that flowed
from his pen."

He believes, in fact, that there is clear evidence that Shakespeare had read *King Leir* carefully not long before he wrote
his own play.   Elsewhere, Greg pointed out two apparent
echoes of *King Leir* in *Hamlet;* and from this he deduces
that Shakespeare must have read the old play in manuscript.[2]
But is it really necessary to suppose that Shakespeare had
read *King Leir?*   If echoes of Coleridge's reading could
coalesce years later in *The Ancient Mariner*, echoes which are
in some instances closer than anything of *Leir* in *Lear*, why
could not Shakespeare have got all he needed from memories
of the old play which he might have seen performed in
1594, or before?   From such a performance, ten or fifteen
years before, he might well have recalled the main outlines
of the piece, as well as a few vivid scenes and chance phrases.
It might even be suggested that there is a possibility that
Shakespeare acted in *King Leir;* and as Perillus is on the
stage when all save one of the above parallel passages are
spoken, that may have been Shakespeare's role.

Shakespeare had doubtless read Holinshed's account,
and seen the cut illustrating Cordeilla's suicide with a
dagger; but he borrowed little from it.   Goneril's line—

" Sir, I love you more than word can wield the matter "—
is fairly close to Holinshed's version—

" she loued him more than toong could expresse; "

---

[1] *Op. cit.* p. 397.
[2] *T.L.S.* 9 March 1940.   The passages are *Leir* 1467 ff. and *Ham.* III. iii.
73 ff.; *Leir* 2453-62 and *Ham.* v. i. 16 ff.   The second of these seems to be
a valid parallel; but it is possible that Shakespeare and the author of *Leir*
both echoed the Ur-*Hamlet.*

but Cordelia's answer—

> " I love your majesty
> According to my bond; no more nor less "

is not, except in the last few words, very close to Holinshed—

" I protest vnto you, that I haue loued you euer, and will continuallie (while I liue) loue you as my naturall father . . . assertaine your self, that so much as you haue, so much you are worth, and so much I loue you, and no more."

From Holinshed, too, Shakespeare may have derived the ducal titles of Cornwall and Albania, though he gives Goneril and Regan to the alternative husbands. Perrett has suggested that Cordelia's avowal of disinterestedness (IV. iv. 23 ff.)—

> " O dear father,
> It is thy business that I go about; . . .
> No blown ambition doth our arms incite,
> But love, dear love, and our aged father's right."—

was inserted in the play because in Holinshed's account Cordeilla is not entirely disinterested—

" Aganippus caused a mightie armie to be put in readinesse, and likewise a great nauie of ships to be rigged, to passe ouer into Britaine with Leir his father in law, to see him againe restored to his kingdome. It was accorded, that Cordeilla should also go with him to take possession of the land, the which he promised to leaue vnto hir, as the rightfull inheritour after his decesse, notwithstanding any former grant made to hir sisters or to their husbands in anie maner of wise."

Greg shows [1] that the treatment of a foreign invasion of England was a ticklish business for a dramatist of Shakespeare's day, and he argues that Cordelia persuaded her husband

---

[1] *M.L.R.* 1940, pp. 431-46. Greg seeks to show that when France and Cordelia " planned their invasion, they cannot possibly have known of Lear's rejection by his elder daughters, for the simple reason that it had not yet happened "; and he suggests that France " incensed at some fresh insult to Cordelia, departed in a rage, determined to wrest by force her portion from . . . Albany and Cornwall. Such is the situation when France and Cordelia land at Dover." This is to scrutinize the chronology of the play too curiously, for an invasion could not in any case be planned and executed in the two or three days that have elapsed since the first scene of the play—as Greg himself points out.

" to abandon his purpose of wresting a portion of the kingdom for himself and retire to his own land, thus leaving her free to use his army in defence of her father."

From Spenser's account in *The Faerie Queene*, Shakespeare probably derived the form of Cordelia's name and also her death by hanging, a method of suicide dictated to Spenser by his need of a rhyme:

> " And ouercommen kept in prison long,
> Til wearie of that wretched life, her selfe she hong."

Many critics have echoed Johnson's complaint that

" Shakespeare has suffered the virtue of Cordelia to perish in a just cause, contrary to the natural ideas of justice, to the hope of the reader, and, what is yet more strange, to the faith of the chronicles."

But in all the sources known to have been used by Shakespeare, with the one exception of the old play, Cordelia commits suicide. By telescoping the battle fought by Cordelia to restore Lear to the throne with the one in which she is captured by her foes, Shakespeare humanizes the plot. He gives Cordelia a comforter in prison, " the father she herself has saved from despair." [1] He removes " the cruel feature which Geoffrey's story shares with the Greek tale of Antigone ": Cordelia is slain—but not by herself. It has been suggested that Gloucester's words (IV. vi. 39)—

> " My snuff and loathed part of nature should
> Burn itself out "—

may have been derived from Spenser's lines—

> " But true it is, than when the oyle is spent,
> The light goes out, and weeke is throwne away ";

but the comparison of human life to a lamp was a commonplace.

There is some evidence that Shakespeare had read John Higgins's account of Cordila in the 1574 edition of *The Mirror for Magistrates*. The agreement that Lear

> " threescore knightes and squires
> Should alwayes haue, attending on him still at cal "

***

[1] R. W. Chambers, *King Lear*, 1940, p. 21.

may be compared with Goneril's reference to " a hundred knights and squires "; and the subsequent reductions of the train were followed by Shakespeare. Higgins makes Cordila tell how, on hearing of the ill-treatment of her father, she

> " besought my king with teares vpon my knee,
>   That he would aide my father ";

and Cordelia says (IV. iv. 26) that France

" My mourning and importun'd tears hath pitied."

The lines contrasting Cordila's former life with that in prison—

" From sight of princely wights, to place where theues do dwel:
   From deinty beddes of downe, to be of strawe ful fayne '

may be compared with Cordelia's lines (IV. vii.)—

> " And wast thou *fain*, poor father,
>   To hovel thee with swine and rogues forlorn,
>   In short and musty *straw*? "—

and the vision of Despair, inciting Cordila to suicide, may be compared with Edmund's lines—

> " To lay the blame upon her own despair,
>   That she forbid herself."

Higgins, alone of the authors Shakespeare is likely to have read, speaks of the " king of *Fraunce* "; he, unlike the author of *Leir*, Spenser, and Holinshed, uses the form " Albany "; he alone gives the evil sisters their Shakespearean husbands; and his spelling of Gonerell is nearer to Shakespeare's than Gonorilla or Gonorill. His King of France " deemde that vertue was of dowries all the best "; and Shakespeare's declares that " She is herself a dowry " [1] (I. i. 241). Higgins, finally, provided a hint for " What need one? " [2] (II. iv. 265)

---

[1] Greg compares Holinshed's words, " onlie moued thereto . . . for respect of hir person and amiable vertues."

[2] Greg compares Holinshed again: " scarslie they would allow him one seruant to wait vpon him."

The above discussion of Shakespeare's treatment of his sources owes a good deal to the exhaustive work by W. Perrett, *The Story of King Lear*, 1904. Cf. pp. 189, 214-5, 274. He points out that " & squires " is omitted in the 1587 edition of *The Mirror for Magistrates* in the first of the above quotations, and that Cordila's tears are omitted from the second passage. This would seem to prove that Shakespeare used the 1574 or 1575 editions of *The Mirror*: but in the lines—

> " Bereaude him of his seruantes all saue one,
> Bad him content him self with that or none."

It is likely that the old play gave Shakespeare the idea of writing on King Lear; but he had long been familiar there is one passage in the 1587 edition, and not in the earlier ones, which is close to Cordelia's speech (I. i. 95-104):—

> " For nature so doth binde and duty mee compell,
> To loue you, as I ought my father, well.
> Yet shortely I may chaunce, if Fortune will,
> To finde in heart to beare another more good will.
> Thus much I sayd of nuptiall loues that ment."

Shakespeare, as Mr. Perret suggests, might have derived Cordelia's lines from Camden's *Remaines* (1605): " Yet she did think that one day it would come to pass that she should affect another more feruently, meaning her Husband, when she was married, who, being made one flesh with her, she was to cleave fast to, forsaking Father and Mother, kiffe and kin." The only other evidence that Shakespeare had read Camden's *Remaines* is the Fool's remark (I. iv. 208), " That's a shealed peascod," which may be compared with Camden's reference to Richard II's device of " a Pescod branch with the cods open, but the Pease out, as it is vpon his Robe in his Monument at Westminster." Shakespeare, perhaps, might have picked this up for some other source; and he could easily have invented, or borrowed from the marriage service, Cordelia's reference to conjugal duties. The possibility that Shakespeare consulted two editions of *The Mirror for Magistrates* is supported by another faint parallel with the 1587 edition which substitutes " Their former loue and friendship waxed cold " for the line in the 1574 edition, " Thought well they might, be by his leaue, or sans so bolde." Cf. I. ii. 110, " Love cools, friendship falls off." (Cf. note on III. vi. 6-7.)

Perrett also argues (*op. cit.* pp. 280 ff.) that Shakespeare, led by a marginal note in Holinshed, had also consulted Geoffrey who describes the distribution of two-thirds of the kingdom immediately after Goneril and Regan have given their answers. Only two accessible sources (Geoffrey and Perceforest) suggest that there was to be an unequal division, the best share going to Cordelia. The pretexts for reducing Lear's train are also to be found in Geoffrey, and in no other known version accessible to Shakespeare. Perrett thinks that Geoffrey's Lear is closer to Shakespeare's in character than any other; and he points out some possible verbal echoes (cf. I. i. 252, 255; I. ii. 186). Shakespeare might have invented these details independently, or used another source no longer extant. Perrett's analysis of the various versions of the Lear story is nevertheless very informative. These versions include those of Henry of Huntingdon (1139), Wace (1155), Layamon (c. 1205), Robert of Gloucester (1300), Robert Mannyng (1338), Caxton (1480), Fabyan (1516), Polydore Vergil (1534), Stow (1565), and some forty others. D. F. Atkinson (*E.L.H.*, 1936, pp. 63-6) has suggested the possibility that Shakespeare was influenced by Gerard Legh's *The Accedens of Armory*, 1562, fol. 165. Legh emphasizes Leir's rage at Cordeilla's answer: " his irefull hart straight braided out wrothful wordes of wreke and reuenge: enforcyng her to shun the rage, thus thundered out against her." In none of the versions certainly used by Shakespeare does Lear tell Cordelia to avoid his presence; but such a detail requires no source.

with the versions of Holinshed and Spenser, and also with *The Mirror for Magistrates*. As we have seen, he was cheerfully eclectic in his use of sources, combining details and phrases from each. On the one hand he rejected the happy ending of *King Leir*, and gave form to its formlessness; on the other hand he rejected the undramatic elements of the versions of Spenser, Holinshed, and Higgins, in which the defeat and suicide of the heroine come as an epilogue irrelevant to the story of Lear himself. The suicide of Cordelia would have been intolerable to a sensitive audience, and her murder necessitated the punishment of the guilty: Goneril and Regan could not be suffered to escape, if Cordelia were to die; and Lear could not, without anticlimax, be restored to the throne. Out of a moral story with a happy ending and an irrelevant, despairing epilogue, Shakespeare created a homogeneous tragedy. Some of the means of bringing about this transformation were to be found in the source of the underplot.

It is well known that the story of the Paphlagonian King in Sidney's *Arcadia* provided Shakespeare with the Gloucester underplot. Sidney drew special attention to the episode,[1] with the remark that it was

" worthy to be remembered for the unused examples therein, as well of true natural goodnes, as of wretched ungratefulness."

Gloucester's words (I. i. 32)—

" He hath been out nine years, and away he shall again "—

may have been suggested by the remark that Plexirtus was " called home by his father." [2] Edgar's disguise as a beggar may have been prompted by the plight of the Paphlagonian King, with alms his " onelie sustenaunce." [3] The storm may be derived from the " haile," " the pride of the wind," and " the tempests furie " of " so extreame and foule a storme." [4] Gloucester's reference to " unnatural dealing " (III. iii. 2) may be taken from Sidney's phrase describing the " vnnaturall dealings " of the wicked

---

[1] F. Pyle, *M.L.R.*, October 1948, pp. 449-55.   [2] Cf. Pyle, *op. cit.*
[3] Cf. Pyle, *op. cit.*   [4] Cf. Appendix, p. 243.

son.   Regan's complaint that the blinded Gloucester moves all hearts against them (IV. v. 10) and her promise that

> " Preferment falls on him that cuts him off "

may be derived from the words of Leonatus—

" In deede our state is such, as though nothing is so needfull vnto vs as pittie, yet nothing is more daungerous vnto vs, then to make our selues so knowne as may stirre pittie."

The duel between Edgar and Edmund may be traced to Shakespeare's preoccupation with the chivalric *Arcadia*.[1] Both Gloucester and Lear die partly of joy. Gloucester's " flawed heart," on his becoming reconciled to Edgar,

> " Alack! too weak the conflict to support!
> 'Twixt two extremes of passion, joy and grief,
>   Burst smilingly ";

and Lear dies believing that Cordelia, after all, lives. The hint for both scenes is to be found in Sidney's words [2]—

" After he had kist him, and forst his sonne to accept honour of him (as of his newe-become subiect) euen in a moment died, as it should seeme; his hart broken with vnkindnes & affliction, stretched so farre beyond his limits with this excesse of comfort, as it was able no longer to keep safe his roial spirits."

Shakespeare, then, took rather more than the bare bones of the underplot from *Arcadia*. The characters, too, of the blind King, and of the good son, Leonatus, are not unlike those of Gloucester and Edgar. Edmund, in his relations with Goneril and Regan, exhibits characteristics which are not to be found in Plexirtus; and, while he is flamboyantly hypocritical in the early part of the play, there is no reason to suspect the genuineness of his repentance in the last scene, in contrast to Plexirtus who in defeat merely

" thought better by humblenes to creepe, where by pride he could not march."

Mr. Fitzroy Pyle has argued further that [3] the main plot of the play may also be influenced by *Arcadia*, not merely in

---

[1] F. Pyle, *op. cit.*

[2] R. W. Chambers, *King Lear*, 1940, p. 44 and Perrett, *op. cit.* p. 212. Shakespeare uses the word *long-engraffed* (I. i. 297); both Sidney and Florio use *engraffed*.   Cf. also note on IV. i. 10.   [3] *Op. cit.*

the parallelism of the good and evil children in both plots—
a father receiving kindness from the child he has wronged
and evil from the child he has favoured—but also because
Sidney's story is more tragic than that of *King Leir*. It
presents

" evil at the height of its power, ruthless, tyrannical, utterly
destructive and sadistic, drying up through fear the springs of
human feeling in ordinary men. Goodness, in the persons of
the two principal characters, is intellectually far inferior, suffers
in consequence grievous affliction of mind and body, and shows
strength only in resignation, kindness of heart, and service gladly
given. In the handling of the story there is a hint of that
largeness of scope and suggestiveness that belongs to high tragedy.
. . . Surely it would seem that in transforming the *King Leir*
play Shakespeare's imagination was fired less by it than by the
' source ' of his Gloucester plot."

Sidney's king does not live happily ever after; and it is
pointed out in different parts of *Arcadia* [1] that

" To be fit to govern country or dependants we must learn to
govern ourselves, that whoever breaks the marriage bond
' dissolues al humanitie,' and that the laws fold us within assured bounds, ' which once broken mans nature infinitely
rangeth '."

Shakespeare, Mr. Pyle concludes, made this familiar
doctrine

" the basis of his whole play and explored it in all its ramifica-
tions—even to the length asserted by Sidney, that when the
bounds of law are broken we should be glad ' we may finde any
hope that mankind is not growen monstrous '."

Another critic has suggested that the Gloucester plot
may have been influenced by another chapter in *Arcadia*.[2]
The story of Plangus, son of the King of Iberia, introduces
a stratagem similar to Edmund's when he wishes to persuade his father of Edgar's guilt—

" He would bring him into a place where he should heare all
that passed. . . . The poore Plangus (being subiect to that only
disadvantage of honest harts, credulitie) was perswaded by him."

---

[1] Pyle, *op. cit.* and Sidney, *Works*, ed. Feuillerat, ii. 175, 94, 195-6.
[2] D. M. McKeithan, *University of Texas Bulletin*, 8 July 1934, pp. 45-9.
Cf. Sidney, *op. cit.* II. xv. 249-9, 246-7 and *Lear*, I. ii. 36-90.

Later on, Plangus is discovered, as Edmund describes Edgar, " in the dark, his sharp sword out "—

" The frightened old man called his guard, who found indeed *Plangus* with his sword in his hand."

Plangus's stepmother defends him to his father in such a way as to make the latter more suspicious. She would tell him—

" I dare take it upon my death, that he is no such sonne, as many of like might have bene, who loved greatnes so well, as to build their greatnes upon their fathers ruine."

Soon, we are told,

" all *Plagus* actions began to be translated into the language of suspition."

Shakespeare would have found this story only a few pages after that of the Paphlagonian King.

Between the stories of the Paphlagonian King and of Plangus there is a dialogue in *terza rima* between Plangus and Basilius, which is supposed to be versified by Basilius himself from an actual conversation. The general tenor of the debate between the two men about the rights and wrongs of suicide, on the justice of the gods, and on the slaughter of the innocent, may have caught Shakespeare's eye before he wrote of the attempted suicide of Gloucester and of the death of Cordelia. Plangus, like Gloucester, contemplates suicide because he thinks that men are merely

> " Balles to the starres, and thralles to Fortunes raigne;
>> Turnd from themselves, infected with their cage,
>> Where death is feard, and life is held with paine.
> Like players pla'st to fill a filthy stage.
>> Where chaunge of thoughts one foole to other shewes,
>> And all but jests, save onely sorrowes rage.
> The child feeles that; the man that feeling knowes,
>> With cries first borne, the presage of his life,
>> Where wit but serves, to have true tast of woes . . .
> Griefe onely makes his wretched state to see
>> (Even like a toppe which nought but whipping moves)
>> This man, this talking beast, this walking tree.
> Griefe is the stone which finest judgement proves:
>> For who grieves not hath but a blockish braine,
>> Since cause of griefe no cause from life removes."

With these lines may be compared several passages in *King
Lear*—

> " As flies to wanton boys, are we to the gods;
> They kill us for their sport."   (IV. i. 36-7)

> " O! our lives' sweetness,
> That we the pain of death would hourly die
> Rather than die at once! "   (v. iii. 184-6)

> " I am even
> The natural fool of fortune."   (IV. vi. 192-3)

> " We came crying hither:
> Thou know'st the first time that we smell the air
> We waul and cry. . . .
> When we are born, we cry that we are come
> To this great stage of fools.   This' a good block! "
>   (IV. vi. 180-5)

> " Howl, howl, howl, howl!   O, ye are men of stones! "
>   (v. iii. 257)

It will be noticed that Sidney's " blockish " follows soon
after " stage " and " fools," just as Lear's obscure word
" block " follows immediately after " stage of fools."   The
cause of Plangus's grief is that Erona, whom he loves, has
been unjustly condemned to death.   Basilius, however,
warns Plangus not to blaspheme and argues, much as
Edgar does, that if we could see clearly we should know
that the gods were just.   Plangus's repeated question,
" Must *Erona* dye? ", and his complaint that the gods fail
to answer prayers—

> " Let doltes in haste some altars faire erect
> To those high powers, which idly sit above,
> And vertue do in greatest need neglect "—

may be compared with the juxtaposition of Albany's prayer
for the safety of Lear and of Cordelia, and Lear's entrance
with her dead body.   There is also a resemblance between
Basilius's words—

> " But such we are with inward tempest blowne
> Of mindes quite contrarie "—

and Lear's remark (III. iv. 12) about the tempest in his mind.[1]

---

[1] Cf. Muir and Danby, *N.Q.*, 4 February 1950, pp. 49-51.   See also notes
on IV. vi. 139 and IV. iii. 18.

Yet another critic has argued that Shakespeare derived " one of his best-known images " and perhaps " some of the interpretations of God and nature found in King Lear " from an episode in the third book of *Arcadia;* but the two conceptions of nature to be found both in *King Lear* and *Arcadia* are also to be found elsewhere.[1]

Lamb thought that " the situation of Andrugio and Lucio " in Marston's *Antonio and Mellida* (III. i.) resembled that of Lear and Kent.[2] There is a closer parallel with the same dramatist's *The Malcontent* (IV. iii.), in which Pietro, in disguise, describes his own feigned suicide by leaping from a cliff into the sea. This scene may have given a hint to Shakespeare when he wrote of Gloucester's attempted suicide.[3] Some details of the mad scenes in *Titus Andronicus* are repeated in *King Lear*. Marcus kills a fly with " slender gilded wings " (III. ii. 61. Cf. *Lear*, IV. i. 36, IV. vi. 115); Titus gets Lucius to try his skill at archery (IV. iii. Cf. *Lear*, IV. vi. 87); he solicits the gods for justice (IV. iii. 15, 39, 49-51, 79); he produces an imaginary petition (IV. iii. 105. Cf. *Lear*, IV. vi. 140) and he uses the words [4]—

" I am not mad; I know thee well enough."

The Aaron-Tamora-Saturninus triangle resembles the later triangle of Edmund-Goneril-Albany; and Aaron has something in common with Edmund.

Shakespeare's use of two other books, Harsnett's *Declaration* and Florio's translation of Montaigne, is discussed in the Appendix.[5]

This account of the sources of the play may serve to throw some light on Shakespeare's method of creating a unity from heterogeneous materials. When he amplified and complicated his original fable, his *donnée*, he pressed

---

[1] William A. Armstrong, *T.L.S.*, 14 October 1949. Cf. Sidney, *op. cit.* III. x. 406-10 and *Lear*, IV. i. 36-7, IV. ii. 32-3, IV. iii. 34-6.

[2] C. Lamb, *Specimens*, 1890, p. 66.

[3] Seneca's *Thebais* opens with a long scene in which Oedipus asks Antigone to let him stumble over a precipice.   [4] IV. vi. 179.

[5] Shakespeare took Edgar's dialect in IV. vi. from *The London Prodigal*, a play performed by his company. Roland M. Smith (*M.L.Q.* 1946 pp. 153 ff.) argued that Shakespeare derived some details of the play from R. Johnson's *Tom a Lincolne* (1607); but the resemblances appear to be fortuitous.

into his service incidents, ideas, phrases, and even words from books and plays; and the remarkable richness of texture apparent in *King Lear* may be explained, at least, in part, by Shakespeare's use of such a method. It is difficult to agree with Mr. Richard H. Perkinson who, while admitting Shakespeare's purposeful rearrangement of his material, asserts [1] that he was

" content to utilize the loose episodic structure associated with the chronicle play,"

and that he deliberately sacrificed the probability of his sources. The play, far from exhibiting any signs of loose, episodic structure, is more closely knit than any of the tragedies, except *Othello*.

4. *King Lear*, 1605-1950

King Lear, as we have seen, was probably performed early in 1605, with Burbage in the title-role and Armin as the Fool. A few years later we hear of the play being performed by Sir Richard Cholmeley's players at Gowthwaite Hall in Yorkshire on Candlemas 1609-10. The actors, who were apparently recusants, used the published Quarto. Lear was probably played by Christopher Simpson, the Fool by William Harrison, and Cordelia by Thomas Pant.[2]

---

[1] *Philological Quarterly*, xxii (1943), 315-29. It will have been noticed that in none of the fifty or sixty versions of the Lear story in existence before Shakespeare's play does the old king go mad. This may well have been Shakespeare's own invention; but he may have been acquainted with the story of Sir Brian Annesley, a gentleman pensioner of Queen Elizabeth, who in October 1603 was " altogether unfit to govern himself or his estate." Two of his daughters, Lady Wildgoose and Lady Sandys, tried to get him certified as insane, so that they could get his estate; but the youngest daughter, Cordell, wrote to Cecil, claiming that her father's services to the late queen " deserved a better agnomination, than at his last gasp to be recorded and registered a Lunatic," and urging that he and his estate be put under the care of Sir James Croft. When Annesley died, the Wildgooses contested the will, but it was upheld by the court of Chancery. A few years later, early in 1608, Cordell Annesley married Sir William Harvey, the widower of the Dowager Countess of Southampton, and thus the step-father of Shakespeare's patron. It is possible, therefore, that Lear's madness was suggested to the poet by the madness of Annesley and the loyalty of his Cordelia. (Cf. G. M. Young, *Today and Yesterday*, 1948, pp. 300-1; Salisbury MSS. ix., 1930, 262, 266; C. C. Stopes, *The Third Earl of Southampton*, 1922, p. 274.)

[2] Cf. Sisson, *R.E.S.*, 1942, pp. 134-43.

To judge from the records of performances, the play seems to have been less popular than *Hamlet* or *Othello*. After the Restoration, it was acted by Betterton who first used the text more or less as Shakespeare wrote it and then, after 1681, Tate's notorious adaptation which held the stage for a century and a half. Garrick, though he omitted many of Tate's additions, retained the interpolated love scenes between Edgar and Cordelia, and also the happy ending. Addison complained that the play in Tate's version had lost half its beauty; [1] but the actors cannot be severely blamed since several critics approved of the happy ending. Samuel Johnson himself confessed—

" I was many years ago so shocked by Cordelia's death, that I know not whether I ever endured to read again the last scenes of the play till I undertook to revise them as editor."

At the beginning of the nineteenth century, critical opinion turned against the happy ending, and Lamb attacked it in a famous essay [2]—

" It is not enough that Cordelia is a daughter, she must shine as a lover too. Tate has put his hook into the nostrils of this Leviathan, for Garrick and his followers, the showmen of the scene, to draw the mighty beast about more easily. A happy ending!—as if the living martyrdom that Lear had gone through —the flaying of his feelings alive, did not make a fair dismissal from the stage of life the only decorous thing for him. If he is to live and be happy after, if he could sustain this world's burden after, why all this pudder and preparation—why torment us with all this unnecessary sympathy? As if the childish pleasure of getting his gilt robes and sceptre again could tempt him to act over again his misused station—as if at his years, and with his experience, anything was left but to die."

In 1823, Kean, influenced mainly by Lamb and Hazlitt, restored the tragic ending, though he still kept the love-scenes, and still excluded the Fool. It was not until 1838 that Macready, with some misgivings, reintroduced the Fool. Later in the century, there was a notable production

---

[1] Cf. *The Spectator*, 16 April 1711. D. Nichol Smith, *Shakespeare in the Eighteenth Century*, 1928, pp. 20-5, has an account of the versions of *King Lear* between 1681 and 1823.

[2] *Works* (ed. W. Macdonald), iii. p. 33.

in which the stars were Henry Irving and Ellen Terry; and during the last twenty years there have been several notable Lears, including Gielgud, Devlin, Wolfit, and Olivier. In the 1950 season at Stratford-on-Avon, Geilgud gave a magnificent performance, which was prevented from achieving its full effect only by the unsatisfactory staging of the storm scenes.

There is comparatively little criticism of the play before the nineteenth century. Joseph Warton's papers in *The Adventurer* (1753-4) and Richardson's *Essays* (1784) are not without interest; and if Warton complains that the plot of Edmund against his brother " destroys the unity of the fable," that the blinding of Gloucester ought not to be exhibited on the stage, and that the cruelty of the daughters is too savage and unnatural, he calls attention to many good qualities in the play, including the judicious contrast between the assumed madness of Edgar and the real distraction of Lear.

With Lamb's essay, mentioned above, Coleridge's lectures, Hazlitt's *Characters of Shakespeare's Plays* (1817), and occasional comments by Keats and Shelley, we arrive at a conception of the play not essentially different from that generally held to-day. Schlegel was the first to realize the dramatic function of the underplot (1808). There have been scores of interpretations of the play since the Romantic period, including those of Dowden (1875), Bradley (1904), Swinburne (1909), Wilson Knight (1930), R. W. Chambers (1940), Bickersteth (1947), Heilman (1948), and Danby (1949), to all of which we shall have occasion to return.

5. THE PLAY

Exasperated by the difference between his experience as a reader of *King Lear* and his experience of Tate's version in the theatre, Lamb proclaimed that the play could not be represented on the stage. Bradley, likewise, argued that it was too huge for the stage. Other critics have followed suit; and it has recently been stated [1] that

---

[1] Tucker Brooke, *Essays on Shakespeare*, 1948, p. 57.

" by the verdict of criticism and theatrical experience alike, King Lear is a poor stage play."

A few critics have realized that a poor stage play is, when all qualifications have been made, a poor play. This, in fact, was Thackeray's opinion [1]—

" We all found the play a bore. . . . It is almost blasphemy to say that a play of Shakespeare's is bad; but I can't help it, if I think so."

Professor Allardyce Nicoll argued some years ago [2] that

" Shakespeare, through exhaustion or haste, had failed to think out the scheme and possibilities of King Lear as he had thought out and considered the scheme and possibilities of Othello ":

and Mr. J. Middleton Murry complains that the play is lacking in poetic spontaneity.[3] Shakespeare, he believes, was " working against his natural bent." He was " spurring his imagination, which in consequence was something less than imagination." In spite of the pains lavished by Shakespeare on the play, Mr. Murry thinks that Coriolanus is much finer, and that it represents

" the return from effort to spontaneity, from artefact to creation, from inhumanity to humanity."

Perhaps the explanation of this singular judgment is to be found in Murry's belief that Shakespeare had experienced his plays before writing them. He found it intolerable to believe, we may suppose, that Shakespeare had experienced the suffering that lies at the heart of King Lear, just as once, as he confesses, he averted his eyes from the Crucifixion. That this is a plausible explanation can be seen from remarks he lets slip in his chapter on the play. He speaks of Shakespeare's " uncontrollable despair " of his " horrible primitive revulsion against sex." The play is an " exploitation of partial despair," " an enforced utterance " made at a time when silence would have been " more wholesome and more natural." It was Shakespeare's " deliberate prophylactic against his own incoherence." Murry's verdict remains astonishing if only because he so seldom disagrees

---

[1] Letters, ed. Ray, 1945, ii. 292.   [2] Studies in Shakespeare, 1927, p. 157.
[3] J. M. Murry, Shakespeare, 1936, pp. 337-51.

with Keats; and Keats has described for us in unforgettable lines his own sensations about the play [1]—

" Once again the fierce dispute
Betwixt damnation and impassion'd clay
Must I burn through ";

and in one of his letters he declared [2] that

" The excellence of every art is in its intensity, capable of making all disagreeables evaporate, from their being in close relationship with Beauty and Truth. Examine *King Lear*, and you will find this exemplified throughout."

This intensity has been recognized by most competent critics, and it was this that led Coleridge to call the play [3] " the most tremendous effort of Shakespeare as a poet," and made Shelley describe [4] it as " the most perfect specimen of dramatic poetry existing in the world." It might, nevertheless, be a great poem and a bad stage play, either because it makes impossible demands on the actor, or because of alleged faults of construction more apparent to the spectator than to the reader. Yet in our own time the play has been strikingly successful on the stage, the role of Lear having been filled creditably, and even brilliantly, by actors who have failed in the supposedly easier parts of Macbeth and Othello; and few readers of Harley Granville-Barker's *Preface* would be prepared to deny the adequacy of Shakespeare's dramatic technique or the actability of the play. Lamb thought that the storm scenes were the most difficult to perform; but if Lear is permitted to act the storm (as his speeches suggest he should) and if the stage effects are neither too realistic nor too clever, the scenes can be overwhelming.[5]

[1] *Poems*, ed. H. W. Garrod, p. 482.
[2] *Letters*, ed. M. B. Forman, 1948, p. 71.
[3] Coleridge, *Table Talk*, 29 December 1822.
[4] Shelley, *A Defence of Poetry*, 1909, p. 134.
[5] The invention of electric light and the banishment of realistic scenery has simplified the producer's task since the days of Garrick; but in Komisarjevsky's Stratford production a film of storm clouds projected on the cyclorama effectually distracted our attention from what was being said by the actors. On the other hand, those who try to suggest the storm solely by means of canned music have seldom or never obtained satisfactory results. Thunder and lightning are necessary, and if they are used to punctuate, rather than to accompany Lear's words, they need not prevent us from hearing a single one of them.

The mad scenes are perhaps more difficult because some members of every audience are inclined to laugh. The omission of the trial of Goneril and Regan from the Folio has been taken to indicate that this scene was unsuccessful in Shakespeare's lifetime. This would not be at all surprising since the Elizabethans were prepared to find madness entertaining. Even Granville-Barker had doubts about the actability of this scene: [1] but though few members of an audience would spot the Horatian allusions and the Latin puns, the symbolic significance of the trial of the two daughters by a mad beggar, a dying Fool, and a serving-man is perfectly clear. *He hath put down the mighty from their seat, and hath exalted the humble and meek.*

No performance of a great play, or of a great piece of music, can be ideal; but a performance, if not too defective, can give us an experience we should not get from a reading of the text or a perusal of the score at home. Drama, especially, is a communal art, requiring an audience to participate in the performance; and Bradley, with all his critical insight, missed something in his ideal theatre of the mind, that his valet might have got in the gallery of the Lyceum theatre.

It is worth noting that the alleged theatrical weaknesses of the play have been analysed most effectively by Bradley himself who yet seems to have had little experience of the play in the theatre. He complains of the structural weakness of the fourth act and of the first part of the fifth, of the disadvantages of the double action, which in his opinion outweighed the advantages, and of a number of gross improbabilities.[2] He points out, for example, that Edgar would be unlikely to write to Edmund when he could speak with him, and that Gloucester would have noticed the improbability; that Gloucester had no need to go to Dover for the purpose of committing suicide; and that it is strange that he should show no surprise when Edgar drops into dialect during his encounter with Oswald; that there is no good reason why Edgar should not reveal himself to his father, or why Kent should preserve his disguise until the

---

[1] *Prefaces to Shakespeare*, 1927, I. 227.   [2] *Op. cit.*, 1922, pp. 254-8, 445.

last scene; that Edmund, after he has received his fatal wound, delays unnecessarily in telling of the danger to Lear and Cordelia; and that it is absurd for Edgar to return from his hiding-place to soliloquize in his father's castle. Now it is perfectly true that the scene between the mad king and the blinded Gloucester is strictly supererogatory to the plot, but it is never felt to be superfluous, even from the theatrical point of view. Parts of the underplot, especially that which concerns Edmund's intrigues with Goneril and Regan, are not presented in detail, and we are left to piece it together from hints and guesses: this is not a dramatic fault since it has the effect of concentrating our attention on Lear himself. Most of the improbabilities mentioned by Bradley would not be noticed in the theatre, and they cannot therefore detract from the effectiveness of *King Lear* as a stage play. Apart from this, there is something to be said in defence of every one of the improbabilities. Edmund's forged letter, which he pretended was thrown through the window, might be regarded as a more plausible method of broaching conspiracy than by word of mouth because the writer could deny his handwriting, or pretend he was making an assay of his brother's virtue; and Gloucester, having swallowed a camel, was not likely to strain at a gnat. Gloucester decides to jump off Dover cliff primarily because Shakespeare wants all his characters to congregate at Dover for the last act of the play. But it may be argued that the reiterated question, " Wherefore to Dover? ", recalls the cliff to Gloucester's mind, and in his half-crazed state he has an irrational urge to end his life there. The case-histories of suicides contain stranger obsessive characteristics than this. Nor does it seem necessary that Gloucester should express surprise when Edgar begins to speak in dialect. Either he could appear surprised without words, or he could assume that his other senses had become imperfect with the loss of his sight. Shakespeare had prepared the way by making Gloucester comment, earlier in the scene, on the improvement in Poor Tom's speech. Edgar, in real life, would perhaps have revealed himself to his father; but the conventions of romance and of poetic drama do not always coincide with those of real life. Shakespeare reconciles the two by making Edgar refer to his conduct as a " fault," or miscalculation. He had wished, we may suppose, not only to overcome his father's desire for suicide, but also to convince him that the gods were not spiteful. He may also have delayed the revelation of his identity in order to impose a penance on his father, and to guarantee the genuineness and permanency of his repentance. R. W. Chambers, not altogether fancifully, thinks that Gloucester, guided by Edgar, is climbing the mountain of Purgatory [1]—

" We begin to see the world as Keats saw it—not so much as a Vale of Tears as a Vale of Soul-making."

There is, too, a suggestion that Edgar wished to rehabilitate himself in the eyes of the world, and punish Edmund, before revealing himself. There is nothing improbable in any of these motives, and the dramatist is bound to explain only those things that would otherwise seem incredible. Indeed, a certain mystery in the characters prevents them from seeming mechanical, just as in real life we can classify our acquaintances, not our friends. A similar defence may be offered of Kent's wish to conceal his identity. Edmund's delay in revealing the danger to Lear and Cordelia may be explained by his loyalty to Goneril, or by the gradual workings of repentance; [2] and Edgar appears to return to his father's courtyard only on a stage with representational scenery—on Shakespeare's own stage the presence of Kent in the stocks would be forgotten, and the audience would certainly not assume that Edgar was in the neighbourhood of the castle. [3]

[1] *Op. cit.* p. 48. Cf. Keats, *Letters*, 1948, pp. 355 ff.

[2] Cf. Masefield, *Shakespeare*, p. 193 and G. W. Knight, *The Wheel of Fire*, 1949, p. 206.

[3] Bradley has other perplexities, to which I append short answers. (1) Why should Edgar meekly avoid his father? (Because Edmund had made him believe that his life is in danger.) (2) Lear speaks of having to dismiss fifty followers, though Goneril has not mentioned a number. (Perhaps Lear hears during his brief absence from the stage that Goneril had dismissed half his train before consulting him on the matter; or maybe he is a telepathist.) (3) Lear and Goneril both send off messengers and tell them to bring back an answer, though both are following them with the greatest speed. (Presumably both Goneril and Lear expected to meet their returning messengers on the road. Kent and Oswald, however, are both commanded by Regan to follow her to Gloucester's house.) (4) Why does Burgundy rather than France

The improbabilities, then, are unlikely to be noticed during a performance; and those detected in the study can be explained away in the study. On the question of time, indeed, as we have seen,[1] Shakespeare preserves a calculated vagueness. We are allowed to think that the King of France invades Britain because of the ill-usage Lear has received from Goneril and Regan, though he could not have heard of Lear's sufferings before the invasion had been set in motion. If we notice the impossibility we are driven to believe that the motive of the invasion is to recover by force Cordelia's share of the kingdom; but this is later contradicted by Cordelia's own claim that the invasion is entirely in her father's interest. This confusion, which could be avoided only by slowing up the action, was the result of cunning rather than carelessness. The same thing may be said of Shakespeare's treatment of place. The vagueness is apparently designed [2]

" to prevent topographical difficulties impeding the rapidity of the action."

have the first refusal? (Because Lear does not wish to insult France by offering Cordelia's hand without a dowry.) (5) Why does Shakespeare neglect to tell us about the fate of the Fool? (There is no particular reason, except novel-readers' insatiable curiosity, why we should be told. It is appropriate that the professional jester should fade out when he is no longer needed.) (6) When Lear arrives at Gloucester's house the Fool implies that most of his train have deserted him; but Regan says that he is attended with a desperate train, and we hear in Act III that he has thirty-six knights in quest of him. (Shakespeare wished to give the impression in II. iv. that Lear was deserted by his followers. The thirty-six " hot questrists " seem to have just arrived at Gloucester's house in III. vii., following Lear from Goneril's; but even if they had arrived earlier, and they are the desperate train mentioned by Regan, who is hardly a reliable witness, they might be regarded by Kent as a small train compared with Lear's accustomed escort.) (7) In IV. iii., Kent refers to a letter sent to Cordelia, though it had been a verbal message (III. i.). (He may have sent a letter as well as a verbal message, or Shakespeare may have forgotten, or hoped that his audience had.) (8) Kent, on finding the King in the storm, does not halloo as he had arranged to do. (Either the actor could insert an halloo, or else the King's plight made Kent forget the arrangement.) (9) Cordelia does not reveal Kent's identity to the gentleman, in spite of the promise in III. i. (Perhaps Shakespeare changed his mind.)

It may be admitted that in Nos. 7, 8 and 9, Shakespeare was guilty of trivial inconsistencies; but they would certainly not be noticed during a performance. And it may be worth while to mention that all three relate to two scenes that are textually unreliable. There are cuts in III. i. in both Q and F; and IV. iii. is omitted by F altogether.

[1] Cf. p. xxxiii *ante*.   [2] Greg, *M.L.R.*, 1940, p. 432.

So much for the alleged faults of *King Lear* as an acting play. We may turn now to broader questions of interpretation.

R. G. Collingwood has remarked [1] that

" apart from the idea of the family, intellectually conceived as a principle of social morality, the tragedy of Lear would not exist."

One theme of the play, expressed in plot and underplot, is the parent-child relationship. To a child, the father may be " both loved protector and unjustly obstructing tyrant "; and to a parent the child may be " both loving supporter of age and ruthless usurper and rival." [2] This ambivalent attitude is distributed between the good and evil children of Lear and Gloucester.[3] Lear has reached the age when he should " renounce love, choose death, and make friends with the necessity of dying." [4] The play opens with his decision to abdicate, so that he may crawl unburthened towards death; but the love-test he imposes shows that he still retains the desire for love, and his actions in the first scene reveal only too plainly that he wishes to retain the authority he is ostensibly renouncing. This is a universal theme; for though, since a king has more to renounce than a subject, Lear's royalty is important, yet, as Goethe pointed out [5]—

" *Ein alter Mann ist stets ein König Lear,*"

because he is reluctant to admit that the young have lives of their own to lead, and because there is always a conflict between youth and age. Children often seem to their parents to be ungrateful; and the old must in some degree be deserted by the young. But in *King Lear* such common human feelings are magnified. The selfishness and ingratitude of children, no longer trammelled by the restraints

---

[1] *The Principles of Art*, 1938, p. 295.

[2] M. Bodkin, *Archetypal Patterns in Poetry*, 1934, pp. 15-16.

[3] In *The Master Builder* the ambivalence is expressed in the single figure of Hilda who is loved and feared by Solness, and who loves and destroys him.

[4] S. Freud, *Collected Papers*, iv. (1934), 236. Cf. G. Orwell, *Polemic*, March 1947; W. Empson, *The Structure of Complex Words*, 1951, p. 125.

[5] Goethe, *Gedichte*, 1925, ii. 103. (" An aged man is always a King Lear.") The poem is quoted by G. Landauer, *Shakespeare*, 1920, ii. 127.

of morality nor modified by filial affection, are projected
into the monstrous figures of Goneril and Regan; and
family bickering is enlarged into an internecine struggle,
destroying the peace of Britain, and accompanied by a
storm in the cosmos itself.

The play is not only a tragedy of parents and children,
of pride and ingratitude: it is also a tragedy of kingship.
Power corrupts not only the possessor's capacity for loving,
but the spontaneity of others' love. He can never be sure
that the professed love of friends and relations is disinterested, since it may easily be purposeful flattery. What
is more, the appetite for flattery grows by what it feeds on;
those who refuse to flatter are hated and banished, while
the flatterers are rewarded. In the first scene of the play,
Lear is a foolish old man who has been described [1] with
pardonable exaggeration as an

" arrogant old idiot, destitute of any decent human quality and
incapable of any reasonable act,"

who is led in the vanity of dotage to stage a scene to gratify
his craving for affection. When Cordelia refuses to barter
her love for material profit, Lear banishes both her and the
one man who dares to take her part. This violation of the
duties of kingship is the initial deed from which the tragedy
springs. As the play progresses, Lear's subconscious realiza-
tion that he has committed a sinful mistake gradually rises
into his consciousness. The cruelty of Goneril and Regan
makes him admit that he has banished the one daughter
who loved him disinterestedly; but it is not until near the
end of the second act that he experiences an emotion not
purely egotistical—when he argues the difference between
the bare animal necessities and human needs. In the storm,
more sinned against than sinning, Lear learns " the art of
our necessities," and so becomes aware of the common
humanity he shares with the poor naked wretches. He
exhorts pomp to "shake the superflux to them," as Gloucester
was later to pray that distribution should

> " undo excess,
> And each man have enough."

[1] By Bridie.

The repetition is significant, and it completely disproves Schücking's argument that as Shakespeare elsewhere displays little social sense we should not assume that Lear in acquiring this compassion was being purified.[1] Shakespeare, after all, was not cut off from the Christian tradition, with its insistence on the duty of charity;[2] and though he doubtless believed in an hierarchical rather than in an equalitarian society, there is no reason to think that he would have looked on the wish of Lear and Gloucester to shake the superflux to the less fortunate as a symptom of madness.

Yet Lear, on the appearance of Poor Tom, does go mad. Obsessed as he is with the thought of filial ingratitude, it needs only a little shock to drive him over the frontiers of sanity. The Bedlam beggar provides him with a living example of the poverty he has been pitying; and by tearing off his clothes he identifies himself with unaccommodated man, the "poor, bare, forked animal." In one sense this is the central moment of the play—a dramatic answer to the Psalmist's question: "What is man that Thou art mindful of him?" Stripped of his proud array, stripped of everything except the basic necessities, man's life is cheap as beast's. But this is only an interim report on the human condition: it is not the answer provided by the play as a whole.

In the trial scene, Lear is concerned with justice—"a kind of wild justice"—and with the cause of hardness of heart. When he next appears, in the fourth act, we see him in a new stage of self-knowledge. He realises that he has been flattered like a dog, and that a king is merely a man. He inveighs against sex, partly because, as the Elizabethans knew, certain kinds of madness are accompanied by such an obsession, and partly because sexual desire has led to the birth of unnatural children, if indeed their unnaturalness does not prove that their mother's tomb sepulchres an adulteress. Lear returns to the subject of justice and authority in his next long speech. "A dog's obeyed in office." All men are sinners, and successful

---

[1] Schücking, *Character Problems in Shakespeare's Plays*, 1922, p. 186.
[2] Cf. J. F. Danby, *Shakespeare's Doctrine of Nature*, 1949, pp 185-9.

men cloak their crimes and vices by the power of gold. Justice is merely an instrument of the rich and powerful to oppress the poor and weak. But since all are equally guilty, none does offend. Since all are miserable sinners, all have an equal right to be forgiven. This speech continues the analysis of authority begun in *Measure for Measure;* and, as I have suggested elsewhere, the praise of Order and the analysis of Authority may be regarded as the thesis and antithesis of the Shakespearian dialectic.[1] It has often been observed that Lear's diatribes on sex and gold resemble the invective of the disillusioned Timon.

The old Lear died in the storm. The new Lear is born in the scene in which he is reunited with Cordelia. His madness marked the end of the wilful, egotistical monarch. He is resurrected as a fully human being. We can tell from his protest—

" You do me wrong to take me out of the grave "—

that the awakening into life is a painful process. After the reconciliation, Lear makes only two more appearances. In the scene in which he is being led off to prison he has apparently overcome the desire for vengeance: he has left behind him all those attributes of kingship which had prevented him from attaining his full stature as a man; he has even passed beyond his own pride. At the beginning of the play, he is incapable of disinterested love, for he uses the love of others to minister to his own egotism. His prolonged agony and his utter loss of everything free his heart from the bondage of the selfhood. He unlearns hatred, and learns love and humility.[2] He loses the world and gains his soul— " Nothing can be made of nothing"

" We two alone will sing like birds i' the cage;
    When thou dost ask me blessing, I'll kneel down,
    And ask of thee forgiveness."

The play is not, as some of our grandfathers believed, pessimistic and pagan: it is rather an attempt to provide

[1] Cf. K. Muir, *Modern Quarterly Miscellany*, 1947, pp. 64-6. I have borrowed several phrases from this article, " *Timon of Athens* " and the *Cash-Nexus*.

[2] Cf. W. H. Auden's description of parabolic art; but in a later essay, *Horizon*, August 1949, p. 87, Auden argues strangely that since Lear repents he is not a tragic hero.

an answer to the undermining of traditional ideas by the new philosophy that called all in doubt.[1] Shakespeare goes back to a pre-Christian world and builds up from the nature of man himself, and not from revealed religion, those same moral and religious ideas that were being undermined. In a world of lust, cruelty and greed, with extremes of wealth and poverty, man reduced to his essentials needs not wealth, nor power, nor even physical freedom, but rather patience, stoical fortitude, and love; needs, perhaps, above all, mutual forgiveness, the exchange of charity, and those sacrifices on which the gods, if there are any gods, throw incense—

" A life of sins forgiven, of reciprocated charity, of clear vision, and of joyous song—what is this but the traditional heaven transferred to earth? "

asks Bickersteth.[2] J. C. Maxwell is right when he says[3] that

" *King Lear* is a Christian play about a pagan world. . . . The fact that Shakespeare can assume in his audience a different religious standpoint from that of any of his characters gives him a peculiar freedom, and makes possible an unusual complexity and richness."

Some have thought that Shakespeare, as well as Gloucester, believed that

" As flies to wanton boys, are we to the gods:
They kill us for their sport."

Others have supposed that he would have subscribed to Kent's exclamation that the stars governed our condition; or, more plausibly, that he would have agreed with Edgar's stern summing-up—

" The gods are just, and of our pleasant vices
Make instruments to plague us."

But all these, and other, statements about the gods are appropriate to the characters who speak them, and to the

---

[1] T. Spencer, *Shakespeare and the Nature of Man*, 1943, pp. 135 ff.

[2] *The Golden World of " King Lear*," 1947, p. 10.

[3] *M.L.R.* xlv. (April 1950), 142 ff. E. Welsford, *The Fool*, 1935, p. 268, points out " that the metaphysical comfort of the Scriptures is deliberately omitted, though not therefore necessarily denied." See also Oscar J. Campbell, E.L.H., June 1948.

immediate situation in which they are spoken. Shakespeare remains in the background; but he shows us his pagan characters groping their way towards a recognition of the values traditional in his society.

In spite of Swinburne's eloquent pages on *King Lear*,[1] Shakespeare's vision of the world was not essentially pessimistic. The tragic writer is necessarily selective; and it would be as foolish to regard the author of the Romances as optimistic, as to suppose that the author of the Tragedies was necessarily a pessimist. Heroes of Romances survive; heroes of Tragedies usually die. Nor is the world of the tragedies, the world of *King Lear* in particular, exclusively evil. In the other scale we have to put the loyalty of Kent and the Fool, the fortitude and forgiveness of Edgar and Cordelia, the humanity of Cornwall's servant. Nor does evil finally triumph, for the will to power is self-destructive.[2] Heilman shows that the " reason in madness " theme is balanced by that of " madness in reason." The three wicked children are all destroyed by their superficially sane pursuit of self-interest. They all believe in looking after themselves; they all implicitly deny that we are members one of another; they all assume that man is a competitive rather than a co-operative animal [3]—

" But the paradox is that these free minds, unburdened by any conventional or traditional allegiances, become slaves to the uncontrolled animal desire, mechanisms for the attainment of irrational objectives."

Goneril and Regan become centaurs, their rational minds instruments of the animal body. Their moral code, apparently so efficient and utilitarian,

" ruins the basis of human order . . . destroys the soul of its practitioner ";

and yet, in spite of the dreadful cost, it cannot even ensure success in this world. Edmund, who believes only in his own will, and seems at first to be as ruthless as Iago, is moved by the story of his father's death to do some good

[1] *A Study of Shakespeare*, 1918, pp. 171-2; *Three Plays of Shakespeare*, 1909, p. 16.

[2] J. Macmurray, *The Clue to History*, 1938, p. 237.

[3] *This Great Stage*, 1948, pp. 225-53.

" in spite of his own nature "; and he is constrained to
admit that there is a moral order in the universe.

Yet Shakespeare was certainly in a ruthless mood when
he wrote *King Lear*, and his religious attitude provides no
easy comfort, and makes no concessions to sentimentality.
But we see Cordelia and Kent, uncontaminated by the evil
around them; we see Lear and Gloucester painfully learning wisdom; we see Albany increase in moral stature as
he frees himself from his infatuation; and we see Edgar
change from a credulous fool to a brave and saintly champion. " Pessimism does not consist in seeing evil injure
good," said Heilman justly; it is rather the inability to
see good, " or to discover total depravity, but no grace."
It is not pessimism but realism to recognize that without
Edmunds there could be no Cordelias.

But Cordelia dies. To some critics—and even Bradley
seems to be undecided on the question—it would have been
better if Shakespeare had allowed the miseries of Lear to
be concluded in the reconciliation scene. Such critics, if
mistaken, are at least not so far astray as others who have
pretended that Cordelia's death is a punishment for her
original obstinacy. Her death is even less a fitting punishment for her " fault " than Lear's own agony is an appropriate punishment for his foolishness. It is right that
the final scenes of the play should make us shrink, but wrong
that we should wish them altered. When Lear banished
Cordelia and when Gloucester committed adultery they
unleashed horrors—treachery, blindness, madness, murder,
suicide and war—and the innocent are at least as vulner-
able as the guilty. Indeed, it may be said, it is because
of her very virtues that Cordelia is chosen to be a victim of
the ruthless destiny that broods over the tragic scene, just
as in the old legends it was always the pure and innocent
who were chosen to propitiate the dragon, and just as in
ancient Mexico it was always the most beautiful of the captives who were slain on the bloody altar of Tezcatlipoca.
Cordelia's honesty is not the best policy; and her virtue
is literally its own reward. Of those critics who complain
that she died guiltless we can only enquire if they would
rather she had died guilty. There is, of course, something

gratuitous and superogatory about her death, since it could have been averted if Edmund had spoken a few minutes earlier; and Shakespeare seems to underline the futility of Albany's prayer for the safety of Lear and of Cordelia. This does not mean that the gods kill us for their sport: it means simply that they do not intervene to prevent us from killing each other.

But we are mainly concerned with the effect of Cordelia's death on Lear himself. It destroys his dream of a happy life in prison, and it hastens his final dissolution; though his actual death-blow is not his bereavement but his joy when he imagines that Cordelia is not dead after all. That joy was based on an illusion. The earlier joy of reconciliation, however short-lived, was not an illusion: it was the goal of Lear's pilgrimage. His actual death was comparatively unimportant: and a happy ending (in the conventional sense) was unthinkable for one who " had learnt too much too late." [1]

It was Bradley who suggested that the play might be called " The Redemption of King Lear "; and the account given above of the development of his character is partly based on his analysis. Schücking, however, argues [2] that it is not

" really consistent with Shakespeare's philosophy to see in this sequence of events an ascent of the character to a higher plane, a process of purification and perfection."

Lear in his madness

" does little more than follow the beaten track of the melancholy type."

His attacks on society, however profound they may seem, are the result of his mental derangement; and at the end of the play he is not purified by suffering, but rather

" a nature completely transformed, whose extraordinary vital forces are extinguished, or about to be extinguished."

Schücking concludes, therefore, that it shows a complete misunderstanding of the play " to regard Lear as greater at the close than at the beginning." It is true, of course,

---

[1] Mark Van Doren, *Shakespeare*, 1939, p. 250.   [2] *Op. cit.* pp. 186-9.

that some of Lear's most impressive criticisms of society are
spoken in his madness; that he becomes progressively more
feeble; and that in the last scene there are signs of his
approaching dissolution: yet the three moments in the
play crucial to Bradley's theory of Lear's development—
his recognition of error, his compassion for the poor, and
his kneeling to Cordelia—occur either before or after his
madness.[1] His resemblance to the melancholic type [2] is
superficial, though other dramatists had criticized society
through the mouth of a malcontent as Shakespeare did
through the mouth of a madman. Schücking seems to be
only partially aware of the paradox that Lear when ostensibly sane cannot distinguish between Cordelia and her
wicked sisters: he acquires wisdom by going mad, and his
wildest speeches are a mixture of matter and impertinency—
" reason in madness." In the same way, Gloucester before
he lost his eyes was spiritually blind, and could not tell the
difference between a good son and a bad.[3] He confesses
this in the lines—

> " I stumbled when I saw. Full oft 'tis seen,
> Our means secure us, and our mere defects
> Prove our commodities."

The whole play is built on this double paradox, which could
be overlooked only by a critic who was determined to regard
Shakespeare's technique as " primitive." [4]

A good deal of attention has been paid in recent years to
the imagery of *King Lear*. As early as 1879, one industrious
critic pointed out the prevalence of animal imagery—133
separate mentions of sixty-four different animals—and several

---

[1] Cf. I. v. 24; III. iv. 28; IV. vii. 45 ff.

[2] A psychiatrist who took part in a recent amateur production of the
play commented on the clinical accuracy with which Shakespeare depicted
Lear's manic state in IV. vi.

[3] This is why Gloucester's blinding is not an irrelevant horror, and not even
something that should have been described by a messenger. Because of its
importance as a visual symbol it had to be carried out in full view of the
audience. By this means, as J. I. M. Stewart puts it (*Character and Motive in
Shakespeare*, p. 23), Shakespeare achieved " the powerful effect of a suddenly
realized imagery; the oppressive atmosphere of the play here condensing in
a ghastly dew."

[4] Cf. R. B. Heilman, *op. cit.* pp. 41 ff., 173 ff.

later critics have commented on the significance of these figures.[1] This imagery is partly designed to show man's place in the Chain of Being, and to bring out the sub-human nature of the evil characters, partly to show man's weakness compared with the animals, and partly to compare human existence to the life of the jungle. It has been said that a scene by Racine is " the explanation which closes for the time a series of negotiations between wild beasts." There are scenes in *King Lear* to which the description might more aptly be applied. Yet Shakespeare knew, as well as a later poet,[2] that humanity is bound to assert itself:

> " the striped and vigorous tiger can move
> With style through the borough of murder; the ape
> Is really at home in the parish
> Of grimacing and licking; but we have
> Failed as their pupils."

According to Miss Spurgeon,[3] the iterative image of the play is that

" of a human body in anguished movement, tugged, wrenched, beaten, pierced, stung, scourged, dislocated, flayed, gashed, scalded, tortured, and finally broken on the rack."

The image expresses the suffering not only of Lear, but of man; and the suffering itself is perhaps more important than its causes. At times Lear's voice seems to blend with that of Job[4] in demanding of the gods why the righteous man is smitten. Lear is suffering man, *homo patiens;* and throughout the play we hear words that express that suffering by recalling the derivation of *Patience*, and the fortitude needed to bear it.

---

[1] *New Sh. Soc. Trans.*, 1877-9, pp. 385-405; G. W. Knight, *The Wheel of Fire*, 1949, pp. 185 ff.; Spurgeon, *Shakespeare's Imagery*, 1935, p. 342; Bradley, *op. cit.* p. 266; Heilman, *op. cit.* pp. 92 ff., 105 ff. W. H. Clemen, *The Development of Shakespeare's Imagery*, 1951, pp. 133-53.

[2] W. H. Auden, *Another Time*, 1940, p. 52.   [3] *Op. cit.* p. 339.

[4] Cf. Knight, *Op. cit.* p. 191. W. H. Gardner, *Gerard Manley Hopkins*, i. 175, points out that " Job's story is one of trial through suffering, while Lear's is one of purgation; but the stature and bearing of the sufferers give them a universal significance. The storm in *Lear* may be considered as much a symbol of divine intervention and judgement as the lightning and whirlwind which precedes the voice of God in *Job*." That Shakespeare was recalling, perhaps unconsciously, the story of Job can be guessed from Lear's references to boils.

" You heavens, give me that patience, patience I need! "
" I will be the pattern of all patience."
" I will endure."
" Thou must be patient."
" Men must endure . . ."
" The wonder is he hath endur'd so long."

We have already referred to the significance of the images relating to the blinding of Gloucester, and to the double paradox of reason in madness and madness in reason. Another recurrent theme is that of clothes,[1] civilized man being contrasted with essential man. This cluster of ideas shows how wealth can pervert justice, and it reminds us that the lady clad in proud array ought to consider the plight of the poor naked wretches. The rights of the poor, the weak, and the aged are contrasted in the play with the doctrine of the survival of the fittest; and if we are to believe Danby,[2] Shakespeare presents two contrasting views of nature—the traditional view of Hooker and Bacon, which assumes that nature is benignant, rational, and divinely ordered; and the view of the rationalists that man is governed by appetite and self-interest. There is nothing impossible in the assumption that Shakespeare was conscious, in a wider sense, of the two conceptions of nature; for he would have found them in Montaigne, in Sidney, and in Holland's preface to his translation of Pliny. H. F. there contrasts the pagan and the Christian views of nature—

" And though Pliny and the rest were not able by Nature's light to search so far as to find out the God of Nature, who sitteth in the glorie of light which none attaineth, but contrariwise in the vanitie of their imagination bewrayed the ignorance of foolish hearts, some doting upon Nature herselfe, and others upon speciall creatures as their God."

Something has been said of the underplot in the section of the introduction dealing with sources. Schlegel explained that its function was to universalize the tragedy [3]—

---

[1] Cf. p. liv *ante*, and Heilman, *op. cit.* pp. 67 ff.

[2] *Op. cit.* pp. 20 ff. Danby goes on to suggest that Shakespeare was thus dramatizing the conflict between medieval society and nascent capitalism.

[3] *Lectures on Dramatic Art*, 1808.

" Were Lear alone to suffer from his daughters, the impression
would be limited to the powerful compassion felt by us for his
private misfortune.　But two such unheard-of examples taking
place at the same time have the appearance of a great com-
motion in the moral world; the picture becomes gigantic, and
fills us with such alarm as we should entertain at the idea that
the heavenly bodies might one day fall from their appointed
orbits."

Coleridge complained of the gross improbability of the
opening situation of the play; [1] but the improbability is
acceptable during a performance because of the artistic
law that two improbabilities are easier to accept than one.
Furthermore, as Dowden pointed out, [2]

" one story of horror serves as a means of approach to the other,
and helps us to conceive its magnitude."

Wilson Knight has written eloquently on the grotesque
element in the play; [3] and he points out that the Fool
" sees the potentialities of comedy in Lear's behaviour."
Most critics have tended to sentimentalize the Fool; and
Granville-Barker remarks justly that the producer to-day is
faced with the difficulty that the Fool " is all etherealized
by the Higher Criticism." [4]　We are usually told that by
his jests the Fool tries to take Lear's mind off his obsession
with his daughters' ingratitude.　Nothing could be further
from the truth.　Nearly every one of his jests reminds Lear
of the sorrow that is gnawing at his heart.　He may " labour
to outjest " his master's " heart-struck injuries "; but it
might almost be said that these jests, coming on top of
Lear's afflictions, and concerned as they are with the afflictions, help to drive him mad.　He stands, perhaps, for
worldly common sense; [5] he is not without malice, [6] and
he can never forgive Lear's treatment of Cordelia.　He
began to pine away on Cordelia's banishment, and his
bitter jokes continually remind the King of his injustice.
He is " not merely a touching figure who might easily have
been drawn from life "; he is also " the sage-fool who sees

---

[1] *Shakespearian Criticism*, ed. Raysor, i. 59.
[2] *Shakespeare His Mind and Art*, 1879, p. 265.
[3] *Op. cit.* pp. 160 ff.　　　　　　[4] *Op. cit.* p. 200.
[5] Orwell's description cited by Empson.　　[6] Empson, *op. cit.* p. 133.

the truth." [1]   His dramatic function is of great importance.
He provides not so much comic relief as a safety-valve for
the emotions of the audience.   Lear's conduct is absurd,
if judged critically; and the representation of madness is
apt to arouse more laughter than sympathy.   The Fool was
therefore inserted to draw the laughs of the audience, and
so preserve Lear's sublimity.   This is near to Hazlitt's
view.[2]   He declared that

" the contrast would be too painful, the shock too great, but
for the intervention of the fool, whose well-timed levity comes
in to break the continuity of feeling when it no longer can be
borne, and to bring into play again the fibres of the heart just
as they are growing rigid from over-strained excitement."

But Keats was also right when he commented in the margin
of his copy of Hazlitt's book—

" And is it really thus?   Or as it has appeared to me?   Does
not the Fool by his very levity give a finishing-touch to the pathos;
making what without him would be within our heart-reach
nearly unfathomable.   The Fool's words are merely the simplest
translation of Poetry as high as Lear's."

The Fool's character and function are both ambiguous, and
all through the play Shakespeare is continually inverting
the orthodox view of wisdom and foolishness.   In the storm
scenes there is a wild quartet of madness—Lear, Poor Tom,
the Fool, and the elements themselves—in which the Fool
seems almost to stand for sanity.   He fades from the picture
when he is no longer needed, since Lear can act as his own
Fool.   As Miss Welsford says,[3]

" Lear's tragedy is the investing of the King with motley:
it is also the crowning and apotheosis of the Fool."

Hazlitt began his essay on the play with the wish that he
could pass it over, and say nothing about it.   His words
must be echoed by every editor—

" All that we can say must fall far short of the subject, or even
what we ourselves conceive of it."

[1] E. Welsford, *The Fool*, 1935, p. 253.
[2] *Characters of Shakespeare's Plays*, 1926, p. 121.   [3] *Op. cit.* p. 269.

KING LEAR

DRAMATIS PERSONÆ

LEAR, *King of Britain.*
KING OF FRANCE.
DUKE OF BURGUNDY.
DUKE OF CORNWALL, *Husband to Regan.*
DUKE OF ALBANY, *Husband to Goneril.*
EARL OF KENT.
EARL OF GLOUCESTER.
EDGAR, *Son to Gloucester.*
EDMUND, *Bastard son to Gloucester.*
CURAN, *a Courtier.*
OSWALD, *Steward to Goneril.*
Old Man, Tenant to Gloucester.
Doctor.
Fool.
An Officer, employed by Edmund.
Gentleman, Attendant on Cordelia.
A Herald.
Servants to Cornwall.

GONERIL,
REGAN, } *Daughters to Lear.*
CORDELIA,

Knights of Lear's train, Officers, Messengers, Soldiers, and Attendants.

Scene: *Britain.*

KING LEAR

ACT I

SCENE I.—[*A State Room in King Lear's Palace.*]

Enter KENT, GLOUCESTER, *and* EDMUND.

Kent. I thought the King had more affected the Duke
    of Albany than Cornwall.
Glou. It did always seem so to us; but now, in the
    division of the kingdom, it appears not which of
    the Dukes he values most; for equalities are so
    weigh'd that curiosity in neither can make choice
    of either's moiety.
Kent. Is not this your son, my Lord?
Glou. His breeding, Sir, hath been at my charge: I
    have so often blush'd to acknowledge him, that   10
    now I am braz'd to 't.

ACT I

Scene i

A . . . *Palace*] Capell; not in Q, F.   Edmund] *F;* Bastard *Q.*   3.
so] *not in F 2, 3, 4.*   4. kingdom] *F;* kingdomes *Q.*   5. equalities] *Q;*
qualities *F.*   6. neither] nature *Q3.*   11. to 't] *F;* to it *Q.*

Scene i] The opening dialogue
introduces the underplot, and gives
us a glimpse of Kent before his
intervention at l. 120.

1. *had . . . affected*] had more regard for. See *1 Hen. VI.* v. v. 57.

2. *Albany*] Holinshed tells us that
Albany extended "from the river
Humber to the point of Caithness."
Albanacte, who owned it, gave his
name to it.

5. *values*] esteems. Cf. II. ii. 146
and *Hen V.* I. ii. 269.

5, 6. *equalities . . . weigh'd*] equalities, shares are so balanced, one
against the other, or perhaps are so
carefully considered and adjusted.

"Elizabethan usage often pluralizes
abstract nouns when two or more
persons or things are in question."
(Kittredge) F "qualities" has been
accepted by a few editors: it may
be a slip by the compositor, or a
scribal correction (Duthie). But it
may be the correct reading, and
refer to the mental and moral qualities of the dukes.

6, 7. *that . . . moiety*] That the
most careful scrutiny of either share
could not induce either of the dukes
to prefer his fellow's portion to his
own.

6. *curiosity*] the most minute and
scrupulous attention or examination.

3

Kent. I cannot conceive you.

Glou. Sir, this young fellow's mother could; where-
upon she grew round-womb'd, and had, indeed,
Sir, a son for her cradle ere she had a husband   15
for her bed.   Do you smell a fault?

Kent. I cannot wish the fault undone, the issue of it
being so proper. *handsome*

Glou. But I have a son, Sir, by order of law, some
year elder than this, who yet is no dearer in my   20
account: though this knave came something
saucily to the world before he was sent for, yet
was his mother fair; there was good sport at his
making, and the whoreson must be acknowledged.
Do you know this noble gentleman, Edmund?   25

Edm. No, my Lord.

Glou. My Lord of Kent: remember him hereafter as
my honourable friend.

Edm. My services to your Lordship.

cf. Lear's mad scene.

14. round-womb'd] *unhyphened Q, F.*   19. a son, Sir] *F;* Sir a son *Q.*
20. year] yeares *Q 3.*   21. something] somewhat *F 3, 4.*   22. to] *F;* into *Q;*
in *Q 3.*   24. the] he *Q 3.*   25. noble gentleman] Nobleman *F 2, 3, 4.*   26.
Edm.] *F; Bast. Q (and throughout).*   27-9. *Glou. . . . Lordship*] *Glo.*
My services to your Lordship. unrable friend. *Q 3.*   Sennet] *F;* Sound a
Sennet *Q.*   one . . . coronet] *Q; not in F.*

Cf. i. ii. 4, i. iv. 73 *post,* and *Tim.*
iv. iii. 303. See also Baret, *Alvearie,*
1580: " Curiositie, piked (i.e. picked)
diligence."

7. *moiety*] share, not necessarily
half. Cf. *1 Hen. IV.* iii. i. 96:
" Methinks my moiety, north from
Burton here,
    In quantity equals not one of
    yours."

11. *braz'd*] made insensible, hardened, literally " plated with brass."
Cf. *Ham.* iii. iv. 37.

12. *conceive*] Kent uses the word in
the sense of " understand "; Gloucester puns on it in his next speech.
Van Dam thinks the quibble is only
possible if the word is used intran-
sitively, and urges the omission of
you. This improvement is not ab-
solutely necessary.

13. *mother*] Coleridge, *Shakespearean*

Criticism, ed. Raysor, i. 56, says
that Edmund " hears his mother
and the circumstances of his birth
spoken of with a most degrading
and licentious levity." But Kittredge
argues that Edmund, though on the
stage, does not hear this conversation.

16. *fault*] Perhaps a quibble on
the two meanings of the word:
(*a*) misdeed, (*b*) loss of scent by
hounds. Shakespeare often compares sin to a bad smell. Cf.
Ham. iii. iii. 36.

18. *proper*] handsome. Cf. *Oth.*
iv. iii. 35.

19, 20. *some year*] about a year.
Cf. *T.S.* iv. iii. 189.

21. *account*] estimation. Cf. *M.V.*
iii. ii. 157.

21. *knave*] fellow—not implying
moral disapproval.

Kent. I must love you, and sue to know you better.   30
Edm. Sir, I shall study deserving.
Glou. He hath been out nine years, and away he shall
  again.   The King is coming.

Sennet.   Enter one bearing a coronet, KING LEAR, CORN-
    WALL, ALBANY, GONERIL, REGAN, CORDELIA, *and
    Attendants.*

Lear. Attend the Lords of France and Burgundy,
  Gloucester.
Glou. I shall, my Liege.   35
                        [*Exeunt Gloucester and Edmund.*

Lear. Meantime, we shall express our darker purpose.
  Give me the map there.   Know that we have
    divided
  In three our kingdom; and 'tis our fast intent
  To shake all cares and business from our age,
  Conferring them on younger strengths, while we   40

34. the] my *Q.*   35. Liege] *Q;* Lord *F.*   Exeunt . . . Edmund] Capell;
Exit F; *not in Q.*   36. we shall] *F;* we will *Q.*   darker] dark *Q 3.*
purpose] *F;* purposes *Q.* 37. Give . . . there] *F;* The map there *Q;* Give me the
map here *F 3, 4.*   Know that] *F;* Know *Q.*   38. fast] *F;* first *Q.*
39. from our age] *F;* of our state *Q.*   40. Conferring] *F;* Confirming *Q.*
strengths] *F;* years *Q.*

25. *Edmund*] The name was perhaps suggested to Shakespeare by the
Edmund Peckham and the Edmunds
mentioned many times by Harsnett.
   29. *services*] i.e. duty.
   32. *out*] in foreign parts, pushing
his fortunes. Cf. *T.G.* I. iii. 7.
   32-3. *away . . . again*] Perhaps
these words seal Gloucester's doom.
   33. S. D. *Sennet*] A particular
set of notes on the trumpet or cornet,
sounded at the entrance or exit of
a company or procession. It is
distinct from a flourish. Cf. Marston
Antonio and Mellida, I. I: "The
Cornets sound a sennet . . . they
embrace, at which the cornets
sound a flourish."
   33. *coronet*] Intended for Cordelia.
   34. *Attend*] wait on them, usher
into our presence.

36. *our darker purpose*] our more
secret intention, i.e. the plan to
give the best share to the daughter
who loves him most. The coun-
cillors only know of Lear's intention
to divide the kingdom, and of the
shares designed for Goneril and
Regan. Empson, *The Structure of
Complex Words,* p. 127, comments:
"We are directed to the idea of
renunciation by his calling it a
darker purpose; in the eyes of
the world it would be a gloomy
one."
   38. *fast*] fixed, unalterable. Cf.
Cor. II. iii. 192.
   39-41 *To . . . death*] cf. *Leir,* 26-7:
"The world of me, I of the world
      am weary,
  And I would fayne resigne these
      earthly cares."

Unburthen'd crawl toward death. Our son of
   Cornwall,
And you, our no less loving son of Albany,
We have this hour a constant will to publish
Our daughters' several dowers, that future strife
May be prevented now. The Princes, France and
   Burgundy, ~ *forestalled*.   45
Great rivals in our youngest daughter's love,
Long in our court have made their amorous sojourn,
And here are to be answer'd. Tell me, my
   daughters,
(Since now we will divest us both of rule,
possession Interest of territory, cares of state)   50
Which of you shall we say doth love us most?
That we our largest bounty may extend
Where nature doth with merit challenge. Goneril,
Our eldest-born, speak first.
Gon. Sir, I love you more than word can wield the
   matter; *express*   55
   Dearer than eye-sight, space and liberty;

40-5. while . . . now] *F; not in Q.*   45. Princes] *F;* two great Princes *Q;*
Prince *F 3, 4.*   46. youngest] younger *F 2, 3, 4.*   48. me] *not in F 3, 4.*
49-50. Since . . . state] *F; not in Q.*   53. Where . . . challenge] *F;* where merit
doth most challenge it *Q.*   55. love] *F;* do loue *Q.*   word] *F;* words *Q.*
wield] yield *conj. Capell;* weld *conj. Gould.*   56. and] *F;* or *Q.*

43. *constant will* fixed purpose, *certa
voluntas.* Cf. " fast intent " 38 *ante.*

45. *prevented*] forestalled.

50. *Interest*] possession, the present
legal sense. Cf. " interess'd " 85
post and *2 Hen. VI.* III. i. 84.

53. *Where . . . challenge*] Steevens
explains, " Where the claims of
merit are superadded to that of
nature, i.e. birth. Challenge, to
make title to, to claim as one's right."
Cf. *3 Hen. VI.* III. ii. 86. Alterna-
tively Steevens suggests that *nature* =
natural filial affection; but it means
rather " paternal affection," and
merit, in the context, means " filial
affection." Cuningham, *N.Q.* 16
May 1914, suggested that the line

should end " challenge it," the word
" Goneril " being transferred to the
following line.

55. *Sir . . . matter*] more than I can
express in words. Cf. *Titus*, III. ii.
29: " handle the theme "; and
Rich. III. III. vii. 19. See *Leir*, 239:
" Which cannot be in windy words
rehearst."

56. *space and liberty*] " *Space* expresses the idea of ' freedom from
confinement'; *liberty* adds the idea
of ' personal freedom in action ' "
(Kittredge). Craig suggests the
phrase means absolute freedom,
" ample room and verge enough."
It may mean merely " spacious
liberty."

Beyond what can be valued rich or rare;
No less than life, with grace, health, beauty,
  honour;
As much as child e'er lov'd, or father found;
A love that makes breath poor and speech
  unable; *inadequate*   60
Beyond all manner of so much I love you. *inestimably*

Cor. [*Aside.*] What shall Cordelia speak? Love, and
  be silent.

Lear. Of all these bounds, even from this line to this,
shady With shadowy forests and with champains rich'd, *unwooded*
With plenteous rivers and wide-skirted meads, *extensive* 65
We make thee lady: to thine and Albany's issues
Be this perpetual. What says our second daughter
Our dearest Regan, wife of Cornwall?

Reg. I am made of that self metal as my sister,
And prize me at her worth. In my true heart 70 *either I consider myself*
I find she names my very deed of love; *to love you as much, or imperative*

59. as] *F;* a *Q.*   found] *F;* friend *Q.*   62. *Aside*] *Pope; not in Q, F.*
speak] *F;* doe *Q.* 64. shadowy] *F;* shady *Q.* rich'd] *F;* rich *Collier MS.* 64-5.
And with . . . rivers] *F; not in Q.*   66. thee] the *F 3.*   issues] *F;* issue *Q.*
68. of Cornwall] *F;* to Cornwall, speake *Q.* 69. I] *F;* Sir I *Q.*   that self
metal] *F* (*hyphened*)*;* the selfe same metall *Q.* as my sister] *F;* that my sister
is *Q.*   70. me] you *conj. Mason.*   worth.   In . . . heart] *F;* worth
in . . . heart, *Q;* worth in . . . heart.   *Theobald* (*conj. Bishop*).

57. *valued*] estimated. Cf. *C.E.*
I. i. 24.

58. *No . . . life*] Cf. *Leir,* 241: "I
thinke my life inferiour to my loue."

60. *unable*] weak, inadequate. Cf.
Hen. V. Epilogue, 1.

61. *Beyond . . . much*] Johnson explains "beyond all assignable quantity." Kittredge suggests that *manner*
is the emphatic word. Wright thinks
so much refers to the comparisons by
which Goneril had tried to measure
her love.

62. *speak*] The Q "doe" is a
possible reading, but it may be an
actor's substitution, influenced by
226 *post,* "I'll do't before I speak"
and 236-7. "This first speech of
Cordelia's seems to me more attractive and less commonplace if we
have her asking herself what *she* shall

say, and then gently but firmly stilling
the question with two commands to
herself." (Duthie.)

64. *shadowy*] shady. Cf. *T.G.* v.
iv. 2. Henderson compares Florio's
Montaigne, Temple ed. iii. 379,
"shady forrests."

64. *champains*] unwooded plains.
Cf. *T.N.* II. v. 174. The word is
often spelt *champian* and *champion.*

64. *rich'd*] enriched.

65. *wide-skirted*] extensive.

68. *Our . . . Cornwall?*] The Q
addition "Speak" was probably
suggested by 54 *ante* and 86 *post,* but
it completes the line.

69. *self*] same. Cf. IV. iii. 35 and
C. E. v. i. 10.

70. *And . . . worth*] Three explanations have been given (i) I estimate
myself her equal in the amount of

Only she comes too short: that I profess
Myself an enemy to all other joys
Which the most precious square of sense possesses,
And find I am alone felicitate   *made happy*   75
In your dear highness' love.

Cor. [*Aside.*]   Then poor Cordelia!
And yet not so; since I am sure my love's
More ponderous than my tongue.

Lear. To thee and thine, hereditary ever,
Remain this ample third of our fair kingdom,   80
No less in space, validity, and pleasure,   *value*
Than that conferr'd on Goneril.   Now, our joy,

---

72. comes too] *F;* came *Q.*   74. precious] spacious *Keightley.*   square]
spirit *Hanmer;* sphere *Collier MS.*   possesses] *Q;* professes *F.*   75. alone]
all one *Q 3.*   76. Aside] *Pope; not in Q, F.*   78. my] their *conj. Warburton*
ponderous] *F;* richer *Q.* 82. conferr'd] *F;* confirm'd *Q.* Now] *F;* but now *Q.*

---

my affection for you. Cf. *T.C.* iv.
iv. 136. (ii) I estimate my love as
equal to hers. (iii) Value me
(imperative) the same as her. Cf.
Leir, 240, " I prize my loue to you
at such a rate."

71. *my . . . love*] my love as it
actually is.   Delius explains " the
formal legal definition of love."

72. *that*] in that.

74. *most . . . sense*] Variously
explained: (i) sense absolute, sense
in its perfection. Cf. Bodenham,
Belvedere, ed. 1875, p. 73:
" Councell and good advise is
            wisdom's square
And most availing to the life of
            man ";
(ii) the most delicately sensitive part
of my nature (Wright); (iii) the
choicest estimate of sense. Cf. *T.C.*
v. ii. 133 (Moberley); (iv) the most
advantageous position on the board.
Cf. 155 *post* (*N.Q.* 7 Oct. 1905);
(v) most delicate test of one's sensibility can claim as joys; *square*
means " criterion " from the carpenter's square (Kittredge); (vi)
Kinnear, *Cruces Shakespearianae,* 1883,
p. 413, proposes *spirit* for *square.*
Cf. *T.C.* i. i. 58 and iii. iii. 106;

Perhaps the soundest explanation
would be a combination of (iii) and
(v), for the quotation " To square the
general sex By Cressid's rule "
suggests a connection with the carpenter's square.

74. *possesses*] A few editors keep F
reading, which is likely to be a
compositor's error from the proximity
of " profess " (72).   Verity says that
professes strikes a wrong note, since
Regan does not mean to doubt the
reality of sensuous joys but to emphasize that she is hostile to them
because she knows the higher joy
of loving and being loved by Lear—
the greater the joys, the greater her
devotion in rejecting them for love
of her father.

75. *felicitate*] made happy. Cf.
suffocate (for suffocated) *T.C.* i. iii.
125.

78 *ponderous*] Perhaps suggested
by " metal " (69). Cordelia cannot
produce golden words, cannot " coin
her heart in words," but her heart
has love of a better and weightier
metal.

81. *validity*] value. Cf. *A.W.* v.
iii. 192.

Although our last, and least; to whose young
　　love
The vines of France and milk of Burgundy
possessed Strive to be interess'd; what can you say to draw　85
A third more opulent than your sisters? Speak.
Cor. Nothing, my lord.
Lear. Nothing?
Cor. Nothing.
Lear. Nothing will come of nothing: speak again.　　90
Cor. Unhappy that I am, I cannot heave
My heart into my mouth: I love your Majesty
According to my bond; no more nor less.
Lear. How, how, Cordelia! Mend your speech a little,
Lest you may mar your fortunes.
Cor.　　　　　　　　　　　Good my Lord,　95
You have begot me, bred me, lov'd me: I
Return those duties back as are right fit,

---

83. our last and] *F;* the last, not *Q;* our last, not *Pope.* least . . . love] *F;*
least in our deare loue, *Q.* 84-5. The . . . interess'd] *F; not in Q.* interess'd]
Jennens; interest *F.* draw] *F;* win *Q.* 86. speak] *F; not in Q.* 88-9.] *F;*
not in Q. 90. Nothing will] *F;* How, nothing can *Q;* Nothing can *Theobald.*
91. heave] have *Q 3, F 3, 4.* 93. no] *F;* nor *Q.* 94. How . . . Cordelia]
F; Goe to, goe to *Q.* 95. you] *F;* it *Q.* 96. I] *Pope's lineation; I begins*
97 *Q, F.* 97. fit] sit *Q 3.*

83. *our last, and least*] Most editors
follow the Q reading but the very
commonness of the expression would
tend to make an actor substitute it
for the F reading. Cf. *Leir,* 2657-8:
　" To thee last of all,
　Not greeted last, 'cause thy
　　desert was small."
Cordelia was young, and small in
stature.
84. *milk*] pastures, the effect for
the cause (Eccles).
85. *interess'd*] closely connected,
interested, concerned. Cf. Florio,
op. cit. iii. 111: "And favour our
childrens causes against us, as men
interessed in the same."
86. *opulent*] McElwaine (*N.Q.* 25
Nov. 1911) points out that Lear must
assign Cordelia her share during his
life, for on his death she will only
inherit equally with her sisters.

87. *Nothing*] This word is echoed
throughout the play. Henderson
(cf. Appendix, p. 249) refers to
Florio, *op. cit.* iii. 341 and *passim.*
90. *Nothing . . . nothing*] Cf. the
proverbial " *ex nihilo nihil fit.*"
Baldwin, *Shakespeare's Small Latine,*
ii. 543, cites Germbergius, *Carminum
Proverbialium,* 1583, p. 154 and Persius
iii. 84: " de nihilo nihilum, in
nihilum nil posse reverti."
91-2. *heave . . . mouth*] Noble compares *Ecclesiasticus,* xxi. 26: "The
heart of fooles in in their mouth:
but the mouth of the wise is in their
heart."
93. *bond*] filial obligation, bounden
duty. Cf. I. ii. 113 and II. iv. 180.
See Appendix pp. 223, 235 for
parallels in Holinshed, Spenser, and
Leir.
97. *Return . . . fit*] " As they, the

Obey you, love you, and most honour you.
Why have my sisters husbands, if they say
They love you all? Happily, when I shall wed,   100
That lord whose hand must take my plight shall
   carry
Half my love with him, half my care and duty:
Sure I shall never marry like my sisters,
To love my father all.

Lear. But goes thy heart with this?

Cor.   Ay, my good Lord. 105

Lear. So young, and so untender?

Cor. So young, my Lord, and true.

Lear. Let it be so; thy truth then be thy dower:
For, by the sacred radiance of the sun,
The mysteries of Hecate and the night,   110
By all the operation of the orbs
From whom we do exist and cease to be,
Here I disclaim all my paternal care,

---

100. Happily] *F;* Happely *Q 1;* Haply *Q 2.* 104. To ... all] *Q; not in F.*
105. thy ... this] *F;* this with thy heart *Q.* my good] *F;* good my *Q.*   108.
Let] *F;* well let *Q.*   thy truth] *Q, F 1, 2;* the truth *F 3, 4.*   110. mysteries]
F 2; mistresse *Q;* miseries *F.* night] *F;* might *Q.*   111. operation] *Q, F;*
operations *F 2, 3, 4.*

duties, are right and fit to be returned" (Craig). "Those duties
that are most fitting," i.e. those
mentioned in the following line
(Kittredge).

98-104. *Obey . . . my father all*]
Perrett, *op. cit.* argues that Shakespeare may have derived the idea
of these lines from Camden's *Remaines.* But he may have got it
from the 1587 edition of *The Mirror
for Magistrates,* or borrowed it himself direct from the marriage service.
See Introduction, p. xxxvi. Baldwin,
Shakespeare's Petty School, p. 174,
points out that Nowell in his commentary on the Little Catechism
puts "obey" in the forefront as does
Cordelia: "sacra scriptura liberos
iubet parentibus obtemperare, atque
inseruire: parentes timere charissi-
mos eos habere, eos colere et reuereri."

101. *plight*] troth-plight.
104. *all*] exclusively. Cf. *Tim.* I.
i. 139.
108. *thy . . . dower*] Cf. *T.G.* III.
i. 78: "Then let her beauty be her
wedding-dower."
110. *mysteries*] secret rites. Daniel
suggested that the man who prepared
Q for the F edition, wishing to correct
mistresse to *misteries,* wrote *eries* in
the margin, but accidentally drew
his pen through the last six, instead
of only the last five, letters of *mistresse.*
110. *Hecate*] The goddess of the
lower world, and patroness of magic
and witchcraft, as in *Macbeth.* The
word, as usual in Shakespeare, is a
dissyllable. The exception, *1 Hen.
VI.* III. ii. 64, may not be his.
111. *operation*] astrological influence. Cf. *A.C.* II. vii. 30.

Propinquity and property of blood,

And as a stranger to my heart and me   115

Hold thee from this for ever.   The barbarous

   Scythian,

Or he that makes his generation messes

To gorge his appetite, shall to my bosom

Be as well neighbour'd, pitied, and reliev'd,

As thou my sometime daughter.

Kent.   Good my Liege,—   120

Lear. Peace, Kent!

   Come not between the Dragon and his wrath.

   I lov'd her most, and thought to set my rest

   On her kind nursery.   Hence, and avoid my sight!

---

118. to my bosom] *F; not in Q.*   120. Liege-] *Rowe;* Liege. *Q, F.*

---

114. *Propinquity*] close relationship.

114. *property*] closest blood relationship, rising, as it were, to identity of blood (Wright).   Cf. *Rich. II.* I. ii. 1, spoken by Woodstock's brother: "The part I had in Woodstock's blood."

116-18. *The . . . appetite*] The usual explanation of *generation* is "offspring."   Cf. *Matt.* iii. 7.   But Craig suggests it means "parents."   He points out that *progeny* is used in the sense of "ancestors" (*Cor.* I. viii. 12) and cites Chapman, *Byron's Tragedy,* IV. ii. 126-32: "to teach. . . . The Scythians to inter, not eat, their parents."   Perrett cites Harrison, *Description of Britain,* iv, "These Scots were reputed for the most *Scithian*-like and barbarous nation. . . . For both Diodorus . . . & Strabo. . . . do seeme to speake of a parceil of the Irish nation that should inhabit Britain in their time, which were giuen to the eating of man's flesh, and therefore called *Anthropophagi* . . . those Scots . . . who vsed to feed on the buttocks of boies and women's paps, as delicate dishes."

117. *messes*] portions of food.

122. *Dragon*] Lear may refer to the dragon of Britain, which he would wear emblazoned on his helmet (Moberley).   Cf. *The Birth of Merlin,* v. ii. 39-40:

"We have firm hope that tho' our dragon sleep

Merlin will us and our fair Kingdom keep."

But Shakespeare often refers to the dragon as a symbol of savage ferocity, e.g. *Cor.* IV. vii. 23.

122. *wrath*] the object of his wrath.   But J. C. Maxwell suggests to me that "the notion conveyed appears to be that of Lear's wrath as an extension of his personality— a sort of anthropologist's 'mana'— his union with which must remain intact if he himself is to hold together.   A dragon cannot *be* a dragon without his wrath.   The kind of disintegration which Lear is afraid of is what actually takes place."   Maxwell goes on to compare I. i. 169-70.   Cf. *Anglia,* xxxix, p. 45, where Dubislaw quotes Koppel to the same effect and cites *Ham.* III. iv. 112.

123. *set my rest*] stake my all.   Cf. *R.J.* v. iii. 110.   The idiom is taken from the game of primero.   See Gascoigne, *Supposes,* iii. 2: "This amorous cause . . . may be compared to them that play at primero: of whom one, peradventure, shall leese a great sum of money

So be my grave my peace, as here I give   125
Her father's heart from her! Call France. Who
    stirs? *Be comick!*
Call Burgundy.   Cornwall and Albany,
With my two daughters' dowers digest the third; *in corporate*
Let pride, which she calls plainness, marry her.
I do invest you jointly with my power,   130
Pre-eminence, and all the large effects *splendid accompan*
That troop with majesty. Ourself, by monthly
    course, *are associated with*
With reservation of an hundred knights
In rejecting By you to be sustain'd, shall our abode
Lear & knights Make with you by due turn.   Only we shall retain 135
Gon & Regan The name and all th' addition to a king; the sway, *honours*
breaking the Revenue, execution of the rest,
bargain Beloved sons, be yours: which to confirm,
This coronet part between you.

Kent.   Royal Lear,
This is Whom I have ever honour'd as my King,   140
not empty Lov'd as my father, as my master follow'd,
rhetoric. As my great patron thought on in my prayers,—
Cf Kents
suicide

128. dowers] Dowres *F;* dower *Q.*   the] *F;* this *Q.*   130. with] *F;* in *Q.*
135. turn] *F;* turnes *Q.*   shall] *F;* still *Q.*   136. th' addition] *F;* the
additions *Q.*   139. between] *F;* betwixt *Q.*   140. my] a *F 4.*   142.
prayers,—] *Rowe;* praiers. *Q, F.*

before he win one stake, and, at last,
half in anger shall set up his rest,
win it, and after that another, and
another; till, at last, he draw the
most part of the money to his heap,
the other by little and little diminish-
ing his rest, till he come as near the
brink as erst the other was."   But
here, as in the *Romeo and Juliet*
passage, there is a quibble on the
phrase.
124. *nursery*] nursing, tender care.
126. *Who stirs?*] i.e. Be quick!
The courtiers are shocked into
immobility.
128. *digest*] incorporate.
129. *Let . . . her*] Let her pride
be her dowry and win her a husband.

130. *with*] Cf. *2 Hen. IV.* iv. v. 73.
Elsewhere after *invest,* Shakespeare
uses ' in.' Cf. *M.M.* iii. i. 96.
131. *large effects*] splendid accom-
paniments.
132. *troop with*] are associated with.
Cf. *R.J.* i. v. 50.
133. *reservation*] Cf. ii. iv. 254.
The word is a legal term, and means
the action or fact of reserving (for
oneself or another) some right, power,
or privilege.
136. *addition*] honours, titles, cere-
monial observances. Cf. *Mac.* i. iii.
106. The plural form, as in Q, is
more usual; but see *N.E.D.*
137. *revenue*] accented on the
second syllable.

Lear. The bow is bent and drawn; make from the
    shaft.

Kent. Let it fall rather, though the fork invade

    The region of my heart: be Kent unmannerly,   145

    When Lear is mad. What would'st thou do, old

    man?

    Think'st thou that duty shall have dread to speak

    When power to flattery bows? To plainness

    honour's bound

    When majesty falls to folly. Reserve thy state;

    And, in thy best consideration, check   150

    This hideous rashness: answer my life my judgment,

    Thy youngest daughter does not love thee least;

    Nor are those empty-hearted whose low sounds

    Reverb no hollowness.

Lear.   Kent, on thy life, no more.

Kent. My life I never held but as a pawn   155

    To wage against thine enemies; nor fear to lose it,

    Thy safety being motive.

146. mad] *Q 2, F;* man *Q 1.* would'st] *F 4;* wilt *Q;* wouldest *F 1, 2, 3.*
149. falls] *F;* stoops *Q.* reserve thy state] *F;* Reuerse thy doome *Q.* 153.
empty-hearted] *hyphen not in Q, F.* low sounds] *F;* low, sound *Q 1;* low sound
Q 2. 154. Reverb] *F;* Reuerbs *Q.* thy] my *F 3, 4.* 155. as a] *Q;*
as *F.* 156. thine] *F;* thy *Q.* nor] *Q;* nere *F.* fear] fear'd *conj. Furness.*

143. *make from*] avoid.
144. *fork*] a forked head on an
arrow. Ascham, *Toxophilus,* ed.
Arber, p. 135 describes it as " hauing two points stretching forward, and
this Englishmen do call a forke-head."
145. *The . . . heart*] The same
expression is used by Ford in *The
Lady's Trial,* III. iii. 27.
146. *old man*] Kent's bluntness
increases Lear's rage.
148. *plainness*] Cf. II. ii. 102.
149. *Reserve thy state*] Duthie
suggests that the actor who played
Kent was influenced by the lines
in *Leir,* 505-6, 567:
" Cease, good my Lords, and sue
    not to reuerse
    Our censure, which is now
    irreuocable."
" Whose deeds haue not de-
    seru'd this ruthlesse doome."

A conflation of these passages would
account for the Q reading. Kent in
the F reading is here thinking more
of Lear's safety than of the injustice
to Cordelia, though it is this injustice which makes Kent intervene.
150. *best consideration*] as opposed
to the rashness of his first thoughts.
151. *answer . . . judgment*] " Let
my life be answerable for my judgment, or I will stake my life on my
opinion " (Johnson).
154. *Reverb*] Shakespeare probably
coined the word from reverberate.
154. *hollowness*] a quibble on the
two meanings of the word: con-
cavity, and insincerity. Cf. I. ii.
118 and *Ham.* III. ii. 218. Kittredge
cites the proverb: " Emptie vessels
haue the loudest sounds " (Greene,
George a Greene IV. 4; ed. Collins, ii.
210).

Lear.   Out of my sight!

Kent. See better, Lear; and let me still remain
    The true blank of thine eye.

Lear. Now, by Apollo,—

Kent.   Now, by Apollo, King, 160
    Thou swear'st thy Gods in vain.

Lear.   O, vassal! miscreant!

                             [Laying his hand upon his sword.

Alb., Corn. Dear Sir, forbear.

Kent. Kill thy physician, and thy fee bestow
    Upon the foul disease. Revoke thy gift;
    Or, whilst I can vent clamour from my throat,   165
    I'll tell thee thou dost evil.

Lear.   Hear me, recreant!

    On thine allegiance, hear me!
    That thou hast sought to make us break our vows,
    Which we durst never yet, and with strain'd pride
    To come betwixt our sentence and our power,   170

---

157. motive] *F;* the motiue *Q.*   160. *Lear] Q; Kear F.*   *Kent] Q;*
Lent F.   161. O . . . miscreant] *F;* Vassall, recreant *Q.*   S.D.] *Rowe;*
not in Q, F.   162.] *F; not in Q.*   163. Kill] *F;* Doe, kill *Q.*   163. thy
fee] *F;* the fee *Q.*   164. thy] the *F 3, 4.*   gift] *F;* doome *Q.*   167. thine]
F; thy *Q.*   168. That] *F;* Since *Q.*   vowes] *F;* vow *Q.*   169. strain'd]
F; straied *Q.*   170. betwixt] *F;* betweene *Q.*   sentence] *Q;* Sentences *F.*

---

155. *held*] considered.

155. *pawn*] a stake hazarded in a
wager; the only instance in Shakespeare of its use in this sense. He
usually employs the word in the
sense of pledge, something given in
security. Cf. *T.G.* I. iii. 47. But
see I. ii. 87 and *Cymb.* I. vi. 194,
where pawn (vb) is used in the sense
of stake. Capell thought there was
an allusion to the game of chess,
and there may have been a concealed
pun. Cf. note on *wage* (156).

156. *wage*] to stake, as in a wager;
to risk, to venture. Cf. *Cymb.* I. iv.
144. But the preposition 'against'
suggests that Shakespeare was also
thinking of waging war.

157. *motive*] moving cause.

158. *still*] always.

159. *blank*] the white spot in the
centre of the target, the white.

Cotgrave defines *Blanc* as " the white
or mark of a pair of buts." Kent
implies that he is the wise counsellor,
to whom Lear should look for advice.
There may be a quibble on the white
of the eye in the ordinary sense of
the phrase.

160. *Apollo*] Leir in Layamon's
The Brute also invokes Apollo. The
pagan setting is necessary to Shakespeare's conception of the story.

161. *miscreant*] Perhaps, as Wright
suggests, the word is used in its
original sense of misbeliever. Kent
had apparently referred contemptuously to the gods.

163. *Kill*] Before this word *Q*
inserts " Doe "; this may be a F
omission, or an actor's addition.

166. *recreant*] one who proves false
to his allegiance.

168. *That*] seeing that.

packed up
y Hib s
corn.

Which nor our nature nor our place can bear,
Our potency made good, take thy reward.
Five days we do allot thee for provision
To shield thee from disasters of the world; *misfortunes*
And on the sixth to turn thy hated back   175
Upon our kingdom: if on the tenth day following
Thy banish'd trunk be found in our dominions,
The moment is thy death. Away! By Jupiter,
This shall not be revok'd.

Kent. Fare thee well, King; sith thus thou wilt appear, 180
Freedom lives hence, and banishment is here.
[*To Cordelia.*] The Gods to their dear shelter take thee,
    maid,

---

172. made] *Q 1, F;* make *Q 2, 3.*   173. Five] *F;* Foure *Q.*   174.
disasters] *F;* diseases *Q;* defeascs *Q 3;* distresses *conj. Kinnear.*   175. sixth]
F 4; sixt *F;* fift *Q.*   176. on] *not in F 2, 3, 4;* one *Q 3.*   tenth] seventh
Collier MS.   180. Fare] *F;* Why fare *Q.*   sith] *F;* since *Q.*   thus]
Q 1, F; not in Q 2, 3.   181. Freedom] *F;* Friendship *Q.*   182. S.D.]
Hanmer. dear shelter] *F;* protection *Q.* thee, maid] thee Maid *F;* the maid *Q.*

---

169 *strain'd*] forced, unnatural,
used beyond its province Cf. *R.J.*
II. iii. 19; *2 Hen. IV.* I. i. 161; *M.A.*
IV. i. 254.

172. *Our . . . reward*] Malone
explains: " As a proof that I am not
a mere threatener, that I have power
as well as will to punish, take the
due reward of thy demerits." Craig
suggests: " You want me to take
back my power. Well I do, and
you must take the consequences."
Nichol Smith, more simply, paraphrases: " our royal authority being
maintained." So Coleridge, *op. cit.*
i. p. 61, says that Kent's opposition
displays " Lear's moral incapability
of resigning the sovereign power in
the very moment of disposing of it."
But I think the phrase means " our
power backed up by those to whom
it has been delegated, Cornwall
and Albany." This is substantially
Steeven's explanation. Pope and
Boswell, accepting the reading of
Q 2, assume that the line means:
" Take thy reward in another
sentence which shall make good,

shall establish, that power." The
rhyme take—make is, however,
ugly.

174. *disasters*] misfortunes. Many
editors prefer Q ' diseases,' and
Malone thought the F printer
altered it because he did not know
that diseases " meant the slighter
inconveniences, troubles, or distresses
of the world." Duthie, however,
points out that the word *disease* occurs
ten lines earlier, and that the Q
reading may be a recollection.

176. *tenth*] Collier MS. proposes
" seventh " and P. A. Daniel suggests
" se'nth," believing that the sense
of the passage requires this alteration.
It would certainly be more logical.

178. *Jupiter*] Perrett cites Harrison,
Description of Britain, ix, on the
religion of the ancient inhabitants.
They " honoured the said *Samothes*
himselfe vnder the name of *Dis* and
Saturne; also *Jupiter, Mars . . .
Apollo, Diana* and . . . *Hercules.*"

180-7. *Fare . . . country new*] Craig
comments: " After the storm comes
the equanimity of Kent's · rhymed

That justly think'st and hast most rightly said!
[*To Goneril and Regan.*] And your large speeches may
    your deeds approve,
That good effects may spring from words of love.   185
Thus Kent, O Princes! bids you all adieu;
He'll shape his old course in a country new.   [*Exit.*
of speaking plainly

Flourish. Re-enter GLOUCESTER, *with* FRANCE,
    BURGUNDY, *and Attendants.*

Glou. Here's France and Burgundy, my noble Lord.
Lear. My Lord of Burgundy,
    We first address toward you, who with this king   190
    Hath rivall'd for our daughter. What, in the
        least,
    Will you require in present dower with her,
    Or cease your quest of love?
Bur.   Most royal Majesty,
    I crave no more than hath your Highness offer'd,
    Nor will you tender less.
Lear.   Right noble Burgundy,   195
    When she was dear to us we did hold her so,
    But now her price is fallen.   Sir, there she stands:

---

    183. justly think'st] *F;* rightly thinks *Q;* justly thinks *F 4.*   hast] *Q 1, F;*
hath *Q 2.*   rightly] *F;* iustly *Q.*   184. S.D.] *Hanmer; not in Q, F.*
And . . . speeches] *Q, F;* And you, large speechers, *Capell.*   187. *Exit*] *F;*
not in Q.   188. Glos.] *Q; Cor. F.*   189. of] *Q 1, F;* or *Q 2.*   190. toward] *F;*
towards *Q;* this] *F;* a *Q.*   193. Most] *F; not in Q.*   194. hath] *F;* what
Q, F 3, 4.   196. did hold] held *F 2, 3, 4.*   197 fallen] fall'n *F 3, 4.*

lines." The lines sum up the situation, and point the moral.

    184. *approve*] prove true. Cf. II. ii. 163.

    185. *effects*] deeds.

    187. *shape . . . new*] Kent means that he will, in a foreign land, pursue his old ways of speaking plainly. For "shape his course" see Marlowe, *Edward II.* IV. v. 3 "Shape we our course to Ireland."

    187. S.D. *Flourish*] See note on 33 *ante.*

    188. *Here's*] A singular verb is often used, especially where it precedes the subjects.

    190. *address*] address myself.

    190. *this*] Duthie argues for the Q reading. "Burgundy will want a large dowry since he, a Duke, has had the temerity to set up as rival to a King." But the same point would be made by stressing *king.*

    191. *rivall'd*] competed.

    196. *so*] i.e. 'dear' at a high price. "While we loved her, we were ready to give her a large dowry."

If aught within that little-seeming substance,
Or all of it, with our displeasure piec'd,
And nothing more, may fitly like your Grace,   200
She's there, and she is yours.   *please by its fitness*

Bur.   I know no answer.

Lear. Will you, with those infirmities she owes,
Unfriended, new-adopted to our hate,
Dower'd with our curse and stranger'd with our oath,
Take her, or leave her?   205

Bur.   *Noone can chose.*   Pardon me, royal Sir;
Election makes not up in such conditions.

Lear. Then leave her, sir; for, by the power that
          made me,
I tell you all her wealth. [*To France.*] For you,
          great King,
I would not from your love make such a stray
To match you where I hate; therefore beseech you   210

---

198. little-seeming] *Collier (conj. S. Walker); unhyphened Q, F.*   199.
with our] *without Q 3.*   piec'd] *pierc'd Pope.*   200. more] *F; else Q.*
202. will] *F; Sir will Q.*   204. Dower'd] *F; Couered Q.*   205. Take
her] *Take leave F 3, 4.*   206. in] *F; on Q.*   208. S.D.] *Pope; not in Q, F.*

---

198. *that . . . substance*] Johnson
thinks *little seeming* is equivalent to
' ugly '; Steevens thinks that *seeming*
means ' specious '; Wright takes the
phrase to refer to Cordelia's small
size; Kittredge paraphrases: " That
little creature, who seems to be something *real*, but is in fact a mere vain
semblance of reality." He suggests
that *seeming-substance* might be hyphened. Craig, I think correctly,
suggests that Lear is referring ironically to Cordelia's blunt professions
of sincerity which she had just
contrasted with her sister's alleged
insincerity. As Schmidt points out,
substance commonly means *reality* in
opposition to *shadow*. I take the
phrase to mean, therefore, " this
genuine creature, who refuses to
flatter." Cf. II. ii. 96 ff. where
Cornwall is similarly ironical at
Kent's expense.

199. *piec'd*] attached to it, in
addition to it. Cf. III. vi. 2 and
Cor. II. iii. 220.

200. *may . . . Grace*] may please
by its fitness. Cf. II. ii. 91.

202. *owes*] owns. Cf. I. iv. 126.

204. *stranger'd*] made a stranger,
disowned.

206. *Election . . . up*] " Election
comes to no decision," as in the
phrase " make up one's mind "
(Wright). " No one can choose."

206. *in such conditions*] on such
terms. Schmidt, *Zur Textkritik,* p. 14,
defended the F reading ' in ' because
' conditions ' referred to the ' qualities ' of Cordelia described by Lear,
203-5. Cf. *Hen. V.* IV. i. 108,
A.Y.L.I. I. i. 48.

208. *For*] as for.

209. *make . . . stray*] stray so far.

210. *To*] as to. Cf. *Rich. III,* III.
ii. 27.

210. *beseech*] I beseech.

T'avert your liking a more worthier way
Than on a wretch whom Nature is asham'd
Almost t'acknowledge hers.

France.   This is most strange,
That she, whom even but now was your best object,
The argument of your praise, balm of your age,   215
The best, the dearest, should in this trice of time
Commit a thing so monstrous, to dismantle
So many folds of favour.   Sure, her offence
Must be of such unnatural degree
That monsters it, or your fore-vouch'd affection   220
Fall into taint; which to believe of her,
Must be a faith that reason without miracle
Should never plant in me.

211. T'avert] *F;* to auert *Q.*   213. t' acknowledge] *F;* to acknowledge *Q.*
214. whom] *F;* that *Q;* who *F 2.*   best] *Q; not in F.*   216. The best, the]
F; Most best, most *Q.*   218. folds] fouls *Q 3.*   220. your fore-vouch
affection] *F;* you for voucht affections *Q.*   221. Fall] *F;* Falne *Q.*   223.
Should] *F;* Could *Q.*

211. *T'avert . . . way*] to turn your
affections from the unworthy person
on whom they are now placed, and
place them on a better person.
211. *more worthier*] Shakespeare frequently uses the double comparative.
214. *whom*] The F reading is un-
grammatical, but not without parallels in Shakespeare. Presumably
France began to say "whom you
loved most" and changed the construction in the middle of the sentence.
214. *best object*] main object of love.
215. *argument*] subject, theme. Cf.
M.A. II. iii. 11.
216. *The best, the dearest*] This, the
F reading, may be a sophistication,
but as the Q reading is not demon-
strably better there is no good reason
for adopting it. For the double
superlative cf. *Ham.* II. ii. 122.
217. *dismantle*] strip off.
218-21. *Sure . . . taint*] Malone,
who accepted Q reading, explains:
"Either her offence must be monstrous, or if she has not committed
any such offence, the affection you

always professed to have for her
must be tainted and decayed."
Craig, following Johnson in assuming
that *or* signifies *ere*, explains: "She
must surely have committed some
unspeakably horrid act, ere the
warm affection you always professed to hold her in, should thus
suddenly have changed to hate."
But F *fall* makes perfectly good
sense. Maxwell, following Delius,
interprets: "Either she has committed a monstrous offence, or your
fore-vouch'd affection must *now* be
discredited as having been all along
unjustified." As the second *must*
can be understood there is no need
to emend *affection* to *affections*, or
fall to *falls*, as Duthie and Johnson
suggest.
220. *monsters it*] makes it a monster.
221. *her*] emphatic (Kittredge).
222. *reason without miracle*] perhaps
a reference to the controversy about
natural religion, as in Montaigne,
op. cit. iii. *passim.*

Cor.　~~you are angry because~~ I yet beseech your Majesty,
~~even if you~~　(If for I want that glib and oily art
　　　To speak and purpose not, since what I well
　　　　intend,　*proclaim*　　　　　　　　225
　　　I'll do 't before I speak), that you make known
　　　It is no vicious blot, murther or foulness,
　　　No unchaste action, or dishonour'd step,
　　　That hath depriv'd me of your grace and favour,
　　　But even for want of that for which I am richer,　230
　　　A still-soliciting eye, and such a tongue
　　　That I am glad I have not, though not to have it
　　　Hath lost me in your liking.

Lear.　　　　　　　　　　　　　Better thou
　　　Hadst not been born than not t' have pleased me　*arrogance*
　　　　better.

France.　Is it but this? a tardiness in nature　　　235
　　　Which often leaves the history unspoke
　　　That it intends to do?　My Lord of Burgundy,
　　　What say you to the lady?　Love's not love
　　　When it is mingled with regards that stand

225. well] *Q;* will *F.*　226. make known] *F;* may know *Q.*　227. murther or] *Q, F;* nor other *Singer (Collier MS).*　　　228. unchaste] *F;* vncleane *Q.*　230. richer] *F;* rich *Q.*　　　231. still-soliciting] *hyphened Theobald.*　　　232. That] *F;* As *Q.*　233. Better] *F;* Goe to, goe to, better *Q.*　233-4. Better . . . better] *Divided as by Pope; F ends line at* had'st, *Q at* borne.　　234, t'have] *F;* to haue *Q.*　　235. but] *F;* no more but *Q.*　236. Which] *F;* That *Q.* leaves] loves *Q 3.*　　237. intends to do] intends *conj. A. Walker.*　　238. Love's] *F;* Loue is *Q.*　239. regards] *F;* respects *Q.* stand] *Pope;* stands *Q, F.*

224. *If for*] even if you are enraged with me because.
225. *purpose not*] i.e. to do what I
have promised.
227. *murther or*] Cordelia, with
scorn, mentions the worst vices she
can think of—vices which might
have justified Lear's treatment of
her. The Collier emendation is
unnecessary, and absurd: for, as
Kittredge points out, "vicious blot"
is not a definite kind of "foulness."
Cordelia mentions murder and un-
chastity as two examples of a vicious
blot.
228. *dishonour'd*] dishonourable.
230. *for which*] for want of which.

231. *still-soliciting*] always cadging.
233. *lost*] ruined. Cf. *A.C.* IV. xii.
29.
233. *liking*] Cordelia deliberately
uses a colder word than love.
235. *tardiness in nature*] natural
reticence (Kittredge).
236. *history*] account. Schmidt explains as "communication of what
is in the heart or inner life of man,"
comparing *M.M.* I. i. 29.
238. *What . . . to*] i.e. Will you
have. Cf. *T.S.* IV. iii. 17. "What
say you to a neat's foot."
238-40. *Love's . . . point*] Cf.
Sonnet, cxvi. 2-6.
239. *regards*] considerations. Cf.

Aloof from th' entire *essential* point.   Will you have her?   240
She is herself a dowry.

Bur.   Royal King,
Give but that portion which yourself propos'd,
And here I take Cordelia by the hand,
Duchess of Burgundy.

Lear. Nothing: I have sworn; I am firm.   245

Bur. I am sorry, then, you have so lost a father
That you must lose a husband.

Cor.   Peace be with Burgundy!
Since that respect and fortunes are his love,
I shall not be his wife.

France. Fairest Cordelia, that art most rich, being poor; 250
Most choice, forsaken; and most lov'd, despis'd!
Thee and thy virtues here I seize upon:
Be it lawful I take up what's cast away.
Gods, gods! 'tis strange that from their cold'st
        neglect
My love should kindle to inflam'd respect.   255
Thy dowerless daughter, King, thrown to my chance,
Is Queen of us, of ours, and our fair France:

---

241. a dowry] *F;* and dowre *Q.*   King] *F;* Leir *Q.*   245. I am firm] *F;*
not in *Q.*   248. respect and fortunes] *F;* respects of fortune *Q.*   256. my] *F;*
thy *Q.*

Oth. I. i. 154. The Q reading was
doubtless suggested by 248 *post.*

239. *stand*] Though Q and F agree
on the reading *stands,* and though a
plural subject often has a singular verb,
the line sounds better without the s.

240. *entire*] essential, single.

248. *respect and fortunes*] mercenary
considerations—an example of hendiadys.   Duthie denies that the
phrase means the same as the Q
reading, but he does not give his
own interpretation.   Perhaps the F
version means "what people think
of me, and what my dowry is."
Cf. *Ham.* II. ii. 192-3:

    "The instances that second
            marriage move
    Are base respects of thrift, but
        none of love."

Heilman, *op. cit.* p. 308, points out
that *regards, respect,* and *despis'd* are
all derived from words of seeing,
and that Shakespeare may have
"embedded a number of bilingual
puns" in these lines.

250-1. *most rich . . . despis'd*] Noble,
Shakespeare's Biblical Knowledge, compares 2 *Corin.* vi. 10: "As poore, and
yet making many rich: as hauing
nothing, and yet possessing all
things."

252. *I seize upon*] Perrett, *op. cit.*
p. 280, compares Geoffrey of Monmouth's phrase "se vero tantum-
modo puellam captare."

255. *My . . . respect*] Perrett cites
Geoffrey again: "amore virginis
inflammatus."

256. *chance*] lot.

Not all the dukes of wat'rish Burgundy
Can buy this <u>unpriz'd</u> precious maid of me. *unappreciated by others*
Bid them farewell, Cordelia, though unkind:　　260
Thou losest here, a better where to find.

Lear. Thou hast her, France; let her be thine, for we
Have no such daughter, nor shall ever see
That face of hers again; therefore be gone
Without our grace, our love, our benison.　　265
Come, noble Burgundy.

　　　　　[*Flourish. Exeunt Lear, Burgundy, Cornwall,
　　　　　　Albany, Gloucester, and Attendants.*

France. Bid farewell to your sisters.
Cor. The jewels of our father, with wash'd eyes
Cordelia leaves you: I know you what you are;
And like a sister am most loth to call　　270
Your faults as they are named. Love well our father:
To your professed bosoms I commit him:
But yet, alas! stood I within his grace,
I would prefer him to a better place.
So farewell to you both.　　275

---

258. of] *F;* in *Q.*　　259. Can] *F; Shall Q.*　　266. Flourish] *F; not in Q.*
Exeunt . . . Attendants] *Capell; Exit Lear and Burgundy Q; Exeunt F.*
268. The] *Q, F; Ye Rowe.*　　271. Love] *F;* vse *Q.*　　274. prefer] perfer *F ℓ.*

258. *wat'rish*] a quibble: abounding in streams, and weak, diluted. Cf. *Oth.* III. iii. 15. R. A. Law, *Studies in Philology*, 1936, p. 222, suggests that Shakespeare may have had historical characters in mind. Sargeaunt, *N.Q.*, 27 March 1909, suggests unnecessarily that we should read *Duke's*.

159. *unpriz'd precious*] unappreciated by others, but precious in my sight.

260. *though unkind*] though they have treated you with unnatural cruelty. Staunton thinks Shakespeare may have intended *unkinn'd*, i.e. forsaken by thy kindred. He compares *V.A.* 203.

261. *here . . . where*] "These have the power of nouns" (Johnson).

265. *benison*] blessing.

268. *The*] i.e. You, the. Several editors follow Rowe's emendation, but though 'the' and 'ye' are often difficult to distinguish in MSS. cf. *J.C.* v. iii. 99 where the article is used in a vocative phrase (Kittredge).

268. *wash'd*] i.e. with tears. Cf. *M.N.D.* II. ii. 93.

271. *as . . . nam'd*] by their true ugly names. Cf. "To call a spade a spade."

272. *professed*] "Cordelia commits her father to the love which her sisters had professed, not to that which they really feel" (Delius).

274. *prefer*] advance (cf. *Rich. III.* IV. ii. 182), or recommend (cf. *Cymb.* II. iii. 49-51).

Reg. Prescribe not us our duty.

Gon.   Let your study
Be to content your lord, who hath receiv'd you
At Fortune's alms; you have obedience scanted,
And well are worth the want that you have wanted.

Cor. Time shall unfold what plighted cunning hides; 280
[compricated]
Who covers faults, at last with shame derides.
Well may you prosper!

[Note break-
down of verse
from formality to plotting]

France.   Come, my fair Cordelia.
                  [*Exeunt France and Cordelia.*

Gon. Sister, it is not little I have to say of what most
nearly appertains to us both. I think our father
will hence to-night.   285

Reg. That's most certain, and with you; next month
with us.

Gon. You see how full of changes his age is; the observation we have made of it hath not been little:
he always lov'd our sister most; and with what 290
poor judgment he hath now cast her off appears
too grossly. *[obviously]*

Reg. 'Tis the infirmity of his age; yet he hath ever but
slenderly known himself.

<hr>

276. *Reg.*] F; *Gonorill* Q.   *Gon.*] F; *Regan* Q.   duty] F; duties Q.
279. want] F; worth Q. 280. plighted] pleated Q. 281. covers] Q, F; cover
Jennens.   with shame] F; shame them Q.   282. my] F; not in Q.
283-5. *verse*] Q, F; *prose Capell.*   283. little] F; a little Q.   289. not]
Q; not in F.   292. too] Q, F; too too F 2, 3, 4.   grossly] F; grosse Q.

278. *At . . . alms*] " When fortune
was doling out petty charities, not
bestowing   bounteous   awards "
(Kittredge). Cf. *Oth.* III. iv. 122.
278. *scanted*] stinted, come short of.
279. *And . . . wanted*] and well
deserve (*a*) to be treated unkindly
by your husband, because of your
own lack of affection for your father;
or (*b*) to lose your share of the
kingdom. (*a*) is more probable.
279. *are worth*] Cf. II. iv. 44.
279. *wanted*] gone, or been, without.
280. *plighted*] folded, complicated,
and so, figuratively, dissembling.
Q and F words have the same sense.

Cf. Milton, *Comus*, 301, " plighted "
and *Lucrece*, 93: " Hiding base sin
in pleats of majesty."
281. *Who*] i.e. Time. Most
editors prefer the Q reading of this
line; in which case *Who* means
" Those who."
281-2. *Who . . . prosper*] Noble,
op. cit. compares *Proverbs*, xxviii. 13.
" He that hideth his sinnes, shall
not prosper." The implication is
that Goneril and Regan will not
prosper.
292. *grossly*] obviously.
293-9. *'Tis . . . them*] Cf. *Leir*,
195: " For he, you know, is alwayes
in extremes."

Gon. The best and soundest of his time hath been but 295
    rash; then must we look from his age, to receive
    not alone the imperfections of long-engraffed con-
    dition, but therewithal the unruly waywardness
    that infirm and choleric years bring with them.

Reg. Such unconstant starts are we like to have from 300
    him as this of Kent's banishment.

Gon. There is further compliment of leave-taking be-
    tween France and him. Pray you, let us hit to-
    gether: if our father carry authority with such
    disposition as he bears, this last surrender of his 305
    will but offend us.

Reg. We shall further think of it.

Gon. We must do something, and i' th' heat.

                                    [*Exeunt.*

296. from ... receive] *F;* to receiue from his age *Q.*   297. imperfections] *F;*
imperfection *Q.*   long-engraffed] *hyphened Pope;* long ingraffed *F;* long
ingrafted *Q.*   298. the] *F; not in Q.*   298. the] *F; not in Q.*   300. starts]
Q 1, F; stars *Q 2.*   303. Pray you] Pray *Q.*   let us] *F;* let's *Q.*   hit] *Q;*
sit *F.*   305. disposition] *F;* dispositions *Q.*   307. of it] *F;* on't *Q.*

296. *rash*] hasty, hot-headed.

297. *long-engraffed*] " firmly im-
bedded " (Kittredge).   Q and F
give variants of the same word from
Fr. *greffer.*

297-8. *condition*] disposition.   Cf.
Oth. IV. i. 204.   Goneril's diagnosis
is near to the truth.

300. *unconstant starts*] sudden whims;
a metaphor from horsemanship.   Cf.
Mac. III. iv. 63, and *V.A.* 302.

302. *compliment*] formality.   Cf.
R.J. II. ii. 89.

303. *hit*] agree, act vigorously.
Cf. *Leir*, 1155-6, where Ragan says:
" Yet will I make fayre weather,
    to procure

Conuenient meanes, and then
    ile strike it sure."
Schmidt adopts F ' sit ', explaining
" take counsel together."   Cf. *Per.*
II. iii. 92.

304-5. *carry ... bears*] continues to
wield his authority, in spite of his
abdication, in the way we have just
seen.

305. *last surrender*] Empson, *op. cit.*
p. 128, comments: " a curious remark
that seems to imply previous renun-
ciations."   But *last* means ' recent '.
Cf. *Temp.* v. i. 153.

306. *offend us*] be a nuisance to us.

308. *do*] as opposed to *think.*

308. *i' th' heat*] i.e. strike while the
iron is hot (Steevens).

SCENE II.—[*The Earl of Gloucester's Castle.*]

Enter EDMUND, *with a letter.*

Edm. Thou, Nature, art my goddess; to thy law
My services are bound. Wherefore should I
Stand in the plague of custom, and permit
The curiosity of nations to deprive me,
For that I am some twelve or fourteen moonshines   5
Lag of a brother? Why bastard? Wherefore base?
When my dimensions are as well compact,
My mind as generous, and my shape as true,

Animal Nature jungle Law.
fastidiousness
behind
a Likeness of
father as Edgar
Noble courageous

S.D.] *Pope subst.*   *Scene* II   4. deprive] deprave *conj. A. Walker.*

Scene II

1. *Nature*] William A. Armstrong, *T.L.S.*, 14 Oct. 1949, argues that Shakespeare was influenced by the epicurean atheism of Cecropia in Sidney's *Arcadia* (ed. Feuillerat, pp. 406-7). But the ideas expressed there were not uncommon: they are discussed, for example, by Montaigne. John F. Danby, *op. cit.*, pp. 31-2, points out that "Edmund worships a Goddess of whom neither Hooker nor Bacon would approve. . . . No medieval devil ever bounced on the stage with a more scandalous self-announcement." Draper, *Shakes. Jahr.*, 1938, p. 133, remarks that Edmund in taking Nature for his goddess "so renounces both religion and the laws of human society." See also Heilman, *op. cit.*, pp. 123-8. Kittredge cites Webster, *The Devil's Law Case*, IV. ii. 275-80.

3. *Stand . . . custom*] stand on, be dependent on pestilential custom. Wright aptly quotes from the Prayer-Book version of *Ps.* xxxviii. 17: "And I truly am set in the plague." See the Montaigne passage quoted in the Appendix, p. 251.

4. *curiosity*] squeamishness, false delicacy, over-particularity or fastidiousness. Cf. I. i. 6 *ante*. "The nice distinctions which the laws of nations make in defiance of nature and common sense" (Kittredge).

4. *deprive me*] debar me, keep me out of my rights. Cf. *Hystorie of Hamblet*, iv: "rather than he would deprive himself." As Edmund is a younger son, he would not inherit even if he were legitimate. Cf. *A.Y.L.I.* I. i. 49.

5. *For that*] because.

6. *Lag of*] behind in years. Cf. I. i. 20 and *Rich. III.* II. i. 90.

6. *base*] *Bastard* has apparently no etymological connection with the adj. *base*, though 'base son' was used for 'bastard.' Edmund is protesting against the assumption that he is low and vile because he is illegitimate.

7. *dimensions*] proportions. Cf. *M.V.* III. i. 62, and Tourneur, *The Atheist's Tragedy*, v. ii. 165-6:

"Me thinks, my parts, and my dimentions, are
As many, as large, as well compos'd as his."

7. *compact*] put together, made. Cf. *T.A.* v. iii. 88.

8. *generous*] gallant, high-spirited, courageous, befitting a person of noble birth. Cf. *T.C.* II. ii. 154.

8. *as true*] as truly stamped, hit off, as true a likeness of my father. Cf. *W.T.* v. i. 127. Kittredge thinks it means symmetrical.

chaste

As honest madam's issue?   Why brand they us
With base?   with baseness?   bastardy?   base,
    base?   10
Who in the lusty stealth of nature take   *cf stolen hours of*
More composition and fierce quality   *lust oth*
Than doth, within a dull, stale, tired bed,
Go to th' creating a whole tribe of fops, *fools*
Got 'tween asleep and wake?   Well then,   15
Legitimate Edgar, I must have your land:
Our father's love is to the bastard Edmund
As to th' legitimate.   Fine word, " legitimate "!   *The motivation of Edmund.*
Well, my legitimate, if this letter speed,
And my invention thrive, Edmund the base   20
Shall top th' legitimate—:   I grow, I prosper;   *It is a grudge cf*
Now, gods, stand up for bastards!   *Iago's sexual jealousy*

10. with . . . base] *F;* with base, base bastardie *Q.* 13. dull, stale] *F;* stale,
dull *Q.*   tired] *F;* lyed *Q 1;* lied *Q 2.*   14. to] *not in F 3, 4.*   th' creating]
F; the creating of *Q;* creating *Pope.*   15. asleep] *Capell;* a sleepe *Q 1, F;* sleepe
Q 2; a-sleep *Pope.*   then] *F;* the *Q.*   18. Fine . . . " legitimate "] *F; not in Q.*
21. top] *Capell (conj. Edwards);* tooth' *Q;* to'th' *F;* toe *Hanmer;* be *Pope.*

9. *honest*] chaste.
11. *lusty . . . nature*] Cf. *Oth.* III.
iii. 338: " stolen hours of lust."
12. *More composition*] a fuller mixture.   The Bastard in *King John*
(I. i. 88) has a " large composition."
12. *fierce quality*] more energetic
quality.
13. *dull . . . tired*] Referring to the
occupants of the marriage bed, and
their relations.
14. *th' creating*] Abbott points out
that " although this is a noun, and
therefore preceded by ' the,' yet it
is so far confused with the gerund
as to be allowed the privilege of
governing a direct object."
14. *fops*] fools; not, as after the
Restoration, dandies.
19. *speed*] prosper.
21. *Shall top th' legitimate*] This
emendation was first suggested by
Edwards in his *Canons of Criticism*,
and first adopted by Capell. Greg
argues that " if the tail of the ' p '
were for any reason obscured, ' top '

would   naturally   be   misread   as
' too '."   Capell aptly points out
that ' top ' is opposed to ' base '
(by a quibble), and connected with
' grow,' which has no natural introduction unless preceded by ' top.'
Duthie shows that although the F
reading might be taken to mean
" shall attack my legitimate brother,"
Edmund is acting against him any-
way by means of the letter.   The
context requires a word meaning
' overthrow ' or ' surpass.'   Johnson,
following Hanmer, explained " toe
the legitimate " as " kick him out
. . . or to supplant him."   Tannenbaum, *S.A.B.*, Jan. 1941, supports
this reading, and cites *M.V.* I. iii.
119: " And foot me as you spurn
a stranger cur."   On the whole,
' top ' would seem to be preferable;
and certainly an actor would find
it easier to say with the right note of
triumph.
22. *stand up*] Heilman, *op. cit.* p.
314, suggests that there is a punning
reference to tumescence.

Enter GLOUCESTER.

Glou. Kent banish'd thus! And France in choler parted!
And the King gone to-night! prescrib'd his power! *restricted*
Confin'd to exhibition! All this done   25
Upon the gad!—Edmund, how now! What news?

Restricted to an allowance suddenly

Edm. So please your Lordship, none.

eagerly   [*Putting up the letter.*
Glou. Why so earnestly seek you to put up that letter?
Edm. I know no news, my Lord.
Glou. What paper were you reading?   30
Edm. Nothing, my Lord.
Glou. No? What needed then that terrible dispatch of
it into your pocket? The quality of nothing hath
not such need to hide itself. Let's see: come; if
it be nothing, I shall not need spectacles.   35
Edm. I beseech you, Sir, pardon me; it is a letter
from my brother that I have not all o'erread, and
for so much as I have perus'd, I find it not fit for
your o'erlooking. *inspection*
Glou. Give me the letter, sir.   40

24. Prescrib'd] *F;* subscribd *Q.*   25. done] gone *F 2, 3, 4.*   27. S.D.]
Rowe; not in Q, F.   28. Why] Whe *F 2.*   32. needed] *F;* needes *Q.*
terrible] *F, Q 2;* terribe *Q 1.*   34. hide] hid *Q 3.*   37. and] *F; not in Q.*
39. o'erlooking] *F;* liking *Q.*

23. *And . . . parted*] In the recorded
parting between Lear and France,
there is no appearance of any choler
in France; but another interview
is spoken of (i. i. 302), and France
is described as 'hot-blooded.' Greg
suggests, *M.L.R.*, 1940, p. 444, that
France, "incensed at some fresh
insult to Cordelia, departed in a
rage, determined to wrest by force
her portion from . . . Albany and
Cornwall." Cf. note to iv. iii. 3.
24. *to-night*] last night (Greg).
24. *prescrib'd*] limited, restricted,
confined within bounds (*N.E.D.*)
This meaning is rare. The Q reading
subscribed is explicable as an anticipa-
tion of iii. vii. 64, also spoken by
Gloucester.

25. *Confin'd to exhibition*] Restricted
to an allowance. Cf. the use of the
term ' exhibition ' as a minor scholarship tenable at a university, and
T.G. i. iii. 69.
26. *Upon the gad*] suddenly, as if
pricked by a gad or goad. Cf. *T.A.*
iv. i. 103 and *Timon*, iii. vi. 73,
" with that spur " = with the same
alacrity.
28. *earnestly*] eagerly. Cf. *T.C.*
iv. ii. 41.
28. *put up*] i.e. in his pocket.
31. *Nothing*] cf. note on i. i. 87.
32. *terrible dispatch*] fearful haste.
36. *pardon me*] excuse me from
showing it to you.
39. *o'erlooking*] inspection. Cf.
v. i. 50.

Edm. I shall offend, either to detain or give it. The
　　contents, as in part I understand them, are to
　　blame.

Glou. Let's see, let's see.

Edm. I hope, for my brother's justification, he wrote　　45
　　this but as an essay or taste of my virtue. test

Glou. [Reads.] *This policy and reverence of age makes the
　　world bitter to the best of our times; keeps our fortunes
　　from us till our oldness cannot relish them.　I begin to
　　find an idle and fond bondage in the oppression of aged*　50
　　*tyranny, who sways, not as it hath power, but as it is
　　suffer'd.　Come to me, that of this I may speak more.
　　If our father would sleep till I wak'd him, you should
　　enjoy half his revenue for ever, and live the beloved of
　　your brother,* EDGAR.—Hum! Conspiracy! "Sleep　　55
　　till I wak'd him,—you should enjoy half his
　　revenue." My son Edgar! Had he a hand to
　　write this? a heart and brain to breed it in?
　　When came you to this? Who brought it?

Edm. It was not brought me, my Lord; there's the　　60
　　cunning of it; I found it thrown in at the case-
　　ment of my closet.

Glou. You know the character to be your brother's?
　　　　　　　　　　writing

46. virtue] *F*; virtue. *A letter Q.*　　47. S.D.] *F*; *not in Q.*　　*and reverence*]
F; *not in Q.*　　48. the best] best *F 2, 3, 4.*　　55. Sleep] *F*; Slept *Q.*
wak'd] wakt *Q*; wake *F.*　　58. brain] a brain *Rowe.*　　59. you to this] *F*;
this to you *Q, F, 3, 4.*

46. *essay . . . taste*] The words
are synonymous, meaning 'test.' To
take the 'assay' of a dish was to
taste it. Cf. *2 Hen. IV.* II. iii. 52 and
K.J. v. vi. 28. See Appendix, p. 251.

47. *This . . . age*] the policy of
reverencing age—hendiadys
(Schmidt).　'Policy' suggests that
it is a clever trick on the part of
the aged (Kittredge).

48. *bitter*] Whiter, in an unpublished note, points out that the word
was suggested by *taste* (46), and that
it suggests *relish.*

48. *best . . . times*] best years of our
lives. Cf. I. i. 295.

49. *relish*] appreciate.　Cf. *M.M.*
III. i. 34-8.

49-51. *to find . . . tyranny*] I begin
to feel that to be thus oppressed by
an aged and tyrannical father is
nothing but a state of vain and
foolish servitude.

50. *find*] feel.

51-2. *who . . . suffer'd*] who is able
to rule not by its strength but by
our tameness in putting up with it.
Cf. *T.C.* I. iii. 137: "Troy in our
weakness stands, not in her strength."
See also *J.C.* I. iii. 104-5.

51. *sways*] rules. Cf. I. i. 136.

63. *character*] handwriting.　Cf.
Ham. IV. vii. 52.

Edm. If the matter were good, my Lord, I durst
  swear it were his; but, in respect of that, I would   65
  fain think it were not.
Glou. It is his?
Edm. It is his hand, my Lord; but I hope his heart is
  not in the contents.
Glou. Has he never before sounded you in this business?   70
Edm. Never, my Lord. But I have heard him oft
  maintain it to be fit that, sons at perfect age, and
  fathers declin'd, the father should be as ward
  to the son, and the son manage his revenue.

65. respect] *Q 2, F;* respect, *Q 1.*   67. It is] *Q 1, F;* Is it *Q 2.*   his?]
Q; his F.   68. but] *not in F 2, 3, 4.*   70. Has] *F;* Hath *Q.*   before] *F;*
hertofore *Q.*   71. heard him oft] *F;* often heard him *Q.*   73. declin'd] *F;*
declining *Q.*   the father] *F;* his father *Q.*   73. ward] a ward *Q 3.*   his] *F;*
the *Q.*

70. *sounded*] a nautical metaphor.
73. *declin'd*] past their prime. Cf.
Oth. III. iii. 265.
73-4. *the father . . . revenue*] Sullivan
points out in his introduction to
Pettie, *The Civile Conversation of . . .
Guazzo* (1581 ed. 1925) that there is
a long passage in the third conversation (*op. cit.* ii. 65-73) on the foolishness of fathers who cling to their
power and possessions: " The father
is so desirous of keping his paternall
jurisdiction, that though his children
bee arived to mans estate, and be
perfectly accomplished every way,
yet he will alowe them neither more
living, nor more liberty then they
had when they were children. . . .
I thinke they have just cause to bee
mal contents, who knowing themselves to be sufficient men, and to
be so taken of every man, are
neverthelesse used by their father
like children: and therefore I
cannot blame them greatly, if in
stead of loving him, they complaine
of death for delaying the execution
of that judgement, which so long
before was pronounced agaynst him
. . . adding, that his living, will do
him no good when it falleth into his
handes, for that, by course of nature,
he shall be constrained to forgoe it
againe. . . . If that come by the
fault of age, I will not say that such
men were wel worthy to dwel
amongst the Caspians, who when
the father is arrived to the age of
threescore and ten, kill him presently,
and give him to beastes to eat."
Similar sentiments are expressed by
Montaigne. Cf. Appendix, p. 251,
and Florio, *op. cit.* iii. 96-107:
" It is meere injustice to see an old,
crazed, sinnow-shronken, and nigh
dead father . . . to enjoy so many
goods as would suffice for the preferment and entertainment of many
children, and in the meane while,
for want of meanes, to suffer them
to lose their best dayes and yeares
. . . ; whereby they are often cast
into dispaire, to seeke, by some way
how unlawfull soever to provide for
their necessaries . . . But a father
over-burthened with yeares . . . .
ought willingly to distribute and
bestow them amongst those, to
whom by naturall decree they
belong."
73-4. *as . . . to*] under the guardian-
ship of.

Glou. O villain, villain! His very opinion in the 75
letter! Abhorred villain! Unnatural, detested,
brutish villain! worse than brutish! Go, sirrah,
seek him; I'll apprehend him. Abominable
villain! Where is he?

Edm. I do not well know, my Lord. If it shall 80
please you to suspend your indignation against
my brother till you can derive from him better
testimony of his intent, you should run a certain
course; where, if you violently proceed against
him, mistaking his purpose, it would make a great 85
gap in your own honour, and shake in pieces the
heart of his obedience. I dare pawn down my
life for him, that he hath writ this to feel my
affection to your honour, and to no other pretence
of danger. 90

Glou. Think you so?

Edm. If your honour judge it meet, I will place you
where you shall hear us confer of this, and by an
auricular assurance have your satisfaction; and
that without any further delay than this very 95
evening.

Glou. He cannot be such a monster—

Edm. Nor is not, sure.

Glou. —to his father, that so tenderly and entirely
loves him. Heaven and earth! Edmund, seek 100

77. sirrah] *F;* sir *Q.*   I'll]Ile *F;* I *Q 1;* I, *Q 2;* Ay *Camb.*   83. his]
F; this *Q.*   should] *Q, F;* shall *Q 2.*   86. own] *not in F 2, 3, 4.*   88.
that] *F; not in Q.*   writ] *F;* wrote *Q.*   89. other] *F;* further *Q.*   93. of]
not in F 3, 4.   97. monster—] *Dyce;* Monster. *Q, F.*   98–100. Nor . . .
earth!] *Q; not in F.*

76. *abhorred*] detestable.

76. *detested*] detestable.

83-4. *you . . . course*] you would
be adopting a safe plan.

84. *where*] whereas.

86. *gap*] breach. Cf. *W.T.* IV.
iv. 198.

87. *pawn*] stake. Cf. I. i. 155.

88. *feel*] test. Cf. *Hen. V.* IV. i. 131.

89-90. *pretence of danger*] dangerous
intention. Cf. *T.G.* III. i. 47.

94. *auricular*] Shakespeare would
know the expression " auricular confession." It is used, for example, in
the preface of Brooke's *Romeus and
Juliet.* Florio, too, uses the word
' auricular.' Cf. Appendix, p. 250.

worm your way into his confidence

him out; wind me into him, I pray you: frame
the business after your own wisdom. I would
unstate myself to be in a due resolution.

at once

Edm. I will seek him, Sir, presently; convey the
business as I shall find means, and acquaint you 105
withal.

Glou. These late eclipses in the sun and moon portend
no good to us: though the wisdom of Nature
can reason it thus and thus, yet Nature finds
itself scourg'd by the sequent effects. Love 110
cools, friendship falls off, brothers divide: in cities,
mutinies; in countries, discord; in palaces,
treason; and the bond crack'd 'twixt son
and father. This villain of mine comes under
the prediction; there's son against father: the 115
King falls from bias of nature; there's father
against child. We have seen the best of our

102. the] *F;* your *Q.*   103. to] *Q 1, F;* ro *Q 2.*   104. will] *F;*
shall *Q.*   105. find] *F;* see *Q.*   109. it] *F; not in Q.*   112. discord] *F;*
discords *Q.* in palaces] *F;* palaces *Q.*   113. treason] treasons *Q 3.* and] *F;*
not in Q.   'twixt] *F;* betweene *Q.*   114-20 This . . . graves] *F; not in Q.*

101. *wind me into him*] worm your
way into his confidence for me
(Kittredge). ' Wind ' is to make
cautious, indirect advances. Cf.
Cor. III. iii. 64. There is a good description of the process in Polonius's
instructions to Reynaldo, *Ham.* II.
i. 1-68.

101. *frame*] fashion, manage. Cf.
W.T. V. i. 91; *2 Hen. IV.* IV. i. 180.

103. *unstate myself*] forfeit my rank
and fortune. Cf. *A.C.* III. xiii. 30.

103. *to . . . resolution*] to be convinced of his innocence, or even of
his guilt, and so freed from uncertainty. Cf. *Oth.* III. iii. 180.

104. *presently*] at once.

104. *convey*] manage.

107-20. *These . . . graves*] See
Introduction p. xxi. and Appendix,
p. 252.

108. *the wisdom . . . Nature*] natural
philosophy, man's reason, scientific
knowledge.

109. *can . . . thus*] can offer explanations of eclipses.

109-10. *yet . . . effects*] yet the
natural world of man is afflicted by
the disasters that follow.

111. *falls off*] revolts. Cf. *1. Hen.
IV.* I. iii. 94.

112. *mutinies*] riots, insurrections.

113. *bond*] Cf. I. i. 93.

115-17. *there's son . . . child*] Noble
compares *Mark* xiii, 12. Hart,
Shakespeare and the Homilies, quotes
Homilies, 1640, pp. 295-6: "The
brother to seek, and often to work
the death of his brother, the son of
his father, the father to seek or procure the death of his sons being at
man's age, and by their faults to disinherit their innocent children, and
kinsmen their heirs for ever."

116. *falls . . . nature*] goes against
natural instincts. The metaphor is
from bowls. Cf. *K.J.* II. i. 574-80.

117-18. *best . . . time*] Cf. I. ii. 48.

time: machinations, hollowness, treachery, and
all ruinous disorders follow us disquietly to our
graves. Find out this villain, Edmund; it shall 120
lose thee nothing: do it carefully. And the
noble and true-hearted Kent banish'd! his offence,
honesty! 'Tis strange. _foolishness_ [*Exit.*

Edm. This is the excellent foppery of the world, that,
when we are sick in fortune, often the surfeits of 125
our own behaviour, we make guilty of our disasters the sun, the moon, and stars; as if we were
villains on necessity, fools by heavenly compulsion,
knaves, thieves, and treachers by spherical predominance, drunkards, liars, and adulterers by an 130
enforc'd obedience of planetary influence; and
all that we are evil in, by a divine thrusting on.
An admirable evasion of whoremaster man, to lay
lascivious his goatish disposition to the charge of a star!
My father compounded with my mother under 135
the dragon's tail, and my nativity was under
Ursa major; so that it follows I am rough and
lecherous. Fut! I should have been that I am
had the maidenliest star in the firmament twinkled
on my bastardizing. Edgar— 140

Enter EDGAR.

120. villain] villanie *Q 3.* 123. honesty] *F;* honest *Q.* 'tis] *F;*
strange *Q.* S.D.] *F; not in Q.* 125. surfeits] *F;* surfeit *Q.* 127. stars] *F;*
the stars *Q.* on] *F;* by *Q.* 129. treachers] *F;* trecherers *Q.* spherical] *F;*
spiritual *Q.* 134. to] *Q; not in F.* a star] *F;* stars *Q.* 138. Fut] *Q;*
not in *F;* Tut *Jennens.* 139. maidenliest] *F 3;* maidenlest *Q, F 1, 2.* in] *F;*
of *Q.* 140. bastardizing] *F;* bastardy *Q.* Edgar] *Q; not in F.*

118. *hollowness*] falseness, insincerity. Cf. I. i. 154.
119. *disquietly*] Cf. Appendix, p.
250. ' unquietly.'
124. *foppery*] stupidity.
125. *surfeits*] natural evil results,
as indigestion follows over-eating.
Cf. *Cor.* IV. i. 46.
128. *on*] by. Cf. *L.L.L.* I. i. 149.
129. *treachers*] traitors. Cf. Spenser,
F.Q. II. i. 12.
129-30. *spherical predominance*] be-

cause a particular planet was most
powerful at the hour of our birth.
Cf. *A.W.* I. i. 211.
131. *divine . . . on*] supernatural
impelling or incitement. Cf. *Macb.*
I. iii. 130: " supernatural soliciting."
134. *goatish*] lascivious. Cf. *Oth.*
III. iii. 180.
138. *Fut!*] 'Foot or 'Sfoot; Pooh!
140. *bastardizing*] extra-marital
conception. The word is used by
Florio. Cf. Appendix, p. 250.

and pat he comes, like the catastrophe of the old
comedy: my cue is villanous melancholy, with
a sigh like Tom o' Bedlam. O! these eclipses
musical do portend these divisions. *Fa, sol, la, mi.* scale
modulation *Edg.* How now, brother Edmund! What serious 145
contemplation are you in?

Intimate *Edm.* I am thinking, brother, of a prediction I read
this other day, what should follow these eclipses.
scene *Edg.* Do you busy yourself with that?
of *Edm.* I promise you the effects he writes of succeed 150
brothers. unhappily; as of unnaturalness between the
child and the parent; death, dearth, dissolutions
of ancient amities; divisions in state; menaces and
maledictions against King and nobles; needless
Suspicious diffidences, banishment of friends, dissipation 155
of cohorts, nuptial breaches, and I know not what.
Edg. How long have you been a sectary astronomical?

believer/student

141. and pat] *Steevens;* and out *Q;* Pat *F.*   142. my cue] *F;* mine *Q.*
143. sigh] *Q 2, F;* sith *Q 1.*   Tom o'] *F;* them of *Q.*   144. do portend]
portent *Q 3.*   144. Fa . . . mi] *F; not in Q.*   149. with] *F;* about *Q.*
150. you] *not in F 2, 3, 4.*   writes] *F;* writ *Q.*   151-57. as . . .
astronomical] *Q; not in F.*   153. amities] *Q 1;* armies *Q 2.*   155. dissipation
of cohorts] denegation of contracts *conj. Kinnear.*   156. cohorts] courts *Steevens;*
comforts *Jennens.*

143. *Tom o' Bedlam*] Tom was the
name generally assumed by the
bedlam beggar, or Abraham man.
Cf. Audeley, *Fraternitye of Vagabondes,*
1565, ed. 1880. p. 1: "An Abraham
man is he that walketh bare armed,
and bare legged, and fayneth himself
mad, and caryeth a packe of wool,
or a stycke with baken on it, or such
lyke toy, and nameth himselfe poore
Tom." See also Jonson, *The Devil
is an Ass,* v. ii. 35, "Your best song's
Tom o' Bethlem." Harsnett also
mentions Bedlamites.
144. *Fa . . . mi*] Some have supposed that these musical notes may
have been suggested to Edmund by
the word 'division,' which had the
sense of musical modulation. Cf.
1 Hen. IV. iii. i. 211. A similar
play on the two meanings of the

word will be found in Beaumont and
Fletcher, *The Coronation,* iii. i.: ed.
Waller, viii. 269.
    " Is it not pitty any division
    Should be heard out of Musick? "
It has also been suggested (*Notes
and Queries,* 23 June 1928) that
" Edmund is evidently about to say
' Father,' but when he hears the
sound of the first part of the word,
his mischievous nature prompts him
to supply, instead, the remaining
syllables of the diabolical progression."
In any case, Edmund sings to himself so as to pretend that he is un-
aware of Edgar's approach.
148. *this other day*] the other day.
150. *succeed*] turn out.
155. *diffidences*] suspicions, cases of
mutual distrust. Cf. *1 Hen. VI.*
iii. iii. 10.

Edm. When saw you my father last?

Edg. The night gone by.

Edm. Spake you with him?   160

Edg. Ay, two hours together.

Edm. Parted you in good terms? Found you no
displeasure in him by word nor countenance?

Edg. None at all.

Edm. Bethink yourself wherein you may have offended   165
him; and at my entreaty forbear his presence until
some little time hath qualified the heat of his displeasure, which at this instant so rageth in him
that with the mischief of your person it would
scarcely allay.   170

Edg. Some villain hath done me wrong.

Edm. That's my fear. I pray you have a continent
forbearance till the speed of his rage goes slower,
and as I say, retire with me to my lodging, from
whence I will fitly bring you to hear my Lord   175
speak. Pray ye, go; there's my key. If you do
stir abroad, go arm'd.

Edg. Arm'd, brother!

---

158. When] *F;* Come, come, when *Q.*   159. The] *F;* Why, the *Q.*
161. Ay] I *F; not in Q.*   163. nor] *F;* or *Q.*   165. may] *not in F 3, 4.*
166. until] *F;* till *Q.*   170. scarcely] *F;* scarce *Q.*   172. fear] *F;* feare
brother *Q.*   172-9. I . . . Brother] *F; not in Q.*   176. ye] *F;* you *Rowe.*

155-6. *dissipation of cohorts*] Craig
remarks that "this does not read
like Shakespeare," and suggests that
he may have written "disputation
of consorts," i.e. wrangling among
comrades. *But,* as Kittredge points
out, "The word *cohorts* fits the era
of the play as Shakespeare seems to
have imagined that era . . . though
the fabulous Lear's reign was long
before" the Roman occupation.
Schmidt thinks that these lines
151-57, peculiar to Q, are spurious,
since they contain six words to be
found nowhere else in Shakespeare.
But of these *menace* (as a noun) and
dissipation are to be found in Florio's
Montaigne, *malediction, astronomical*

and *cohort* were not uncommon, and
Shakespeare uses elsewhere in the
play words cognate to *unnaturalness.*
It may be added that Florio also
uses *sectary.* The cohorts were melt-
ing away, presumably by the desertion of the soldiers.

157. *sectary astronomical*] believer
in, or student of, astrology.

166. *forbear . . . presence*] avoid
meeting him.

167. *qualified*] mitigated. Cf. *Oth.*
II. iii. 31.

172-3. *have . . . forbearance*] restrain your feelings, and keep away.
Cf. 166 *ante.*

175. *fitly*] opportunely. Cf. *Tim.*
III. iv. 111.

Cf Iago & protestation of honesty (handwritten)

Edm. Brother, I advise you to the best. I am no honest
intention (handwritten) man if there be any good meaning toward you; 180
I have told you what I have seen and heard;
but faintly, nothing like the image and horror of it;
pray you, away.
Edg. Shall I hear from you anon?   185
Edm. I do serve you in this business.   [*Exit Edgar.*
A credulous father, and a brother noble,
Whose nature is so far from doing harms
That he suspects none; on whose foolish honesty
Jungle (handwritten) My practices ride easy! I see the business.
law (handwritten) Let me, if not by birth, have lands by wit: 190
of Nature (handwritten) All with me's meet that I can fashion fit.   [*Exit.*

Any means justifies the end. (handwritten)

179. best] *F;* best, goe arm'd *Q.*   180. toward] *F;* towards *Q.*   186.
S.D.] *Q 1; after 196 Q 2; Exit (after 197) F.*

SCENE III.—[*A Room in the Duke of Albany's Palace.*]

Enter GONERIL, *and* OSWALD, *her Steward.*

Gon. Did my father strike my gentleman for chiding
of his Fool?
Osw. Ay, Madam.

Scene III

S.D. *A Room . . . Palace*] Capell; *The Palace Rowe; not in Q, F. Oswald,
her steward*] Collier; *Gentleman Q 1; A Gentleman Q 2; Steward F.*   3. *Osw.*
Collier; *Gent. Q; Stew. F.*   Ay] I *F;* Yes *Q.*

180. *meaning*] intention.
182. *faintly*] euphemistically.
182. *image and horror*] horrible
reality—the horror which an exact
description would fill you with.
186. *credulous father*] Geoffrey of
Monmouth uses the expression
credulus ergo pater about Lear (Perrett,
op. cit. p. 280).
189. *practices*] intrigues.
189. *ride*] Cf. *T.N.* III. iv. 318,
W.T. I. ii. 94.

191. *All . . . fit*] To me everything
is fitting and justifiable that I can
utilize for my purposes; the end
justifies the means.
191. *fashion fit*] make fitting.

Scene III

1-2. *chiding . . . Fool*] Empson,
op. cit. p. 129, comments: "So it is
the Fool who causes the beginning of
the storm against Lear, rather than his
shadowy train of deboshed knights."

Gon. By day and night, he wrongs me; every hour
  He flashes into one gross crime or other, *Hence* 5
  That sets us all at odds: I'll not endure it:
  His knights grow riotous, and himself upbraids us
  On every trifle.   When he returns from hunting
  I will not speak with him; say I am sick:
  If you come slack of former services,   10
  You shall do well; the fault of it I'll answer.

Osw. He's coming, Madam; I hear him.   [*Horns within.*

Gon. Put on what weary negligence you please,
  You and your fellows; I'd have it come to question:
  If he distaste it, let him to my sister,   15
  Whose mind and mine, I know, in that are one,
  Not to be over-rul'd.   Idle old man, *foolish*
  That still would manage those authorities
  That he hath given away!   Now, by my life,
  Old fools are babes again, and must be us'd   20
  With checks as flatteries, when they are seen abus'd. *rebukes as*
  Remember what I have said.   *well as kind words when*

Osw.   Well, Madam. *they are seen*
                                                to err

But this is as part of the bargain

4. night, he] F; night he Q.   7. upbraids] Q 2, F; obrayds Q 1.   12. S.D.]
Capell; not in Q, F.   14. fellows] F; fellow seruants Q 1; fellow-seruants
Q 2.   to] F; in Q.   15. distaste] F; dislike Q.   my] F; our Q.
17–21. Not . . . abus'd] Q; not in F.   21. checks . . . abus'd] like flatt'rers
when they're seen t'abuse us *Theobald.*   22. have said] F; tell you Q.   Well]
F; Very well Q.

4. *By . . . night*] Probably an oath.
Cf. *Hen. VIII.* i. ii. 213. But Craig
explains the phrase as " at all times."
Kittredge points out that Lear
swears by day and night, i. i. 109-10.

5. *flashes*] Cf. *Ham.* ii. i. 33.

5. *crime*] offence.

8. *hunting*] In the story of Lear as
told in Layamon's *Brut.* the two
dukes covenanted with Lear " that
they would provide for the king
Hawks and hounds that he might
ride over all the country and live in
bliss while he lived."   Lear's hunting
is mentioned elsewhere in the poem.

10. *come . . . services*] are less serviceable, less duteous to him, than you
formerly were. Cf. ii. iv. 247 and
Oth. iv. iii. 88.

11. *answer*] be answerable for.

14. *to question*] to be discussed.

15. *distaste*] dislike. Cf. *T.C.* ii.
ii. 66.   See note to i. iv. 2 *post.*

17. *idle*] foolish.

21. *With . . . abus'd*] With rebukes
as well as soothing words, when they
(the old fools) are seen to be deluded.
Tyrwhitt thought the antecedent
of *they* was *flatteries,* but Kittredge
argued that this " interpretation
forces one to emphasize *they,* and
that spoils the metre." Johnson
points out a play on the words *used*
and *abused,* and he explains: " Old
men must be treated with checks,
when as they are seen to be deceived
with flatteries."

Gon. And let his knights have colder looks among you;
What grows of it, no matter; advise your fellows so:
opportunities I would breed from hence occasions, and I shall,   25
That I may speak: I'll write straight to my sister
To hold my very course. Prepare for dinner. [*Exeunt.*

25-6. I would . . . speak] *Q; not in F.*   27. very] *Q; not in F.*   S.D.] *Q;*
Exit F.

SCENE IV.—[*A Hall in the same.*]

Enter KENT, *disguised.*

Kent. If but as well I other accents borrow,
Disguise That can my speech defuse, my good intent   *render indistinct*
on the side May carry through itself to that full issue
of good. For which I raz'd my likeness. Now, banish'd Kent,
If thou canst serve where thou dost stand con-
demn'd,   5
(wish?) So may it come, thy master, whom thou lov'st,
ie So let it Shall find thee full of labours.
come

Scene IV

S.D. *A Hall . . . same*] *Capell; not in Q, F.*   *disguised*] *Rowe; not in*
Q, F.   1. well] *Q 1;* will *F.*   2. That] *Q, F;* And *Rowe, Pope, Johnson,*
Theobald.   defuse] *Q, F;* disuse *Rowe, Pope, Johnson;* diffuse *Theobald;*
deface *Capell;* disguise *conj. Jennens.*   6. So . . . come] *F; not in Q.*   7.
labours] *F;* labour *Q.*   Horns within] *F; not in Q.*

25. *breed*] cf. *grows* in the previous
line and I. ii. 58, III. vi. 78.
25. *occasions*] opportunities.   Cf.
Oth. II. i. 246.
26. *straight*] immediately.

Scene IV

2. *defuse*] disorder, confuse, render
indistinct, speak broad, disguise.
Cf. *Hen. V.* v. ii. 61, " defused attire";
M.W. IV. iv. 54, " diffused (i.e.
uncouth) song." Dyce cites Palsgrave, *Lesclarcissement;* " *Dyffuse* harde
to be vnderstande, *diffuse.*" Wright
cites Lyly, *Euphues,* ed. Arber, p. 64:
" defused determination"; and
Armin, *Nest of Ninnies,* 1880, p. 48:

" it is hard that the taste of one
Apple should distaste the whole
lumpe of this defused Chaios."
2-4. *my . . . likeness*] I may be able
to carry out the good purpose which
made me so disguise myself, i.e. to
attend on the King.
4. *raz'd . . . likeness*] obliterated
my former appearance. As Kent
had probably shaved his beard,
there may be a quibble on *raz'd* and
razor.
6. *So . . . come*] Either a paren-
thetical wish, referring to Kent's
hope of serving his master, or else
it may mean " so it may happen
that."

Horns within.   Enter LEAR, *Knights, and
Attendants.*

Lear. Let me not stay a jot for dinner: go, get it
    ready.   [*Exit an Attendant.*
    How now! what art thou?   10
Kent. A man, Sir.
Lear. What dost thou profess?   What would'st thou
    with us?
Kent. I do profess to be no less than I seem; to serve
    him truly that will put me in trust; to love him   15
    that is honest; to converse with him that is wise,
    and says little; to fear judgment; to fight when
    I cannot choose; and to eat no fish.
Lear. What art thou?
Kent. A very honest-hearted fellow, and as poor as   20
    the King.
Lear. If thou be'st as poor for a subject as he is for a
    King, thou art poor enough.   What would'st
    thou?
Kent. Service.   25
Lear. Who would'st thou serve?
Kent. You.
Lear. Dost thou know me, fellow?
Kent. No, Sir; but you have that in your counten-
    ance which I would fain call master.   30

Knights] *Rowe; not in Q, F.*   Attendants] *F; not in Q.*   9. S.D.]
Malone; not in Q, F.   17. says] say *Steevens.*   19. art] are *F 2.*
22. be'st] *F;* be *Q.*   he is] *Q;* hee's *F.*   23. thou art] *Q 2, F;* thar't *Q 1.*
26. Who] Whom *F 2, 3, 4.*

8. *stay*] wait. Cf. *T.G.* I. ii. 131.
jot] moment.
    12. *What . . . profess*] What is
your job? Lear uses *profess* " in the
sense of *trade* or *calling.*" Kent replies in the sense of *assertion* (Delius).
    16. *converse*] consort. Accented on
the first syllable.
    17. *fear judgment*] by an earthly, or
a heavenly, judge. Cf. *Ps.* i. 6
(cited Noble, *op. cit.*).
    17-18. *when . . . choose*] when I
must. Cf. *A.W.* I. i. 158.
    18. *eat no fish*] Two explanations

(*a*) I am a loyal protestant (Warburton).   Cf. Marston *The Dutch
Courtezan,* I. ii (ed. Wood, p. 76):
" Yet I trust I am none of the wicked
that eate fish a Fridaies." (*b*) I
am no weakling (Capell). Cf. *2 Hen.
IV.* IV. iv. iii. 99: " these demure boys
who never come to any proof; for
thin drink doth so over-cool their
bloods, and making many fish meals."
From *R.J.* I. i. 36, it seems possible
that Kent's meaning is indecent.
    29-30. *countenance*] bearing—not
merely ' face ' (Kittredge).

Lear. What's that?

Kent. Authority.

Lear. What services canst thou do?

Kent. I can keep honest counsel, ride, run, mar a
curious tale in telling it, and deliver a plain   35
message bluntly; that which ordinary men are
fit for, I am qualified in, and the best of me is
diligence.

Lear. How old art thou?

Kent. Not so young, Sir, to love a woman for singing,   40
nor so old to dote on her for anything; I have years
on my back forty-eight.

Lear. Follow me; thou shalt serve me; if I like thee
no worse after dinner I will not part from thee
yet. Dinner, ho! dinner! Where's my knave?   45
my Fool? Go you and call my Fool hither.

                            [*Exit an Attendant.*

                    Enter OSWALD.

You, you, sirrah, where's my daughter?

Osw. So please you,—   [*Exit.*

Lear. What says the fellow there? Call the clotpoll
back.   50
                            [*Exit a Knight.*

Where's my Fool, ho? I think the world's
asleep.

                    Re-enter Knight.

How now! where's that mongrel?

Knight. He says, my Lord, your daughter is not well.

Lear. Why came not the slave back to me when I   55
call'd him?

---

31. What's] What's is *Q 3.*   33. services] service *Q 3.*   thou] *Q 2, F;*
not in *Q 1.*   34. counsel] counsailes *F 2, 3, 4.*   40, Sir] *F;* not in Q.
43. thou] that *F 2.*   me;] *Rowe;* me, *Q, F.*   46. S.D.] *Capell; Enter
Steward* (47) *Q, F.*   47. You, you] *F;* you *Q.*   48. S.D.] *Dyce;* not in
Q, F.   50. S.D.] *Dyce;* not in *Q, F.*   54. daughter] *Q;* Daughters *F 1, 2.*

34. *keep . . . counsel*] keep an
honourable secret.

35. *curious*] elaborate, complicated,
elegant, nice.

40. *to love*] as to love.

45. *knave*] boy. Cf. I. i. 21.

48. *So please you*] Oswald is carry-
ing out instructions. Cf. I. iii. 13.

49. *clotpoll*] clod-pate, blockhead.
Cf. *T.C.* II. i. 128 and *T.N.* III. iv. 208.

Knight. Sir, he answered me in the roundest manner,
   he would not.

Lear. He would not!

Knight. My Lord, I know not what the matter is;   60
   but, to my judgment, your Highness is not
   entertain'd with that ceremonious affection as
   you were wont; there's a great abatement of kindness appears as well in the general dependants
   as in the Duke himself also and your daughter.   65

Lear. Ha! say'st thou so?

Knight. I beseech you, pardon me, my Lord, if I be
   mistaken; for my duty cannot be silent when
   I think your Highness wrong'd.

Lear. Thou but rememb'rest me of mine own con-   70
   ception: I have perceived a most faint neglect of
   late; which I have rather blamed as mine own
   jealous curiosity than as a very pretence and
   purpose of unkindness: I will look further into't.
   But where's my Fool? I have not seen him this two   75
   days.

Knight. Since my young Lady's going into France,
   Sir, the Fool hath much pined away.

Lear. No more of that; I have noted it well. Go you,
   and tell my daughter I would speak with her.   80
                                          [*Exit an Attendant.*
   Go you, call hither my Fool.   [*Exit an Attendant.*

---

59. me] *not in F 3, 4.*   57. He] *Q 2, F; A Q.*   63-4 of kindness] *F;*
not in Q.   69. wrong'd] *Q, F.; is wronged Q 2.*   70. mine] *my F 3, 4.*
72. mine] *my F 4.*   74. purpose] *F; purport Q.*   75. my] *F; this Q.*
80-1. S.D.] *Dyce; not in Q, F.*   81. *Re-enter Oswald] Collier; Enter*
Steward F; not in Q.

57. *roundest*] plainest, rudest. Cf.
Ham. III. i. 191.

62. *entertain'd*] treated.

70. *rememb'rest*] remindest. Cf.
W.T. III. ii. 231.

70-1. *conception*] idea.

71. *most faint*] hardly perceptible,
or, more probably, dull languid,
cold, "weary negligence." Cf. I. iii.
13. In *Leir*, 2262, the King speaks
of Gonorill's treatment: "But euery
day her kindnesse did grow cold."

73. *curiosity*] "a puctilious jealousy, resulting from a scrupulous
watchfulness of his own dignity"
(Steevens). Cf. I. i. 6 and I. ii. 4.

73. *very pretence*] an actual intention. Cf. I. ii. 89.

75. *this*] these.

77-8. *Since . . . away*] By this
delicate stroke Shakespeare gives us
an insight into the characters of
Cordelia, Lear and the Fool.

Re-enter OSWALD.

O! you sir, you, come you hither, sir.
Who am I, sir?

Osw. My Lady's father.

Lear. " My Lady's father!" my Lord's knave: you   85
whoreson dog! you slave! you cur!

Osw. I am none of these, my Lord; I beseech your
pardon.

Lear. Do you bandy looks with me, you rascal?

exchange
                                        [*Striking him.*

Osw. I'll not be strucken, my Lord.   90

Kent. Nor tripp'd neither, you base foot-ball player.

                                [*Tripping up his heels.*

Lear. I thank thee, fellow; thou serv'st me, and I'll
love thee.

Kent. Come, sir, arise, away! I'll teach you differences: away, away! If you will measure your   95
lubber's length again, tarry; but away! Go
to; have you wisdom? [*Exit Oswald.*] So.

Lear. Now, my friendly knave, I thank thee: there's
earnest of thy service.   [*Gives Kent money.*

82. you sir, you] *F 1, 2;* you sir, you sir *Q;* you sir *F 3, 4.*   hither, sir]
F; hither *Q.*   87. these] *F;* this *Q.*   87–8. your pardon] *F;* you pardon
me *Q.*   89. S.D.] *Rowe; not in Q, F.*   90. strucken] *F;* struck *Q.*
91. S.D.] *Rowe; not in Q, F.*   94. arise, away] *F; not in Q.*   96-7. Go to] *F;*
not in Q.   97. S.D.] *Theobald, subst.*   have . . . so] *F;* you haue
wisedome *Q.*   98. my] *F; not in Q.*   99. S.D.] *Capell, subst.*

89. *bandy*] exchange, hit to and
fro, as in the game of tennis. Cf.
II. iv. 177 and *T.S.* v. ii. 172. Cotgrave has: " To bandy against,
at Tennis; and (by metaphor) to
pursue with all insolencie ".

90. *strucken*] struck. Cf. *Cor.* IV.
v. 156

91. *foot-ball*] Football, perhaps
suggested by ' bandy ' (93), was
regarded as a low game in Shakespeare's day. It was played by
idle boys in the streets to the great
annoyance of the citizens.

94-5. *I'll . . . differences*] I'll teach
you your position, the difference
between yourself and the king.

95-6. *measure . . . length*] Cf. *Cym.*
I. ii. 25; *M.N.D.* III. ii. 429; *R.J.*
III. iii. 70.

97. *have . . . wisdom?*] " Are you
in your senses? " Cf. *2 Hen. IV.*
v. v. 49. Or it may simply mean,
" Have you the sense to make
yourself scarce? " Schmidt argues
that this is not a question, but an
imperative. Neither Ff nor Qq
have a question-mark.

97. *so*] that's right!

99. *earnest*] earnest-money, a small
sum paid to secure a bargain, hansel.
Cf. *Macb.* I. iii. 104.

Enter Fool.

Fool. Let me hire him too: here's my coxcomb.   100

[*Offers Kent his cap.*

Lear. How now, my pretty knave! how dost thou?

Fool. Sirrah, you were best take my coxcomb.

Kent. Why, Fool?

Fool. Why? for taking one's part that's out of favour.
Nay, and thou canst not smile as the wind sits,   105
thou'lt catch cold shortly: there, take my coxcomb. Why, this fellow has banish'd two on's
daughters, and did the third a blessing against
his will: if thou follow him thou must needs
wear my coxcomb. How now, Nuncle! Would   110
I had two coxcombs and two daughters!

Lear. Why, my boy?

Fool. If I gave them all my living, I'd keep my coxcombs myself. There's mine; beg another of
thy daughters.   115

Lear. Take heed, sirrah; the whip.

103. *Kent.* Why, Fool?] *Q; Lear.* Why my Boy *F.*   104. one's] *F, Q 2;*
on's *Q.*   that's] that is *F 4.*   106. thou'lt] *F;* thou't *Q.*   107. has] *F;*
hath *Q.*   on's *Q 1, F;* of his *Q 2, 3.*   108. did] *F;* done *Q.*

100. *coxcomb*] the cap of the professional fool. Cf. Minshew, *Ductor
in Linguas,* 1617: "Natural idiots
and fools have, and still accustom
themselves to wear, cock's feathers,
or a hat with the neck and head of a
cock on the top, with a bell thereon."

102. *you were best*] you had better,
Cf. Speed, *Chronicle,* p. 1136: "My
counsel is that you were best to yield."

103. *Kent.*] Wrongly given to
Lear by *F.*

105. *and*] a common variant of
an, meaning if.

105. *smile . . . sits*] back the
stronger side. Cf. II. ii. 76-82 *post.*

106. *catch cold*] be turned out of
doors; or, perhaps, it merely means
"it will be the worse for you."

107-8. *banish'd . . . daughters*] This
may mean that Lear had made
Goneril and Regan independent, and

so lost their love and obedience
(Capell); but the Fool deliberately
uses the word *banish'd,* to glance at
Lear's treatment of Cordelia.

107. *on's*] of his.

108-9. *a blessing . . . will*] By
cursing and banishing Cordelia,
Lear had made her Queen of France,
and saved her from marrying Burgundy.

110. *nuncle*] contracted from *mine
uncle.* "It seems to have been the
customary appellation of the licensed
fool to his superiors" (Nares).

113. *living*] property. Cf. *M.V.*
v. i. 286.

114-15. *There's . . . daughters*]
"Thus he calls Lear a double-dyed
fool" (Kittredge).

116. *whip*] Fools were commonly
whipped. Cf. *A.Y.L.I.* i. ii. 90 ff.

Fool. Truth's a dog must to kennel; he must be
  whipp'd out when the Lady Brach may stand
  by th' fire and stink.

Lear. A pestilent gall to me!   120

Fool. Sirrah, I'll teach thee a speech.

Lear. Do.

Fool. Mark it, Nuncle:

> Have more than thou showest,
> Speak less than thou knowest,   125
> Lend less than thou owest,
> Ride more than thou goest,
> Learn more than thou trowest,

113. gave] give *F 3, 4.*   all my] *F;* any *Q.*   I'd] I'll *Rowe.*   113-14.
coxcombs] *Q 1, F;* coxcombe *Q 2, 3, F 2, 3, 4.*   117. Truth's] *F;* Truth
is *Q.*   dog] *F;* dog that *Q.*   118. the Lady] *F;* Ladie oth'e *Q.*   120, gall]
F; gull *Q.*   123. Nuncle] *F;* vncle *Q.*   126. less] more *Jennens.*

118. *the Lady Brach*] Most editors
follow Steevens in reading *Lady, the
brach,*—Lady being a common name
for hound. Cf. *1 Hen. IV.* III. i. 240.
Brach, in Shakespeare's day, was
generally used as "a mannerly
name for all hound bitches." Sir
Thomas More, *Comfort against Trib-
ulation,* 1573, p. 199: "I am so
cunning that I cannot tell whether
among them a bitch be a bitch,
but as I remember she is no bitch,
but a brach." Archibald Smith,
N.Q., 1858, suggested "lye the
brach," lie being an antithesis to
Truth (117). Duthie conjectures
"Liar the Brach," though retaining
the F reading in his text. He remarks: "It has been implied that
Truth is a dog of low social status—
the Lady Brach is pictured as of
high social status." Perhaps the
antithesis is not between Truth and
Falsehood, but between Truth and
Flattery. Shakespeare often associates dogs with flatterers. There
may even be a suggestion that
Cordelia is truth, and Goneril
and Regan flattering bitches.

120. *A . . . me!*) A passionate
remembrance of Oswald's insolence
(Moberly); "a plague take me for

my folly " in banishing Cordelia
(Craig); or a reference to the Fool's
satirical gibes (Kittredge). Cf.
" bitter Fool " (142).

120. *gall*] irritation, sore, produced by rubbing and chafing.
But the word also means " the
secretion of the liver, bile," something intensely bitter. Cf. previous
note.

124-31. *Have . . . door*] Florio,
Second Fruites, pp. 101-5, has some
similar rhymed proverbs:

> " The bottom of your purse or
>   heart,
>   To anie man do not empart.
>   Do not giue your selfe to plaie,
>   Vnles you purpose to decaie . . .
>   Shun wine, dice, and letchery,
>   Else will you come to beggery."

124. *Have . . . showest*] Don't
parade your wealth.

125. *Speak . . . knowest*] Be reticent,
don't tell all you know.

126. *owest*] ownest. Cf. *Rich. II.*
IV. i. 185.

127. *goest*] walkest. Cf. *Sonnets,*
cxxx. 11.

128. *Learn . . . trowest*] don't
believe all you hear; or " Ascertain
much, and don't indulge in guessing "
(Tovey).

Set less than thou throwest;
Leave thy drink and thy whore,　　　130
And keep in-a-door,
And thou shalt have more
Than two tens to a score.

Kent. This is nothing, Fool.

Fool. Then 'tis like the breath of an unfee'd lawyer; 135
you gave me nothing for't. Can you make no
use of nothing, Nuncle?

Lear. Why, no, boy; nothing can be made out of
nothing.

Fool. [*To Kent.*] Prithee, tell him, so much the rent 140
of his land comes to: he will not believe a Fool.

Lear. A bitter Fool!

Fool. Dost thou know the difference, my boy, between a bitter Fool and a sweet one?

Lear. No, lad; teach me.　　　145

Fool.　　　That lord that counsell'd thee
　　　To give away thy land,
　　　Come place him here by me,
　　　Do thou for him stand:
　　　The sweet and bitter fool　　　150
　　　Will presently appear;

131. in-a-door] *Capell;* in a doore *Q, F;* in dore *F 3, 4.*　　134. Kent] *F;*
Lear Q.　　135. 'tis] *F;* not in *Q;* it is *F 4.*　　136. gave] *F;* give *F 3, 4.*
for't] for it *Q 2, 3.*　　137. Nuncle] *F;* vncle *Q.*　　140. S.D.] *Rowe; not in*
Q, F.　　143. thou] *F; not in Q.*　　144. one] *F;* foole *Q.*　　146-61. That . . .
snatching] *Q; not in F.*

129. *Set . . . throwest*] Don't stake
all your winnings at a single throw.

131. *in-a-door*] indoors.

132-3. *And . . . score*] Meaning, I
suppose, that for each pound one
would have more than twenty
shillings.

134. *nothing*] Cf. notes to I. i. 87
and I. iv. 136-9.

135. *Then . . . lawyer*] See Appendix, p. 251.

136. *you . . . for't*] Cf. *Leir,* 654:
" He lou'd me not, and therfore
gaue me nothing."

142. *bitter*] sarcastic. Cf. 120 *ante.*

146. *That lord*] Skalliger, a lord
in the old play, who gives advice
to Leir about the division of the
kingdom, may have been in Shake-
spear's mind here; but Kittredge
thinks the Fool implies that nobody
gave Lear such idiotic advice.

149. *Do . . . stand*] Impersonate
him. Hanmer read " Or do ";
White argued for " And do "; the
Cambridge editors suggested the
line should read: " Do thou there
for him stand."

151. *presently*] at once.

The one in motley here,
The other found out there.

Lear. Dost thou call me fool, boy?

Fool. All thy other titles thou hast given away; that 155
thou wast born with.

Kent. This is not altogether Fool, my Lord.

Fool. No, faith, lords and great men will not let me;
if I had a monopoly out, they would have part
on't: and ladies too, they will not let me have 160
all the fool to myself; they'll be snatching.
Nuncle, give me an egg, and I'll give thee two
crowns.

Lear. What two crowns shall they be?

Fool. Why, after I have cut the egg i' th' middle and 165
eat up the meat, the two crowns of the egg.
When thou clovest thy crown i' th' middle, and
gav'st away both parts, thou bor'st thine ass on
thy back o'er the dirt: thou hadst little wit in thy
bald crown when thou gav'st thy golden one 170
away. If I speak like myself in this, let him be
whipp'd that first finds it so. ~ foolishly

159. out] *Q;* on't *Pope.*   160. on't, and ladies] *Capell;* an't, and Ladies
Q 1 corr.; an't, and lodes *Q 1 uncorr.;* on't, and lodes *Q 2, 3.*   161. the]
Q 1; not in Q 2, 3.   162. Nuncle ... egg] *F;* giue me an egge Nuncle *Q.*
167. crown] *Q;* Crownes *F.*   168. thine] *F;* thy *Q.*   168-9. on thy] at'h
Q 1.   172. so] sooth *Warburton.*

153. *there*] He points at Lear, who
is the bitter fool.

156. *thou ... with*] i.e. Lear was
a born fool.

158. *No ... me:*] The Fool takes
"altogether fool" to mean not
"entirely a fool," but "one who
has all the folly that there is"
(Kittredge).

159. *monopoly out*] i.e. one granted.
In spite of the Declaratory Act
against monopolies, passed at the
end of Elizabeth's reign, James I
constantly granted them to his
needy courtiers, and there was a

great popular outcry in consequence.

164. *What ... be?*] The answer
to the Fool's riddle is obvious, but
Lear is deliberately acting as a
stooge.

168-9. *thou ... dirt*] The Fool
refers to Æsop's fable of the man,
his two sons, and the ass. Warner
had retold it in *Albion's England*,
1586, 1602.

171. *like myself*] like a fool, foolishly outspoken.

172. *so*] i.e. true. The implication is that Lear himself should be
whipped already.

> *Fools had ne'er less grace in a year;*
> *For wise men are grown foppish,*
> *And know not how their wits to wear,*   175
> *Their manners are so apish.*

Lear. When were you wont to be so full of songs, sirrah?

Fool. I have used it, Nuncle, e'er since thou mad'st thy daughters thy mothers; for when thou gav'st 180 them the rod and putt'st down thine own breeches,

> *Then they for sudden joy did weep,*
> *And I for sorrow sung,*
> *That such a king should play bo-peep,*
> *And go the fools among.*   185

Prithee, Nuncle, keep a schoolmaster that can teach thy Fool to lie: I would fain learn to lie.

Lear. And you lie, sirrah, we'll have you whipp'd.

---

173. grace] *F; wit Q.*   175. And] *F; They Q.*   to] *F; doe Q.*
179. e'er] ere *F; euer Q.*   180. mothers] *F; mother Q.*   182. Then they]
verse by Theobald; prose Q, F.   182-5. for . . . among] *verse F; prose Q.*
185. fools] *Q; Foole F 1, 2.*   187. learn to] *F; learnto Q corr.;* learne *Q*
uncorr.   188. And] *Q 1, F; If Q 2, 3.*   sirrah] *F; not in Q.*

173-6. *Fools . . . apish*] Johnson explains: " There was never a time when fools were less in favour than now, and the reason is they were never so little wanted, for wise men now supply their place." Malone cites Lyly, *Mother Bombie,* II. iii. (ed. Bond iii. p. 191): " I thinke Gentlemen had neuer lesse wit in a yeere."

174. *foppish*] foolish.

176. *apish*] See Appendix, p. 256. The word is also by Armin, *op. cit.,* p. 49.

179. *used it*] made a practice of it. Cf. *Ham.* III. ii. 50.

182-5. *Then . . . among*] Rollins, *M.L.R.,* 1920, p. 87, points out that the Fool is adapting an old ballad:

" Some men for sodayne ioye do wepe,
And some in sorrow syng:

When that they lie in daunger depe,
To put away mournyng."

Steevens compares a song in Heywood's *Rape of Lucrece,* 1608 (*Works* ed. Pearson v. 179):

" Some men for sudden joy gan weep,
But I for sorrow sing."

184. *play bo-peep*] Cotgrave thus translates *Faire les doux yeux.* Harsnett uses the phrase metaphorically. See Appendix, p. 254. The implication is that Lear has blinded himself, hidden himself (i.e. abdicated), or played silly pranks. From Dekker, *Satiromastix* (ed. Pearson, i. 257), the game seems to have been more like hide-and-seek than the modern bo-peep: " Our vnhandsome-fac'd Poet does play at bo-peepes with your Grace, and cryes ' all-hidde ' as boyes doe " (cited Kittredge).

Fool. I marvel what kin thou and thy daughters are:
they'll have me whipp'd for speaking true, thou'lt 190
have me whipp'd for lying; and sometimes I am
whipp'd for holding my peace. I had rather be
any kind o' thing than a fool; and yet I would not
be thee, Nuncle; thou hast pared thy wit o' both
sides, and left nothing i' th' middle: here comes 195
one o' the parings.

Enter GONERIL.   *is doing forehead*

Lear. How now, daughter! what makes that frontlet
on? You are too much of late i' th' frown.
Fool. Thou wast a pretty fellow when thou hadst no
need to care for her frowning; now thou art an O 200
without a figure. I am better than thou art now;
I am a Fool, thou art nothing. [*To Goneril.*]
Yes, forsooth, I will hold my tongue; so your
face bids me, though you say nothing.
  Mum, mum: 205
  He that keeps nor crust nor crum,
  Weary of all, shall want some.
That's a sheal'd peascod.   *eavly*   [*Pointing to Lear.*

190 thou'lt] *F;* thou wilt *Q.*   191. sometimes] *F;* sometime *Q.*   193.
o'] *F;* of *Q.*   194. o'] *F;* a *Q.*   20. i'th] *F;* in the *Q.*   o'] *F;* of *Q.*
198. You] *F;* me thinks you *Q.*   of late] *F;* alate *Q.*   200. frowning] *F;*
frowne *Q.*   now thou] *Q corr., F;* thou thou *Q 1 uncorr., Q 2, 3.*
202-3. S.D.] *Pope; not in Q, F.*   206. nor crust] *F;* neither crust *Q.*   nor
crumb] not crum *F 1, 2.*   208. S.D.] *Johnson; not in Q, F.*

197. *makes*] is doing.

197. *frontlet*] Perrett takes this to
be a " generic name for a coronet or
small crown." Cf. *N.E.D.* But a
frontlet was a band worn either for
ornament, or, at night, to remove
wrinkles. Lear is clearly referring
to Goneril's frowning forehead.
Steevens cites *Zepheria,* 1594, xxvii:

" But now my sunne it fits thou
 take thy set,
And vayle thy face with frownes
 as with a frontlet."

200-1. *an . . . figure*] a mere cipher.
Florio, *Second Fruites,* p. 149, uses

the same conceit: " Doo not you
knowe that nobilitie is now a daies
like vnto a cipher of nothing in
arithmetick, which if it haue no
number added vnto it, it sommes
nothing, euen so if there be no valor,
ritches, or knowledge ioyned vnto
nobilitie, it makes nothing, and is
neither regarded nor honoured."

208. *sheal'd peascod*] shelled pea-
pod. Camden, *Remaines* (ed. 1629,
p. 181, cited Perrett) mentions
Richard II's device of " a Pescod
branch with the cods open, but the
Pease out, as it is vpon his Robe in
his Monument at Westminster."

Gon. Not only, Sir, this your all-licens'd Fool,
   But other of your insolent retinue   210
   Do hourly carp and quarrel, breaking forth
   In rank and not-to-be-endured riots. Sir,
   I had thought, by making this well known unto you,
   To have found a safe redress; but now grow fearful,
   By what yourself too late have spoke and done,   215
   That you protect this course, and put it on
   By your allowance; which if you should, the fault
   Would not 'scape censure, nor the redresses sleep,
   Which, in the tender of a wholesome weal,
   Might in their working do you that offence,   220
   Which else were shame, that then necessity
   Will call discreet proceeding.
Fool. For you know, Nuncle,
   The hedge-sparrow fed the cuckoo so long,
   That it's had it head bit off by it young.   225
   So out went the candle, and we were left darkling.

210. other] *Q, F*; others *Johnson.*   212. and ... Sir] *Craig; without hyphens, Capell;* and (not . . . riots,) Sir *Q;* and (not . . . endur'd) riots Sir. *F 1;* (and . . . endured) riots Sir. *F 2;* (and . . . endured) riots, Sir *F 3, 4.*   213. known] know *F 4.*   216. it] *F; not in Q.*   218. redresses] *F;* redresse *Q.* 221. Which] *F;* that *Q.*   222. Will] *F;* must *Q.*   proceeding] *F;* proceedings *Q.*   223. know] *F;* trow *Q.*   224-5] *verse Pope; prose Q, F.* 225. it's had] *F;* it had *Q, F 2.*   it head] *Q,* *F 1;* its head *F 2, 3, 4.* by it] *F 1, 2;* beit *Q 1, 2;* be it *Q 3;* by it's *F 3, 4.*

211. *carp*] find fault, prate.

212. *rank*] gross, excessive. Cf. *Ham.* I. ii. 136.

214. *safe*] sure. Cf. *3 Hen. VI.* IV. vii. 52.

215. *too late*] Lear has been tardy in reproving his retinue.

216. *put it on*] instigate it. Cf. *Cor.* II. iii. 264.

217. *allowance*] approbation (Malone). Cf. *Oth.* I. i. 128. Huloet, *Dictionary,* 1572, has: "Allowance, acceptation or estimation."

217-22. *which . . . proceeding*] If you should do this, I will censure you for it, and take steps to check the riotous behaviour of your knights. My disciplinary measures, due to my desire to have a healthy state, may well offend you; and I should be accused of lacking in filial duty, were it not that everyone would recognize the necessity of my actions. Goneril's speech is deliberately tortuous, but the meaning is clear.

291. *Which*] i.e. the redresses.

219. *tender*] strong desire for. Cf. *T.G.* IV. iv. 145 and *1 Hen. IV.* v. iv. 49.

224-5. *The . . . young*] This couplet may have been proverbial.

225. *it . . . it*] its . . . its.

226. *So . . . darkling*] Cf. Spenser, *Faerie Queene,* II. x. 30:

"But true it is, that when the oyle
   is spent,
The light goes out, and weeke
   is throwne away;
So when he had resigned his
   regiment,
His daughter gan despise his
   drouping day"

Lear. Are you our daughter?

Gon. I would you would make use of your good wisdom,
Whereof I know you are fraught; and put away
These dispositions which of late transport you   230
From what you rightly are.

Fool. May not an ass know when a cart draws the
horse? Whoop, Jug! I love thee.

Lear. Does any here know me? This is not Lear:
Does Lear walk thus? speak thus? Where are his
  eyes?   235
Either his notion weakens, his discernings
Are lethargied—Ha! waking? 'tis not so.
Who is it that can tell me who I am?

Fool. Lear's shadow.

Lear. I would learn that; for by the marks of sove-   240
reignty, knowledge, and reason, I should be false
persuaded I had daughters.

---

229. I] *F;* Come sir, I *Q.*   your] *F;* that *Q.*   230. which] *F;* that *Q.*
transport] *F;* transforme *Q.*   233. Does] *F;* Doth *Q.*   This] *F;* Why
this *Q.*   234. Does] *F;* doth *Q.*   236. weakens] *F;* weakness *Q.*   his] *F;* or
his *Q;* or's *Craig (conj. S. Walker).*   237. lethargied—*Rowe;* Lethergied. *F;*
lethergie *Q.*   Ha! waking] *F;* sleeping or wakeing, ha! sure *Q.*   239.
assigned to Lear Q.   240-3. I . . . father] *Q; not in F.*   241. false] halfe
conj. Anon.

229. *fraught*] stored.
230. *dispositions*] states of mind,
temperamental fits.
230. *transport*] Cf. *Cor.* I. i. 77.
232-3. *May . . . horse?*] May not
a Fool see that there is something
obviously wrong, when a daughter
gives instructions to her royal father?
233. *Whoop . . . thee*] Possibly, as
Steevens was informed, a quotation
from an old song. Jug is a nickname
for Joan. Presumably there is no
connection between this, and the
more modern refrain " Little brown
jug, don't I love thee? "
236. *notion*] intellectual power.
Cf. *Mac.* III. i. 83.
237. *waking?*] Am I awake?
239. *Lear's shadow*] Cf. *Leir*, 1111:
" And think me but the shaddow
of myselfe."

240-3. *I . . . father*] These two
speeches are omitted by F. Q as-
scribes *Lear's shadow* to Lear himself;
and editors assume that his two
speeches have been erroneously run
together, with the incorporation
of the Fool's intervening words.
Nosworthy, however, thinks that
Lear repeats the Fool's words as a
question. The omission could arise
from the repetition of the words,
and the propinquity of the three
Lears. But it is safer to assume
that Lear ignores the Fool's remark, and follows his own train
of thought.
241. *false*] i.e. falsely. Perhaps
we should hyphen *false-persuaded.*
Shakespeare has ' false-derived ' (*2
Hen. IV.* IV. i. 190) and ' false-played '
(*A.C.* IV. xiv. 19).

Fool. Which they will make an obedient father.
Lear. Your name, fair gentlewoman?
Gon. This admiration, Sir, is much o' th' savour   245
    Of other your new pranks.   I do beseech you
    To understand my purposes aright:
    As you are old and reverend, should be wise.
    Here do you keep a hundred knights and squires;
    Men so disorder'd, so debosh'd, and bold,   250
    That this our court, infected with their manners,
    Shows like a riotous inn: epicurism and lust
    Makes it more like a tavern or a brothel
    Than a grac'd palace.   The shame itself doth speak
    For instant remedy; be then desir'd   255
    By her, that else will take the thing she begs,
    A little to disquantity your train;
    And the remainders, that shall still depend,
    To be such men as may besort your age,
    Which know themselves and you.
Lear.   Darkness and devils! 260
    Saddle my horses; call my train together.
    Degenerate bastard! I'll not trouble thee:
    Yet have I left a daughter.

---

243. they] *Q 3;* they, *Q 1, 2.*   245. This admiration, Sir] *F;* Come, sir, this admiration *Q.*   savour] *Q, F;* fauour *Q 3, Capell.*   247. To] *F; not in Q,* 248. should] *Q 1, F;* you should *Q 2, 3; not in Steevens conj.*   249. a] *Q, F;* one *Q 2, 3.*   250. debosh'd] *F;* deboyst *Q;* debauch'd *Pope.*   253. Makes it] *F;* make *Q.*   or a] *F;* or *Q.*   254. grac'd] *F;* great *Q.* 255. then] *F;* thou *Q.*   258. remainders] *F;* remainder *Q.*   260. Which] *F; that Q 1;* And *Q 2, 3.*

243. *Which*] i.e. *whom,* relating to the ' I ' of Lear's speech.

245. *admiration*] affected astonishment.

246. *other your*] other of your.

248. *should*] Q 2 inserts *you* before this word, but it can be understood from the preceding clause.

250. *disorder'd*] disorderly.

250. *debosh'd*] a variant of *debauched.* Cf. *A.W.* II. iii. 145 and Cotgrave, who thus translates *desbauché.* See Appendix, p. 250.

252. *Shows*] appears. Cf. *Cor.* IV. v. 68.

252. *epicurism*] gluttony, riotous living. Cf. Appendix, p. 250.

253. *tavern . . . brothel*] *tavern* refers to *epicurism* and *brothel* to *lust.*

254. *grac'd*] honourable, the abode of stately decorum, "graced with the presence of a sovereign" (Warburton).

255. *desir'd*] requested.

257. *disquantity*] reduce the size of.

258. *remainders*] those who remain. Cf. *Cym.* I. i. 129.

258. *depend*] attend you as dependants.

259. *besort*] suit. Cf. *Oth.* I. iii. 239.

Gon. You strike my people, and your disorder'd rabble
        Make servants of their betters.   265

                    Enter ALBANY.

Lear. Woe, that too late repents; O! Sir, are you come?
        Is it your will? Speak, Sir. Prepare my horses.
        Ingratitude, thou marble-hearted fiend,
        More hideous, when thou show'st thee in a child,
        Than the sea-monster.
Alb.   Pray, Sir, be patient. 270
Lear. [*To Goneril.*] Detested <u>kite</u>! thou liest.
        My train are men of choice and rarest parts,
        That all particulars of duty know,
        And in the most exact regard support
        The worships of their name. O most small fault, 275

265. S.D.] *F; Enter Duke Q.*   266. Woe] *F; We Q.*   repents] *F;*
repent's *Q 1;* repent's vs *Q 2, 3.*   O . . . come?] *Q; not in F.*   267. Speak
Sir] *F;* that wee *Q.*   my] *F;* any *Q.*   270. *Alb.* Pray . . . patient] *F;*
not in Q.   271. *Lear*] *F; not in Q.*   S.D.] *Rowe; not in Q, F.*   liest] *F;*
list *Q 1;* lessen *Q 2, 3.*   272. train are] *F;* traine, and *Q.*

266. *Woe, that*] Woe to him that.
Florio, *Second Fruites*, p. 165, gives
the proverb:
    "Yet, but too late repents the
        ratt,
    If once her taile be caught by
        the cat."
268. *marble-hearted*] Cf. ' marble-
breasted ' (*T.N.* v. i. 127).
270. *the sea-monster*] ' the ' is the
generic article (Kittredge). Lear
is not referring to any specific monster. Cf. *M.V.* III. ii. 57. Upton
suggests that the reference is to the
hippopotamus, a symbol of impiety
and ingratitude. Plutarch, *Morals*
(tr. P. Holland) p. 1300, mentions
a picture in the temple of Minerva
at Sais, in which is the figure of a
river-horse, denoting " murder, im-
pudence, violence, and injustice."
But the hippo is a river-monster,
not a sea-monster. Other editors
suggests that Lear was referring to
the whale. Craig argues that Shakespeare was thinking of those monsters

of classical antiquity slain by Hercules
and Perseus.
    271. *kite*] Armstrong, *Shakespeare's
Imagination*, 1946, pp. 12, 17, points
out that to Shakespeare the kite
" is a despicable creature symbolic
of cowardice, meanness, cruelty and
death," and he shows that a reference
to the bird is normally accompanied
by allusions to bed, death, spirits,
birds and food. In the present
context we have ' marble-hearted '
(268), ' devils ' (260), and ' epicurism ' (252).
    272. *choice*] choicest, the super-
lative being understood from ' rarest.'
    274-5. *And . . . name*] And are
most particular in living up to the
honourable reputation they have
earned.
    274. *in . . . regard*] the smallest
details. Cf. *Ham.* II. ii. 79.
    275. *worships*] honour. " Ab-
stract nouns are often pluralized
when they refer to more than one
person " (Kittredge).

How ugly didst thou in Cordelia show!
Which, like an engine, wrench'd my frame of nature
From the fix'd place, drew from my heart all love,
And added to the gall.   O Lear, Lear, Lear!
Beat at this gate, that let thy folly in,   280
                              [*Striking his head.*

And thy dear judgment out!   Go, go, my people.

Alb. My Lord, I am guiltless, as I am ignorant
Of what hath moved you.

Lear.   It may be so, my Lord.

Hear, Nature, hear! dear Goddess, hear!
Suspend thy purpose, if thou didst intend   285
To make this creature fruitful!
Into her womb convey sterility!
Dry up in her the organs of increase,
And from her derogate body never spring
A babe to honour her!   If she must teem,   290
Create her child of spleen, that it may live
And be a thwart disnatur'd torment to her!
Let it stamp wrinkles in her brow of youth,
With cadent tears fret channels in her cheeks,

277. Which] *F;* That *Q.*   279. Lear. Lear, Lear!] *F;* Lear, Lear! *Q.*
280. S.D.] *Pope; not in Q, F.*   283. Of . . . you] *F; not in Q.*   284. Hear,
Nature] *F;* Hark, Nature *Q.* Goddess, hear!] *F;* Goddesse *Q.* 292. thwart]
F; thourt *Q.*   disnatur'd] *F;* disuetur'd *Q 1, 2;* disventur'd *Q 3.*   294.
cadent] *F;* accent *Q;* candent (*Warburton*).

277. *engine*] Edwards and later
critics assume that this is the rack;
but Kittredge points out that the
rack does not wrench the human
frame *from its fixed place,* and suggests
that the " figure is that of a building
that is thrown off its foundation
(' the fix'd place ') by a powerful
mechanical contrivance." Maxwell
suggests (privately) that " the picture
called up by the passage, as a whole,
is rather of Lear's frame being prised
apart, once a lever has been introduced far enough to get purchase."
He compares I. i. 169-70.
289. *derogate*] debased, degraded.
Cf. *Cymb.* II. i. 48. The word, like

' sterility ' (287), and ' disnatur'd '
(292), is used by Florio.   Cf. Appendix, p. 250.
290. *teem*] have offspring.
291. *child of spleen*] a child con-
sisting only of spleen.
292. *thwart*] cross-grained, perverse.
292. *disnatur'd*] without natural
affection. Steevens quotes Daniel,
Hymen's Triumph, II. iv. 89:
" I am not so disnatured a man,
    Nor so ill borne, to disesteeme
    her loue."
294. *cadent*] falling.   Perhaps
Shakespeare's coinage.
294. *fret*] wear.

Turn all her mother's pains and benefits   295
To laughter and contempt, that she may feel
How sharper than a serpent's tooth it is
To have a thankless child! Away, away!   [*Exit.*
Alb. Now, Gods that we adore, whereof comes this?
Gon. Never afflict yourself to know more of it: 300
But let his disposition have that scope
~~humour~~ As dotage gives it.

Re-enter LEAR.

Lear. What! fifty of my followers at a clap;
Within a fortnight!
Alb.   What's the matter, Sir?
Lear. I'll tell thee. [*To Goneril.*] Life and death! I
am asham'd   305
That thou hast power to shake my manhood thus,
That these hot tears, which break from me per-
force,
Should make thee worth them. Blasts and fogs
upon thee!
Th' untented woundings of a father's curse
Pierce every sense about thee! Old fond eyes,   310

To deep to be cleaned with tent (lint)

296. that . . . feel] *F, Q 2;* that shee may feele, that she may feele *Q 1.* 298.
away, away!] *F;* goe, goe, my people? *Q.*   S.D.] *F; not in Q.*   300. more
of it] *F;* the cause *Q;* of it *F 2, 3, 4.*   302. As] *F;* That *Q.*   S.D.] *F;
not in Q.*   304. What's] *F;* What is *Q.*   307. which] *F;* that *Q.*   308.
thee . . . Blasts] *F;* the worst blasts *Q.*   308–9. upon thee!/Th' untented] *F;*
vpon the vntender *Q uncorr. Q 2, 3;* vpon the vntented *Q corr.*   310. Pierce]
Q corr., F; Peruse *Q uncorr., Q 2, 3.*   thee. Old] *F;* the old *Q.*

295. *her . . . pains*] Goneril's
maternal cares.
297. *How . . . tooth*] Malone
compares *Ps.* cxl. 3. "They have
sharpened their tongues like a
Serpent."
299. *Gods . . . adore*] Empson,
The Structure of Complex Words, p. 130,
comments: "Perhaps implying that
Nature was not one of the regular
gods and should not be prayed to."
301. *disposition*] humour.
302. *As*] The relative construction

'that . . . as' is found elsewhere
in Shakespeare (Cf. Abbott, 280),
and there is no need to adopt the
Q reading.
303. *fifty*] See Introduction, p.
xxxv.
303. *at a clap*] Shakespeare could
have found the phrase in Harsnett.
See Appendix, p. 254.
309. *Th' untented woundings*] wounds
too deep to be cleaned with a *tent,*
a roll of lint.
310. *fond*] foolish.

If you weep for

Beweep this cause again, I'll pluck ye out,
And cast you, with the waters that you loose, *emit*
To temper clay.　Yea, is 't come to this?
Ha!　Let it be so: I have another daughter,
Who, I am sure, is kind and comfortable: *comforting* 315
When she shall hear this of thee, with her nails
She'll flay thy wolvish visage.　Thou shalt find
That I'll resume the shape which thou dost think
I have cast off for ever.

> [*Exeunt Lear, Kent, and Attendants.*

Gon. Do you mark that?　　　　　　　　　　320

Alb. I cannot be so partial, Goneril,
To the great love I bear you,—

Gon. Pray you, content.　What, Oswald, ho!

[*To the Fool.*] You, sir, more knave than fool, after
your master.

Fool. Nuncle Lear, Nuncle Lear! tarry, take the Fool 325
with thee.

---

311. this cause] *Q, F 1;* thee once *F 2, 3, 4.*　ye] *F;* you *Q.*　312. cast
you] *F;* you cast *Q.*　　　　　　loose] *F 1, 2, Staunton;* make *Q;* lose *F 3, 4.*
313. Yea . . . this?] *Q 1;* Yea, is it . . . this? *Q 2, 3; not in F.*　　314. Ha!
Let it be so] *F; not in Q.* I have another] *F;* Yet haue I left a *Q;* yet I have
left a *Steevens.*　　315. Who] *F;* Whom *Q.*　　319. ever] *F;* euer, thou shalt
I warrant thee *Q.*　　　　　　S.D.] *Capell, subst.; Exit Q 2, F; not in Q 1.*
320. that?] *F;* that my Lord *Q.*　　322. you-] *Theobald;* you. *F;* you, *Q.*
323. Pray you content.] *F;* come sir no more *Q.* What, Oswald, Ho!] *F; not in
Q.*　324. you, sir] *F;* you *Q.*　325. take] *F;* and take *Q.*　326. with thee:
A] *F;* with a *Q.*

---

311. *Beweep*] cf. *Sonnets*, xxix.—2.
The meaning is " If you weep for."

312. *loose*] There is no good reason
for altering the F reading; for
though *loose* is a frequent spelling
of *lose*, the word does not certainly
mean that here. Kittredge interprets: " waste—since these tears
are of no avail." Staunton, retaining *loose*, explains it as ' discharge,' as in the phrase ' to loose
an arrow.' But the word can also
mean ' emit,' and this would seem
to be the sense here. There may,

however, be a quibble on *loose* and
lose.

315. *comfortable*] comforting, ready
to give comfort.　Cf. *A.W.* i. i. 86.

325-6. *take . . . thee*] There is a
double meaning in this: (i) take
me with you, (ii) take the epithet
' fool ' with you. Kittredge remarks
that this was a regular farewell gibe.

329. *Should sure*] should certainly
be sent.

330, 331. *halter . . . after*] pronounced hauter and auter. Cf.
Ellis, *English Pronunciation*, ii. 193-201.

A fox, when one has caught her,
And such a daughter,
Should sure to the slaughter,
If my cap would buy a halter;   330
So the Fool follows after.   [*Exit.*

Gon. This man hath had good counsel. A hundred
knights!
'Tis politic and safe to let him keep
At point a hundred knights; yes, that on every
dream,
Each buzz, each fancy, each complaint, dislike,   335
He may enguard his dotage with their powers,
And hold our lives in mercy. Oswald, I say!

Alb. Well, you may fear too far.

Gon.   Safer than trust too far.
Let me still take away the harms I fear,
Not fear still to be taken: I know his heart.   340
What he hath utter'd I have writ my sister;
If she sustain him and his hundred knights,
When I have show'd th' unfitness,—

Re-enter OSWALD.

                         How, now, Oswald!
What, have you writ that letter to my sister?

Osw. Ay, madam.   345

Gon. Take you some company, and away to horse:
Inform her full of my particular fear;

In armed readiness [margin note]

rather than fear [margin note]

own [margin note]

---

331. S.D.] *F; not in* Q.   332-43. This . . . unfitness] *F; not in* Q.   342.
she] *F;* she'll *F 3, 4.*   343. unfitness,—] *Rowe;* vnfitnesse. *F.*   S.D.] *F;
not in* Q. How now, Oswald] *F;* What Oswald, ho. *Oswald.* Here Madam *Q.*
344. that] *F;* this *Q.*   345. Ay] I *F;* Yes *Q.*   347. fear] *F;* feares *Q.*

---

334. *At point*] in armed readiness.
Cf. *Ham.* I. ii. 200.

335. *buzz*] rumour. Cf. Chapman
The Widow's Tears, II. i (ed. Pearson,
ii. 24): "Thinke 'twas but a Buzz
deuis'd by him to set your braines
a work." See also *Ham.* IV. v. 90:
'buzzers.'

336. *enguard*] protect. Cf. 'en-
steep' (*Oth.* II. i. 70) 'englut'

(*Oth.* I. iii. 57), and 'engirt' (*2 Hen.
IV.* v. i. 99).

337. *in mercy*] in jeopardy. Cf.
the legal term *In misericordia.*

339. *still*] always.

340. *Not . . . taken*] rather than
continue in the fear of being over-
taken by harm.

347. *particular*] own, personal, individual.

And thereto add such reasons of your own
As may compact it more.   Get you gone,
And hasten your return.   [*Exit Oswald.*
                    No, no, my Lord, 350
This milky gentleness and course of yours
Though I condemn not, yet, under pardon,
You are much more attax'd for want of wisdom
Than prais'd for harmful mildness.

Alb. How far your eyes may pierce I cannot tell: 355
Striving to better, oft we mar what's well.

Gon. Nay, then—

Alb. Well, well; th' event.   [*Exeunt.*

350. hasten] *Q corr., F;* after *Q uncorr., Q 2, 3.*   S.D.] *Rowe; not in*
Q, F.   No, no] *F;* now *Q.*   351. milky] *Q corr., F;* mildie *Q*
uncorr., Q 2, 3.   352. condemn] *F;* dislike *Q;* condemn it *Pope.*   353. You
are] *F 2, 3, 4;* Y'are *Q;* Your are *F 1.*   attax'd for] *Duthie (conj. Greg);*
alapt *Q uncorr., Q 2, 3;* attaskt for *Q corr.;* at task for *F.*   354. prais'd]
F; praise *Q.*   356. better, oft] *F;* better ought *Q.*   358. th' event] the
'uent *F;* the euent *Q.*

349. *compact*] confirm, make substantial, fortify.   Cotgrave has:
Affermir; to strengthen, fortifie, confirm, assure, compact.

351. *This . . . yours*] this mild
and gentle course of action of yours—
hendiadys.   Tovey compares *K.J.*
v. ii. 133.

351. *milky*] Cf. *Macb.* I. v. 18.

352. *condemn not*] Pope and most
editors insert 'it' between these
words.   This regularizes the metre;
but as Abbott (*483) points out,
the voice can linger hesitatingly on
'yet' if the F reading is retained.

353. *attax'd*] Greg's emendation.
(*Variants*, pp. 141-2, 153-5).   He
suggests that the copy for Q had
ataxt: this was misread as *alapt* by
the compositor; the corrector

emended to *attaskt:* and this was
emended in the F to *at task.*   H. W.
Crundell, *N.Q.* 26 Jan. 1935, suggests
attach'd, meaning *accused,* and cites
from *N.E.D.* a quotation from Nashe:
"They shall not easily be attached
of any notable absurditie."   The
main objection to the F reading is
that a past participle is needed, or
expected, to balance *praised.*   None
of the three readings ('attaskt,'
'at task for' and 'ataxt') are to
be found elsewhere, but *attax'd* is a
plausible Shakespearian coinage.

354. *harmful mildness*] dangerous
lenity.

356. *Striving . . . well*] Cf. 'let
well alone' and *Sonnet* ciii. 9-10.

358. *th' event*] Let us see what
happens.

SCENE V.—[*Court before the Same.*]

Enter LEAR, KENT, *and Fool.*

Lear. Go you before to Gloucester with these letters.
Acquaint my daughter no further with any
thing you know than comes from her demand
out of the letter. If your diligence be not speedy
I shall be there afore you.   5

Kent. I will not sleep, my Lord, till I have delivered
your letter.   [*Exit.*

Fool. If a man's brains were in's heels, were't not in
danger of kibes?

Lear. Ay, boy.   10

Fool. Then, I prithee, be merry; thy wit shall not
go slip-shod.

Lear. Ha, ha, ha!

Scene v

Court . . . Same] Capell.
Lear, Kent, Gentleman, and Fool F.
8. brains] *Q, F;* brain *Pope.*
F 3, 4.   were't] *Rowe;* wert *Q, F.*

S.D.] *Q 2, 3; Enter Lear Q 1; Enter*
5. afore] *F;* before *Q.*
were] where *Q 1.*   in's] *F;* in his *Q.*
11. not] *F;* ne'er *Q.*

Scene v

1. *Gloucester*] i.e. the town of that name, near which the residence of the Duke was.

1. *these letters*] this letter. Cf. 4 *post.*

3-4. *than . . . letter*] than the perusal of the letter suggests to her to ask you.

3. *demand*] question.

4. *out of*] suggested by.

8. *If . . . heels*] Armin. *op. cit.* p. 56, speaking of "the cleane fooles of this world," says "that the braine is now lodged in the foote, and therevpon comes it that many make their head their foote." Cf. III. ii. 31-4.

8. *brains*] Furness takes the word to be used as a singular, *brains* and *brain* being used more or less interchangeably.

8. *were't*] it = his brain.

9. *kibes*] chilblains, chapped heels, Cf. *Ham.* v. i. 153; and Beaumont and Fletcher, *Love's Cure,* II. i. 120: "scabs, chilblains, and kib'd heels." Kibby is used in Devonshire and Cornwall for *sore, chapped* (Cf. Halliwell, *Dictionary of Archaic and Provincial Words,* 1878). The Fool is referring to Kent's promise to be speedy. Kittredge compares Hoccleve, *Male Regle,* 232, "No more than hir wit were in hire heele."

11-12. *thy . . . slip-shod*] You will never have to wear slippers because of chilblains, for you show you have no wit, even in your heels, in undertaking your journey to Regan.

12. *slip-shod*] slippered, in slipshoes or slippers. Cf. Jonson, *Alchemist,* I. i. 46; "Your feete in mouldy slippers, for your kibes."

Fool. Shalt see thy other daughter will use thee
      kindly; for though she's as like this as a crab's   15
      like an apple, yet I can tell what I can tell.

Lear. What canst tell, boy?

Fool. She will taste as like this as a crab does to a crab.
      Thou canst tell why one's nose stands i' th' middle
      on's face?   20

Lear. No.

Fool. Why, to keep one's eyes of either side's nose, that
      what a man cannot smell out, he may spy into.

Lear. I did her wrong,—

Fool. Canst tell how an oyster makes his shell?   25

Lear. No.

Fool. Nor I neither; but I can tell why a snail has a
      house.

Lear. Why?

Fool. Why, to put's head in; not to give it away to   30
      his daughters, and leave his horns without a
      case.

Lear. I will forget my nature. So kind a father!
      Be my horses ready?

15. she's] she is *Q 2, 3.*   crab's] *F;* crab is *Q.*   16. can tell what] *F;*
con what *Q.*   17. What . . . boy?] *F;* Why, what canst tell, my boy? *Q.*   18.
She will] *F;* sheel *Q.*   does] *F;* doth *Q.*   19. Thou canst] *F;* canst thou
F 3, 4; canst not *Q.*   stands] stande *Q 1.*   20. on's] *F;* of his *Q.*
22. one's] *F;* his *Q.*   of] *F;* on *Q.*   23. he] a *Q 1.*   side's] *Q 1, F;*
side his *Q 2, 3.*   30. put's] *F;* put his *Q.*   to] unto *Q 2, 3.*   31. daughters]
F; daughter *Q.*

15. *kindly*] a play on the two senses
of the word: (i) affectionately,
(ii) after her kind, according to her
nature. Cf. *A.C.* v. ii. 264.

15. *she*] Regan.

15. *this*] Goneril.

16. *as . . . apple*] i.e. she is like
her in appearance. Wright compares Lyly, *Euphues* (ed. Arber),
p. 120: "The sower Crabbe hath
the shew of an Apple as well as the
sweet Pippin."

20. *on's*] of his.

22. *of*] on.   Cf. *T.S.* iv. i. 71:
"Both of one horse."

22. *side's*] side of his.

27. *snail*] see note to iii. iv. 159.

30. *put's*] put his.

31. *horns*] "The Fool does not
mean to call Lear a cuckold: he
simply accepts horns as the inevitable
adornment of married men"
(Kittredge).

33. *forget . . . nature*] i.e. cease to
be a kind father.

Fool. Thy asses are gone about 'em. The reason why 35
the seven stars are no mo than seven is a pretty
reason.

Lear. Because they are not eight?

Fool. Yes, indeed: thou would'st make a good Fool.

Lear. To take 't again perforce! <u>Monster</u> Ingrati- 40
tude!

Fool. If thou wert my Fool, Nuncle, I'd have thee
beaten for being old before thy time.

Lear. How's that?

Fool. Thou should'st not have been old till thou hadst 45
been wise.

Lear. O! let me not be mad, not mad, sweet heaven;
Keep me in temper; I would not be mad!

Enter Gentleman.

How now! Are the horses ready?

Gent. Ready, my Lord. 50

Lear. Come, boy.

Fool. She that's a maid now, and laughs at my departure,
Shall not be a maid long, unless things be cut
shorter. [*Exeunt.*

35. 'em] *F;* them *Q.* 36. mo] *F;* more *Q, F 4.* 39. indeed] *F; not in Q.*
42, thou wert] you wert *F 2;* you were *F 3, 4.* 45. till] *F;* before *Q.* 47.
not mad] *F; not in Q.* 47. heaven:] *F;* heauen! I would not be mad *Q.* S.D.]
Theobald; not in Q, F. 49. How now!] *F; not in Q.* 52. that's a] *F;* that
is *Q;* that is a *Capell.* 53. unless] *F;* except *Q.*

36. *the seven stars*] the Pleiades.
Cf. *1 Hen. IV.* I. ii. 16. See *Amos* v. 8
and *Job* xxxviii. 31, marginal note
in A.V. to Pleiades: " Cimah or the
seven stars." Cf. note to III. iv. 159.
36. *mo*] more.
36. *pretty*] apt, neat.
40. *To . . . perforce*] Either he is,
as Johnson suggests, " meditating
on his resumption or royalty,"
perhaps with the help of Cornwall
and Regan (cf. I. iv. 317-319); or
he is thinking of Goneril's monstrous
ingratitude in taking away the
privileges she had agreed to grant
him (Steevens).

47. *mad*] the first premonition.
48. *in temper*] in my normal condition of mind.
52-3. *She . . . shorter*] addressed to
the audience. Several editors assume that Shakespeare was not
responsible for the couplet. The
maid who sees only the funny side
of the Fool's gibes, and does not
realize that Lear is going on a tragic
journey is such a simpleton that she
won't know how to preserve her
virginity. The rhyme *departure—
shorter* was accurate in Elizabethan
pronunciation. The word *departure*
is a homonymic pun.

ACT II

SCENE I.—[*A Court within the Castle of the Earl of Gloucester.*]

Enter EDMUND *and* CURAN, *meeting.*

Edm. Save thee, Curan.

Cur. And you, sir. I have been with your father, and
given him notice that the Duke of Cornwall and
Regan his Duchess will be here with him this
night.   5

Edm. How comes that?

Cur. Nay, I know not. You have heard of the news
abroad? I mean the whisper'd ones, for they
are yet but ear-bussing arguments.

Edm. Not I: pray you, what are they?   10

Cur. Have you heard of no likely wars toward, 'twixt
the Dukes of Cornwall and Albany?

Edm. Not a word.

Cur. You may do then, in time. Fare you well, sir. [*Exit.*

Edm. The Duke be here to-night! The better! best! 15
This weaves itself perforce into my business.
My father hath set guard to take my brother;

tricky nature

And I have one thing, of a queasy question,
Which I must act.   Briefness and Fortune, work!
Brother, a word; descend: brother, I say!   20

Enter EDGAR.

My father watches: O Sir! fly this place;
Intelligence is given where you are hid;
You have now the good advantage of the night.
Have you not spoken 'gainst the Duke of Cornwall?
He's coming hither, now, i' th' night, i' th'
    haste,   25
And Regan with him; have you nothing said
On his side Upon his party 'gainst the Duke of Albany?
Advise yourself.

Edg.   I am sure on't, not a word.
Edm. I hear my father coming; pardon me;
In cunning I must draw my sword upon you;   30
Draw; seem to defend yourself; now quit you well. *fight well*
Yield; come before my father.   Light, ho! here!

19. I must act] *F;* must aske *Q.*   work *F;* helpe *Q.*   20. S.D.] *So*
Theobald; at 16 Q 1; at 19 Q 2, 3, F.   21. Sir] *F; not in Q.*   24.
'gainst] against *Q 2, 3.*   Cornwall?] *F;*   Cornwall ought *Q.*   27. 'gainst] *F;*
against *Q.*   28. yourself] *F;* your-   *Q.*   30. cunning] *F;* crauing *Q.*
31. Draw] *F; not in Q.*   32. ho] *F; not in Q.*

18. *of . . . question*] of a kind that
requires careful handling, if he is
not to make a mess of it.
  18. *queasy*] sickly, liable to vomit.
  19. *Briefness*] Promptitude, immediate action, speed. Cf. *Per.*
v. ii. 280.
  25. *i' th' haste*] in great haste. For
instances of the use of the definite
article in adverbial phrases, see
Abbott, 91.
  27. *Upon his party*] on his side;
not against him (as in 24 *ante*),
but against Albany. Schmidt gives
several instances where the phrase
means 'upon the side of.' Cf.
K.J. I. i. 34; *Rich II.* III. ii. 203;
Cor. I. i. 238. It is unlikely, therefore, that the passage means "re-

flecting upon his party, which is
soon to be opposed to Albany in
the coming struggle." Craig, however, cites *Macb.* IV. iii. 131:

  " My first false speaking
  Was this upon myself "—

where *upon* means *against.*
  28. *Advise yourself*] consider. Cf.
T.N. IV. ii. 102.
  28. *on't*] of it.
  30. *In cunning*] to avoid the appearance of collusion.
  31. *quit you well*] Give a good
account of yourself, fight well.
Cf. *1 Sam.* IV. 9: "Be strong, and
quit yourselves like men, and fight."
  32. *Yield*] spoken loudly, so as to
be overheard.

Fly, brother.   Torches! torches!   So, farewell.

[Exit Edgar.

Some blood drawn on me would beget opinion

[Wounds his arm.

Of my more fierce endeavour: I have seen drunk-
  ards   35
Do more than this in sport.   Father! father!
Stop, stop!   No help?

Enter GLOUCESTER, *and Servants with torches.*

Glou.   Now, Edmund, where's the villain?
Edm. Here stood he in the dark, his sharp sword out,
  Mumbling of wicked charms, conjuring the moon
  To stand auspicious mistress.
Glou.   But where is he?   40
Edm. Look, Sir, I bleed.
Glou.   Where is the villain, Edmund?
Edm. Fled this way, Sir, when by no means he could—
Glou. Pursue him, ho!   Go after.   *[Exeunt some Servants.*
                     " By no means " what?
Edm. Persuade me to the murther of your lordship;
  But that I told him, the revenging Gods   45

33. brother] *F;* brother flie *Q.*   torches!] *not in F 2, 3, 4.*   S.D.] *F;*
not in Q.   34. S.D.] *Rowe; not in Q, F.*   37. *and . . . torches*] *F; not in Q.*
where's] *F;* where is *Q 1.*   39. mumbling] *F;* warbling] *Q.*   40. stand] *F;*
stand's *Q 1;* stand his *Q 2, 3.*   42. Sir, when] *Q, F;* sir. When *Capell.*
could-] *Q;* could. *F 1.*   43. ho!] *F; not in Q.*   S.D.] *Dyce; not in Q, F.*
44. to the] to *F 3, 4.*   45. revenging] *F;* reuengiue *Q.*

34-5. *beget . . . endeavour*] make
people think I have had a desperate
fight.

35-6. *I . . . sport*] Young gallants,
under the influence of drink, would
wound themselves in order to pledge
the health of their mistresses in blood
mingled with their drink. See, e.g.
Jonson, *Cynthia's Revels,* IV. i. 200-9:
" I would see how *Loue* could worke
. . . by letting this gallant expresse
himselfe . . . with stabbing himselfe
and drinking healths, and writing
languishing letters in his bloud."
Kittredge cites *The Man in the Moone,*
1609 (ed. Halliwell, p. 43): " He

hath let his owne blood . . . and
quaffed an health thereof in praise
of his mistresse."

39. *Mumbling . . . charms*] Edmund
plays on Gloucester's superstitions.

40. *auspicious mistress*] The same
phrase is used in *A.W.* III. iii. 8.

41. *I bleed*] Edmund must gain
time to allow Edgar to escape; he
does not wish to be confronted with
him until Gloucester is convinced
of his guilt.

45. *that*] when that, ' when ' being
understood from 42 *ante.* Cf. I. i.
168, where That = Since that.

'Gainst parricides did all the thunder bend; *aim*
Spoke with how manifold and strong a bond
The child was bound to th' father; Sir, in fine,
Seeing how loathly opposite I stood
To his unnatural purpose, in fell motion, *deadly thrust* 50
With his prepared sword he charges home
unprotected My unprovided body, lanch'd mine arm: *lanced/pierced*
And when he saw my best alarum'd spirits *roused*
Bold in the quarrel's right, roused to th' encounter,
frightened Or whether gasted by the noise I made, 55
Full suddenly he fled.

46. the thunder] *F;* their thunders *Q.*   48. in] *F;* in a *Q.*   50. in] *F;* with *Q.*   52. lanch'd] *Q;* latch'd *F;* lanced *Theobald.*   53. And when] *F;* But when *Q;* But whe'r *Furness (conj. Staunton).*   54. quarrel's right] *Q 2, 3, F;* quarrels, rights *Q 1.*   55. gasted] 'ghasted *Jennens;* gaster'd *conj. Craig.*   56. Full] *F;* but *Q.*

46. *bend*] aim.

49. *loathly opposite*] bitterly opposed (Kittredge).

50. *fell*] deadly, fierce.

50. *motion*] thrust—a fencing term. Cf. *T.N.* iii. iv. 303.

51. *prepared*] unsheathed and ready. Cf. *R.J.* i. i. 116.

51. *charges home*] makes a home thrust at.

52. *unprovided*] unprotected. Cf. *Rich. III* iii. ii. 75.

52. *lanch'd*] pierced, wounded, the old form of *lanced* Wright quotes *Hollyband, French Dictionary,* 1593: "*Poindre,* to stick, to lanch." Duthie defends *latch'd,* the F reading, which could mean ' catch ' ' to pull or strike swiftly off, out, up.' He cites Stewart, *Cronicles* (1858), 383: "Lymnis war lachit hard of be the kne." Here *lachit* means ' struck.' But even if Shakespeare read Stewart when writing *Macbeth* there is no evidence that he had read it before he wrote *King Lear,* and no evidence that the word was used with this meaning in England in Shakespeare's time. The meaning ' caught ' would give tolerable sense, but the Q reading gives a better since it implies that Edgar had drawn blood. The corrector might easily misread *lach'd.*

53. *And*] The Q reading ' But ' is more logical, perhaps; but Edmund is feigning agitation. See next note.

53. *when*] Staunton's suggestion, ' whe'r ' = whether, adopted by Furness is attractive, as it makes a logical construction; but Verity argues that we do not here want symmetry, " the broken, disjointed style of the whole speech being intended to indicate Edmund's feigned agitation."

53. *alarum'd spirits*] energies roused to action, as by a trumpet.

54. *Bold . . . right*] emboldened by the justice of his cause.

55. *gasted*] frightened. Cf. Palsgrave, *Lesclarcissement,* 1530; " I gast him as sore as he was this twelve months." Shakespeare uses ' gastness ' (*Oth.* v. i. 106). Elizabethans erroneously supposed that ' gastfull ' was etymologically connected with ' ghost.' Harsnett, *op. cit.* pp. 137, 73, uses the phrases " gastful opinions " and " God-gastring Giants." (Shakespeare may have intended a quibble on *gasted* and *ghosted;* Edgar, frightened, vanished like a ghost at cock-crow.)

56. *Let . . . far*] However far he flies.

Glou.   Let him fly far:

Not in this land shall he remain uncaught;

And found—dispatch. The noble Duke my master,

My worthy arch and patron, comes to-night:

By his authority I will proclaim it,   60

That he which finds him shall deserve our thanks,

Bringing the murderous coward to the stake;

He that conceals him, death.

Edm. When I dissuaded him from his intent,

And found him pight to do it, with curst speech   65

I threaten'd to discover him: he replied,

" Thou unpossessing bastard! dost thou think,

If I would stand against thee, would the reposal

Of any trust, virtue, or worth in thee

Make thy words faith'd? No: what I should

deny,—   70

As this I would; ay, though thou didst produce

My very character—I'd turn it all

To thy suggestion, plot, and damned practice:

And thou must make a dullard of the world,

---

59. worthy] worth *F 4*.   62. coward] *F;* caytife *Q*.   68. would] *F;* could *Q*. reposal] *F;* reposure *Q*.   70. what I should] *Q;* what should I *F;* what, should I *Schmidt*.   71. ay] I *Q; not in F*.   72. I'ld] I'll *F 4*. 73. practice] *F;* pretence *Q*.

58. *And . . . dispatch*] and when he is found, kill him. Brae, *N.Q.* 1852, argues that *dispatch* means " Get on with your story."

59. *worthy*] honourable.

59. *arch and patron*] chief patron (hendiadys).

62. *Bringing . . . stake*] Craig suggests that it was customary to chain captives to a stake of wood, and he cites Chaucer, *The Knight's Tale*, 1693-4:

" And he that is at meschief, shal be take,
And noght slayn, but he broght un-to the stake."

But Gloucester probably means " Bringing Edgar to the place of execution," not implying that he is to be burned at the stake.

63. *death*] the same elliptical form of expression as 58 *ante*.

65. *pight*] fully determined, from *pitched*.

65. *curst*] sharp, harsh, angry.

67. *unpossessing*] incapable of holding property, and so beggarly.

68. *would*] should.

68. *reposal*] placing.

69. *virtue . . . worth*] or your own virtue, or worth.

70. *faith'd*] credited.

72. *character*] handwriting. Cf. I. ii. 63.

73. *suggestion*] evil instigation. Cf. *Oth.* II. iii. 358 and *Macb.* I. iii. 134.

73. *practice*] treacherous device. Cf. v. iii. 151.

74. *make . . . world*] suppose everyone to be stupid. Cf. *Cymb.* v. v. 265.

If they not thought the profits of my death   75
Were very pregnant and potential spirits
To make thee seek it."
Glou.   O strange and fast'ned villain!
Would he deny his letter, said he?   I never got him.
                                        [*Tucket within.*
Hark! the Duke's trumpets.   I know not why he
   comes.
All ports I'll bar; the villain shall not 'scape;   80
The Duke must grant me that: besides his picture
I will send far and near, that all the kingdom
May have due note of him; and of my land,

---

76. spirits] *F, Rowe, Delius, Schmidt, Harrison;* spurres *Q, most edd.*
77. O strange] *F;* Strong *Q.*   78. said he?] *F; not in Q.*   I . . . him]
Q; not in F.   S.D.] after *seek it*] (77) *F; not in Q.*   79. why] *Q;* wher *F.*
83. due] *F; not in Q.*

---

75. *If . . . thought*] The auxiliary
was not required, when the negative
preceded the verb. Cf. Abbott, *305,
and IV. ii. 2.

76. *pregnant*] obvious, readily con-
ceivable (Craig); ready (Johnson);
productive of something, teeming
with incitements (Furness).

76. *potential*] powerful.

76. *spirits*] Schmidt, almost the
only editor who retains F reading,
interprets 'evil spirits'; it might
mean 'incitements.'   In several
passages in other plays Shakespeare
juxtaposes 'potent' and 'spirits.'
Cf. *Temp.* I. ii. 275 ("potent ministers") *K.J.* II. i. 358 ("potents,
fiery kindled spirits"); *Macb.* IV. i.
76 ("more potent than the first"
spirit); *Ham.* II. ii. 631 ("very
potent with such spirits"); *Ham.* v.
ii. 364 ("The potent poison quite
o'ercrows my spirit"). In view of
these parallels, it is needless to adopt
the Q reading, though Duthie
suggests that the F compositor may
have corrupted *spurres* into *spirits* by
confusion with *profits* in the preceding
line; or that a scribe misread the
playhouse MS. and miscorrected Q.

77. *O strange*] Gloucester is con-

cerned with Edgar's apparent unnaturalness, rather than his reckless-
ness. Cf. Q reading.

77. *fast'ned*] inveterate, hardened.
It is probably a metaphor from the
hardening of cement.

78. *got*] begot.

78. *Tucket*] Gloucester recognizes
the Duke's special trumpet-call.

79. *why*] Kirschbaum, defending
the F reading 'where', argues that
Gloucester "is apprehensive . . .
that Edgar may escape by the open
door through which the duke will
enter." But there is no reason to
think that Edgar is still in the castle
precincts.

80. *ports*] seaports, or, less prob-
ably, means of exit, gates. Cf.
T.C. IV. iv. 113. Craig compares
Kyd, *Soliman and Perseda*, II. i. 332-6:
  "But for Assurance that he may
     not scape,
  Weele lay the ports and hauens
     round about;
  And let a proclamation straight
     be made
  That he that can bring foorth
     the murtherer
  Shall haue three thousand
     Duckets for his paines."

Loyal and natural boy, I'll work the means
To make thee capable.　　　　　　　　　85

Enter CORNWALL, REGAN, *and Attendants.*

Corn. How now, my noble friend! since I came hither,
Which I can call but now, I have heard strange
news.

Reg. If it be true, all vengeance comes too short
Which can pursue th' offender. How dost, my
Lord?

Glou. O! Madam, my old heart is crack'd, it's crack'd.　90

Reg. What! did my father's godson seek your life?
He whom my father nam'd, your Edgar?

Glou. O! Lady, Lady, shame would have it hid.

Reg. Was he not companion with the riotous knights
That tended upon my father?　　　　　　95

Glou. I know not, Madam; 'tis too bad, too bad.

Edm. Yes, Madam, he was of that consort.

Reg. No marvel then though he were ill affected;
'Tis they have put him on the old man's death,

---

85. S.D.] *F, subst.; Enter the Duke of Cornwall Q.*　　87. strange
news] *Q;* strangenesse *F.*　　89. dost] does *F 2, 3, 4.*　　90. O!] *F; not in Q.*
it's] *F;* is *Q.*　　92. nam'd, your] *F;* named your *Q.*　　93. O!] *F;* I *Q.*
95. tended upon] *F;* tends vpon *Q;* tend upon *Theobald;* tended on *Hanmer.*
97. of that consort] *F; not in Q. Capell.*

84. *Loyal and natural*] Cf. III. v. 3
"nature thus gives way to loyalty."
Gloucester is quibbling on the two
meanings of *natural*, 'bastard' and
'feeling natural affection' (opposed
to the unnaturalness of his legitimate
son). But since *natural* could mean
legitimate as well as illegitimate, he
may also imply that Edmund is now
his rightful heir.

85. *capable*] able to inherit. *N.E.D.*
quotes from Guillim, *Heraldry,* 1610,
ii. 5 (1660) 65: "Bastards are not
capable of their father's patrimony."

88. *If . . . vengeance*] Cf. *Leir,* 1582:

"If it be so, that shee doth seeke
reuenge."

97. *Yes*] Kittredge suggests the
word should be "prolonged and
dissyllabic," presumably to fill out
the metre and to suggest Edmund's
feigned hesitation in speaking of
Edgar's guilt.

97. *consort*] set. The accent is on
the second syllable. Cf. *T.G.* IV. i.
64. The word is often used contemptuously. Cf. *R.J.* III. i. 49.

98. *ill affected*] disloyal.

99. *put him on*] incited him to.

To have th' expense and waste of his revenues.   100
I have this present evening from my sister
Been well inform'd of them, and with such cautions
That if they come to sojourn at my house,
I'll not be there.

Corn.   Nor I, assure thee, Regan.
Edmund, I hear that you have shown your father   105
A child-like office.

Edm.   *discover*   It was my duty, Sir.

Glou. He did bewray his practice; and receiv'd
This hurt you see, striving to apprehend him.

Corn. Is he pursued?

Glou.   Ay, my good Lord.

Corn. If he be taken he shall never more   110
Be fear'd of doing harm; make your own purpose,
How in my strength you please.   For you, Edmund,
Whose virtue and obedience doth this instant
So much commend itself, you shall be ours:
Natures of such deep trust we shall much need;   115
You we first seize on.

Edm.   I shall serve you, Sir,
Truly, however else.

Glou.   For him I thank your Grace.

100. th' expense and waste] *F;* these—and wast *Q uncorr., Q 2, 3;* the wast
and spoyle *Q corr.;* the spence and waste *conj. Greg;* the fee and waste *conj. Max-*
well   his] *F, Q corr.;* this his *Q uncorr., Q 2, 3;* not in *F 2, 3, 4.*
105. hear *F;* heard *Q.*   106. It was] *F;* twas *Q;* It is *F 3, 4.*   107.
bewray] *F;* betray *Q.*   112. For] *Q, F 1;* as for *F 2, 3, 4, Jennens.*
113. this instant] *Q, F;* in this instance *Jennens (conj. Heath);* at this instant
conj. Capell.   116. Sir] *F;* not in *Q, Jennens.*

100. *th' expense and waste*] the privilege of spending and squandering.
Greg, *Variants,* pp. 155-6, discusses
the reading of Q 1. He thinks there
is a remote possibility that Shakespeare wrote " the spence and waste,"
th' expence being a F sophistication.
The copy for Q must have been
illegible at this point, but the uncorrected version looks like a genuine
attempt to decipher the copy, the
corrected version being an emendation.

106. *child-like*] filial.

107. *bewray*] discover, disclose.
Cf. *Matt.* xxvi. 73. There is no
suggestion of treachery in this word,
unlike ' betray.'

108. *apprehend*] arrest.

111. *Be . . . harm*] be feared, lest
he should do mischief.

111-12. *make . . . please*] carry out
your plans for his capture, and
make what use you like of my authority and resources for that purpose.

113. *virtue . . . obedience*] virtuous
obedience. Hence the singular vb.

Corn. You know not why we came to visit you,—
Reg. Thus out of season, threading dark-ey'd night: *evil*
    Occasions, noble Gloucester, of some prize, 120
    Wherein we must have use of your advice. *importance*
    Our father he hath writ, so hath our sister,
quarrels Of differences, which I best thought it fit
    To answer from our home; the several messengers
    From hence attend dispatch. Our good old friend,
    Lay comforts to your bosom, and bestow 125
    Your needful counsel to our businesses,
    Which craves the instant use.
Glou.   I serve you, Madam.
    Your Graces are right welcome.
                                    [*Flourish. Exeunt.*

---

119. threading] *F;* threatning *Q.*   120. prize] *F, Q 2, 3;* prise *Q uncorr.;*
poyse *Q corr.;* price *Capell (conj. Johnson).*   123. differences] *F, Q corr.;*
defences *Q uncorr., Q 2, 3.*   best] *F, Q uncorr., Q 2, 3;* lest *Q corr.;*
least *Wright, Camb.*   thought] *Q;* though *F.*   124. home] *F, Q corr.;*
hand *Q uncorr., Q 2, 3.*   127. businesses] *F;* business *Q.*   129.
Flourish] F; not in *Q, F 2, 3, 4.*   Exeunt] not in *Q.*

119. *Thus*] Regan takes the words out of her husband's mouth, and thereby shows that he is subordinate.

119. *threading . . . night*] traversing the darkness, with a quibble on the eye of a needle, and the dark eyes of Night. Heywood, *Love's Mistress,* III. i. 4, speaks of " negro night, the black-eyed Queene " (cited Kittredge).

120. *prize*] importance. Greg, *Variants,* shows that as the Q used as copy for F was here in its corrected state, the F reading must have come from the playhouse MS. and not from the uncorrected Q. The Q compositor misread *o* as *r* in III. iv. 6 (contentious/crulentious); the cor-

rector presumably did the same in the present passage.

123. *differences*] quarrels.

123. *which*] referring, as Delius points out, not to *differences,* but to a letter Lear has *writ.*

123-4. *I . . . home*] She wishes to answer the letters away from home, so that the King cannot quarter himself there before she has consulted with Goneril; who, we learn, is also coming to Gloucester's castle (Cf. II. iv. 186).

124. *from*] away from. Cf. *Ham.* III. ii. 22.

125. *attend dispatch*] are waiting to be dispatched.

128. *craves . . . use*] requires to be done at once.

SCENE II.—[*Before Gloucester's Castle.*]

Enter KENT *and* OSWALD, *severally*.

Osw. Good dawning to thee, friend: art of this house?

Kent. Ay.

Osw. Where may we set our horses?

Kent. I' th' mire.

Osw. Prithee, if thou lov'st me, tell me.   5

Kent. I love thee not.

Osw. Why, then I care not for thee.

Kent. If I had thee in Lipsbury pinfold, I would
  make thee care for me.   *between my teeth*

Osw. Why dost thou use me thus?   I know thee not.   10

Kent. Fellow, I know thee.

Osw. What dost thou know me for?   *scraps*

Kent. A knave, a rascal, an eater of broken meats; a
  base, proud, shallow, beggarly, three-suited,

yearly clothing of servants

Scene II

Before . . . Castle] Capell; *not in* Q, F.   *severally*] F; *not in* Q.
1. dawning] F; deuen Q *uncorr.;* euen Q *corr.,* Q 2, 3.   this] F; the Q.
4. I'th'] F; It'h Q *1;* In the Q *2, 3.*   5. lov'st] F; loue Q.

Scene II

1. *dawning*] It is still dark (cf. 32), and the sun has still not risen by the end of the scene. As Greg suggests, the copy for Q was probably ' dauen,' and the F reading was a substitution of a more common form of the word.

1. *of this house*] a servant here. Cf. North's *Plutarch* (*Coriolanus*), Temple ed., p. 35: " They of the house spying him, wondred what he should be."

8. *Lipsbury pinfold*] A pinfold is a pound, a pen in which stray cattle are confined, Nares suggests the phrase means " between my teeth " (i.e. in my clutches), *Lipsbury* meaning Liptown. In Fletcher, *Wit at Several Weapons,* I. i. ed. Glover ix. 71 " to purchase lipland " means " to procure a kiss "; and Kittredge cites *Lucrece,* 679:

 " Entombs her outcry in her
  lips' sweet *fold.*"

Nosworthy cites Middleton, *The Changeling,* III. iii. " Have you read Lipsius? " Here the name is introduced for the sake of the pun on the first syllable.

13. *A knave . . .*] In this speech Kent attacks Oswald as a cowardly menial who parades as a gentleman (Kittredge).

13. *eater . . . meats*] one who eats up remains of food. Cf. *Cor.* IV. v. 35 and *Cymb.* II. iii. 119.

14. *three-suited*] Cf. Edgar's words. III. iv. 139. Servants were apparently given three suits of clothes a year. Wright quotes Jonson, *The Silent Woman,* III. i. 38-42: " Who giues you your maintenance, I pray you? Who allowes you your horse-meat, and man's meat? your three sutes of apparell a yeere? your foure paire of stockings, one silke, three worsted? "

attire of debts

hundred-pound, filthy worsted-stocking knave; 15
a lily-livered, action-taking, whoreson, glass-
*vaim*gazing, super-serviceable, finical rogue; one-
*over officious*trunk-inheriting slave; one that wouldst be a bawd
in way of good service, and art nothing but the
composition of a knave, beggar, coward, pandar, 20
and the son and heir of a mongrel bitch: one
whom I will beat into clamorous whining if thou
deni'st the least syllable of thy addition.

Osw. Why, what a monstrous fellow art thou, thus to
rail on one that is neither known of thee nor 25
knows thee!

Kent. What a brazen-fac'd varlet art thou, to deny
thou knowest me! Is it two days since I tripp'd
up thy heels and beat thee before the King?
Draw, you rogue; for though it be night, yet 30
the moon shines: I'll make a sop o' th' moonshine of you.　　　　　　　　　　*[Drawing his sword.*

---

14. three-suited] *F;* three suyted *Q uncorr.;* three shewted *Q corr., Q 2, 3.*
16. action-taking] *F;* action-taking knaue, a *Q.* 17. super-serviceable, finical] *F.*
super finicall *Q.* 18. one-trunk-inheriting] *F 3;* one trunk-inheriting *F 1, 2;*
no hyphens *Q.* 21. one] *F; not in Q.* 22. clamorous] *Q, F 3, 4;*
clamours *F 1, 2.* 23. deni'st] *F;* denie *Q.* thy] *F;* the *Q.* 24.
Why] *F; not in Q.* 25. that is] *F;* that's *Q.* 28. since] *F;* agoe since *Q.*
28-9. tripp'd . . . thee] *F;* beat thee, and tript vp thy heeles *Q.* 30. yet] *F; not in*
Q. 31. o'th'] *F;* of the *Q.* of] *F;* a' *Q.*　　S.D.] *Rowe; not in Q, F.*

15. *hundred-pound*] probably a hit at James I's profuse creation of knights. Steevens quotes Middleton, *The Phoenix,* IV. iii. 55: " How's this? am I used like a hundred-pound gentleman? "

15. *worsted-stockings*] Cf. Jonson's words quoted in note on l. 14. Gentlemen wore silk stockings.

16. *lily-livered*] white-livered, without blood in it, and hence cowardly. Cf. *Macb.* v. iii. 15; *2 Hen. IV.* IV. iii. 113; *M.V.* III. ii. 86; *T.N.* III. ii. 65-7.

16. *action-taking*] one who goes to law, instead of fighting.

16-17. *glass-gazing*] vain, foppish. Cf. *Rich. III.* I. i. 15.

17. *super-serviceable*] above his work

(Wright); over-officious (Johnson); ready to serve his master in dishonourable ways, " a bawd in the way of good service " (Kittredge).

17. *finical*] affectedly fastidious.

17-18. *one-trunk-inheriting*] possessing only one trunkful of effects.

20. *composition*] compound, mixture.

21. *heir*] inheriting the mongrel bitch's characteristics.

23. *thy addition*] the titles I've given you. Cf. I. i. 136.

31-2. *a sop . . . moonshine*] the ground is drenched in moonlight, and Kent proposes to pierce him with his sword, to allow the moonlight, or the reflection of the moon in a pond, to soak into him, as when

You whoreson cullionly barber-monger, draw.

Osw. Away! I have nothing to do with thee.

Kent. Draw, you rascal; you come with letters   35
against the King, and take Vanity the puppet's
part against the royalty of her father. Draw,
you rogue, or I'll so carbonado your shanks:
draw, you rascal; come your ways.ᵛ *cut of neat*

Osw. Help, ho! murther! help!   40

Kent. Strike, you slave; stand, rogue, stand; you
neat slave, strike.   [*Beats him.*

Osw. Help, ho! murther! murther!

33. You] *F;* draw you *Q.*   cullionly] cully only *Q 3.*   35. come with] *F;*
bring *Q.*   41. strike] *F, Q uncorr.;* strike? *Q corr.*   S.D.] *Rowe;*
not in Q, F.   43. murther, murther] *F;* murther, helpe *Q.*   S.D.] *Furness;*
Enter Bastard, Cornewall, Regan, Gloster, Servants F; Enter Edmund with his rapier
drawn, Gloster, the Duke and Dutchesse Q.

a piece of toast or a wafer is set
floating in a prepared drink. Or
perhaps, as Entwisle suggests, Kent
means to steep Oswald in his own
blood, "by the consenting light of
the moon." The existence of a
dish, called "eggs in moonshine"
(eggs fried in oil or butter, covered
with slices of onions and seasoned
with verjuice, nutmeg and salt)
made Farmer and others suppose
that there was a quibbling reference
to a dish with a similar name.
Nosworthy compares Porter, *Two
Angry Women of Abington* (1599),
2333; "Ile cut thee out in collops
and egges."

33. *cullionly*] rascally, base, vile;
from cullion. Cf. *T.S.* iv. ii. 20.

33. *barber-monger*] a constant patron
of the barber's shop.

36. *Vanity*] Vanity was a common
character in the old Moralities, which
were often performed in puppet-
shows. Marlowe, *The Jew of Malta*,
ii. iii. (881), mentions Lady Vanity.
Cf. Jonson, *Volpone*, ii. iii. 21 and
The Devil is an Ass, i. i. 42. Kent is,
of course, referring to Goneril.

38. *carbonado*] to scotch, or cut
cross-wise, a piece of meat before

broiling or grilling it. Cf. *Cor.* iv.
v. 199. It was frequently used in a
metaphorical sense. Cf. Nashe, *Have
With You to Saffron Walden*, ed.
McKerrow, iii. 17: "I will deliuer
him to thee, to be scotcht and car-
bonadoed."

39. *come your ways*] come along.
Cf. *Ham.* i. iii. 135. The phrase is
still current in Northern England.

42. *neat*] elegant, foppish (cf.
Chapman, *All Fools*, v. ii. "that
neate spruce slaue"); or, perhaps,
as Walker suggests, pure, unmixed,
as in the phrase "neat wine"; or
Shakespeare may have had both
meanings in mind.

44. *Part!*] Grant White, following
Dyce's conjecture, took the unitali-
cised 'Part' of F to be a S.D., and
nearly all later editors have done the
same. Schmidt, one of the few
editors who retains *Part* in the text,
has to argue that Kent quibbles on
the word in his "with you," i.e.
"I will depart with you." This is
barely possible; but the interpretation given below is more probable,
and to keep *Part* in the text thus
separates the retort from the words
that evoke it.

Enter EDMUND, *with his rapier drawn.*

Edm. How now! What's the matter? Part!

Kent. With you, goodman boy, if you please: come,　45
I'll flesh ye; come on, young master.

Enter CORNWALL, REGAN, GLOUCESTER, *and Servants.*

Glou. Weapons! arms! What's the matter here?

Corn. Keep peace, upon your lives:
He dies that strikes again. What is the matter?

Reg. The messengers from our sister and the King.　50

Corn. What is your difference? speak.

Osw. I am scarce in breath, my Lord.

Kent. No marvel, you have so bestirr'd your valour.
You cowardly rascal, nature disclaims in thee:
a tailor made thee. *Your shar is in your cloths*　55

Corn. Thou art a strange fellow; a tailor make a
man?

---

44. Part] *F; not in Q; Parts them Grant White.*　　45. if] *F; and Q;*
an *Staunton.*　　　46. ye] *F; you Q.*　　S.D.] *Staunton; see S.D. 43 ante.*
51. What is] *F; whats Q.*

44. *matter*] subject of the quarrel.

45. *With you*] i.e. the quarrel is with you.

45. *goodman boy*] a title of mock respect to an impudent youth. Cf. *R.J.* I. v. 79.

46. *flesh*] initiate. It was originally a hunting term. See Palsgrave, *Lesclarcissement;* " Flesche as we do an hounde, when we give him any parte of a wyld beast, to encourage him to run well." The word was often used in connection with fighting. Cf. *1 Hen. IV.* v. iv. 133, and Beaumont and Fletcher, *Wit at Several Weapons,* I. i. (ed. Glover, ix. 78)

" The first that flesht me a Soldier, Sir,
was that great battel of *Alcazar* "

51. *difference*] quarrel. Cf. II. i. 123.

53. *your valour*] Craig suggests that this may be a mock title, and he compares *T.C.* I. iii. 176.

54. *disclaims in thee*] renounces any claim to have produced you. Cf. Jonson, *The Case is Altered,* v. xii. 67-8:
" *Count F.* Is not *Rachel* then thy daughter?
Jaq. No, I disclaime in her."
Gifford points out that two instances of *disclaim in* Jonson's *Every Man in his Humour* were altered to *disclaim* in the Jonson Folio, and he suggests that the phrase was becoming obsolete.

55. *a . . . thee*] proverbial. Cf. *Cym.* IV. ii. 81; Jonson, *The Staple of News,* I. ii. 110-11: " Thence comes your prouerbe; The Taylor makes the man." Apperson, *English Proverbs,* pp. 616-17, gives some variants and see *Ham.* III. ii. 37 ff.

Kent. A tailor, sir: a stone-cutter or a painter could
not have made him so ill, though they had been
but two years o' th' trade.   60
Corn. Speak yet, how grew your quarrel?
Osw. This ancient ruffian, Sir, whose life I have
spar'd at suit of his grey beard,—
Kent. Thou whoreson zed! thou unnecessary letter!
My Lord, if you will give me leave, I will tread   65
coarse this unbolted villain into mortar, and daub the
wall of a jakes with him. Spare my grey beard,
you wagtail?
Corn. Peace, sirrah!
You beastly knave, know you no reverence?   70

58. A] *F;* I, a *Q.*   59. they] *F;* hee *Q.*   60. years] *F;* houres *Q.*
o'th] *F 3;* oth' *F 1, 2;* at the *Q.*   61. *Corn.*] *F; Glost. Q.*   62. This] The
F 3, 4.   63. grey beard,—] *Rowe;* gray-beard.   *Q, F 1, 2;* gray beard.
F 3.   65. you will] *F;* you'l *Q.*   67. wall] *F;* walles *Q.*   a jakes] Iaques
Q 3.   69. sirrah] *F;* sir *Q.*   70. know you] *F;* you haue *Q.*

60. *years*] Greg, *Editorial Problem*,
p. 91, points out that the Q reading
is a vulgarization. " Shakespeare
knows that art is long." Nosworthy
compares Porter, *Two Angry Women
of Abington*, 1786-8: " thou whorson
refuge of a Taylor, that wert prentise
to a Taylor halfe an age, and because
if thou hadst serued ten ages thou
wouldst prooue a botcher ".
60. *o' th' trade*] Duthie cites *M.M.*
II. i. 192.
64. *thou . . . letter*] this title is
given to the letter Z because it was
generally ignored in the dictionaries
of the time. Baret omits it altogether in his *Alvearie*, and Rider in
his *Dictionary*, ed. 1640, says it is
not used in Latin. Jonson, *English
Grammar*, ed. Herford and Simpson,
viii. 492 writes: " Z is a letter often
heard amongst us, but seldome
seene." Jonson was echoing Mul-
caster's *Elementarie*, 1582.
66. *unbolted*] Tollet says that unbolted mortar is made of unsifted
lime, the lumps of which have to
be broken up by treading on them
with wooden shoes. But ' coarse ' is

a curious epithet to apply to Oswald,
the glass-gazing, finical, barber-
monger; and Kittredge explains
" this fellow who is a rascal through-
and-through." Perhaps a quibble
is intended: an unbolted villain
might be a released or unrestrained
one; or, since *unbolt* is used in the
sense of *reveal* (*Tim.* I. i. 51), unbolted
might mean *apparent*. It has been
suggested to me that since Boult
(in *Pericles*) has a name suitable to
his trade, *unbolted* might be taken
to mean ' effeminate ' or ' impotent.'

66. *mortar*] Steevens compares
Massinger, *A New Way to Pay Old
Debts*, I. i: " I will . . . tread you
into mortar."

67. *jakes*] privy.

68. *wagtail*] Cf. silly-ducking, 104
post. Kittredge comments that the
wagtail is so called " from the spas-
modic up-and-down jerking of its
tail. Oswald is too scared to stand
still." Kent may merely mean that
Oswald is obsequious.

70. *beastly*] beast-like, irrational,
and perhaps disgusting.

Kent. Yes, sir; but anger hath a privilege.

Corn. Why art thou angry?

Kent. That such a slave as this should wear a sword,
Who wears no honesty. Such smiling rogues as
    these,
Like rats, oft bite the holy cords a-twain   75
Which are too intrince t' unloose; smooth every
    passion
That in the natures of their lords rebel;
Being oil to fire, snow to their colder moods;
Renege, affirm, and turn their halcyon beaks
With every gale and vary of their masters,   80
Knowing nought, like dogs, but following.

---

71. hath] *F;* has *Q.*   74. Who] *F;* That *Q.*   75. the holy] *F;* those *Q.*
a-twain] *F 3;* a twain *F 1;* in twain *Q.*   76. too intrince] *Capell;* t'intrince *F;*
to intrench *Q.*   t'unloose] *F;* to inloose *Q.*   78. Being] *F;* Bring *Q.*   fire]
F; stir *Q.*   their] *Q;* the *F.*   79. Renege] *F 2, 3, 4;* Reneag *Q;* Reuenge
F 1.   80. gale] *Q;* gall *F 1.*   81. dogs] *F;* dayes *Q.*

---

71. *anger . . . privilege*] Cf. *K.J.*
iv. iii. 32.

75. *holy cords*] natural bonds of
affection. Editors think that the
reference is to the bonds between
parent and child; but the context
suggests that Kent is referring to
the bonds of matrimony.

76. *intrince*] abbreviated from *in-
trinsicate* (cf. *A.C.* v. ii. 307), from
Ital. *intrinsecato,* but confused in
sense with *intricato* (*N.E.D.*). Wright
thinks it is a compound of *intrinsic*
and *intricate.* It means intricate,
involved, entangled, tightly drawn.

76. *smooth*] flatter. Cf. *Rich. III.*
I. iii. 48; *R.J.* III. ii. 98; *T.A.* v. ii.
140.

78. *Being*] Both Q and F readings
make excellent sense. Duthie
explains: " Kent means that the
flatterers *are* oil to the flame of their
masters' wrath, that they feed it
and keep it burning . . . just as when
their masters are in, say, a melancholy mood . . . the flatterers are

snow to that mood." He compares
2 Hen. VI. v. ii. 51 ff.

79. *Renege*] deny. Cf. *A.C.* I. i. 8.

79-80. *turn . . . gale*] This refers
to the belief that the halcyon, or
kingfisher, if hung up by the tail or
beak, would turn with the wind.
T. Lupton, *Tenth Book of Notable
Things,* says that " A little byrde
called the King's Fisher, being
hanged up in the ayre by the neck,
his nebbe, or bill, will be always
direct or straight gainst the wind."
Cf. Marlowe, *The Jew of Malta,* I. i.
38-9:
" But now how stands the wind?
    Into what corner peeres my
        Halcions bill? "
Sir Thomas Browne exposed the
belief as a vulgar error; but, according to Green, *Shakespeare and
the Emblem Writers,* p. 393, it was
still prevalent in some parts of
England in the middle of the nineteenth century.

80. *gale and vary*] varying gale
(hendiadys).

A plague upon your epileptic visage!
Smoile you my speeches, as I were a Fool?
Goose, if I had you upon Sarum plain,
I'd drive ye cackling home to Camelot.   85
Corn. What! art thou mad, old fellow?
Glou. How fell you out? say that.
Kent. No contraries hold more antipathy
Than I and such a knave.
Corn. Why dost thou call him knave? What is his
fault?   90
Kent. His countenance likes me not.
Corn. No more, perchance, does mine, nor his, nor hers.
Kent. Sir, 'tis my occupation to be plain:
I have seen better faces in my time
Than stands on any shoulder that I see   95
Before me at this instant.
Corn.   This is some fellow,
Who, having been prais'd for bluntness, doth affect

---

83. smoile] *F 1, 2, 3, Q;* smile *F 4.*   84. if] *Q 2, 3, F;* and *Q 1.*
85. drive ye] *F;* send you *Q.*   90. What is his fault?] *F;* What's his offence? *Q.*
92. does] doth *Q 2, 3.*   nor . . . nor] *F;* or . . . or *Q.*   95. Than] *Q 2;*
Then *Q 3, F;* That *Q.*   96. Some] *F;* a *Q.*

82. *epileptic*] Oswald pale, and trembling with fright, was yet smiling and trying hard to put on a look of lofty unconcern.

83. *Smoile*] Q and F agree here substantially. Presumably Kent remembers to speak in dialect, and unless the passage is corrupt he means " smile at."

83. *as . . . Fool?*] as if I were a professional jester, trying to make you laugh; or, less likely, as if I were foolish, and your butt.

84-5. *Goose . . . Camelot*] Camelot, the residence of King Arthur, has been identified with Winchester (cf. Malory, *Morte Darthur*, ii. 19). Others suppose Camelot to have been in Somerset or Wales; and there are said to have been flocks of geese on the moors near the former site. Capell thought that there was an allusion to a " Winchester goose,"

a syphilitic swelling (so called because the Southwark brothels were on land " within the jurisdiction of the Bishop of Winchester ") or a person suffering therefrom. E. A. Armstrong, *Shakespeare's Imagination*, pp. 57-65, shows that the goose often appears as part of a chain of ideas, including disease, bitterness, seasoning, and restraint. In this context we have 'plague' (82), 'lily-livered' (16, rather remote), 'saucy' (98), and 'cords' (75). Cf. II. iv. 46-64, where some of the same associations recur. But the allusions to the Winchester goose was probably unconscious, and is not likely to have been noticed by an audience.

91. *likes*] pleases. Cf. I. i. 200.

95. *shoulder*] Shoulder is often, if not always, employed by Shakespeare for the part between the shoulders.

A saucy roughness, and constrains the garb
Quite from his nature: he cannot flatter, he,
An honest mind and plain, he must speak truth: 100
And they will take it, so; if not, he's plain.
These kind of knaves I know, which in this plain-
        ness
Harbour more craft and more corrupter ends
Than twenty silly-ducking observants,
That stretch their duties nicely.   105
Kent. Sir, in good faith, in sincere verity,
Under th' allowance of your great aspect,
Whose influence, like the wreath of radiant fire
On flick'ring Phœbus' front,—
Corn.   What mean'st by this?

100. An . . . and] *F;* He must be *Q.*   101 And] An *Pope.* take it] *F;*
tak't *Q.*   104. silly-ducking] *F;* silly ducking *Q.*   106. faith] *F;* sooth *Q,*
Steevens.   in] *F;* or in *Q.*   107. great] *F;* graund *Q.*   109. on] *F;*
in *Q.*   flick'ring] *Duthie;* flicking *F;* flitkering *Q;* flickering *Pope.*   front,
—] *Rowe;* front. *Q, F.*   by] *F;* thou by *Q.*

98-9. *constrains . . . nature*] forces
on himself a demeanour, a character,
quite opposed to what is really his
(Craig). But it is more likely that
his = its, and that Cornwall means
that Kent "distorts the style of
straightforward speaking quite from
its nature, which is sincerity; whereas
he makes it a cloak for craft"
(Clarke).

98. *garb*] style, manner, fashion,
especially of speech; it does not
mean "fashion of dress."

103. *harbour*] Abbott *412 points
out that the two nouns connected
by 'of' (*kind of knaves*) seem regarded
as a compound noun with plural
termination.

103. *more . . . ends*] Shakespeare
often uses the double comparative.
Ridley points out that Cornwall
has given an admirable character
sketch of Iago.

104. *silly-ducking*] ludicrously obsequious. Cf. 'silly-stately' *1 Hen.
VI.* IV. vii. 72.

104. *observants*] obsequious attendants.

105. *stretch . . . nicely*] are particular to carry out their courtly
duties punctiliously.

107-9. *Under . . . front*] Florio, *A
Worlde of Wordes,* 1598, uses the same
affected language in his Epistle
Dedicatory: "But as to me, and
manie more the glorious and gracious
sunne-shine of your Honor hath
infused light and life: so may my
lesser borrowed light, after a principal respect to your benigne aspect,
and influence, affoorde some lustre
to some others."

107. *allowance*] approval. Cf. I. iv.
217.

107. *aspect*] the accent is on the
second syllable. Kent is quibbling
on the two meanings of the word
(i) appearance, (ii) the relative positions of the heavenly bodies as they
appear to an observer . . . and the
influence attributed thereto (Onions).

108. *influence*] astrological power
exercised by the heavenly bodies:
Kent implies ironically that Cornwall
is a heavenly body.

109. *front*] forehead.

Kent. To go out of my dialect, which you discommend 110
    so much.   I know, sir, I am no flatterer: he that
    beguil'd you in a plain accent was a plain knave;
    which for my part I will not be, though I should
    win your displeasure to entreat me to 't.
Corn. What was th' offence you gave him?   115
Osw. I never gave him any:
    It pleas'd the King his master very late
    To strike at me, upon his misconstruction;
    When he, compact, and flattering his displeasure,
    Tripp'd me behind; being down, insulted, rail'd,   120
    And put upon him such a deal of man,
    That worthied him, got praises of the King
    For him attempting who was self-subdu'd;
    And, in the fleshment of this dread exploit,
    Drew on me here again.
Kent.   None of these rogues and cowards 125

in league with the King [margin annotation]
made himself out such a hero [margin annotation]
assaulting [margin annotation]

    110. dialect] *F;* dialogue *Q.*   114. to 't] to it *Q 2, 3.*   115. What was
th'] *F;* what's the *Q.*   119. compact] *F;* coniunct *Q.*   121. man] *F;* man,
that *Q.*   124. fleshment] *F;* flechuent *Q.*   dread] *Q;* dead *F.*

    110. *dialect*] manner of speaking,
language.
    111-12. *he . . . accent*] the type of
man Cornwall has been describing,
96-105.
    113-14. *though . . . to 't*] This has
not been explained satisfactorily.
"Though I should win you, dis-
pleased as you now are, to like me
so well as to entreat me to be a
knave" (Johnson). "Though I
should so far win over, appease,
your wrath, that you should entreat
me to answer it again" (Craig).
"I will not be a plain knave, though
as a great inducement to be such,
though to entreat me, induce me, to
it, I should win your displeasure, a
thing far more desirable in my eyes
than your favour" (Craig, alterna-
tively). "Even if I could induce
you to lay aside your displeasure so
far as to beg me to be one" (Kittredge). Schmidt suggests, I think
rightly, that "your displeasure" is
the opposite to the usual style of
address, "your grace." The passage

might then mean: "Though I should
convert your grace, who are not
gracious to me, to a more amiable
frame of mind, so that instead of
being annoyed with me you actually
entreat me to be a plain knave, i.e.
a flatterer."
    119. *compact*] in league with the
King. The *Q* reading means the same.
    120. *being . . . insulted*] exulted
over me when I was down. Cotgrave
defines *insulter,* "to insult, crow,
vaunt, or triumph over." Cf.
A.Y.L.I. III. v. 36.
    121. *put . . . man*] made himself
out such a hero.
    122. *worthied him*] won honour for
himself (Kittredge); gave him the
appearance of worth (Craig). Abbott
derives *worthied* from the adj.;
Schmidt from *worthy* = hero; Perrett
from ME *wurthien* = dignify.
    123. *For . . . who*] for assailing
one who.
    124. *fleshment*] the action of ' flesh-
ing '; hence, the excitement resulting from a first success. Cf. II. ii. 48.

But Ajax is their fool. *[handwritten: they consider themselves superior to Ajax]*

Corn.   Fetch forth the stocks!
You stubborn ancient knave, you reverend braggart,
We'll teach you.

Kent.   Sir, I am too old to learn.
Call not your stocks for me; I serve the King,
On whose employment I was sent to you;   130
You shall do small respect, show too bold malice
Against the grace and person of my master,
Stocking his messenger.

Corn.   Fetch forth the stocks!
As I have life and honour, there shall he sit till
   noon.

Reg. Till noon! till night, my Lord; and all night too. 135
Kent. Why, Madam, if I were your father's dog,
   You should not use me so.

Reg.   Sir, being his knave, I will.
Corn. This is a fellow of the self-same colour *[handwritten: kind]*
Our sister speaks of.   Come, bring away the stocks.

                                     [*Stocks brought out.*

126. Fetch . . . Stocks] *F;* Bring forth the stocks, ho? *Q.*   127. ancient] *F;*
ausrent *Q uncorr.;* miscreant *Q corr. Q 2, 3.*   reverend] vnreuerent *Q 2, 3.*
128. Sir] *F; not in Q.*   130. employment] *F;* imployments *Q.*   131. shall]
F; should *Q.*   respect] *Q;* respects *F.*   133. Stocking] *F;* Stobing *Q uncorr.;*
Stopping *Q corr.*   137. should] *F;* could *Q.*   138. self-same colour] *F;* selfe
same nature *Q 1;* same nature *Q 2, 3.*   139. speaks] speake *Q 1.*   S.D.]
Dyce; after 137 F; not in Q.

126. *But . . . fool*] Ajax is (by their
own account) a fool in comparison
with *them* (Kittredge).   "Ajax in
bragging is a fool to them" (Capell).
In *Troilus and Cressida* Ajax is treated
as a fool by the rogue and coward,
Thersites.

127. *stubborn*] rough, fierce.
127. *reverend*] aged.
132. *grace and person*] i.e. an insult to
the Crown, and a personal insult too.
133. *stocks*] G. M. Young points
out, *T.L.S.*, 30 Sept., 1949, p. 633,
that in the Rawdon Hastings MSS.
iv there are "some briefe notes of
orders to be observed" in the household of the fifth Earl of Huntingdon
(who succeeded in 1604).   Kent's

punishment was "strictly in accord-
ance with the discipline observed in
a great house of the time." Young
quotes, p. 327: "Whosoever shall
be unseemly stout or urge any
quarrell in mealetyme and will not
be silenced . . . that he be presently
taken from the table and carryed to
the porter's lodge, and there to be
sett in the stockes. . . . That if any
doe unseemly behave themselves towards there betters, the offence to
be punnyshed first by the stockes."
137. *should*] would.
138. *colour*] kind, complexion. Cf.
A.Y.L.I. I. ii. 107.
139. *bring away*] bring here, bring
along. Cf. *M.M.* II. i. 41.

Glou. Let me beseech your Grace not to do so.   140
His fault is much, and the good King his master
Will check him for't: your purpos'd low correction
Is such as basest and contemned'st wretches
For pilf'rings and most common trespasses
Are punish'd with: the King must take it ill,   145
That he, so slightly valued in his messenger,
Should have him thus restrained.
Corn.   I'll answer that.
Reg. My sister may receive it much more worse
To have her gentleman abus'd, assaulted,
For following her affairs.   Put in his legs.   150
                          [Kent is put in the stocks.
Corn. Come, my Lord, away.
                [Exeunt all but Gloucester and Kent.
Glou. I am sorry for thee, friend; 'tis the Duke's
    pleasure,
Whose disposition, all the world well knows,
Will not be <u>rubb'd</u> nor stopp'd: I'll entreat for thee.
Kent. Pray, do not, Sir.   I have watch'd and travell'd
    hard;   155
Some time I shall sleep out, the rest I'll whistle.
A good man's fortune may grow out at heels:
Give you good morrow!
Glou. The Duke's to blame in this; 'twill be ill taken.
                                [Exit.

impeeded [margin annotation]

141-5. His . . . with] *Q; not in F.*   143. contemned'st] *Capell;* contaned *Q uncorr.;* temnest *Q corr., Q 2, 3.*   145. must] *Q;* his master, needs must *F.* 146. he] *F;* he's *Q, F 3, 4.*   149. gentleman] Gentlemen *Q 1.*   150. For . . . legs] *Q; not in F.*   S.D.] *Pope; after 147 Rowe; not in Q, F.*   151. Come . . . away] *F, Q 2, 3;* Come, my good lord, away *Q 1 (assigned to Regan).* S.D.] *Dyce;* Exit *Q 2, F; not in Q 1.*   152. Duke's] *Q;* Duke *F 1.*   155. Pray] *F;* Pray you *Q.*   156. out] ont *Q 1.*   159. taken] *F;* tooke *Q.* S.D.] *not in Q 1.*

142. *check*] rebuke.
144. *pilferings*] Cf. Appendix, p. 250.
147. *answer*] be answerable for.
149. *assaulted*] Cf. Appendix, p. 250.
151. *Come . . . away*] Q gives these words to Regan.   But, as Kirchbaum points out, Cornwall sees that Gloucester is reluctant to leave Kent, and orders him to follow.   " Nevertheless, Gloucester remains, though obviously nervous."
154. *rubb'd*] impeded.   A *rub* in bowls is an obstacle by which a bowl is diverted from its proper course.
155. *watch'd*] gone without sleep.
158. *Give*] i.e. God give.
159. *taken*] received.

Kent. Good King, that must approve the common
                    saw,   160
     Thou out of heaven's benediction com'st
     To the warm sun!   *from better to worse*
     Approach, thou beacon to this under globe,
     That by thy comfortable beams I may
     Peruse this letter.   Nothing almost sees miracles,   165
     But misery: I know 'tis from Cordelia,
     Who hath most fortunately been inform'd
     Of my obscured course; and shall find time

---

165. miracles] *F; my* rackles *Q uncorr.; my* wracke *Q corr., Q 2, 3;*
167. most] not *Q uncorr.*   168-9. shall . . . From] shee'll . . . For *conj.*
Daniel; she'll . . . From *Staunton.*

---

160. *approve*] confirm.

161-2. *heaven's . . . sun!*] This
proverb, derived presumably from
those who leave the shade to go into
the hot sun, and so go from better
to worse is to be found in Heywood,
Proverbs (1546), ed. 1874, p. 115:
" In your running from him to me,
          yee runne
     Out of God's blessing into the
          warme sunne."
It is to be found in Lyly, *Euphues*
(ed. Arber, pp. 196, 320), in Holinshed, *Chronicles* (1577, ed. i. 33), and
in Pettie, *Petite Pallace* (ed. 1908,
ii. 146). Kittredge cites Howell,
Dendrologia, 1640, p. 13: " And now
I am come from God's blessing to
the warme Sun, who is a little too
prodigall of his beames here."
P. L. Carver, *M.L.R.*, 1930, p. 478,
shows that in translating *Ab equis
ad asinos*, Palsgrave, *Acolastus*, has
" from the hall into the kitchen, or
out of Christe's blessing into a
warme sonne (now I am well pro-
moted) " i.e. humiliated or degraded.
Carver therefore interprets Kent's
words: " You are destined to learn
in all its bitterness the meaning of
the proverb which speaks of ex-
changing power and dignity for
impotence and humiliation." This
is doubtless correct, though the
proverb does not always have the
implication of humiliation. Cf. *Leir,*
1154: " he came from bad to worse."

163. *under globe*] Cf. "lower world,"
Rich II. III. ii. 38.

164. *comfortable*] comforting, help-
ful.

165-6. *Nothing . . . misery*] for,
when we are in despair, any relief
seems miraculous (Kittredge).   Cf.
IV. i. 2-6.

168. *obscured*] in disguise.

168. *course*] course of action.

168-70. *and . . . remedies*] The
passage is probably corrupt. Jennens
started the idea that Kent was reading
to himself divided portions of Cordelia's letter.   It would not be light
enough to make out the words clearly.
Perhaps, too, as White suggests,
Kent is too sleepy to concentrate.
Staunton's reading of *she'll* for *shall*
is unnecessary, since *who* is understood; unless, indeed, Kent is saying
that he will himself find time.
E. Sullivan, *T.L.S.*, 20 Dec. 1923,
suggests that *From* = away from
(cf. II. i. 24) and that the passage
means that Cordelia " removed as
she is from the lawless state of things
prevailing her, will be sure to find
time when seeking to provide remedies." This is not very satisfactory,
as from III. i. 30 it looks as though

From this enormous state, seeking to give
Losses   their   remedies.   All   weary   and   o'er-
   watch'd,   170
Take vantage, heavy eyes, not to behold
This shameful lodging.
Fortune, good night; smile once more; turn thy
   wheel!   [*He sleeps.*

170. their] and *Q uncorr.*   o'erwatch'd] *F;* ouerwatch *Q 1;* ouer-watcht
Q 2, 3.   171. Take] Late *Q uncorr.*   173. smile . . . turn] *F;* Smile, once more
turne *Q 1, 2;* Smile one more turne *Q 3.*   (*Lines divided after* night *Q, F.*)

SCENE III.—[*A Wood.*]

Enter EDGAR.

Edg. I heard myself proclaim'd;
And by the happy hollow of a tree   *opportune*
Escap'd the hunt.   No port is free; no place,
That guard, and most unusual vigilance,
Does not attend my taking.   Whiles I may 'scape,   5
I will preserve myself; and am bethought
have the idea

Scene III

1. heard] *F;* hear *Q.*   4. unusual] vnusall *Q 2, 3, F 1, 2.*   5. Does] *F.*
dost *Q.*   taking. Whiles] *F;* taking while *Q.*

this letter informs Kent that France
is planning an invasion. Cuningham,
N.Q. 28 March 1914, wanted to
emend *From* to *Form* = Restore.
In any case, the meaning of the
passage is that Cordelia will somehow
intervene.

169. *enormous*] out of the norm,
irregular, lawless.   Not used elsewhere by Shakespeare.   Cf. Appendix, p. 250.

169. *state*] state of things.

170. *o'er-watched*] Cf. 155 *ante*, and
J.C. IV. iii. 241.

171-2. *Take . . . lodging*] Take the
opportunity afforded by sleep of not
seeing the stocks.

Scene III

S.D.] F has no scene division,
and presumably Kent remained on
the stage during Edgar's speech,
though he must not be supposed
to be in the immediate neighbourhood of the castle.   It is possible
that F text represents a version of
the play performed on a platform,
without an inner stage or gallery.
See *R.E.S.* 1940, pp. 300-3; 1946,
p. 229.

2. *happy*] opportune.

3. *port* Cf. II. i. 80.

5. *attend my taking*] await to capture me.

6. *am bethought*] have got the idea.

To take the basest and most poorest shape
That ever penury, in contempt of man,
Brought near to beast; my face I'll grime with filth,
Blanket my loins, elf all my hairs in knots,⠀⠀⠀⠀⠀10
And with presented nakedness outface
The winds and persecutions of the sky.
The country gives me proof and precedent
Of Bedlam beggars, who, with roaring voices,
Strike in their numb'd and mortified bare arms⠀⠀*insensible*⠀15⠀*to pain*
Pins, wooden pricks, nails, sprigs of rosemary;
And with this horrible object, from low farms,
Poor pelting villages, sheep-cotes, and mills,
Sometime⠀⠀with⠀⠀lunatic⠀⠀bans,⠀⠀sometime⠀⠀with
⠀⠀⠀⠀prayers,

10. elf] *F;* else *Q, F 2;* put *F 3, 4.* ⠀⠀⠀hairs] *F;* hair *Q, F 4.*⠀⠀⠀in] *F;* with *Q.*⠀⠀12. winds] *F;* wind *Q.*⠀⠀persecutions] *F;* persecution *Q.*⠀⠀15. Strike] *Q, F;* Stick *Furness (conj. S. Walker)*⠀⠀and] *not in Q uncorr.*⠀⠀bare] *Q; not in F.*⠀⠀16. Pins] *Q, F;* Pies *Q uncorr.*⠀⠀17. from] *Q, F;* frame *Q uncorr.*⠀⠀farms] *F;* seruice *Q.*⠀⠀18. sheep-cotes] *Q;* sheeps-coates *F.*⠀⠀19. Sometime] *Q;* Sometimes *F.*⠀⠀sometime] sometimes *F 2, 3, 4.*

8. *in . . . man*] to show how contemptible a creature man is.

10. *elf*] tangle into elf-locks; matted hair, caused by neglect, was called 'elf-locks,' and elves were blamed for them. Cf. *R.J.* i. iv. 89-91. In an anonymous pamphlet, *O per se O*, possibly by Dekker, reprinted in Judges, *The Elizabethan Underworld*, p. 371, the Abram cove is described as "a lusty strong rogue . . . his hair long and filthily knotted, for he keeps no barber."

11. *presented*] exposed to view, as on a stage.

11. *outface*] brave. Cf. *M.V.* iv. ii. 17.

13. *proof*] example.

15. *numb'd*] Cf. Appendix, p. 250.

15. *mortified*] made insensible to pain. Dekker, *Bellman of London*, 1608, ed. 1904, p. 99, describes an Abraham man: "You see pinnes stuck in sundry places of his naked flesh, especially in his armes, which paine hee gladly puts himselfe to . . . onely to make you beleeue he is

out of his wits. He calls himselfe by the name of *Poore Tom.*" See also Appendix, pp. 254-5.

15. *bare*] Kirschbaum regards this word as an interpolation, a recollection of "presented nakedness" (l. 11).

16. *pricks*] skewers.

16. *sprigs*] Cf. Appendix, p. 250.

17. *object*] spectacle. Cf. v. iii. 238.

17. *low*] lowly. Cf. *A.Y.L.I.* ii. iii. 68.

18. *pelting*] petty, paltry. Cf. *Rich. II.* ii. i. 60; and Golding, tr. Ovid's *Metamorphoses*, viii. 804-5:
⠀⠀"one cotage afterward
Receyved them, and that was but
⠀⠀a pelting one in deede."

19. *bans*] curses.

19-20. *Poor . . . Tom!*] Edgar practises the Bedlam beggar's whine (Kittredge).

19. *Turlygod*] Nothing is known of this name, though some have supposed it to be a corruption of Turlupin, the name given to a sect of half-mad beggars in Paris *cir.* 1600,

Enforce their charity. Poor Turlygod! poor
Tom!   20
That's something yet: Edgar I nothing am.   [*Exit.*

20. Turlygod] *Q, F;* Tuelygod *Q uncorr.*

SCENE IV.—[*Before Gloucester's Castle.   Kent
in the Stocks.*]

Enter LEAR, *Fool, and Gentleman.*

Lear. 'Tis strange that they should so depart from home,
And not send back my messenger.
Gent.   As I learn'd,
The night before there was no purpose in them
Of this remove.
Kent.   Hail to thee, noble master!
Lear. Ha!   5
Mak'st thou this shame thy pastime?
Kent.   No, my Lord.

Scene IV

Before . . . Castle] *Pope, subst.; not in Q, F.*   *Kent . . . stocks*]
Dyce; not in Q, F.   S.D.] *F; Enter King Q 1; Enter King and a Knight
Q 2, 3.*   1. home] *F;* hence *Q.*   2. messenger] *Q;* Messengers *F 1, 2.*
Gent.] *F;* Knight. *Q.*   3. in them] *F; not in Q.*   4. this] *F;* his *Q,*
5. Ha!] *F;* How, *Q.*   6. thy] *Q;* ahy *F 1.*   No my Lord.] *F; not in Q.*

who used to perform their religious
services naked. C. Mackay, *Glossary
of Obscure Words and Phrases,* 1887,
pp. 429-30, suggests that the word
is an anglicized form of *Tuir-le-guid,*
" one who beseeches or importunes
for alms with a doleful pertinacity."
Guid in Gaelic signifies importunity,
and *Tuir* means " to relate with
a mournful cadence, to whine, to
chant dolefully." Roland M.
Smith, *M.L.Q.,* 1946, p. 168, re-
jects this interpretation and suggests
the word is derived from the Ir.
Toirdhealbhach God, which means
'stammering Turley' or possibly 'mad
Turley' (reading *gealt* for *god*). None
of these suggestions is satisfactory.
19-20. *poor Tom*] Cf. I. ii. 143 and
note to l. 15 above.

21. *That's . . . am*] There is some
hope for me as Poor Tom; I am
nothing, I am doomed, as Edgar.
Or possibly the words mean merely
" I am no longer Edgar."

21. *am*] the rhyme, owing to the
pronunciation of Tom, was probably
a good one.

Scene IV

1-2. *'Tis . . . messenger*] Cf. *Leir,*
1355-6:

" I wonder that the Messenger
    doth stay,
Whom we dispatcht for Cambria
    so long since."

4. *remove*] change of residence.
Cf. *A.W.* v. iii. 131.

Fool. Ha, ha! he wears cruel garters. Horses are
    tied by the heads, dogs and bears by th' neck,
    monkeys by th' loins, and men by th' legs:
    when a man's over-lusty at legs, then he wears   10
    wooden nether-stocks.

Lear. What's he that hath so much thy place mistook
    To set thee here?

Kent.   It is both he and she,
    Your son and daughter.

Lear. No.   15

Kent. Yes.

Lear. No, I say.

Kent. I say, yea.

Lear. No, no; they would not.

Kent. Yes, they have.   20

Lear. By Jupiter, I swear, no.

Kent. By Juno, I swear, ay.

---

7. he] *F;* looke he *Q.*   8. tied] tide tide *F 2.*   heads] *F;* heeles *Q.*
10. man's] *Q;* man *F;* man is *F 2, 3, 4.*   10. then] hen *Q 2;* when *Q 3.*
19-20. *Lear.* No . . . have] *Q; not in F.* 22. *Kent.* By . . . ay. *Lear*] *F; not in Q.*

---

7. *cruel*] a pun on *cruel* and *crewel,*
i.e. thin, worsted yarn. Cf. *Two
Angry Women of Abington,* 1599
(Malone Soc. 489-90):
    " heele haue
    His Cruel garters crosse about the
      knee."
Greene, *Menaphon* (ed. Arber, p. 36),
has the same pun: " with his sheep-
hook fringed with cruel to signifie
he was chief of the savages."

7-9. *Horses . . . legs*] Cf. Harsnett,
Appendix, p. 255.

10. *over-lusty at legs*] too much of
a vagabond (Kittredge).   Cf.
Dekker, *The Seven Deadly Sins of
London,* ed. Arber, p. 31: " tradesmen
as if they were dancing galliards are
lusty at legs and never stand still."
See also Massinger, *Virgin Martyr,*
IV. ii. 13; Middleton, *Blurt Master
Constable,* I. i. 91.

11. *nether-stocks*] stockings. What
we now call knee-breeches were
then called upper-stocks. Kittredge
cites Harington, *Apology,* ed. 1814,
p. 26: " Wooden stocks were fitter
for them than silk stockings." The
same jest is made by Lyly, *Mother
Bombie,* v. iii.

13. *To*] as to.

15-22. *No . . . ay*] These lines are
a conflation of Q and F. Kirschbaum
argues that the reporter restates
21-2 in 19-20, then recollects 21
and attaches it to Lear's next speech.
But the two speeches omitted by F
are so effective in their context that
it is difficult to believe they were
added by the actors. Duthie remarks
that the effect of climax in the passage
seems to bear the stamp of Shakespearian calculation.

Lear.   They durst not do't,
They could not, would not do't; 'tis worse than
    murther,
To do upon respect such violent outrage.
Resolve me, with all modest haste, which way   25
Thou might'st deserve, or they impose, this usage,
Coming from us.

Kent.   My Lord, when at their home
I did commend your Highness' letters to them,
Ere I was risen from the place that show'd
My duty kneeling, came there a reeking post,   30
Stew'd in his haste, half breathless, panting forth
From Goneril his mistress salutations;
Deliver'd letters, spite of intermission,
Which presently they read: on whose contents
They summon'd up their meiny, straight took horse;   35
Commanded me to follow, and attend
The leisure of their answer; gave me cold looks:
And meeting here the other messenger,
Whose welcome, I perceiv'd, had poison'd mine,
Being the very fellow which of late   40
Display'd so saucily against your Highness,
Having more man than wit about me, drew:
He rais'd the house with loud and coward cries.

22-3. do 't] do it *Q 2, 3*.   23. could . . . would] *F;* would . . . could *Q.*
26. might'st] may'st *Q.*   impose] *F;* purpose *Q.*   31. panting] *Q;*
painting *F.*   32. salutations] salutation *F 2, 3, 4.*   34. whose] *Q;* those *F.*
35. meiny] *F;* men *Q.*   40. which] *F;* that *Q.*

24. *upon respect*] There are two
explanations: (i) upon the respect
due to the king's messenger (Johnson) or upon Respect, personified
(Malone); (ii) deliberately.   Cf.
K.J. iv. ii. 214:
    " when, perchance, it frowns
    More upon humour than advised
    respect."
Cf. also *Ham.* iii. i. 68.
25. *Resolve*] satisfy, answer.   Cf.
Rich. III. iv. ii. 26.
25. *modest*] becoming, sober, reasonable. Cf. iv. vii. 5.
26. *might'st*] could'st.

28. *commend*] commit, deliver. Cf.
A.W. v. i. 31.
33. *spite of intermission*] though my
business was interrupted and the
answer delayed which I was to
receive.
34. *presently*] immediately.
35. *meiny*] household, servants.
See Appendix, p. 254.
41. *display'd*] acted ostentatiously.
42. *more . . . wit*] more courage
than sense.
42. *drew*] drew his sword.
43. *rais'd . . . house*] awakened the
servants.

Your son and daughter found this trespass worth
The shame which here it suffers.   45
Fool. Winter's not gone yet, if the wild-geese fly that
    way.

        Fathers that wear rags
          Do make their children blind,
        But fathers that bear bags   50
          Shall see their children kind.
        Fortune, that arrant whore,
        Ne'er turns the key to th' poor.

But for all this thou shalt have as many dolours
for thy daughters as thou canst tell in a year.   55
Lear. O! how this mother swells up toward my heart;
   Hysterica passio! down, thou climbing sorrow!
   Thy element's below.   Where is this daughter?
Kent. With the Earl, Sir; here within.
Lear. Follow me not; stay here.   [*Exit.*

---

45. The] *F;* This *Q.*   46-55. winter's . . . year] *F; not in Q.*   46. wild]
F 2; wil'd *F 1.*   55. for thy] *F;* for thy deare *F 2, 3, 4;* from thy deare
Theobald; from thy *Singer.*   57. *Hysterica*] *F 4; Historica Q, F 1, 2;*
Hystorica F 3. 59. here] *F; not in Q.* 60. here.] *F;* there? *Q 1;* there. *Q 2, 3.*
S.D.] *F; not in Q.*

46. *wild-geese*] Cf. note on II. ii. 84
and *saucily* (41), *blind* (49), *dolours*
(54) and *stocks* (64).   Roland M.
Smith, *M.L.Q.,* 1946, p. 165, compares *Buile Suibhne;*
" Cold is the night tonight—
    I have heard the cry of the wild-
      goose."
The resemblance is probably accidental.

50. *bear bags*] hang on to the
money-bags.

53. *turns the key*] opens the door.
Cf. III. vi. 67.

54. *dolours*] a pun on dollars, the
English name for the Spanish peso
and the German thaler. Cf. *Temp.*
II. i. 19 and *M.M.* I. ii. 50.

55. *for*] on account of, owing to.

55. *tell*] a quibble, the word
meaning both *relate* and *count.*

56-7. *mother . . . Hysterica passio*]
The symptoms of this malady are
described by Drayton, *Polyolbion,* vii.

19-28.   Richard Mainy, one of the
people mentioned in Harsnett's pamphlet, suffered from the mother, and
it is alluded to more than once.
See Appendix, p. 253.   Edward
Jordan, *A Brief Discourse of a Disease
called the Suffocation of the Mother,*
1605, p. 5, writes: " This disease
is called by diverse names amongst
our authors, *Passio Hysterica, Suffocatio,
Priefocatio,* and *Strangulatus uteri,
Caducus Matricis,* i.e. in English, the
Mother or the Suffocation of the
Mother, because, most commonly, it
takes them with choking in the throat;
and it is an affect of the mother or
wombe, wherein the principal parts
of the bodie by consent do suffer
diversely according to the diversitie
of the causes and diseases wherewith
the matrix is offended."   Craig
thinks the word may be only a
contradiction of *smother.*

58. *element*] proper place.

Gent. Made you no more offence but what you speak   61
    of?

Kent. None.
    How chance the King comes with so small a
    number?

Fool. And thou hadst been set i' th' stocks for that
    question, thou'dst well deserv'd it.   65

Kent. Why, Fool?

Fool. We'll set thee to school to an ant, to teach thee
    there's no labouring i' th' winter. All that follow
    their noses are led by their eyes but blind men;
    and there's not a nose among twenty but can   70
    smell him that's stinking. Let go thy hold when
    a great wheel runs down a hill, lest it break thy
    neck with following; but the great one that
    goes upward, let him draw thee after. When a
    wise man gives thee better counsel, give me mine   75
    again: I would have none but knaves follow it,
    since a Fool gives it.

*of fortunes
displeasure*

*He says one
thing meaning
the opposite.
He sees the
truth in Lear. He will not desert L. and would not wish Kent to do so.*

61. but] *F; then Q.*   62. None] *F; no, Q.*   63. the] *Q; the the F.*
number] *F; traine Q.*   64. And] *Q 1, F; If Q 2, 3; An Pope.*   70. twenty]
F; a 100 Q.   stinking] sinking *conj. Mason.*   73. following.] *F; following
it, Q.*   74. upward] *F; vp the hill Q.*   76. have] *Q; hause F 1.*

61. *Made . . . offence*] For examples
of this form, see *M.M.* iv. ii. 198-9;
A.Y.L.I. iii. v. 117.

63. *How chance*] How does it
happen that.

67. *ant*] the ant lays up a store
of food during the summer, and the
Fool implies that in the winter of
Lear's fortunes his followers have
deserted him, because they can no
longer make anything out of him.
Cf. the verses 81-6 below. Alterna-
tively, or additionally, he may be
telling Kent that he is foolish to
remain with the King. Baldwin,
*Shakespeare's Small Latine and Lesse
Greeke,* i. 620-1, points out that
Shakespeare may have been influenced by the fable of the Fly
and the Ant as told by Camerarius:

" *At ego aestate mediocri labore exerceor,
vt hyeme quietam & securam vitam possim
degere.* "

71. *stinking*] Mason wished to
emend to *sinking,* with which
Steevens compared *A.C.* iii. x. 26.
Malone defended *stinking,* and compared *A.W.* v. ii. 4-6: " I am now,
sir, muddied in fortune's mood, and
smell somewhat strong of her strong
displeasure." Those who can see
that the king is ruined have deserted
him, and even the blind should be
able to smell the stench of fortune's
displeasure.

76. *have*] J. Sledd, *M.L.N.,* 1940,
p. 595, suggests that the F reading,
hause, may be a variant of *halse,*
meaning *beseech* or *abjure,* and derived
from O.E. *halsian.*

That sir which serves and seeks for gain,
 And follows but for form,
Will pack when it begins to rain,   80
 And leave thee in the storm.
But I will tarry; the Fool will stay,
 And let the wise man fly:
The knave turns Fool that runs away;
 The Fool no knave, perdy.   85

Kent. Where learn'd you this, Fool?

Fool. Not i' th' stocks, Fool.

Re-enter LEAR, *with* GLOUCESTER.

Lear. Deny to speak with me! They are sick! They
 are weary!
 They have travell'd all the night! Mere fetches, ay,   *tricks*

78. That sir] That, sir, *F 4.*   which] *F; that Q.*   and seeks] *F; not in Q.*
80. begins] begin *Q 1.*   81. the] a *F 4.*   82. But] And *F 3, 4.*   84-5. The
knave ... knave] The fool turns knave that runs away, The knave no fool *Collier*
(*conj. Johnson*).   87. Fool] *F; not in Q.*   S.D.] *Capell, based on Q;*
after 85 F.   89. have] *F; not in Q.*   all the night] *F; hard to night Q.*
fetches, ay] *conj. Capell;* fetches *F;* Iustice I *Q.*

78. *sir*] man.

79. *faorm*] Cf. *M.M.* II. iv. 12 and
Oth. I. i. 50. The man is "trimmed
in forms and visages of duty," but
has no inner feelings of loyalty.
He serves because of his master's
rank.

80. *pack*] be off.

82-5. *But ... perdy*] Enid Welsford,
The Fool, 1935, pp. 255-6, 267,
commenting on these lines, and
rejecting Johnson's emendation,
shows that the Fool, like Erasmus in
The Praise of Folly, is playing upon
the various meanings and relations
of the words 'fool' and 'knave.'
His decision to stay with Lear is
"the unambiguous wisdom of the
madman who sees the truth." He
does not wish Kent to follow his
advice to desert the King, for it is
only the advice of a fool. "The
knave who runs away comes out
into the open, and is at once seen

as the abject contemptible ludicrous
creature that he has always been.
The fool is at least true to himself."
Kittredge similarly interprets: "The
fellow that forsakes his master is
(from the point of view of the higher
wisdom) a fool, since true wisdom
implies fidelity; and the fool who,
like me, remains faithful is, at all
events, no knave."

87. *Not ... Fool*] Kent, too, is a
loyal fool, and not a politic knave.

88. *Deny*] refuse.   Cf. *Rich. III.*
v. iii. 343.

89. *fetches*] tricks, subterfuges, ruses,
acts of tacking (nautical).

89. *ay*] This may be an interpolation by the actor, or an accidental
omission by F.   On the whole,
although there is no reason why the
line should be made regular, it is
improved by the retention of this
word.

signs

The images of revolt and flying off. desertion   90
Fetch me a better answer.

Glou.   nature   My dear Lord,
You know the fiery quality of the Duke;
stubborn   How unremovable and fix'd he is
In his own course.

Lear. Vengeance! plague! death! confusion!   95
Fiery! what quality?   Why, Gloucester, Gloucester,
I'd speak with the Duke of Cornwall and his wife.

Glou. Well, my good Lord, I have inform'd them so.

Lear. Inform'd them! Dost thou understand me, man?

Glou. Ay, my good Lord.   100

Lear. The King would speak with Cornwall; the dear
father
Would with his daughter speak, commands, tends
service: offers
Are they inform'd of this?   My breath and
blood!
Fiery! the fiery Duke!   Tell the hot Duke that—
No, but not yet; may be he is not well: 105
Infirmity doth still neglect all office   duty

---

95. plague! death!] *F;* death, plague *Q.*   96. Fiery! what quality?] *F;*
what fierie quality, *Q.*   98-9. Well . . . man?] *F; not in Q.*   101. father]
fate *Q uncorr.*   102. with his] with the *Q uncorr.*   commends, tends] *F;*
come and tends *Q uncorr.;* commands her *Q corr., Q 2, 3.*   103. Are . . .
blood!] *F; not in Q.*   104. Fiery . . . Duke] *F;* The fierie Duke *Q uncorr.;*
Fierie Duke *Q corr.*   that—] *F;* that Lear *Q.*   105. No] mo *Q uncorr.*
108. commands] command *Q 1.*

90. *images*] signs, symbols. The
word, Craig suggests, may here be
dissyllabic, though this is surely
improbable.

90. *flying off*] revolt, desertion.
Cf. *A.C.* II. ii. 155.

92. *quality*] nature, disposition.
Cf. *T.N.* III. i. 70.

93. *unremoveable*] stubbornly firm.
Cf. *Tim.* v. i. 227.

102. *commands, tends*] The corrected reading of Q, *commands her seruice*
could not have been in the copy, for
the original compositor could not
have misread *her* as *tends.* Although

F here may have been printed from
an uncorrected sheet, and *tends* may
therefore be a reproduction of a
Q error, the word makes sense.
Schmidt suggests that it is an aphetic
form of *attends:* Greg, that it means
offers. Lear commands her service,
tenders his own; and this may be
taken as a conciliatory afterthought,
or as an ironical reinforcement of
his words. Cf. Greg, *Variants,* pp.
161-2 and Duthie, *op. cit.* pp. 143-4.

104. *hot*] hot-tempered, passionate.

106. *office*] duty.

Whereto our health is bound; we are not our-
    selves
When Nature, being oppress'd, commands the
    mind
To suffer with the body.   I'll forbear;
And am fall'n out with my more headier will,   110
To take the indispos'd and sickly fit
For the sound man.   Death on my state! where-
    fore   [*Looking on Kent.*
Should he sit here?   This act persuades me
That this remotion of the Duke and her
Is practice only.   Give me my servant forth.   115
Go tell the Duke and's wife I'd speak with them,
Now, presently: bid them come forth and hear me,
Or at their chamber-door I'll beat the drum
Till it cry sleep to death.   119
Glou. I would have all well betwixt you.   [*Exit.*
Lear. O me! my heart, my rising heart! but, down!
Fool. Cry to it, Nuncle, as the cockney did to the eels

---

112. S.D.] *Johnson; not in Q, F.*   116. Go] *F; not in Q.*   I'd] Ile *Q.*
120. S.D.] *F; not in Q.*   121. O me . . . down] *F;* O my heart, my heart *Q.*

110. *am . . . will*] am angry with
my more headlong impulse.
110. *headier*] impetuous or headlong, rather than headstrong. Cf.
Ascham, *Toxophilus*, ed. Arber, p. 85:
" Wales being headye, and re-
belling many yeares against us."
111. *To take*] for taking.
112. *my state*] my royal power.
114. *remotion*] keeping aloof, as in
Tim. IV. ii. 346. But Lear may be
referring to their removal. Cf.
II. iv. 4.
115. *practice*] craft, trickery.
115. *forth*] out of the stocks.
117. *presently*] at once.
119. *Till . . . death*] till the noise
of the drum has been the death of
sleep, so that they gave up all idea
of sleeping. Cf. *Macb.* II. ii. 42.
120. *; . . . well*] Cf. *Leir*, 831,
" I feare that all things go not well."
122. *cockney*] Halliwell and Dyce
suspect that there is an allusion to

some lost story. A cockney could
be a spoilt child, a cook, a Londoner,
or an affected woman. Cotgrave
defines *Coquine* as a beggar woman,
also a cockney, *simper-de-cockit*, nice
thing. Meres, *Wit's Treasury*, 1598,
cited *N.E.D.*, has: " Many cockney
and wanton women are often sick."
The present use of the word is difficult to determine, as affected woman,
cook, and Londoner would all fit
the context. Perhaps the heroine
of the story was all three. She was
so unfamiliar with eels that she did
not know that they should be killed
before cooking. Cf. Lyly, *Euphues*,
ed. Arber, p. 103; " But why cast
I the effects of this vnnaturalnesse in
thy teeth, seeing I my selfe was the
cause? I made thee a *wanton*, and
thou hast made me a foole: I
brought thee vp like a *cockney*, and
thou hast handled me like a *cockes-
combe*." J. C. Maxwell points out

when she put 'em i' th' paste alive; she knapp'd
'em o' th' coxcombs with a stick, and cried
" Down, wantons, down! " 'Twas her brother 125
that, in pure kindness to his horse, buttered his
hay.

Re-enter GLOUCESTER, *with* CORNWALL, REGAN,
and Servants.

Lear. Good morrow to you both.
Corn.   Hail to your Grace!
                                      [*Kent is set at liberty.*
Reg. I am glad to see your Highness.
Lear. Regan, I think you are; I know what reason   130
I have to think so: if thou shouldst not be glad,
I would divorce me from thy mother's tomb,
Sepulchring an adult'ress. [*To Kent.*] O! are you
      free?

123. she] hee *F 2, 3, 4.*   'em] *F;* vm *Q 1;* them *Q 2, 3, F 4.*   i' th']
F; it'h *Q 1;* vp i' th *Q 2, 3.*   123-4. knapp'd 'em o' th'] *F;* rapt um ath *Q.*
125. her] his *F 3, 4.*   127. S.D.] *F, subst.; Enter Duke and*
Regan Q.   128. *&c.*   *Corn.*] *F; Duke Q.*   S.D.] *F; not in Q.*
130. you] *Q;* your *F.*   132. divorce] deuose *Q uncorr.*   mother's] *Q;*
Mother *F.*   tomb] fruit *Q uncorr.*   133. S.D.] *Rowe; not in Q, F.*
O] *F;* Yea *Q.*

to me that the italicized words re-
appear in the present context, and
that the situation recalls that of
Euphues, where Ferardo complains
of his daughter's ingratitude: " I
had thought that my hoary haires
should haue found comforte by thy
golden lockes, and my rotten age
great ease by thy rype years . . .
Would I had neuer lyued to be so
olde, or thou to be so obstinate. . . .
Is this the comfort that the parent
reapeth for all his care? Is obstinacy payed for obedyence, slubberne-
nesse, rendred for duetie, malycious
desperatenesse, for filiall feare? "
123. *knapp'd*] rapped. Jamieson
Scottish Dictionary, defines knap as
" to strike smartly, as ' knap the
nail on the head '." Cf. *Ps.* xlvi. 9.
125. *Down . . . down!*] Down, you

playful creatures, down (Kittredge).
But even without Robert Graves'
poem of this title one might suspect
that the phrase was equivocal.
126-7. *buttered his hay*] A common
trick of cheating ostlers was to grease
the hay of horses committed to their
care; the horses, disliking grease,
were kept from feeding, and the
ostler could steal their provender.
The cockney's brother, however, did
it in all innocence.
128. *Good morrow*] It is now evening, so that Lear's greeting is ironical.
132. *mother's tomb*] At the opening
of *King Leir,* there is a reference to
the funeral of the Queen.
133. *Sepulchring*] as being the
sepulchre of. The accent is on the
second syllable.

Some other time for that. [*Exit Kent.*] Beloved Regan,
Thy sister's naught: O Regan! she hath tied　　　135
Sharp-tooth'd unkindness, like a vulture, here.

> [*Points to his heart.*

I can scarce speak to thee; thou'lt not believe
With how deprav'd a quality—O Regan!

Reg. I pray you, Sir, take patience. I have hope
You less know how to value her desert　　　140
Than she to scant her duty.

Lear.　　　　　　　　Say? how is that?

Reg. I cannot think my sister in the least
Would fail her obligation. If, Sir, perchance
She have restrain'd the riots of your followers,
'Tis on such ground, and to such wholesome end,　145
As clears her from all blame.

Lear. My curses on her!

Reg.　　　　　　　O, Sir! you are old;
Nature in you stands on the very verge
Of her confine: you should be rul'd and led
By some discretion that discerns your state　　150
Better than you yourself. Therefore I pray you
That to our sister you do make return;

---

134. S.D.] *See p. 258.*　　135. sister's] sister is *Q;* tied] tired (*Sympson*).
136. S.D.] *Pope; not in Q, F.*　137. thou'lt] *F;* thout *Q.*　138. With how
deprav'd] *F;* Of how depriued *Q corr., Q 2;* Of how deptoued *Q uncorr.* quality
—] *Rowe;* quality. *F;* qualitie, *Q.*　139. you] *F; not in Q.*　141. scant] *F;*
slacke *Q.*　141-6. *Lear.*　Say . . . blame.] *F; not in Q.*　148. in] *F;*
on *Q.*　149. her] *Q;* his *F 1.*　151. you] *F; not in Q.*

---

136. *like a vulture* an allusion to
the torture of Prometheus. See
Appendix, p. 255.

137. *quality*] manner, disposition.

139-41. *I . . . duty*] Johnson and
other critics (inc. Greg. *T.L.S.*
9 Nov. 1933) have pointed out that
Shakespeare says the opposite of
what he intends. But the double
negative does not, here and frequently in Shakespeare, make an
affirmative. Regan means: " I
hope you undervalue her dutifulness,
rather than that she has come short

in it." Perhaps Shakespeare meant
Regan to say the opposite of this,
and so tell the truth against her will.

141. *scant*] Cf. I. i. 278; II. iv. 177;
III. ii. 67.

149. *confine*] assigned limit; or
Regan may mean that Lear is
imprisoned in the flesh and about
to be released by death.

150. *discretion*] the abstract for
the concrete, i.e. discreet person.
Cf. ' houseless poverty,' III. iv. 26.

150. *state*] condition of mind; or,
your dependent position.

Say you have wrong'd her.

Lear.   Ask her forgiveness?
Do you but mark how this becomes the house:
" Dear daughter, I confess that I am old;   155
Age is unnecessary: on my knees I beg   [*Kneeling.*
That you'll vouchsafe me raiment, bed, and food."

Reg. Good sir, no more; these are unsightly tricks.
Return you to my sister.

Lear. [*Rising.*] *deprived*   Never, Regan.
She hath abated me of half my train;   160
Look'd black upon me; struck me with her tongue,
Most serpent-like, upon the very heart.
All the stor'd vengeances of Heaven fall
On her ingrateful top!   Strike her young bones,
                         head

153. her.] *F;* her Sir? *Q.*   154. but] *F; not in Q.*   156. S.D.] *Dyce; not in Q, F.*   159. Never] *F;* No *Q.*   161. black] back *Q 2, 3.*

154. *house*] the royal house (Perrett); family relations (Kittredge).

155-7. *Dear . . . food*] Heilman, *op. cit.* pp. 142-3, says that Lear is here " the ironic critic of a violation of Nature which is symbolized by the father's being a suppliant to his child . . . Lear's ironic prayer is a ruthlessly logical display of the doctrine of the survival of the fittest . . . age is a crime in a world where the chief value is physical force."

156. *Age . . . unnecessary*] old people are useless.   Johnson explained: " Old age has few wants."

160. *abated*] deprived, curtailed. Hilda M. Hulme, *M.L.R.*, 1951, p. 322, shows that the word was used in Warwickshire in this sense.

161. *struck . . . tongue*] Cf. *Leir,* 1048: " I will so toung-whip him."

163. *stor'd vengeances*] Cf. Beaumont and Fletcher, *The Coxcomb,* I. i. 22: " Let all the stored vengeance of heaven's justice."

164. *top*] head.

164. *young bones*] Cf. *Leir,* 844-7:

" *Leir.* Alas, not I: poore soule,
      she breeds yong bones,
And that is it makes her so
      tutchy sure.
Gon. What, breeds young bones
      already! you will make
An honest woman of me then,
      belike."

The same expression, " young bones," for unborn progeny, is to be found in Tourneur, *The Atheist's Tragedy,* IV. iii. 172, and in Ford, *The Broken Heart,* II. i. Kellett, *Suggestions,* p. 40, remarks that " the curse gains greatly in meaning if we assume that Shakespeare's Lear, like the old playwright's Leir, knew or suspected that Goneril had already an unborn child." Kittredge declares that the context makes it certain that the young bones are Goneril's own; and Perrett urges that since the embryo is well protected, it could not be hurt by taking airs. But this is not a decisive objection. Cf. *Ham.* I. i. 163. Perrett's other objection, that Lear would not curse an innocent unborn child, is invalid. Cf. I. iv. 290 ff.

intechiug

You taking airs, with lameness!

Corn.   Fie, Sir, fie!   165

Lear. You nimble lightnings, dart your blinding flames
Into her scornful eyes! Infect her beauty,
You fen-suck'd fogs, drawn by the pow'rful sun,
To fall and blister her!

Reg. O the blest Gods! so will you wish on me,   170
When the rash mood is on.

Lear. No, Regan, thou shalt never have my curse:
Thy tender-hefted nature shall not give

gentle / tender hearted

165. Fie, Sir, fie!] *F;* Fie fie sir *Q.*   166. *Lear.*] *Q 2; Le. F; not in Q.*
169. blister her] *Muir;* blister *F;* blast her pride *Q;* blister pride *Schmidt;* blister
her pride *Duthie.*   171. is on] *F; not in Q.*   173. Thy] *F;* The *Q,* tender-
hefted] *F;* tender hested *Q 1, 2;* tender hasted *Q 3;* tender-hearted *Rowe.*

165. *taking*] infecting, blasting.
Cf. *M.W.* iv. iv. 32 and Palsgrave,
op. cit. "taken, as children's limbs
are by the fairies."

168. *fen-suck'd*] sucked up from
the fens by the heat of the sun.
Cf. *M.N.D.* ii. i. 90. In another
passage, *Temp.* ii. ii. 1-2, Shakespeare
uses five words that appear together
in the present context:
   " All the infections that the sun
         sucks up
   From bogs, fens, flats on Prosper
         fall."

169. *blister her*] The Q reading is
unlikely to be right, because it was
deliberately corrected by F; but
the F reading is not convincing as
it stands. Schmidt's *blister pride*
is easier to speak, and the compositor
may have thought that *pride* as well
as *blast her* was marked for deletion.
Duthie's reading, *blister her pride*,
if the -er of *blister* is elided as he
suggests, would be indistinguishable
in the theatre from *blister pride*. The
reading in the text can be spoken
with plenty of venom. For a similar
use of *blister* cf. *Temp.* i. ii. 323:
" blister you all o'er "; and *Ham.*
iii. iv. 42-4. Duthie argues that
the Q reading is a memorial corruption (cf. i. iv. 308). But it must
be admitted that *blast* and *infection*

were also closely associated in
Shakespeare's mind, and *blast* and
blister were probably thought to have
a common derivation, so that the
substitution of one for the other would
be simple enough. It is not impossible that Shakespeare suggested
or allowed an emendation which by
some accident never got into the
prompt-book. Nosworthy conjectures
blister o'er.

173. *tender-hefted*] set in a delicate
' haft ' or bodily frame; hence
womanly, gentle. (*N.E.D.*) Florio
uses the word *hafted*, ' handled '
(Cf. Appendix, p. 250). Shakespeare
elsewhere (*W.T.* ii. i. 45) uses *heft*
to mean ' heaving,' as in retching;
and Steevens, followed by Kittredge,
explains: " heaved (i.e. moved,
swayed) by tender emotions only."
Schmidt (*Lexicon*) suggests the word
means ' tender-handled,' gentle to
touch or approach, affable. If the
Q reading *tender hested* were accepted, it might mean, since *hest* =
command, commanded by tender-
ness, " a nature which is governed
by gentle dispositions." I am not
satisfied with any of these explanations. Wright cites Cotgrave, *op.
cit.;* " *Emmanché:* . . . Helued, set
into a haft. *Lasche emmanché:* Lazie,
idle, slothfull, weake, feeble, loose

Thee o'er to harshness: her eyes are fierce, but thine
Do comfort and not burn. 'Tis not in thee   175
To grudge my pleasures, to cut off my train,
To bandy hasty words, to scant my sizes, *allowances*
And, in conclusion to oppose the bolt
Against my coming in: thou better know'st
The offices of nature, bond of childhood,   180
Effects of courtesy, dues of gratitude;
Thy half o' th' kingdom hast thou not forgot,
Wherein I thee endow'd.

Reg.   Good sir, to th' purpose.
Lear. Who put my man i' th' stocks?   [*Tucket within.*
Corn.   What trumpet's that?
Reg. I know't, my sister's: this approves her letter,   185
That she would soon be here.

Enter OSWALD.

                    Is your Lady come?
Lear. This is a slave, whose easy-borrow'd pride

174. Thee] the *Q 1.*   o'er] are *Q 3.*   182. o' th'] *F;* of the *Q.*
183. S.D.] *F, after 183; not in Q.*   185. sister's] sister *Q 3.*   letter] *F;*
letters *Q.*   186. S.D.] *Dyce; Enter Steward (after that, 184) Q, after*
stocks *F.*   187. easy-borrow'd] *hyphened Theobald.*

ioynted, faint-hearted." But he
does not draw the conclusion that
if *lasche emmanché* can mean ' faint-
hearted,' then *tender-hefted* may
reasonably be taken to mean ' tender-
hearted.'

175. *Do . . . burn*] Malone compares
Tim. v. i. 134.

177. *bandy*] Cf. i. iv. 89 and
note.

177. *sizes*] allowances. Cotgrave,
op. cit., defines *Mesure:* " scantling,
rule, square, proportion, size." A
sizar is a poor scholar who used to
obtain allowances from the college
buttery-hatch. In *Leir*, Perillus
complains (763):

" His pension she hath halfe re-
        strain'd from him."

Skalliger urges Gonorill (801):

" The large allowance which he
hath from you . . .
        Therefore abbridge it halfe."

180. *offices*] duties.

180. *bond of childhood*] a child's
duty to her parents.

181. *Effects*] workings, manifesta-
tions. Cf. *Hen. VIII.* ii. iv. 86.

185. *I know't*] Regan probably
recognized some distinguishing note
or tune (Steevens). Cf. *Oth.* ii. i. 180.

185. *approves*] confirms, is in ac-
cordance with. Cf. ii. ii. 160.

187. *easy-borrow'd*] " borrowed
without the trouble of doing anything to justify it " (Moberly), as
one who borrows money without
offering any security. Perhaps
Theobald was wrong to hyphen the
words; *easy* may mean ' coolly-
impudent.'

Dwells in the fickle grace of her he follows.
Out, varlet, from my sight!
Corn.   What means your Grace?
Lear. Who stock'd my servant? Regan, I have good
  hope   190
Thou didst not know on't.   Who comes here?

Enter GONERIL.

O Heavens,
If you do love old men, if your sweet sway
Allow obedience, if you yourselves are old,
Make it your cause; send down and take my part!
[*To Goneril.*] Art not asham'd to look upon this
  beard?   195
O Regan! will you take her by the hand?
Gon. Why not by th' hand, sir?   How have I offended?
All's not offence that indiscretion finds
And dotage terms so.
Lear.   O sides! you are too tough;
Will you yet hold?   How came my man i' th'
  stocks?   200
Corn. I set him there, Sir; but his own disorders
Deserv'd much less advancement.
Lear.   You! did you?
Reg. I pray you, father, being weak, seem so.
If, till the expiration of your month,
You will return and sojourn with my sister,   205

188. fickle] *Q;* fickly *F 1, 2;* sickly *F 3, 4.*   he] a *Q 1.*   190. *Lear]*
F; Gon. Q.   stock'd] *F;* struck *Q.*   191. on 't] *F;* ant *Q 1, 2.*   S.D.]
Johnson; at 189 Q, F.   192. your] *F;* you *Q.*   193. you] *F; not in Q.*
195. S.D.] *Johnson; not in Q, F.*   196. will you] *F;* wilt thou *Q.*   201.
Sir] *not in Q 2, 3.*

188. *fickle*] The F reading was probably due to a remembrance of l. 111 *ante.*

193. *Allow*] approve of. Cf. *allowance* I. iv. 217.

198. *finds*] deem (Fr. *trouver*), detects.

199. *dotage*] Heilman, *op. cit.* p. 141, says that this " is Goneril's favourite word for age: it is her way of deny- ing that age has dignity or deserts, and that it has a place in Nature; she conceives of it only as a state which compels submission to her and her sister's desires."

199-200. *O . . . hold*] Cf. *A.C.* IV. xiv. 39.

201. *disorders*] misconduct.

202. *advancement*] promotion, honour.

    Dismissing half your train, come then to me:
    I am now from home, and out of that provision
    Which shall be needful for your entertainment.
Lear. Return to her? and fifty men dismiss'd?
    No, rather I abjure all roofs, and choose   210
    To wage against the enmity o' th' air;
    To be a comrade with the wolf and owl,
    Necessity's sharp pinch! Return with her!
    Why, the hot-blooded France, that dowerless took
    Our youngest born, I could as well be brought   215
    To knee his throne, and, squire-like, pension beg
    To keep base life afoot. Return with her!
    Persuade me rather to be slave and sumpter *pack horse*
    To this detested groom.   [*Pointing at Oswald.*
Gon.   At your choice, Sir.
Lear. I prithee, daughter, do not make me mad: 220
    I will not trouble thee, my child; farewell.
    We'll no more meet, no more see one another;
    But yet thou art my flesh, my blood, my daughter;
    Or rather a disease that's in my flesh,
    Which I must needs call mine: thou art a boil, 225
    A plague-sore, or embossed carbuncle, *swollen*

q. mad speech on women.

211. o' th'] of the *Q.*   212. owl] howl *Collier.*   214. hot-blooded] hot bloud in *Q.*   216. beg; bag *Q 1.*   217. afoot] *Q;* a foote *F.*   219. S.D.] *Johnson, subst.*] *not in Q, F.*   220. I] *F;* Now I *Q.*   224. that's in] *F;* that lies within *Q.*

211. *wage*] combat, contend.

212. *owl*] Collier, following the Collier MS., read *howl.* This is not an improvement, in spite of the lines quoted by Collier in support of it, *A.W.* III. ii. 119-21.

213. *Necessity's . . . pinch*] Cf. Florio's words, Appendix, p. 251.

214. *hot-blooded*] passionate. Cf. I. ii. 23.

216. *knee his throne*] Schmidt explains " to travel thither on the knees." Cf. *Cor.* v. i. 5 and *Leir*, 2294:
" Ide creepe along, to meet him
    on my knee."
But the phrase is more likely to mean " kneel before his throne."

218. *sumpter*] packhorse, or possibly pack-horse driver. In Florio, *op. cit.* ii. 143, the word has the former meaning. Cotgrave defines *Sommier* " a Sumpter horse, and generally any toyling and load-carrying drudge or groom."

225. *boil*] Cotgrave (s.v. *Bosse*) gives it as a synonym of 'plague-sore.'

226. *embossed*] swollen, tumid, knobbed like the boss of a shield. Palsgrave has " Botch, a sore; *bosse de pestilence* "; and Cotgrave, " *Embosser*, to swell, or arise in bunches, hulches, knobs; to grow knottie, or knurrie."

In my corrupted blood. But I'll not chide thee;
Let shame come when it will, I do not call it;
I do not bid the thunder-bearer shoot,   *Jupiter*
Nor tell tales of thee to high-judging Jove.   230
Mend when thou canst; be better at thy leisure;
I can be patient; I can stay with Regan,
I and my hundred knights.

Reg.   Not altogether so;
I look'd not for you yet, nor am provided
For your fit welcome. Give ear, Sir, to my sister; 235
For those that mingle reason with your passion
Must be content to think you old, and so—
But she knows what she does.

Lear.   Is this well spoken?

Reg. I dare avouch it, sir: what! fifty followers
Is it not well? What should you need of more?   240
Yea, or so many, sith that both charge and danger
Speak 'gainst so great a number? How, in one
        house,
Should many people, under two commands,
Hold amity? 'Tis hard; almost impossible.

Gon. Why might not you, my Lord, receive attendance 245
From those that she calls servants, or from mine?

Reg. Why not, my Lord? If then they chanc'd to
        slack ye   *come short of their duty*
We could control them. If you will come to me,
For now I spy a danger, I entreat you
To bring but five-and-twenty; to no more   250
Will I give place or notice.

---

226. or] *F;* an *Q.* 229. thunder-bearer] *F;* thunder bearer *Q.* 230. high-judging] *F;* high iudging *Q.* 233. so] *F;* so sir *Q.* 234. look'd] *F;* looke *Q.* 235. sir] *not in Q 2, 3.* 237. you old] *F;* you are old *Q.* so—] *Rowe;* so, *Q, F.* 238. spoken] *F;* spoken now *Q.* 242. Speak] *F;* Speakes *Q.* one] *F;* a *Q.* 247. chanc'd] *F;* chanc'st *Q.* ye] *F;* you *Q.*

229. *thunder-bearer*] Jupiter.
230. *high-judging*] that is supreme judge; or "judging in heaven" (Schmidt). There is the same ambiguity in "high heaven" (*M.M.* II. ii. 121).

236. *mingle . . . passion*] dilute your passionate words with a little common sense, examine them in the cold light of reason.
247. *slack you*] come short of their duty towards you. Cf. *Oth.* IV. iii. 88.

Lear. I gave you all—
Reg.   And in good time you gave it.
Lear. Made you my guardians, my depositaries,   ~~stewardesses~~
    But kept a reservation to be follow'd   ~~trustees.~~
    With such a number.   What! must I come to you 255
    With five-and-twenty?   Regan, said you so?
Reg. And speak't again, my Lord; no more with me.
Lear. Those wicked creatures yet do look well-favour'd   ~~good~~
    When others are more wicked; not being the   ~~looking~~
        worst
quantity   Stands in some rank of praise.   [*To Goneril.*] I'll
        go with thee: 260
    Thy fifty yet doth double five-and-twenty,
False   And thou art twice her love.
quantitative   *Gon.*   Hear me, my Lord.
value.   What need you five-and-twenty, ten, or five,
    To follow in a house where twice so many
    Have a command to tend you?
Reg.   What need one? 265
Lear. O! reason not the need; our basest beggars
    Are in the poorest thing superfluous:
    Allow not nature more than nature needs,
    Man's life is cheap as beast's.   Thou art a lady;
    If only to go warm were gorgeous,   270

---

254. kept] keep *F 3, 4.*   258. look] *F;* seem *Q.*   well-favour'd]
hyphened *Q 2;* unhyphened *Q 1, F 1, 2.*   260. S.D.] *Hanmer; not in*
Q, F.   265. need] *F;* needes *Q.*   266. need] *F;* deed *Q.*   269. life is] *F;*
life as *Q 1;* life's as *Q 2, 3.*

252. *I . . . all*] Cf. *Leir,* 2144:
" Ah, cruell *Ragan,* did I giue thee
all? "

253. *guardians . . . depositaries*]
stewardesses and trustees.   Cf.
Appendix, p. 251.

254. *reservation*] a saving clause.
Cf. I. i. 133.

258-60. *Those . . . praise*] Steevens
compares *Cymb.* v. v. 215-17.

258. *well-favour'd*] good-looking.

264. *follow*] be your attendants.

266. *reason not*] do not argue about.
Heilman, *op. cit.* p. 169, commenting

on this speech, observes that " Lear
not only defines the effect upon
humanity of the use of mere need
as a measuring stick for perquisites,
but he shrewdly demonstrates that
his daughters do not themselves
observe the canon of need."

267. *Are . . . superfluous*] have,
however little they possess, something
above what is necessary for bare
existence. Cf. IV. i. 67 and III. iv. 35.

270-2. *If . . . warm*] If it were
gorgeous merely to be warm, you
would not need the fashionably
scanty attire you are now wearing.

Why, nature needs not what thou gorgeous wear'st,
Which scarcely keeps thee warm.   But, for true
     need,—
You Heavens, give me that patience, patience I
     need!—
You see me here, you Gods, a poor old man,
As full of grief as age; wretched in both!   275
If it be you that stirs these daughters' hearts
Against their father, fool me not so much   *do not make me*
To bear it tamely; touch me with noble anger,   *such a fool*
And let not women's weapons, water-drops,   *as—*
Stain my man's cheeks!   No, you unnatural hags, 280
I will have such revenges on you both
That all the world shall—I will do such things,
What they are, yet I know not, but they shall be
The terrors of the earth.   You think I'll weep;
No, I'll not weep: 285
I have full cause of weeping,   [*Storm heard at a
     distance.*] but this heart
Shall break into a hundred thousand flaws
Or ere I'll weep.   O Fool! I shall go mad.
          before   [*Exeunt Lear, Gloucester, Gentleman, and Fool.*

271. wear'st] *F;* wearest *Q.*   274. man] *F;* fellow *Q.*   275. grief] gteefe
Q 2.   277. so] *F;* to *Q 1, 3;* too *Q 2.*   278. tamely] *F;* lamely *Q.*
279. And] *F;* O *Q.*   282. shall-] *Q 2,*   *F;* shall, *Q.*   283. are, yet] *Q 2;*
are yet, *F;* are yet *Q 1.*   286. S.D.] *Capell; Storm and Tempest F; not in Q.*
287. into a hundred thousand] *F;* in a *100.* thousand *Q 1;* in a thousand *Q 2.*
flaws] flowes *Q.*   288. Or ere] Ere *Q 2.*   S.D.] *See p. 258; Exeunt Lear,
Leister . . . Q; Exuent F; Exeunt Lear, Gloucester, Kent, and Fool Q 2.*

272. *But . . . need*] Lear is about
to explain the difference between
true need and the perverted needs
of fashionable women, when he
breaks off to pray for his own chief
need at the moment—Patience or
fortitude.

277. *fool*] Empson, *op. cit.* p. 134,
remarks that " the heavens themselves, in this break-up of the human
order, are becoming fools like everyone else, only malicious ones." But
the passage probably means " do
not make me such a fool as."

282-4. *I will . . . earth*] Ritson cites

Golding's *Ovid's Metamorphoses,* vi.
784-5:
     " The thing that I doe purpose on
          is great, what ere it is;
     I know not what it may be yet."
286. S.D.] The Heavens answer.
287. *flaws*] fragments.   Bailey,
Eng. Dict., 1721, thus defines the
word.   The word was also used by
Shakespeare to mean ' crack '
(*L.L.L.* v. ii. 415), and also ' gust
of passion ' (*Macb.* III. iv. 63).   There
may be a quibble on two or three
of these meanings here.
288. *or ere*] before;   both words
separately also mean ' before.'

Corn. Let us withdraw, 'twill be a storm.

Reg. This house is little: the old man and 's people   290
   Cannot be well bestow'd. *lodged*

Gon. 'Tis his own blame; hath put himself from rest,
   And must needs taste his folly.

himself *Reg.* For his particular, I'll receive him gladly,
   But not one follower.

Gon.   So am I purpos'd. 295
   Where is my Lord of Gloucester?

Corn. Follow'd the old man forth. He is return'd.

Re-enter GLOUCESTER.

Glou. The King is in high rage.

Corn.   Whither is he going?

Glou. He calls to horse; but will I know not whither.

Corn. 'Tis best to give him way; he leads himself.   300

Gon. My Lord, entreat him by no means to stay.

Glou. Alack! the night comes on, and the bleak winds
   Do sorely ruffle; for many miles about
   There's scarce a bush.

Reg.   O! Sir, to wilful men,
   The injuries that they themselves procure   305
   Must be their schoolmasters. Shut up your doors;
   He is attended with a desperate train,

290. and's] *F 2, 3, 4,* an'ds *F;* and his *Q.*   295. *Gon.*] *F; Duke Q.*
purpos'd] *F;* puspos'd *Q 1.*   297. *Corn.*] *F; Reg. Q.*   S.D.] *Dyce; after*
296. *Q, F.* 298-9. rage . . . whither] *F;* rage, and wil I know not whether *Q.*
300. *Corn.*] *F; Reg. Q.*   best] *F;* good *Q.*   302. bleak] *Q;* high *F.*
303. ruffle] *F;* russell *Q;* rustle *Capell.*   304. There's] There is *Q 3.*   scarce]
F; not *Q.*

291. *bestow'd*] lodged.
   292. *'Tis . . . hath*] F takes over
the defective punctuation of Q
(Duthie). Both omit the semicolon.
   292. *hath*] ' he ' is understood.
   292. *rest*] repose of mind.
   294. *For his particular*] As far as he
personally is concerned.
   300. *give him way*] give him his
own way, let him go.
   300. *he . . . himself*] he insists on
having his own way (Kittredge).

302. *bleak*] The F reading may
be an echo of *high* (l. 298).
   303. *ruffle*] to bluster, to be noisy
and turbulent. The word is used
by Harsnett. Cf. Appendix, p. 253.
   307. *with*] by.
   307. *desperate train*] It is not clear
where Lear's knights are supposed
to go, or if he brought them with
him. Cf. II. iv. 63. Perhaps Regan
is making a fictitious excuse for her
conduct.

And what they may incense him to, being apt
To have his ear abus'd, wisdom bids fear.
Corn. Shut up your doors, my Lord; 'tis a wild night: 310
My Regan counsels well: come out o' th' storm.

                                                        [*Exeunt.*

308. to] too *Q 2, 3, F 1.*   310. wild] wil'd *F 1, 2.*   311. Regan] Reg
Q 1.   o' th'] *F 3, 4;* oth' *F 1, 2;* at'h *Q 1;* ath *Q 2, 3.*

308. *incense*] provoke, instigate.
309. *To . . . abus'd*] Cf. I. iii. 21.
309. *wisdom*] As Heilman points
out (*op. cit.* p. 233) Regan means by
wisdom, looking out for oneself.
" Here a veritable exaggeration of

cool sanity is transmuted into moral
madness."
310. *Shut . . . doors*] Gloucester, in
spite of his feelings, (cf. III. vii. 62 ff.)
obeys.

ACT III

SCENE I.—[*A Heath.*]

A storm, with thunder and lightning.   Enter KENT
and a Gentleman, meeting.

Kent. Who's there, besides foul weather?
Gent. One minded like the weather, most unquietly.
Kent. I know you.   Where's the King?
Gent. Contending with the fretful elements;
    Bids the wind blow the earth into the sea,   5
    Or swell the curled waters 'bove the main,
    That things might change or cease; tears his white
      hair,
    Which the impetuous blasts, with eyeless rage,
    Catch in their fury, and make nothing of;
    Strives in his little world of man to out-storm   10

The to-and-fro-conflicting wind and rain.
This night, wherein the cub-drawn bear would
    couch, *lie in lair*
The lion and the belly-pinched wolf
Keep their fur dry, unbonneted he runs,
And bids what will take all. *gamblers cry*

Kent.   But who is with him?   15

Gent. None but the Fool, who labours to out-jest *exercise with jokes'?*
His heart-strook injuries.

Kent.   Sir, I do know you;
And dare, upon the warrant of my note, *on the strength of*
Commend a dear thing to you.   There is division, *my observation of you*
Although as yet the face of it is cover'd   20
With mutual cunning, 'twixt Albany and Cornwall;
Who have—as who have not, that their great stars
Thron'd and set high?—servants, who seem no less, *spies*
Which are to France the spies and speculations *spies (abstract)*
Intelligent of our state.   What hath been seen,   25

entrust
important

giving information

11. to-and-fro-conflicting] *hyphened Capell.*   13. belly-pinched] *hyphened*
Pope.   17. heart-strook] *F;* heart strooke *Q.*   18. note] *F;* Arte *Q.*
19. Commend] Commended *Q 3.*   20. is] *F;* be *Q.*   22-9. Who have . . .
furnishings] *F; not in Q.*   23. Thron'd] *F;* Throne *Theobald.*

Complaint, 7: "Storming her world
with sorrow's wind and rain." This
line contains the same reference to
the microcosm, and the Q compositor elsewhere confused c/t and
m/n (cf. collations IV. ii. 12, II. i. 124).

11. *to-and-fro-conflicting*] swaying
about in mad, angry conflict. Cf.
IV. vii. 32 and *Tim.* IV. iii. 230.

12. *cub-drawn*] sucked by her cubs,
and so ravenous and ferocious. Cf.
A.Y.L.I. IV. iii. 115, 127. Kittredge
compares *Arden of Feversham*, II. ii.
118-20:
  "Such mercy as the staruen
      Lyones,
    When she is dry suckt of her
        eager young,
    Showes to the prey that next
        encounters her."

12. *couch*] lie in its lair.
14. *unbonneted*] Cf. *Oth.* I. ii. 23.
15. *take all*] the cry of the gambler,

staking all on a last throw. Cf. *A.C.*
IV. ii. 8

16-17. *labours . . . injuries*] to drive
out, exorcise them by jesting; or
perhaps, to outdo the greatness of
his master's wrongs by the wild
extravagance of his jests.

17. *heart-strook*] Cf. II. iv. 161.

18. *upon . . . note*] on the strength
of my observation, knowledge of you.

19. *Commend*] entrust.

19. *dear*] important.

20. *is*] Q has *be*: but the indicative
may be used for subjunctive since
there is no reference to futurity, and
since no element of doubt is involved
(Duthie).

23. *who . . . less*] who do not seem
less than servants, i.e. spies.

24. *speculations*] spies; the abstract
used for the concrete, as in II. iv. 150.

25. *Intelligent*] giving information.
Cf. III. v. 11 and III. vii. 12.

Either in snuffs and packings of the Dukes,
Or the hard rein which both of them have borne
Against the old kind King; or something deeper,
Whereof perchance these are but furnishings—
But, true it is, from France there comes a power   30
Into this scatter'd kingdom; who already,
Wise in our negligence, have secret feet
In some of our best ports, and are at point
To show their open banner. Now to you:
If on my credit you dare build so far   35
To make your speed to Dover, you shall find

27. have] *F 2, 3, 4;* hath *F 1.*   30-42. But . . . office to you] *Q;* not in *F.*
31. scatter'd] *Q;* shatter'd *Hanmer.*   32. feet] *Q 1;* fee *Q 2;* see *Q 3;*
sea *Pope;* seat *conj. Upton;* foot *Capell.*

26. *snuffs*] resentments, quarrels, huffs. The word was often used in quibbles, since it could also mean a burning candlewick. Cf. *M.N.D.* v. i. 254; *L.L.L.* v. ii. 22; *1 Hen. IV.* i. iii. 41.

26. *packings*] plots, intrigues. Cf. *T.S.* v. i. 121 and *Cymb.* III. v. 80. See also *Leir,* 1932: " There is good packing ' twixt your King and you '." The word is connected with the vb. *pack*, to plot, scheme, intrigue; and *pack* in this sense may be derived either from sb. *pack* (in sense of *gang*) or *pack* (of cards). " To pack cards with " is to make a cheating arrangement with. Cf. *A.C.* IV. xiv. 19, where there may be a quibble on the two senses.

27. *the . . . borne*] how inflexibly firm, how stiff-necked they have been; or perhaps it means " the cruel way they have proceeded."

29. *furnishings*] trimmings, pretexts. Schmidt remarks: " Whether these incomplete sentences are due to the poet, or to the style in which the scene has been transmitted to use, cannot be decided." As 22-9 are lacking in Q, and 30-42 in F (the compositor may have thought the marginal addition of 22-9 was meant to be substituted for 30-42, beside

which it was written) it is quite possible that a line or two have been omitted from both texts at this point, in which Kent's sentence was completed. Or Shakespeare may have intended him to break off in the middle of his explanation. Any explanation of France's invasion that detracted from its disinterestedness would have been dramatically wrong. On the other hand, France could not have heard by this time of ill-usage of Lear sufficient to justify an invasion. Shakespeare's manipulation of time for dramatic ends compelled him to be ambiguous and vague on the subject of the French invasion. If, however, we follow Steevens and most later editors in putting a semicolon after *state* (25), the *what* in that line might be taken to mean " namely, to note and report what." In which case the sense would be completed at *furnishings.*

30. *power*] army.

31. *scatter'd*] divided, unsettled, disunited (Johnson).

32. *have . . . feet*] have gained a secret foothold. Cf. III. vii. 45.

33. *at point*] ready. Cf. I. iv. 334.

35. *my credit*] your trust in me.

36. *To*] as to.

Some that will thank you, making just report
Of how unnatural and bemadding sorrow
The King hath cause to plain.
I am a gentleman of blood and breeding,   40
And from some knowledge and assurance offer
This office to you.
Gent. I will talk further with you.
Kent.   No, do not.
For confirmation that I am much more
Than my out-wall, open this purse, and take   45
What it contains.   If you shall see Cordelia,—
As fear not but you shall—show her this ring,
And she will tell you who that fellow is
That yet you do not know.   Fie on this storm!
I will go seek the King.   50
Gent. Give me your hand. Have you no more to
    say?
Kent. Few words, but, to effect, more than all yet;
    That, when we have found the King, in which your
        pain
    That way, I'll this, he that first lights on him
    Holla the other.   [*Exeunt severally.* 55

43. further] *F;* farther *Q 1, 2.*   44. I am] *F;* I *Q.*   47. fear] doubt
Q 2, 3.   48. that] *F;* your *Q.*   53. in . . . pain] *F; not in Q.*   54. That
. . . this] *F;* Ile this way, you that *Q.*   55. S.D.] *Theobald; Exeunt Q, F.*

37. *making*] for making.
37. *just*] accurate.
38. *bemadding*] maddening.   Cf.
Cymb. II. ii. 37 'madding.'
39. *plain*] complain of.
41. *assurance*] trustworthy information.

42. *office*] service, duty (i.e. the
journey to Dover).
45. *out-wall*] exterior.   Cf. *T.N.*
I. ii. 48 and *Sonnet* cxlvi. 4.
48. *fellow*] companion.
52. *to effect*] in importance.
53-4. *in which . . . this*] in which
task, you go that way, while I go this.

SCENE II.—[*Another part of the Heath.*]   *Storm still.*

Enter LEAR *and Fool.*

Lear. Blow, winds, and crack your cheeks! rage! blow!

You cataracts and hurricanoes, spout

Till you have drench'd our steeples, drown'd the
cocks!

You sulph'rous and thought-executing fires,

Vaunt-couriers of oak-cleaving thunderbolts,   5

Singe my white head! And thou, all-shaking
thunder,

Strike flat the thick rotundity o' th' world!

Scene II

S.D. *Another . . . Heath*] *Capell.*   *Storm still*] *F; not in Q. 1.*
winds] *F; wind Q.*   2. cataracts] caterickes *Q.*   hurricanoes] Hyrricano's
F 1; Hircanios *Q 1, 2;* Hercantos *Q 3.*   3. our] *F; The Q.*   drown'd]
Q; drown *F.*   4. thought-executing] *F; unhyphened Q.*   5. of] *F;*
to *Q.*   6. Singe] sing *Q 2, 3.*   all-shaking] *unhyphened Q.*   7. Strike] *F;*
Smite *Q.*   o' th'] *F; of the Q.*

Scene II

1-5. *Blow . . . thunderbolts*] For
Harsnett parallels see Appendix,
p. 253.

2. *cataracts*] the flood-gates of the
heavens, the earliest meaning of the
word (cf. *Gen.* vii. 11); or possibly
'waterspouts.'   Eden, *West India*,
1555 (ed. Arber, p. 386), mentions
"that in certeyne places of the sea,
they sawe certeyne stremes of water
which they caule spoutes faulynge
owt of the ayer into the sea. . . . Sum
phantasie that these shoulde be the
catractes of heaven whiche were all
opened at Noe's flood."

2. *hurricanoes*] this form of the
word is rare.   Cf. *T.C.* v. ii. 272:

"The dreadful spout,
Which shipmen do the hurricano
call."

The word has been found in this
sense in only one other passage,
Drayton, *Mooncalfe*, 1627, 494:

"As that which men the hurricane
call."

Drayton may have been echoing
Shakespeare.

3. *drown'd*] submerged.

3. *cocks*] weathercocks.

4-5. *You . . . thunderbolts*] Pringle
Barret, *M.L.N.* 1928, pp. 316-17,
compares *Temp.* I. ii. 201-3:

"Jove's lightnings, the precursors

O' th' dreadful thunderclaps, more
momentary

And sight-outrunning were not."

4. *thought-executing*] Barret points
out that Johnson's explanation,
"doing execution with rapidity
equal to thought," is supported by
the parallel passage in *The Tempest*.
Moberly, however, explains "execut-
ing the thought of him who casts you."

5. *Vaunt-couriers*] forerunners, har-
bingers, heralds.   Originally the
word meant the foremost scouts in
an army.   Cf. 'precursors' in the
passage quoted from *The Tempest*.

5. *oak-cleaving thunderbolts*] a favour-
ite image of Shakespeare's. Cf., e.g.
Temp. v. i. 44-6; *M.M.* II. ii. 115-16;
Cor. v. iii. 153.

7. *rotundity*] Delius thinks that from
the context "the roundness of
gestation" as well as the sphere of
the globe is here suggested.

Crack Nature's moulds, all germens spill at once
That makes ingrateful man!

Fool. O Nuncle, court holy-water in a dry house is   10
better than this rain-water out o' door. Good
Nuncle, in, ask thy daughters blessing; here's a
night pities neither wise men nor Fools.

Lear. Rumble thy bellyful! Spit, fire! spout, rain!
Nor rain, wind, thunder, fire, are my daughters: 15
I tax you not, you elements, with unkindness;
I never gave you kingdom, call'd you children,
You owe me no subscription: then let fall
Your horrible pleasure; here I stand, your slave,
A poor, infirm, weak, and despis'd old man.   20
But yet I call you servile ministers,
That will with two pernicious daughters join
Your high-engender'd battles 'gainst a head
So old and white as this. O, ho! 'tis foul.

8. moulds] *F;* Mold *Q.*   9. makes] *F;* make *Q.*   10. holy-water] *F;*
unhyphened Q.   11. this rain-water] *F;* the Rain-water *F 3, 4; un-*
hyphened Q.   o'] *F;* a *Q.*   12. ask] *F;* and ask *Q.*   13. wise men]
wisemen *F;* wise man *Q.*   Fools] *F;* foole *Q.*   14. bellyful] *Malone;* belly
full *Q, F.*   16. tax] *F;* taske *Q.*   18. then] *F;* Why then *Q.*   22. will
. . . join] *F;* haue . . . ioin'd *Q.*   23. high-engender'd] *F; unhyphened Q.*
battles] *F;* battel *Q.*   24. O, ho!] *F;* O *Q.*

8. *moulds*] the moulds used by
Nature in forming men.

8. *germens*] the germs or seeds of
matter. Cf. *Macb.* IV. i. 59 and
W.T. IV. iv. 488-9. Lear wishes to
prevent the birth of any more people,
so that the ungrateful race of man
will die out.

8. *spill*] destroy.

9. *ingrateful*] ungrateful.

10. *court   holy-water*]   flattery.
Malone cites Cotgrave, *op. cit.*
Eau beniste de Cour. "Court holy
water; . . . faire words, flattering
speeches, glosing, soothing, palpable
cogging." The phrase is used by
Florio (see Appendix, p. 251), and
Harsnett makes frequent mention of
holy-water. Eliot, *Ortho-Epia*
Gallica, explains: " I shall be
sprinckled with the Court holy-
water, that is to say, I shall haue a

deluge of ceremonies, but as many
apes tailes as dinners and breakefasts."

12. *ask* . . . *blessing*] ask a blessing
from your daughters. Cf. v. iii.
10 with its two objects.

14. *thy bellyfull*] to thy heart's
content. The storm here, is in the
opening line of the scene, personified.

15. *fire*] dissyllabic.

16. *tax*] to bring a charge of
something against. Cf. I. iv. 353 and
M.M. v. i. 312. Moberly compares
A.Y.L.I. II. vii. 174.

18. *subscription*] allegiance, submission, obedience. Cf. I. ii. 24
(Q) and III. vii. 65.

21. *ministers*] agents.

23. *high-engender'd*] engendered in
the heavens. Kittredge thinks there
is also a suggestion of the meaning
' sublime.'

23. *battles*] battalions.

Fool. He that has a house to put's head in has a good   25
    head-piece.
              The cod-piece that will house
              Before the head has any,
              The head and he shall louse;
              So beggars marry many.   30
              The man that makes his toe
              What he his heart should make,
              Shall of a corn cry woe,
              And turn his sleep to wake.
For there was never yet fair woman but she   35
made mouths in a glass. *mu trer*

              Enter KENT.

Lear. No, I will be the pattern of all patience;
    I will say nothing.
Kent. Who's there?

25. put's] *F;* put his *Q.*   31. The] That *F 3, 4.*   33. of] *F;* haue *Q.*
35. but] hut *Q uncorr.*   36. S.D.] *F after 37 Q.*   37. pattern] patience
F 3, 4.

25. *put's*] put his.
26. *head-piece*] a pun (*a*) a helmet,
a covering for the head, (*b*) a head,
i.e. brain.
27. *cod-piece*] part of male attire,
worn by men in front of the close-
fitting hose; it is here used for the
phallus.
27-30. *The . . . many*] The man
who satisfies his sexual appetites
before he has a house to live in will
end up by marrying a wife, and share
her lice.   Danby, *op. cit.* p. 111,
suggests that l. 30 refers to the
beggar's long train of doxies, and he
compares the rake's progress described by Edgar III. iv. 85 ff., of
the proud gallant who becomes a
naked Bedlamite.   But Poor Tom
was perhaps a servingman, not a
courtier.
31-4. *The . . . wake*] The man who
cherishes a mean part of his body to
the exclusion of what is really worth

cherishing, shall suffer lasting harm,
and from the very part he so foolishly
cherished.   The Fool is glancing at
Lear's folly in casting out Cordelia
and enriching her evil sisters.
Kittredge quotes Greene, *Euphues
his Censure,* 1587 (ed. Grosart, vi. 191):
"Finding it folly to sett that at his
heart which other set at their heele."
35-6. *For . . . glass*] Probably an
irrelevant piece of nonsense, "such
as was often used to distract attention
from too keen a piece of satire."
(Kittredge, following Furness.)   The
Fool is referring to the habit women
have of practising pretty faces in a
mirror; and may be glancing
obliquely at the vanity and hypocrisy
of Goneril and Regan.
37. *I . . . patience*] Cf. *Leir,* 755-6:
"But he, the myrrour of mild
    patience,
Puts vp all wrongs, and neuer
    giues reply."

Fool. Marry, here's grace ~~The King~~ and a cod-piece; that's   40
a wise man and a Fool.

Kent. Alas! Sir, are you here? things that love night
Love not such nights as these; the wrathful skies
~~terrify~~ Gallow the very wanderers of the dark,   ~~wild beasts~~
And make them keep their caves. Since I was man   45
Such sheets of fire, such bursts of horrid thunder,
Such groans of roaring wind and rain, I never
Remember to have heard; man's nature cannot
  carry ~~bear~~
Th' affliction nor the fear.

Lear.   ~~turmoil~~ Let the great Gods,
That keep this dreadful pudder o'er our heads,   50
Find out their enemies now. Tremble, thou
  wretch,
That hast within thee undivulged crimes,
Unwhipp'd of Justice; hide thee, thou bloody
  hand,

---

41. wise man] *Pope;* wiseman *Q, F.*   42. are] *F;* sit *Q.*   44.
wanderers] *F;* wanderer *Q.* 45. make] *F;* makes *Q.* 47. never] *F;* ne're *Q.*
49. fear] *F;* force *Q.*   50. pudder] *F;* Powther *Q 1;* Thundring *Q 2, 3.*

---

40. *grace*] the King's grace, i.e. the King; or an honourable man.

40. *cod-piece*] Douce remarks that the Fool " was usually provided with this unseemly part of dress in a more remarkable manner than other persons."

41. *a wise . . . Fool*] " He leaves it to Kent to decide which is which " (Kittredge). After the Fool's allusion to the King as a codpiece in l. 27, the audience, too, will share the ambiguity.

44. *Gallow*] terrify. It is now used only in S.W. Midland dialect, and by whale-fishers.

44. *wanderers . . . dark*] wild beasts.

45. *And . . . caves*] Cf. III. i. 12.

46. *bursts*] peals.

48. *carry*] bear, endure.

49-60. *Let . . . sinning*] Baldwin,

op. cit. ii. 532, compares Juvenal, *Satires,* xiii. 223-6.

50. *pudder*] hubbub, turmoil. Lamb preferred this reading to that of Q. Steevens quotes Beaumont and Fletcher, *The Scornful Lady,* II. ii. (ed. Glover, i. 251):
  " Some fellows would have cryed now, and have curst thee,
    and faln out with their meat,
      and kept a pudder."
Mr. F. Kermode calls my attention to the *pothering pole* used in Herefordshire for knocking down cider apples. He suggests that Lear may be alluding to the shower of missiles from above when the pothering pole is plied. This, however, is improbable.

51. *Find . . . now*] " by the terror which such offenders must show " (Kittredge).

53. *of*] by.

Thou perjur'd, and thou simular of virtue
That art incestuous; caitiff, to pieces shake,   55
That under covert and convenient seeming
Has practis'd on man's life; close pent-up guilts,
Rive your concealing continents, and cry
These dreadful summoners grace. I am a man
More sinn'd against than sinning.

Kent.   Alack! bare-headed!   60
Gracious my Lord, hard by here is a hovel;
Some friendship will it lend you 'gainst the
    tempest;
Repose you there while I to this hard house,—
More harder than the stones whereof 'tis rais'd,
Which even but now, demanding after you,   65
Denied me to come in,—return and force
Their scanted courtesy.

Lear.   My wits begin to turn.
Come on, my boy. How dost, my boy? Art cold?
I am cold myself. Where is this straw, my fellow?
The art of our necessities is strange,   70

54. simular] *F*; simular man *Q 1, 2*; simulier man *Q 3*. 55. to] *F*; in *Q*. 57. Has] *F*; hast *Q*.   58. concealing continents] *F*; concealed centers *Q*. 60. than] *F 4*; then *F 1, 2, 3*; their *Q*.   63. while] *F*; whilst *Q*.   64. harder than] *F*; hard then is *Q*.   stones] *F*; stone *Q*.   65. you] *F*; me *Q*. 67. wits begin] *F*; wit begins *Q*.

54. *perjur'd*] perjured one, perjurer.

54. *simular*] simulator, counterfeiter. This is more common as adj. (hence the Q reading) but *N.E.D.* quotes Tindale: "Christ . . . calleth them ypocrites, that is to saye Simulars."

55. *caitiff*] wretch.

55. *to . . . shake*] Cf. *A.W.* IV. iii. 192.

56. *seeming*] hypocrisy. Cf. *M.M.* II. iv. 150.

57. *practis'd on*] plotted against. Cf. *Hen. V.* II. ii. 99.

57. *guilts*] crimes.

58. *Rive . . . continents*] burst the covering that hides you. Cf. *A.C.* IV. xiv. 40.

58-9. *cry . . . grace*] cry for mercy

from the dread ministers of vengeance; a summoner was an officer who haled offenders before the ecclesiastical courts.

59-60. *I . . . sinning*] I, as opposed to the hypocritical sinners described in this speech.

62. *lend*] afford.

63. *hard*] cruel.

65. *Which*] the owners of which; or the people in it. Cf. II. ii. 1.

65. *demanding after*] asking for.

66. *Denied . . . in*] refused me admittance. Cf. *W.T.* v. ii. 139.

70. *The . . . strange*] Necessity has a strange power of transforming, like that of the Alchemists who changed lead into gold. Florio, *op. cit.* vi. 299 says: "Nature hath like a kinde mother observed this,

And can make vile things precious.   Come, your
   hovel.
Poor Fool and knave, I have one part in my heart
That's sorry yet for thee.

Fool.   *He that has and a little tiny wit,*
      With hey, ho, the wind and the rain,   75
      Must make content with his fortunes fit,   *cf. p 43*
      Though the rain it raineth every day.

Lear. True, boy.   Come, bring us to this hovel.
                     [*Exeunt Lear and Kent.*

Fool. This is a <u>brave</u> night to cool a courtezan.

               fine

I'll speak a prophecy ere I go: 80
When priests are more in word than matter;
When brewers mar their malt with water;
When nobles are their tailors' tutors;
No heretics burn'd, but wenches' suitors;
When every case in law is right;   85
No squire in debt, nor no poor knight;

---

71. And] *F;* that *Q.*   vile] *Pope;* vilde *Q, F.*   your] *F;* you *Q.*
72. in] *F;* of *Q.*   73. That's sorry] *F;* That sorrowes *Q.*   74. has and]
F has *Q.*   75. hey, ho] height-ho *F 2, 3, 4.*   77. Though] *F;* for *Q.*
78, boy] *F;* my good boy *Q.*   S.D.] *Capell;* Exit *F;* not in *Q.*   79-96.
This . . . time] *F;* not in *Q.*

that such actions as shee for our
necessities hath enjoyed unto us,
should also be voluptuous unto us."
(Cited G. C. Taylor. See Appendix,
p. 249).

74. *He . . . wit*] An adaptation
of Feste's Song, *T.N.* v. i. 398, and
probably sung by the same actor.
The Fool may be referring to Lear,
or to himself.

78. *True*] Lear admits that he
must make his happiness fit his
fortunes.

78. *bring*] conduct.

79. *brave*] fine, suitable. This
line, and the rest of the scene is
omitted by Q, and some have thought
it to be an interpolation.

80. *a prophecy*] The verses that
follow are a parody of some pseudo-
Chaucerian verses to be found in
Puttenham, *Arte of English Poesie*

(ed. Arber, p. 232).   Thynne's
edition of Chaucer prints them as
follows:

  " When faithe fayleth in preestes
     sawes
  And lordes hestes are holden for
     lawes
  And robbery is holden purchace
  And lechery is holden solace
  Than shal the londe of albyon
  Be brought to great confusyon."

Warburton pointed out that 81-4
refer to the actual state of affairs,
while 85-90 are Utopian.   He
suggested, perhaps rightly, that 91-2
should be inserted after 84.

83. *tutors*] teaching them their
job.   Kittredge cites *T.S.* iv. iii.
86 ff.

84. *burn'd*] there is a punning
reference to the pox.

When slanders do not live in tongues;
Nor cut-purses come not to throngs;
When usurers tell their gold i' th' field;
And bawds and whores do churches build;   90
Then shall the realm of Albion
Come to great confusion:
Then comes the time, who lives to see't,
That going shall be us'd with feet.
This prophecy Merlin shall make; for I live   95
before his time.   [*Exit.*

SCENE III.—[*A Room in Gloucester's Castle.*]

Enter GLOUCESTER *and* EDMUND, *with lights.*

Glou. Alack, alack! Edmund, I like not this unnatural
dealing. When I desir'd their leave that I
might pity him, they took from me the use of
mine own house; charg'd me, on pain of perpetual
displeasure, neither to speak of him, entreat for   5
him, or any way sustain him.
Edm. Most savage and unnatural!
Glou. Go to; say you nothing. There is division
between the Dukes, and a worse matter than
that. I have receiv'd a letter this night; 'tis   10
dangerous to be spoken; I have lock'd the
letter in my closet. These injuries the King

Scene III

A . . . *Castle*] Rowe, subst.; not in Q, F.   *Enter . . . Edmund*]
F; Enter Gloster and the Bastard Q.   with lights] Q; not in F.   3.
took] tooke me Q 1.   4. perpetual] F; their Q; their perpetual *Jennens.*
6. or] F; nor Q.   8. There is] F; There's a Q.   9. between] F; betwixt Q.

89. *tell*] count.
90. *do . . . build*] as a sign of repentance.
94. *going . . . feet*] feet shall be
used for walking.
95. *Merlin*] Shakespeare probably
derived his knowledge of Merlin's
prophecies from Holinshed. Bethell,
*Shakespeare and the Popular Dramatic
Tradition,* 1946, p. 86, points out
that the Fool's concluding remark

makes him step out of the remote
period as a contemporary.

Scene III

1-2. *unnatural dealing*] Sidney uses
the phrase " vnnaturall dealings " in
the story Shakespeare used for his underplot. Cf. Introduction, p. xxxvii.
3. *pity*] take pity on, relieve.
6. *sustain*] care for.
9. *worse*] i.e. the French invasion.

now bears will be revenged home; there is part
of a power already footed; we must incline to
Seek　the King.　I will look him and privily relieve　15
him; go you and maintain talk with the Duke,
that my charity be not of him perceiv'd.　If
he ask for me, I am ill and gone to bed.　If I
die for it, as no less is threatened me, the King,
my old master, must be reliev'd.　There is　20
strange things toward, Edmund; pray you,
be careful.　　　　　　　　　　　　　　*[Exit.*

Edm.　This courtesy, forbid thee, shall the Duke
Instantly know; and of that letter too:
This seems a fair deserving, and must draw me　25
That which my father loses; no less than all:
The younger rises when the old doth fall.　　*[Exit.*

13. there is] *F;* ther's *Q.*　14. footed] *F;* landed *Q.*　15. look] *F;* seeke *Q.*
18. If] *F;* though *Q.*　19. for it] *F;* for't *Q.*　21. strange things] *F;* some
strange thing *Q.*　25. draw me] draw to me *Q 2, 3.*　27. The] *F;* then *Q.*
doth] *F;* doe *Q.*

SCENE IV.—[*The Heath.　Before a Hovel.*]

Enter LEAR, KENT, *and Fool.*

Kent.　Here is the place, my Lord; good my Lord, enter:
The tyranny of the open night's too rough
For nature to endure.　　　　　　　*[Storm still.*
Lear.　　　　　　　　Let me alone.
Kent.　Good my Lord, enter here.
Lear.　　　　　　　　Wilt break my heart?

Scene IV
The Heath . . . Hovel] Rowe, subst.; not in Q, F.　　　3 S.D.]
F; not in Q.　　4. here] *F; not in Q.*

13. *home*] to the full.　　　　　　　20. *is*] a singular verb is often
14. *footed*] landed.　Cf. III. i. 32　followed by a plural subject.　There
and note.　　　　　　　　　　　　is no need to adopt the Q reading.
14. *incline to*] take the side of.　21. *toward*] impending.
Cf. *W.T.* I. ii. 304.　　　　　　　23. *forbid*] forbidden.
15. *look*] seek for.　Cf. *A.Y.L.I.*　25. *fair deserving*] an action which
II. v. 34.　　　　　　　　　　　　will deserve to be rewarded.
17. *of*] by.
18-19. *If . . . it*] Gloucester, who　　　　　*Scene* IV
had earlier offered reasons of policy
(12-15), now displays some moral　2. *open night*] night in the open.
stamina for the first time.　　　　4. *Wilt . . . heart?*] Steevens
　　　　　　　　　　　　　　　　suggests that Lear is addressing his

Kent. I had rather break mine own. Good my Lord,
    enter.   5
Lear. Thou think'st 'tis much that this contentious storm
    Invades us to the skin: so 'tis to thee;
    But where the greater malady is fix'd,
    The lesser is scarce felt. Thou 'ldst shun a bear;
    But if thy flight lay toward the roaring sea,   10
    Thou 'ldst meet the bear i' th' mouth. When the
      mind's free
    The body's delicate; this tempest in my mind
    Doth from my senses take all feeling else
    Save what beats there—filial ingratitude!
    Is it not as this mouth should tear this hand   15
    For lifting food to 't? But I will punish home:
    No, I will weep no more. In such a night
    To shut me out? Pour on; I will endure.
    In such a night as this? O Regan, Goneril!
    Your old kind father, whose frank heart gave
      all,—   20
    O! that way madness lies; let me shun that;
    No more of that.
Kent.   Good my Lord, enter here.

6. contentious] *F;* crulentious *Q uncorr. Q 2, 3;* tempestious *Q corr.*   7.
skin: so] *Rowe;* skinso: *F 1; skin so:* F *2;* skin, so: *F 3, 4;* skin, so *Q.*
9. Thou'dst] *F;* thou wouldst *Q 2, 3.*   10. thy] they *F 1.*   lay] light *F 4.*
roaring] *F;* raging *Q uncorr., Q 2, 3.*   11. i' th'] *F;* it'h *Q.*   12. this]
Q corr.; the *Q uncorr., Q 2, F;* not in *Q 3.*   14. beats] *Q corr., F;* beares *Q*
uncorr., Q 2, 3.   there—] *Singer;* their *Q;* there, *F 1, 2;* there. *F 3, 4,*
Rowe; there: *Delius, Schmidt.*   15. this hand] his hand *F 3, 4.*   16. to
't] to it *Q 2, 3.*   home] *F;* sure *Q.*   17-18. In . . . endure] *F;* not in *Q.*
20. gave] *F;* gaue you *Q.*   22. here] *F;* not in *Q.*

own heart; but Lear's next speech explains the meaning. He thinks that by remaining outside in the storm, he will have his thoughts distracted from the ingratitude which will otherwise break his heart.

8-9. *But . . . felt*] Cf. *Cymb.* IV. ii. 243.

11-14. *When . . . ingratitude*] Cf. Appendix, p. 252.

11. *free*] at ease. Cf. *Oth.* III. iii. 340; Middleton and Rowley, *A*
Fair Quarrel, I. i. 399: "Then 'tis no prison when the mind is free."

12. *delicate*] sensitive, averse to pain.

14. *beats*] a quibble: (*a*) throbs, think laboriously. Cf. *Temp.* I. ii. 176, (*b*) rage, as of a tempest.

14. *there—filial ingratitude*] As Delius pointed out, "filial ingratitude" is in apposition to "what beats there."

16. *home*] Cf. III. iii. 14.

Lear. Prithee, go in thyself; seek thine own ease:
This tempest will not give me leave to ponder
On things would hurt me more.   But I'll go in.   25
[*To the Fool.*] In, boy; go first.   You houseless
   poverty,—
Nay, get thee in.   I'll pray, and then I'll sleep.
                                        [*Fool goes in.*

Poor naked wretches, whereso'er you are,
That bide the pelting of this pitiless storm,
How shall your houseless heads and unfed sides,   30
Your loop'd and window'd raggedness, defend you
From seasons such as these?   O! I have ta'en
Too little care of this.   Take physic, Pomp;
Expose thyself to feel what wretches feel,
That thou mayst shake the superflux to them,   35
And show the Heavens more just.
Edg. [*Within.*] Fathom and half, fathom and half!
Poor Tom!   [*The Fool runs out from the hovel.*
Fool. Come not in here, Nuncle; here's a spirit.
Help me! help me!   40

---

23. thine own] *F;* thy one *Q 1;* thy owne *Q 2.* 26. S.D.] *Johnson; not in Q.*
26-7. In, boy . . . sleep] *F; not in Q.*   poverty—] *Rowe;* pouertie. *F.*   27.
S.D.] *Johnson;* Exit *F* (*after 26*); *not in Q.*   29. storm] *F;* night *Q.*   37-8.
Fathom . . . Tom] *F; not in Q.*   37. S.D.] *Theobald; not in F.*   38. S.D.]
Theobald (*after 40*); Enter Edgar and Foole (*after 36.*) *F.*

26. *houseless poverty*] the abstract for the concrete; the phrase is expanded in 28 ff.

27. *pray*] the prayer is not to the gods, but to the poor.

29. *bide*] endure.   Cf. *T.N.* II. iv. 97.

30-1. *How . . . raggedness*] D. G. James, *The Life of Reason,* 1949, p. 147, comments: " If the reader will read the . . . lines carefully, and will bear in mind that ' house ' is two words and not one, having in its second and little known meaning the sense of ' textile covering '; if also he will consider the phrases ' unfed sides ' and ' loop'd and window'd raggedness,' he will see what a fusion of ideas is here; the

body as the house of the soul and the house as protection for the body are ideas fused in the way I have spoken of."

31. *loop'd and window'd*] full of holes and openings.   The original meaning of window appears to have been *wind-eye,* i.e. eye, or hole, to admit the wind.

33-6. *Take . . . just*] Cf. Gloucester's words, IV. i. 66-71.

35. *superflux*] superfluity.   Cf. Appendix, p. 253.

36. *And . . . just*] Cf. *Leir,* 1909, " The heauens are iust "; and v. iii. 170.

37. *Fathom . . . half*] suggested by the floods of rain.

Kent. Give me thy hand.   Who's there?

Fool. A spirit, a spirit: he says his name's poor Tom.

Kent. What art thou that dost grumble there i' th' straw?
Come forth.

Enter EDGAR *disguised as a madman.*

Edg. Away! the foul fiend follows me! Through   45
the sharp hawthorn blow the winds. Humh!
go to thy bed and warm thee.

Lear. Didst thou give all to thy daughters?
And art thou come to this?

Edg. Who gives any thing to poor Tom? whom the   50
foul fiend hath led through fire and through
flame, through ford and whirlpool, o'er bog and

42. A spirit, a spirit] *F;* A spirit *Q.*   name's] name is *Q 2, 3.*   43. i' th']
F; in the *Q.*   44. S.D.] *Capell; not in Q, F.*   46. blow] *F;* blowes *Q.*
winds] *F;* cold wind *Q.*   Humh!] *F;* Humph *Rowe; not in Q.*   47. bed] *F;*
cold bed *Q.*   48. Didst . . . daughters?] *F;* Hast thou giuen all to thy two
daughters? *Q; Didst . . . two daughters? Singer.* 51. through fire] *Q:* though
Fire *F 1.*   51-2. through flame] *F; not in Q.*   52. ford] foord *Q;* Sword *F;*
Swamp *Collier MS.*   whirlpool] *F;* whirlipoole *Q 1, 2.*

45-6. *Through . . . winds*] Cf.
" The Friar of Orders Grey," l. 95
(see Percy's *Reliques*):
   " Through the hawthorn blows
      the cold wind,
   And drizzly rain doth fall."
   46. *Humh!*] E. A. Armstrong, *op. cit.*
p. 45, points out that " Shakespeare
uses the word in twenty contexts and
in twelve of these there is death or
sleep imagery." Cf. I. ii. 55-6.
   47. *go . . . thee*] Cf. *T.S.* Induction,
i. 10, where nearly the same words
are used: " Go by, Jeronimy; go
to thy cold bed, and warm thee."
In this parallel passage, as Theobald
points out, there are allusions to
Kyd's *Spanish Tragedy* (ed. Boas III.
xii. 31; II. v. 1). See also note on
III. iv. 101 *post.* The Q reading,
accepted by most editors, was probably
a corruption caused by the familiarity
of the *Shrew* passage, or " an interpolation by the actor to get an
effective antithesis " (Duthie).
Staunton says the phrase " go to

thy cold bed " means only " go cold
to bed."
   48. *Didst . . . daughters?*] Empson,
op. cit. p. 137, comments: " Madness
has come.   No doubt the appearance of the wild Edgar . . . is the
accident that made him unable to
shun it any longer."
   50. *gives*] Edgar takes his cue from
Lear's *give* (48).
   50-4. *whom . . . pew*] Theobald
pointed out that the substance of
these lines is to be found in Harsnett's
Declaration. Cf. Appendix, p. 256.
Steevens quoted Marlowe, *Doctor
Faustus,* ed. Tucker Brooke, 632-4:
   " then swordes and kniues,
   Poyson, gunnes, halters, and in-
      venomd steele
   Are layde before me to dispatch
      my selfe."
Kittredge cites Greene and Lodge,
A Looking Glass for London, 1594 (ed.
Collins, i. 204) S.D. " The Euill
Angel tempteth him, offering the
knife and rope."

quagmire; that hath laid knives under his
pillow, and halters in his pew; set ratsbane
by his porridge; made him proud of heart,   55
to ride on a bay trotting-horse over four-inch'd
chase bridges, to course his own shadow for a traitor.
Bless thy five wits! Tom's a-cold. O! do de,
shiver. do de, do de. Bless thee from whirlwinds, star-
blasting, and taking! Do poor Tom some charity,   60
whom the foul fiend vexes. There could I have
him now, and there, and there again, and there.

　　　　　　　　　　　　　　　　　　[*Storm still.*

Lear. What! has his daughters brought him to this
　　pass?

53. hath] *F;* has *Q.*　　55. porridge] *F;* pottage *Q.*　　56. trotting-horse]
hyphened Steevens.　　　　four-inch'd] *hyphened Capell.*　　　　58, 59. Bless] *Q;*
Blisse *F.*　　58-9. O . . . de] *F; not in Q.*　　59-60. star-blasting] *F;* starre-
blusting *Q.*　　62. and there] *F, Q 2;* and there and and *Q 1.*　　　　there
again] here again *F 4.*　　62. and there] *F; not in Q.*　　S.D.] *F; not in Q.*
63. What! has] *Duthie;* Ha's *F 1;* Has *F 2, 3;* Have *F 4;* What, *Q;* What!
have *Theobald.*　　　　64. Would'st] *F;* didst *Q.*　　　　'em] *F;* them *Q.*

54. *pew*] " a gallery in a house or
outside a chamber window " (Kittredge).

55. *porridge*] broth. The modern
meaning of the word was not used
in Shakespeare's day.

56. *trotting-horse*] a horse trained
to trot and amble in a stately and
measured fashion.

56-7. *four-inch'd   bridges*] Cf.
Jonson, *The Magnetic Lady,* v. viii.
(ed. Herford and Simpson, vi. 589):

" a poore Squire . . .
　That talk'd in's sleepe; would
　　walke to Saint Iohn's wood,
And Waltham Forrest, scape by
　all the ponds,
And pits i' the way; run over
　two-inch bridges;
With his eyes fast, and i' the
　dead of night! "

57. *course*] chase.

58. *Bless*] Duthie cites *N.E.D.*
" *bliss* vb . . . trans. To give joy
or gladness to . . . to gladden, make
happy." The word became blended
with *bliss* in the 16th-17th centuries,

but was derived from O.E. *blissian.*
But see III. vi. 59, where the more
usual word is employed, and III.
iv. 59 where *bless* is more appropriate.

58. *five wits*] Malone points out
that in Hawes, *The Pastime of
Pleasure,* xxiv. 2, the five wits are
enumerated as common wit, imagination, fantasy, estimation and memory.
Cf. Sir John Davies, *Nosce Teipsum*
(ed. Grosart, 1876, pp. 70 ff.) for
a similar list. The five wits were
sometimes confused with the five
senses, but Shakespeare distinguishes
between them, as Malone points
out. Cf. Sonnets, cxli. 9-10:
" But my five wits nor my five
　　senses can
　Dissuade one foolish heart from
　　serving thee."

59. *do . . . de*] He is presumably
shivering. Cotgrave defines *Friller,*
" To shiuer, chatter, or didder for
cold."

59-60. *star-blasting*] Cf. Harsnett,
Appendix, p. 255.

60. *taking*] infection, evil in-
fluences. Cf. II. iv. 165.

Couldst thou save nothing? Would'st thou give
   'em all?

Fool. Nay, he reserv'd a blanket, else we had been 65
   all sham'd.

Lear. Now all the plagues that in the pendulous air
   Hang fated o'er men's faults light on thy daughters!

Kent. He hath no daughters, Sir.

Lear. Death, traitor! nothing could have subdu'd nature 70
   To such a lowness but his unkind daughters.
   Is it the fashion that discarded fathers
   Should have thus little mercy on their flesh?
   Judicious punishment! 'twas this flesh begot
   Those pelican daughters.   75

[handwritten marginal note: with the power of fate]

68. light] *F;* fall *Q.*

67-8. *Now . . . faults*] Boswell cites *Tim.* v. iii. 108-9; Schmidt compares *The Birth of Merlin,* iv. i. 220 (*Shakes. Apoc.*):

   " Knowest thou what pendulous
     mischief roofs thy head? "

But there is a closer parallel with Harsnett, *op. cit.* p. 159. Cf. Appendix, p. 256.

68. *fated*] invested with the power of fatal determination (Johnson). Cf. *A.W.* i. i. 232, " the fated sky."

70. *subdu'd nature*] reduced his natural powers.

73. *little . . . flesh*] referring either to Edgar's wretchedness, or, more likely, to the pins and thorns in his flesh.

75. *pelican*] Cf. *Leir,* 512-13:

   " I am as kind as is the Pellican
     That kils it selfe, to saue her
     young ones liues."

Wright quotes *Batman vppon Bartholome,* ed. 1582, fol. 186: " The Pellican loueth too much her children. For when the children bee haught, and begin to waxe hoare, they smite the father and the mother in the face, wherfore the mother smiteth them againe and slaieth them. And the thirde daye the mother smiteth her selfe in her side that the bloud runneth out, and sheddeth that hot bloud vppon the bodies of her children. And by virtue of the bloud the birdes that were before dead, quicken againe." Green, *Shakespeare and the Emblem Writers,* p. 395, cites Whitney, *Choice of Emblems,* p. 87:

   " The Pellican, for to reuiue her
     younge,
   Doth pierce her breast, and
     geue them of her blood."

He also cites Reusner, ii. 73, where the pelican is compared to a king:

   " For people and for sanctioned
     law heart's life a king will
     pour;
   So from this blood of mine do I
     life to my young restore."

In some references to the pelican, it is said that the mother bird does not revive her young ones with her blood, but feeds them with it. Cf. *Edward III,* iii. v. 110-13 (*Shakes. Apoc.* p. 90):

   " A Pellican, my Lord,
   Wounding her bosome with her
     crooked beak,
   That so her nest of young ones
     may be fed
   With drops of blood that issue
     from her hart."

Lear seems to go further, and imply that the young pelicans strike at the

Edg. Pillicock sat on Pillicock hill:
Alow, alow, loo, loo!

Fool. This cold night will turn us all to fools and
madmen.

Edg. Take heed o' th' foul fiend.   Obey thy parents;   80
keep thy word's justice; swear not; commit not
with man's sworn spouse; set not thy sweet
heart on proud array.   Tom's a-cold.

Lear. What hast thou been?

Edg. A servingman, proud in heart and mind; that   85

76. on] one *Q 3*.   Pillicock] *F;* pelicocks *Q 1, 2;* pelicacks *Q 3*.   77.
Alow, alow] *F;* Halloo, halloo *Theobald;* a lo *Q*.   80. o'th'] *F;* at' h *Q 1;* of
the *Q 2, 3*.   81. word's justice] words lustice *F 1;* words iustly *Q;* word, Justice
F 2, 3, 4.   word justly *Pope*.   82. set not] set on *F 3, 4*.   82-3. sweet
heart] *Q;* Sweet-heart *F*.

breasts of the old ones, to drain their
life out.   Green, *op. cit.* p. 426, on
l. 76, quotes Augustine, *Confessions*,
I. xii.   " De peccante me ipso juste
retribuebas mihi.   Jussisti enim, et
sic est, ut poena sua sibi sit omnis
inordinatus animus " (by my own
sin Thou didst justly punish me).
With this may also be compared
v. iii. 170-1.   Finally, a writer in
N.Q. 15 Oct. 1904, pp. 310-11, points
out that St. Thomas Aquinas refers
in Dante's *Paradiso*, xxv. 113, to
" nostro Pellicano," i.e. Christ.

76. *Pillicock . . . hill*] Collier cites
Ritson, *Gammer Gurton's Garland*:

" Pillycock, Pillycock sat on a hill;
   If he's not gone, he sits there
      still."

This may belong to a later date than
Edgar's rhyme, which was doubtless
suggested by *pelican*.   Pillicock was a
term of endearment, meaning ' darling ' (Florio), ' prettie knaue ' (Cotgrave).   But it is also used as a
synonym for phallus.   Cf. Rabelais
(Tudor Translations), i. 56; Florio,
World of Words, thus translates *Puga*.

77. *Alow . . . loo!*] Variously
explained.   " A wild ' halloo ' as
if he were calling a hawk."   Cf.
Ham. I. v. 116 (Kittredge); " A
cry to excite dogs " (Craig).   Cf.

T.C. v. vii. 10; " the noise of the
Bedlam's horn " (Perrett).   Perhaps
it is intended as the refrain of the
song.

80-3. *Obey . . . array*] Edgar recites
a kind of catechism.

81. *word's justice*] Most editors
adopt Pope's improvement of the Q
reading but Schmidt, Harrison, and
Duthie follow F.   Duthie interprets:
" Keep the justice of thy words."
Schmidt, similarly: " Be as just in
deeds as in words." (Cf. Catechism:
" To be true and iuste in al my deal-
ynge.")   Perhaps in this passage,
depending for its effect on echoes
from the scriptures and the prayer-
book, the simpler reading is to be
perferred.

81. *commit*] i.e. adultery, as in the
7th Commandment, and *Oth.* IV. ii.
72.

83. *proud array*] Noble, *op. cit.*
compares *1 Tim.* ii. 9: " Likewise
also the women, that they aray
themselues in comely apparell . . .
not in braided heare, either golde,
or pearles, or costly aray."

85. *servingman*] Knight supposes
this to be a *cavaliere servente*, a lover
(Cf. *T.G.* II. iv. 106).   Schmidt
supposes it to be used in the ordinary
sense of servant.   Craig quotes

curl'd my hair, wore gloves in my cap, serv'd
the lust of my mistress' heart, and did the act of
darkness with her; swore as many oaths as I
spake words, and broke them in the sweet face
of Heaven; one that slept in the contriving of   90
lust, and wak'd to do it. Wine lov'd I deeply,
dice dearly, and in woman out-paramour'd the
Turk: false of heart, light of ear, bloody of
hand; hog in sloth, fox in stealth, wolf in greedi-
ness, dog in madness, lion in prey. Let not the   95
creaking of shoes nor the rustling of silks betray
thy poor heart to woman: keep thy foot out of
brothels, thy hand out of plackets, thy pen from

91. deeply] *Q;* deerely *F.*   93-4. of hand] hand *F 2;* handed *F 3, 4.*   96.
rustling] *F;* ruslngs *Q 1;* ruslings *Q 2, 3.*   silks] sickles *Q 3.*   97. woman]
F; women *Q.*   98. brothels] *F;* brothell *Q.*   plackets] *F;* placket *Q.*

Cocles, *Physiognomie,* Sig. A, iii. 9:
" A courtier or servingman." Shakespeare may have intended either, as
Edgar's account would fit either a
fashionable lover or a servant who
turned his good looks to account.

86. *curl'd my hair*] Malone cites
a Harsnett passage. See Appendix,
p. 254.

86. *wore . . . cap*] favours from his
mistress. Cf. *T.C.* iv. iv. 73.

90. *contriving*] plotting, presumably in his sleep.

91-2. *Wine . . . woman*] Cf. Florio,
Second Fruites, p. 105:

" Shun wine, dice, and letchery,
    Else will you come to beggery."

92. *out-paramour'd*] had more mistresses than.

92-3. *the Turk*] the Grand Turk,
the Sultan.

93. *light of ear*] credulous of evil,
ready to listen and receive malicious
reports (Johnson). Kittredge cites
The Schole-House of Women, 43-9
(ed. Hazlitt, *Early Popular Poetry,* iv.
107):

" So light of eare they be and
    sowre,

That of the better they neuer
    record,
The worse reherce they word
    by word."

94-5. *hog . . . prey*] The Seven
Deadly Sins were often figured under
the names of animals. Malone cites
a Harsnett passage. Cf. p. 254.
Florio, *Second Fruites,* p. 165, has a
similar list: " lyon for surguedry,
goate for letcherie, dragon for
crueltie."

95. *prey*] preying.

96. *creaking*] Creaking shoes were
fashionable. Kittredge cites Rowley,
A Shoo-maker a Gentleman, ii. i, in
which a shoemaker tells Leodice that
he has made her a " tunable heele "
. . . "A creake Madam, for a Musicall
creake nere a Boy in Feversham yet
went beyond me."

97-9. *keep . . . books*] Florio,
Second Fruites, pp. 99-105, has a
number of similar injunctions.

98. *plackets*] a placket was an
opening in a petticoat, jocosely
derived by Middleton (*Any Thing
for a Quiet Life,* ii. ii) from " *placet:
a placendo,* a thing or place to please."
It was also used as a synonym for
wench.

lenders' books, and defy the foul fiend. Still
through the hawthorn blows the cold wind; 100
says suum, mun, hey no nonny. Dolphin my
boy, boy; sessa! let him trot by.   [*Storm still.*
Lear. Thou wert better in a grave than to answer

99. books] F; booke Q.   100. the hawthorn] thy Hawthorn F 3, 4.   101.
says suum, mun] F; not in Q.   hey no nonny] Eccles; ha, no, nonny Steevens;
hay no on ny Q; nonny F.   102. boy, boy] F; boy, my boy Q.   sessa!] Malone;
sesey F; cease Q 1; cease Q 2; ceas Q 3.   S.D.] F; not in Q.   103. Thou]
F; Why thou Q.   a] F; thy Q.

99. *lenders*] moneylenders.

101. *suum*] imitating the noise of
the wind.

101. *hey no nonny*] presumably the
refrain of a song. Cf. *M.A.* ii. iii.
71. Whiter in an unpublished note
points out that in Fletcher, *The
Humorous Lieutenant,* iv. iv (ed.
Glover and Waller, ii. 347) the
phrase is used, as here, in proximity
to *placket:*

"Was that brave Heart made to
   pant for a placket? . . .
That noble Mind to melt away
   and moulder
For a hey nonny nonny!"

See also *The Wit of a Woman,* 1604,
C. l. v: "These dauncers sometimes
do teach them trickes above trench-
more, yea and sometimes such
lavoltas, that they mount so high,
that you may see their hey nonny,
nony no." Drayton, *Shepherd's
Garland,* 1593 (ed. Hebbel, i. 55)
speaks of "These noninos of filthie
ribauldry." J. M. Nosworthy
suggests, privately, that the Q reading may be the best a reporter or
compositor could do with 'Hay-
ronomy' or 'heyronomy' (i.e.
Jeronimy, Hieronimo). This and
iii. iv. 47 echo a passage from
The Taming of the Shrew, in which
Shakespeare gibes at *The Spanish
Tragedy:* but in neither place does
he use the name Hieronimo, unless
Nosworthy's conj. is sound.

101. *Dolphin*] Steevens gives a

stanza from an old ballad written
on some battle fought in France, in
which Dolphin is the Dauphin.
This was probably a fabrication;
but as Jonson, *Bartholomew Fair,* v.
iv. (ed. Herford and Simpson, vi.
127) uses the phrase "hee shall be
Dauphin my boy" it is clear that
Edgar was quoting from some song
or ballad, unless Jonson was
echoing Edgar. J. Crow has called
my attention to the Newcastle Play
of Noah (*The Non-Cycle Mystery
Plays,* ed. O. Waterhouse, 1909,
p. 25) which contains the following
lines:

"I pray to Dolphin,
   prince of dead,
Scald you all in
   his lead."
According to Holthausen, *Dolphin*
means 'Dauphin' in this context,
and he is identified with the devil
because of the English hatred of the
French. Edgar has just spoken of
the fiend.

102. *sessa!*] Cf. *T.S.* Induction, 6;
"let the world slide, sessa." Cf.
also iii. vi. 74 and iv. vi. 205 *post.*
It is probably a mere interjection,
perhaps an incitement to speed.
Johnson thought it was the Fr.
word *cessez,* pronounced *cessey,* and
meaning "be quiet, have done."
From the context and iii. vi. 74, it
would seem to mean rather "Off
you go!"

103. *Thou . . . better*] It would be
better for you to be.

with thy uncover'd body this extremity of the
skies. Is man no more than this? Consider 105
him well. Thou ow'st the worm no silk, the
beast no hide, the sheep no wool, the cat no per-
fume. Ha! here's three on 's are sophisticated; *adultera*
thou art the thing itself; unaccommodated man
is no more but such a poor, bare, forked animal 110
as thou art. Off, off, you lendings! Come;
unbutton here.

[Tearing off his clothes.

105. than] *F;* but *Q.*   108. Ha] *F; not in Q.*   on's] ones *Q 2, 3*
11. lendings] *Q corr., F;* leadings *Q uncorr., Q 2, 3.*   111-12. Come . . .
here] *F;* come on bee true *Q uncorr., Q 2, 3;* come on *Q corr.*   112. S.D.]
Rowe; not in Q, F.   113. contented] *F;* content *Q.*   'tis] *F;* this is *Q.*
114. wild] wide *Jennens (conj. Capell).*

104. *answer*] encounter, bear the
brunt. Cf. *Cor.* i. iv. 52.
104. *extremity*] extreme severity.
Cf. *W.T.* v. ii. 129.
105-6. *Is . . . well*] Noble, *op. cit.*
compares *Heb.* ii. 6. " What is man,
that thou shouldest bee mindful of
him? or the sonne of man, that thou
wouldest consider him? "
106-11. *Thou . . . lendings*] G. C.
Taylor cites the following passages
from Florio's Montaigne: " Miserable man; whom if you consider
well what is he? " " Truely, when
I consider man all naked . . . I
finde we have had much more
reason to hide and cover our nakedness than any creature else. We may
be excused for borrowing those which
nature had therein favored more
than us . . . and under their spoiles
of wooll, of haire, of feathers, and
of silke, to shroud us." " And
that our wisedome should learne
of beasts, the most profitable docu-
ments, belonging to the chiefest
and most necessary parts of our
life. . . . Wherewith (with reason)
men have done, as perfumers doe
with oyle, they have adulterated
her with so many argumentations,
and sofisticated her." To these
passages may be added: " man is

the onely forsaken and out-cast
creature, naked on the bare earth . . .
having nothing to cover and arme
himselfe withall but the spoile of
others; whereas Nature hath clad
and mantled all other creatures,
some with huskes . . . with wooll, . . .
with hides . . . and with silke . . .:
whereas man only (Oh silly wretched
man) can neither goe, nor speake,
nor shift, nor feed himselfe, unlesse
it be to whine and weepe onely,
except hee be taught " (*op. cit.*
iii. 250, 268; vi. 189-90; iii. 215-16).

107. *beast*] ox, or similar animal.
107. *cat*] the civet cat.
108. *sophisticated*] adulterated. See
note to 106-11 above. Shakespeare
does not use the word again.
109. *unaccommodated*] without the
trappings of civilization. Cf. *2 Hen.
IV.* iii. ii. 72-7; *Oth.* i. iii. 239;
M.M. iii. i. 14. It is never used by
Shakespeare in the modern sense.
110. *forked*] two-legged. Falstaff,
2 Hen IV. iii. ii. 334, calls Shallow
" a forked raddish with a head
fantastically carved upon it."
111. *lendings*] borrowed articles.
112. *unbutton here*] Lear wishes to
identify himself with the poor naked
wretches, unaccommodated men.

Fool. Prithee, Nuncle, be contented; 'tis a ~~naughty~~ *wicked*
night to swim in. Now a little fire in a wild
field were like an old lecher's heart; a small 115
spark, all the rest on 's body cold. Look! here
comes a walking fire.

Enter GLOUCESTER, *with a torch.*

Edg. This is the foul Flibbertigibbet: he begins at
curfew, and walks till the first cock; he gives   *midnight*
the web and the pin, squinies the eye, and makes 120   *Cataract*
the hare-lip; mildews the white wheat, and
hurts the poor creature of earth.   *nearly ripe*
    Swithold footed thrice the old;
    He met the night-mare, and her nine-fold;

116. on's] *F;* in *Q.*   112. S.D.] *F (after 112); Enter Gloster Q.*
118. foul] *F;* foule fiend *Q.* Flibbertigibbet] *F;* Sriberdegibit *Q uncorr.;* flib-
erdegibek *Q corr.;* Sirberdegibit *Q 2, 3.*   119. till the] *Q;* at *F.*   119. gives]
gins *Q uncorr., Q 2, 3.*   120. and the pin, squinies] *Duthie (conj. Greg);*
and the pin, squints *F;* the pin-queues *Q uncorr.; & the pin, squemes Q corr.;*
the pin-queuer *Q 2;* the pinquever *Q 3;* and the pin, squinies *conj. Anon ap. Cam-*
bridge.   121. hare-lip] *F;* harte lip *Q uncorr., Q 2, 3;* hare lip *Q corr.*
122. earth] the earth *F 3, 4.*   123. Swithold] *F;* swithald *Q;* St Withold
Theobald.   old] wold *Theobald (conj. Bishop).*   124. He . . . night-mare] *Q*
corr., F; a nellthu night more *Q uncorr.;* anelthu night Moore *Q 2;* anelthunight
Moor *Q 3.*   nine-fold] nine foles *conj. Tyrwhitt;* nine foals *conj. Farmer.*

113. *naughty*] wicked.
114. *fire*] presumably he sees
Gloucester's torch. Perhaps the
sequence of thought would be improved if this sentence and the next
were transposed.
  114. *wild*] Jennens' emendation is
unnecessary. *Wild* suggested the
lecher's body, unfruitful, out of
condition. It is just possible that
Shakespeare wrote *vilde* = vile.
  115. *old lecher's*] The Fool does not
know that he is speaking of Gloucester, though the audience, from
the previous scene, expects his
arrival.
  118. *Flibbertigibbet*] The name is
taken from Harsnett. Cf. Appendix,
p. 254.
  119. *first cock*] midnight.
  120. *the web and the pin*] cataract.
Cf. *W.T.* I. ii. 291.   Cotgrave

explains *taye* as " a pin or web in
the eye."   Holland, *Pliny,* 1601,
p. 229, speaks of " eyes dim and
overcast either with the pin and web,
or cataract."
  120. *squinies*] Greg, *Variants,* pp.
165-7, argues that the F ' squints '
may be a sophistication. The word
squiny is used IV. vi. 138; and it is
to be found in Armin, *Nest of Ninnies,*
1608 (ed. 1880, p. 48). In the same
book (p. 45) he uses *squened,* and in
The Italian Taylor (ed. 1880, p. 175)
squeaning.   Armin probably played
the part of the Fool on the first
production of *King Lear.*
  121. *white*] nearly ripe.   Cf.
John, IV. 35: " the fields . . . white
already to harvest."
  123-7. *Swithold . . . aroint thee*]
Kittredge explains these lines as a
charm. " To recite how St. Withold

Bid her alight,   125
And her troth plight,
And aroint thee, witch, aroint thee!

Kent. How fares your Grace?

Lear. What's he?

Kent. Who's there?   What is 't you seek?   130

Glou. What are you there?   Your names?

Edg. Poor Tom; that eats the swimming frog, the
toad, the todpole, the wall-newt, and the water;
that in the fury of his heart, when the foul fiend
rages, eats cow-dung for sallets; swallows the 135
old rat and the ditch-dog; drinks the green
mantle of the standing pool; who is whipp'd
from tithing to tithing, and stock-punish'd, and

---

125. her a-light] *F;* her O light *Q.*   126. troth plight] *Q;* troth-plight *F.*
127. aroynt] *F;* arint *Q.*   witch] *Q corr., F;* with *Q uncorr., Q 2, 3.*
133. todpole] Tod-pole *F;* tode pold *Q uncorr., Q 2, 3;* tod pole *Q corr.;* tadpole *Johnson.*   wall-newt] *Q corr., F;* wall-wort *Q uncorr., Q 2, 3.*
134. fury] fruite *Q 2, 3.*   138. stock-punish'd] *Q;* stockt, punish'd *F.*

---

encountered the demon and her nine fold (her nine offspring) and subdued her, served as a charm against her power. He quotes from Thomas Blundevill, *The Foure Chiefest Offices belonging to Horsemanshippe,* 1571, xxiii, a charm, from "an olde Englyshe writer," containing the lines:

"He walked day so did he night,
 Untill he hir founde,
He hir beate, and he hir bounde,
Till truely hir trouth she him
 plyght,
That she woulde not come within
 the night."

123. *old*] wold.

124. *night-mare*] an incubus, a demon from O.E. *mare.* It has no connection with the word meaning a female horse.

124. *her nine-fold*] Kittredge explains " her nine offspring "; Capell explains " her nine imps of familiars."

127. *aroint*] be gone. Cf. *Macb.* I. iii. 6.

133. *todpole*] tadpole.

133. *wall-newt*] wall-lizard.

133. *water*] i.e. water-newt.

135. *for sallets*] as a substitute for salads.   Hamlet uses the word for " something tasty " (II. ii. 462), and this subsidiary meaning adds point to Edgar's remark.

136. *ditch-dog*] dead dog thrown into a ditch.

136-7. *green mantle*] scum.   Cf. *M.V.* I. i. 89.   Craig suggests it means duckweed, and it may mean water covered with weed.

137-8. *whipp'd . . . tithing*] a tithing was a district containing ten families. Vagabonds, under the statute of 1597, were liable to be whipped and sent from parish to parish, until they reached their own, if that could be determined.

138. *stock-punish'd*] punished by being put in the stocks.   The F reading is awkward as it puts a general word, *punished,* sandwiched between two particular punishments, *stocked* and *imprisoned.*

imprison'd; who hath had three suits to his
back, six shirts to his body,　　　　　　　　140
　　Horse to ride, and weapons to wear,
　　But mice and rats and such small deer,
　　Have been Tom's food for seven long year.
Beware my follower. Peace, Smulkin! peace,
thou fiend!　　　　　　　　　　　　　　145
Glou. What! hath your Grace no better company?
Edg. The Prince of Darkness is a gentleman; Modo
he's called, and Mahu.

---

139. had] *Q; not in F.*　　143. Have] *F;* Hath *Q.*　　144. Smulkin] *F;*
snulbug *Q;* Smolkin *Theobald (Harsnett).*　　148. Mahu] *F;* ma hu—*Q.*

139. *three-suits*] Cf. ii. ii. 14, and
note.

142-3. *But . . . year*] Capell notes
that this couplet is a version of one
in the popular romance, *Bevis of
Hampton* (ed. Kölbing, p. 74):
　" Ratons and myce and soche
　　　smale dere,
　　That was hys mete that seven
　　　yere."

142. *deer*] game.

144. *follower*] familiar, fiend.

144. *Smulkin*] Cf. Harsnett, Appendix, p. 256.

147-8. *The . . . Mahu*] Cf. Harsnett.
Appendix, p. 254. Blunden,
Shakespeare's Significances (Bradby,
Shakespeare Criticism, 1919-35, p.
331) suggests that Modo recalled
a passage in Horace, *Epistles,* ii. i:
　" Ille per extentum funem mihi
　　　posse videtur
　　Ire poeta, meum qui pectus
　　　inaniter angit,
　　Irritat, mulcet, falsis terroribus
　　　implet,
　　Ut magus; et modo me Thebis,
　　　modo ponit Athenis."

Blunden argues that this passage led
to the mention of " learned Theban "
and " good Athenian " (161, 184)
and to the later echo from one of
Horace's Odes (iii. vi. 82). Baldwin,

op. cit. ii. 520, quotes Drant's translation (1567) of Horace's lines:

　" That poet on a stretched rope
　　　may walke and neuer fall,
　　That can stere vp my passions,
　　　or quicke my sprytes at all.
　　Stere me, chere me, or with
　　　false feares of bugges fill vp
　　　my brest,
　　At *Athens* now, and now at
　　　Thebes, by charminge make me
　　　rest."

Baldwin goes on to show that Cooper,
Thesaurus, defines *magus* as " Dictio
Persica, qua apud eos sapiens sig-
nificatur, eos enim Persae magos
vocant, quos Graeci philosophos,
Latini sapientes . . . Cic.　*A wise
man: a great learned philosopher.*"
Cf. " philosopher . . . learned
Theban (158, 161) Persian " (iii.
vi. 82).　This theory may be supported by the fact that the chain of
ideas could have been suggested by
Harsnett, who quotes, and translates,
a passage from Horace's next epistle:

　" Dreames and Magicall affrights,
　　Wonders, witches, walking
　　　sprights,
　　What Thessalian Hags can doe,
　　All this seemes a iest to you."

The two passages are linked by their
mention of terrors and magic.

Glou. Our flesh and blood, my lord, is grown so vile,
  That it doth hate what gets it.   *children v.*   150
                                          parents universality
Edg. Poor Tom's a-cold.

Glou. Go in with me.   My duty cannot suffer
  T' obey in all your daughters' hard commands:
  Though their injunction be to bar my doors,
  And let this tyrannous night take hold upon you,   155
  Yet I have ventured to come seek you out
  And bring you where both fire and food is ready.

Lear. First let me talk with this philosopher.
  What is the cause of thunder?

Kent. Good my Lord, take his offer; go into th'
  house.   160

---

149. blood . . . vile] *F;* bloud is growne so vild my Lord *Q.*   150. gets it]
it gets *F 3, 4.*   152, 177. a-cold] *hyphened Rowe.*   153. T'obey] *F;*
to obey *Q.*   154. Though] Though all *F 3, 4.*   156. fire and food] *F;*
food and fire *Q.*   160. Good my] *F;* my good *Q.*   the house] *Q;* th'
house *F.*

149-50. *Our . . . gets it*] Gloucester, reminded perhaps by some tone or inflection in his son's voice (Cowden Clarke) links Edgar's supposed villainy with that of Goneril and Regan.

149. *Our . . . blood*] humanity, our children.

150. *gets*] begets.

158. *philosopher*] the word could mean a natural scientist.

159. *What . . . thunder?*] This question was much discussed. G. S. Gordon, *Shakespearian Comedy*, 1944, pp. 126-8, points out that Lear mistakes Edgar for a professional wise man, acquainted with the secrets of Nature, such as were formerly kept by all kings.   In the Middle Ages " one of the most popular forms of instructive reading was the dialogue and catechism."   One such dialogue was called *The Book of Sidrach*, or *The Sapience of Nature.* Gordon asserts that a 16th century translation contains such questions

as " What is the cause of eclipses? Why are the planets seven? Why has the snail a house? "   Cf. I. v. 27, 35 where the Fool, reversing the usual procedure, puts the ' reasons of nature ' to his master. *Boccus and Sydrac,* the only version I have seen, contains the question (No. 122) " whereof cometh the thounder? " But though it mentions seven planets (No. 143) and " whereof snayles come " (No. 224) it does not seem to discuss the Fool's other questions. Ovid, *Metamorphoses* (tr. Golding, xv. 74 ff.) tells how Pythagoras taught

" The first foundation of the world:
    the cause of every thing:
What nature was: and what was
    God: whence snow and lyght-
    ning spring:
And whether *Jove* or else the
    wynds in breaking clowdes
    doo thunder:
What shakes the earth: what
    law the starres doo keepe
    theyr courses under."

Lear. I'll talk a word with this same learned Theban.
  What is your study?
Edg. How to prevent the fiend, and to kill vermin.
Lear. Let me ask you one word in private.
Kent. Importune him once more to go, my Lord;   165
  His wits begin t' unsettle.
Glou.   Canst thou blame him?

                                        [*Storm still.*

  His daughters seek his death.   Ah! that good Kent;
  He said it would be thus, poor banish'd man!
  Thou say'st the king grows mad; I'll tell thee,
      friend,
  I am almost mad myself.   I had a son,   170
  Now outlaw'd from my blood; he sought my life,
  But lately, very late; I lov'd him, friend,
  No father his son dearer; true to tell thee,
  The grief hath craz'd my wits.   What a night's this
  I do beseech your Grace,—
Lear.   O! cry you mercy, Sir. 175
  Noble philosopher, your company.
Edg. Tom's a-cold.
Glou. In, fellow, there, into th' hovel: keep thee warm.
Lear. Come, let's in all.
Kent.   This way, my Lord.
Lear.   With him;
  I will keep still with my philosopher.   180

161. talk] take *F 3, 4.*   same] *F;* most *Q.*   164. me] us *F 3, 4.*
165. once more] *F; not in Q.*   166. t'] *F;* to *Q.*   S.D.] *F; not in Q.*
167. Ah] *F;* O *Q.*   171. he] a *Q 1.*   173. true] truth *Q 2, 3.*   174.
hath] has *Q 2, 3.*   175. Grace,—] *Capell;* Grace. *Q, F.*   175-6. mercy,
Sir: Noble] *F;* mercy noble *Q.*   178. into th'] *F;* in't *Q 1.*

161. *learned Theban*] Jonson, *Pan's Anniversary* (ed. Herford and Simpson, vii. 532) uses the words: "Then comes my learned *Theban*, the Tinker, I told you of." This may be an echo of this scene; but it looks as though both Jonson and Shakespeare were using an expression, the meaning of which has been lost.
162. *study*] department of research.
163. *prevent*] use preventative measures against, avoid.

163. *kill vermin*] Blunden, *op. cit.* p. 332, compares III. vi. 22.
171. *outlaw'd . . . blood*] condemned to outlawry, through corruption of blood.   Those subject to attainder (stain or corruption of blood) formerly suffered such loss. Cf. *1 Hen. VI.* III. iii. i. 159.   Gloucester may merely mean, however, that Edgar has been disowned.
174. *The . . . wits*] Cf. III. iv. 78.
175. *cry you mercy*] I beg your pardon.

Kent. Good my Lord, soothe him; let him take the fellow.
Glou. Take him you on.
Kent. Sirrah, come on; go along with us.
Lear. Come, good Athenian.
Glou. No words, no words: hush.   185
Edg.   *Child Rowland to the dark tower came,*
             His word was still: Fie, foh, and fum,
             I smell the blood of a British man.   [*Exeunt.*

186. tower came] *F;* towne come *Q.*

SCENE V.—[*A Room in Gloucester's Castle.*]

Enter CORNWALL *and* EDMUND.

Corn. I will have my revenge ere I depart his house.
Edm. How, my lord, I may be censured, that nature *thought*
      thus gives way to loyalty, something fears me *of*
      to think of.

                    Scene v

A . . . *Castle*] *Capell; not in Q, F.*   1. my] *not in F 3, 4.*   his] *F;* the
Q; this *Hanmer.*

181. *soothe*] humour. Cf. *C.E.*
IV. iv. 82.   The word is used by
Harsnett, *op. cit.* p. 185.

186. *Child . . . came*] Probably a
line from a lost ballad.   The fragments quoted in Jamieson, *Illustra-
tions of Northern Antiquities,* 1814,
p. 402, and Child, *English and
Scottish Ballads,* 1864, i. 245 are
" manifestly of modern composition "
(Kittredge).

186. *Child*] a candidate for knighthood.

186. *Rowland*] Roland, Charle-
magne's nephew, and the hero of
The Song of Roland and other poems.

187. *His . . . still*] Edgar's remark,
meaning " His watchword or motto
was always " (Kittredge).

187-8. *Fie . . . man*] The Giant's
speech from the story of *Jack the
Giant-Killer.*   It is given, by an
intentional incongruity, to the heroic
Child Rowland.   Cf. Nash e, *Hae
with You to Saffron-Walden,* 1596
(ed. McKerrow, iii. 37):

" O, tis a precious apothegmaticall
   Pedant, who will finde matter
   inough to dilate a whole daye
   of the first inuention of *Fy,
   fa, fum,* I smell the bloud of
   an Englishman."
Nashe's words whould serve as a
warning to commentators.   E.
Yardley, *N.Q.* 30 May 1896, attempts to associate Rowland and
the Giant.   Helen was carried off
by a sea-monster and immured in
an enchanted castle.   Her brother,
Childe Rowland, traversed the seas
in quest of her.   She concealed him
during the temporary absence of
the monster.   But the monster, when
he returned, smelt the blood of a
Christian man.

                    Scene v

2. *How . . . censured*] what people
will think of me.

3. *nature*] my natural feelings as a
son.

3-4. *something . . . of*] rather
frightens me.   Cf. *3 Hen. VI.* v. ii. 2.

Corn. I now perceive it was not altogether your   5
    brother's evil disposition made him seek his
    death; but a provoking merit, set a-work by
    a reproveable badness in himself.

Edm. How malicious is my fortune, that I must repent
    to be just! This is the letter he spoke of, which   10
    approves him an intelligent party to the ad-
    vantages of France. O Heavens! that this treason
    were not, or not I the detector!

Corn. Go with me to the Duchess.

Edm. If the matter of this paper be certain, you   15
    have mighty business in hand.

Corn. True or false, it hath made thee Earl of
    Gloucester. Seek out where thy father is, that
    he may be ready for our apprehension.

Edm. [*Aside.*] If I find him comforting the King,   20
    it will stuff his suspicion more fully. [*Aloud.*] I
    will persever in my course of loyalty, though the
    conflict be sore between that and my blood.

Corn. I will lay trust upon thee; and thou shalt find   24
    a dearer father in my love.   [*Exeunt.*

---

10. letter] *Q;* Letter which *F.*   12. this] *F;* his *Q.* were not] *F;* were *Q.*
20. S.D.] *Theobald; not in Q, F.*   21. S.D.] *Duthie; not in Q, F.*
25. dearer] *Q;* deere *F.*   S.D.] *F; Exit Q.*

7-8. *a provoking . . . himself*] "a
provoking merit" has been taken
to mean "a virtue apt to be pro-
voked," "a consciousness of his
own worth which urged him on"
and "an anticipative merit, a
meritorious forestalling of crime by
its punishment." Similarly "badness in himself" has been taken to
mean Edgar's wickedness, and also
Gloucester's. The passage should
probably be interpreted: "Edgar's
reprehensible wickedness was pro-
voked to mete out to Gloucester the
death that he deserved." Although
Gloucester deserved to die, only an
evil son would attempt to murder
his father.

10. *just*] righteous, i.e. that he has
revealed his father's treason.

11. *approves him*] proves him to be.

11. *intelligent party*] intelligencer,
spy, providing information. Some
take it to mean "well informed
of."

11-12. *to the advantages*] for the
assistance.

19. *apprehension*] arrest.

20. *comforting*] used in the legal
sense of "supporting, helping."
Lord Campbell says: "The in-
dictment against an accessory after
the fact, for treason, charges that the
accessory 'comforted' the principal
traitor after knowledge of the
treason."

22. *persever*] continue. The accent
is on the second syllable.

23. *blood*] natural feelings of a son.

SCENE VI.—[*A Chamber in a Farmhouse adjoining
the Castle.*]

Enter GLOUCESTER *and* KENT.

Glou. Here is better than the open air; take it thank-
fully. I will piece out the comfort with what
addition I can: I will not be long from you.
Kent. All the power of his wits have given way to his
impatience. The Gods reward your kindness!   5
                                                [*Exit Gloucester.*

Enter LEAR, EDGAR, *and Fool.*

Edg. Frateretto calls me, and tells me Nero is an
angler in the Lake of Darkness. Pray, innocent,
and beware the foul fiend.

Scene VI

A . . . Castle . . .] *Malone; A Chamber, Rowe; A Chamber, in a Farmhouse.   Theobald; A Room in some of the out-buildings of the Castle.
Capell.*   S.D.] *F; Enter Gloster and Lear, Kent, Foole, and Tom Q.*
4. have] *Q. F; has Pope; hath Capell.*   to his] *F; to Q.*   reward] *F;*
deserue Q; preserve conj. Capell.   5. S.D. *Exit Gloucester*] *Capell;*
Exit (after 3) F; not in Q.   Enter . . . *Fool*] *F; at beginning of scene Q.*
8. and] *F; not in Q.*

Scene VI

S.D.] Perret, comparing III. iv. 160,
suggests that Theobald's placing of
this scene in a farmhouse is wrong.
Perhaps Capell's suggestion, "A
Room in some of the outbuildings
of the Castle" is better.
    2. *piece*] eke. Cf. *M.W.* III. ii. 34.
    4. *have*] Attracted into the plural
by the intervening *wits* (Kittredge).
    6. *Frateretto*] Another name from
Harsnett. See Appendix, p. 254.
    6-7. *Nero . . . Darkness*] Upton
pointed out that according to
Rabelais (ii. 30) Nero played on
the hurdy-gurdy in hell; it was
Trajan who angled (for frogs). But
F. E. Budd, *R.E.S.* (1935), pp. 421-9,
shows that Shakespeare's knowledge
of Nero's angling was taken from
Chaucer, *The Monk's Tale*, ll. 485-6;

and that the mention of Nero was
suggested by Harsnett's *Declaration.*
Immediately after the first mention
of Frateretto, a Fiddler comes in to
provide "musicke in hell." In the
same context, Harsnett mentions
the "*stygian* lake" and "a *Caesars*
humor"; and there are later references to the bottomless pit. See
Appendix, p. 254. Edith Sitwell,
A Notebook on William Shakespeare,
pp. 48-9, suggests "the lake of
darkness" means "the bottomless
depth of human nature" and she
compares *M.M.* III. i. 93:
    "His filth within being cast, he
                would appeare
    A pond as deepe as hell."
She also suggests that Shakespeare
had read Pausanias, *Description of
Greece,* ii. 37, where he describes an

Turning Point.

Fool. Prithee, Nuncle, tell me whether a madman be
    a gentleman or a yeoman?   10
Lear. A King, a King!
Fool. No; he's a yeoman that has a gentleman to
    his son; for he's a mad yeoman that sees his
    son a gentleman before him.
Lear. To have a thousand with red burning spits   15
    Come hizzing in upon 'em—
Edg. The foul fiend bites my back.
Fool. He's mad that trusts in the tameness of a wolf,
    a horse's health, a boy's love, or a whore's oath.   *try in court*
Lear. It shall be done; I will <u>arraign</u> them straight.   *try*20
    [*To Edgar.*] Come, sit thou here, most learned justicer;

9. be] may be *Q 2, 3.*   12-15. Fool. No . . . him.   *Lear.*] *F; not in Q.*
13. mad] *not in F 3, 4.*   16. hizzing] *F;* hiszing *Q 1;* hissing *Q 2, 3.*
'em-] *Theobald;* 'em. *F;* them. *Q.*   17-56. *Edg.* The foul . . . 'scape] *Q;*
not in F.   18. trusts] trust *Q 3.*   19. health] *Q;* heels *Singer (conj. War-*
burton).   21. S.D.] *Capell; not in Q; To the Fool Hanmer.*   justicer]
Theobald; Iustice *Q.*

attempt by Nero to sound the depth
of the Alcyonian Lake, through
which Dionysus went to Hell to
fetch up Semele. It is unlikely that
Shakespeare read Pausanias in the
original, but it is possible that he
read of Nero's experiment elsewhere.
John Berryman, *T.L.S.,* 30 March
1946, points out that Nero was
guilty of matricide, and that Edgar,
who speaks this line, is accused of
parricide. Higgins, in the 1587
edition of *The Mirror for Magistrates*
(*Cordila,* l. 370) mentions the
" darkesome *Stygian lake* ".

12-14. *No . . . before him*] Shakespeare is thought to have secured
a coat of arms for his father. Schmidt
suggests that there is a pun on *mad*
and *made.*

15-16. *To . . . upon 'em*] See
Harsnett, Appendix, p. 255.

16. *hizzing*] This form of *hissing*
" suggests the whizzing sound of
the redhot weapons as they are to
be brandished by a thousand assail-
ants " (Kittredge).

19. *horse's health*] Perhaps his

seller's account of his condition.
But see *T.S.* I. ii. 81 and III. ii. 50-6.
Warburton read " a horse's heels."
Cf. Ray, *Proverbs,* ed. 1879, p. 546:
" Trust not a horse's heels, nor a
dog's tooth."

20. *arraign*] Lear suddenly aban-
dons his intention of using armed
force, and decides to bring his
daughters to trial instead.   R.
Peacock, *The Poet in the Theatre,* 1946,
p. 128, comments on the trial:
" Lear, scarcely rescued from the
fury of nature, his ideas scattered by
suffering, conducts a trial of his
daughters. It is an illumination that
produces from the sub-conscious the
effects of order. At the moment of
greatest breakdown we are given a
judgement that represents amidst
chaos the memory of civilization.
Moral assumptions are at the centre
of tragedy."

21. *justicer*] P. A. McElwaine,
N.Q. 23 Sept. 1911, suggests that
this is a corruption of " Justiciar,"
a high officer in the time of William I,
who took the king's place when

N.B.

[*To the Fool.*] Thou, sapient sir, sit here.   Now, you
     she foxes!

Edg. Look where he stands and glares!   Want'st
     thou eyes at trial, madam?   25
               Come o'er the bourn, Bessy, to me,—

Fool. [*Sings.*]   *Her boat hath a leak,*
                   And she must not speak;
          Why she dares not come over to thee!

Edg. The foul fiend haunts poor Tom in the voice   30
     of a nightingale.   Hoppedance cries in Tom's
     belly for two white herring.   Croak not, black
     angel; I have no food for thee.

[margin annotations: Hunger ; Rumble]

22. S.D.] *Capell; not in Q; To Edgar Hanmer.*   Now] *Q 2, 3; no*
Q 1.   24. he *Q;* she *Theobald.*   Want'st] *Q 2;* wanst *Q 1.*   25-6.
Wanst . . . eyes] *Q:* Wantonizeth thou *conj. Staunton;* Wanton'st thou eyes *Jen-*
nens (conj. Seward).   25. trial] *Q 2, 3;* tral *Q 1.*   26. bourn] *Camb.;*
boorne *Capell;* broome *Q.*   27. S.D.] *Craig (conj. Camb).*   28. speak;]
conj. Schmidt; speake, *Q.*

he was abroad. Cotgrave uses it as
a synonym for " Justice." The word
is actually an emendation of Theobald's. Cf. III. vi. 56 and IV. ii. 79;
also *Cymb.* v. v. 214.

24. *Look . . . glares*] a fiend; or
Lear.

24-5. *Want'st . . . madam?*] Do
you want to have spectators at your
trial, madam? Look where he, a
fiend stands, and glares.   K.D.
(*N.Q.* 2 Dec. 1905) conjectures
" worse than eyes at trol-madam."
Cf. *W.T.* IV. iii. 92. Steevens
explained: " Do you want to at-
tract admiration, even while you
stand at the bar of justice? " Eccles
gave the speech to Lear, changing
he to *she*.

25. *eyes*] Bell, unnecessarily, thought
this represented the crier's proclamation at the opening of court, *Oyez*.

26. *Come . . . me*] from a song in
which a lover calls upon his sweet-
heart to come to him across a stream.
Wager, *The Longer thou Livest the
More Fool thou Art*, quotes from the
same song:

" Com ouer the Boorne besse
   My little pretie Besse,
   Com ouer the Boorne besse to
      me."
(Cf. *Harleian Miscellany*, ed. Park. x.
260.)

26. *bourn*] burn, brook. Capell's
emendation.

27-9. *Her . . . thee*] The Fool
improvises.

30. *The . . . voice*] Edgar pretends
that the Fool's singing is that of a
fiend disguised as a nightingale.

31. *Hoppedance*] Harsnett's form is
' Hoberdidance.'

31. *cries*] His stomach is rumbling
because it is empty. Cf. III. ii. 14.

32. *white herring*] either pickled herring (Steevens); or fresh, unsmoked
herring (Kittredge). Nashe, *Lenton
Stuffe*, 1599 (ed. McKerrow, iii. 204)
speaks of " herrings, which were as
white as whales bone when hee hung
them vp, nowe lookt as red as a
lobster"; and, *op. cit.* p. 223: a
white pickled herring? why it is
meate for a Prince! "

32. *croak*] rumble. Cf. Harsnett
Appendix, p. 256.

Lear for the first time looks onwards. Not quite p110.

SC. VI.]　　　　KING LEAR　　　　133

Kent. How do you, sir? Stand you not so amaz'd: *dumbfounded*
　　Will you lie down and rest upon the cushions?　35
Lear. I'll see their trial first. Bring in their evidence. *those to*
　　[*To Edgar.*] Thou robed man of justice, take thy *testify against them*
　　　place;
　　[*To the Fool.*] And thou, his yoke-fellow of equity,
　　Bench by his side. [*To Kent.*] You are o' th' com-
　　　mission,
　　Sit you too.　　　　　　　　　　　　　　　　40
Edg. Let us deal justly.

　　　　Sleepest or wakest thou, jolly shepherd?
　　　　Thy sheep be in the corn;
　　　　And for one blast of thy minikin mouth,
　　　　Thy sheep shall take no harm.　　　45
　　Purr, the cat is grey.

35. cushions] cushings *Q 1.*　　36. in their] *Q;* in the *Pope.*　　37. S.D.]
Capell; not in Q.　　robed] robbed *Q.*　　38. S.D.] *Capell; not in Q.*　　39.
S.D.] *Capell; not in Q.*　　　o' th'] *Q 2, subst.;* ot'h *Q 1.*　　41-2. justly.
Sleepest] *Theobald;* iustly sleepest *Q 1;* iustly, sleepest *Q 2.*　　46. Purr, the]
Pur the *Q;* Purr! the *most edd.*

34. *amaz'd*] dumbfounded.
36. *their evidence*] those who are to
testify against them.
37. *robed*] Edgar's blanket appears
as judicial robes here, and later (82)
as the Persian attire of a Magus.
38. *yoke-fellow*] partner. Cf.
Henry V. IV. vi. 9. Harsnett uses
several words hyphened with *fellow.*
39. *Bench*] Take your seat on the
bench.
39. *o' th' commission*] commissioned
as a justice. P.A. McElwaine points
out that " we speak of ' commission
of the peace,' but we also speak of
' commission of Assize.' "
42-5. *Sleepest . . . harm*] Probably
a fragment, or an adaptation of an
old song. Steevens quotes from
*Interlude of the Nature of the Four
Elements,* 1510: " Slepyst thou,
wakyst thou geffery coke." Whiter,
in an unpublished note, compares
an obscure passage in *T.G.* I. i. 77-80.
44. *for one blast*] Kittredge explains: " for the time it takes to
play one strain on your shepheard's

pipe." But it is the corn, not the
sheep, which will be harmed; and
the phrase may mean " if only you
will blow one strain on your pipe,
your precious sheep will leave the
cornfield, whatever damage they
may have done." It may refer,
ironically, to the shepherd's shout,
rather than to his pipe.
44. *minikin*] delicate, dainty, feat,
concinnus. It was also a musical term,
as in the apocryphal Marlowe poem,
ed. Cunningham, 1870, p. 271:
　" I cannot lisp, nor to some fiddle
　　sing,
　　Nor run upon a high stretched
　　minikin."
Here it means the thin string of gut
used for the treble string of the lute
or viol, and hence shrill (*N.E.D.*).
46. *Purr*] The name was probably
suggested by the name of one of
Harsnett's demons (see Appendix,
p. 254); but Edgar is referring to a
demon or familiar in the shape of
a grey cat, and this may be its noise,
rather than its name.

Cf. First scene, Lear sane: judges
falsely. Lear mad judges rightly

134   KING LEAR   [ACT III.

Lear. Arraign her first; 'tis Goneril. I here take
    my oath before this honourable assembly, she
    kick'd the poor King her father.

Fool. Come hither, mistress. Is your name Goneril?   50

Lear. She cannot deny it.

Fool. Cry you mercy, I took you for a joint-stool.

Lear. And here's another, whose <u>warp'd</u> looks proclaim *unnatu*
    What <u>store</u> her heart is made on. Stop her there!
    Arms, arms, sword, fire! Corruption in the place!   55
    False justicer, why hast thou let her 'scape?

stock
(of evil
passions)

Edg. Bless thy five wits!

Kent. O pity! Sir, where is the patience now
    That you so oft have boasted to retain?

Edg. [*Aside.*] My tears begin to take his part so much,   60
    They mar my counterfeiting.

Lear. The little dogs and all,
    Tray, Blanch, and Sweetheart, see, they bark at me.

Edg. Tom will throw his head at them. Avaunt, you
    curs!
                                    65

---

48. she] *not in* Q *1.*   52. joint-stool] ioyne stoole Q *1.*   54. store] stuff
conj. Jennens; stone Collier (*conj. Theobald*).   made on] *Capell;* made an
Q; made of *Theobald.*   59. retain] remain F *3, 4.*   60. S.D.] *Rowe; not in*
Q, F.   61. They] F; Theile Q *1;* They'l Q *2, 3.*

52. *Cry . . . stool*] This proverbial
expression is found in J. Withal,
Short Dictionary, 1554: " Antehac te
cornua habere putabam, I cry you
mercy, I took you for a joyn'd stool."
It was a facetious apology for over-
looking a person, " a ridiculous
instance of making an offence worse,
by a foolish and improbable
apology " (Nares). Steevens cites
Lyly, *Mother Bombie,* IV. ii: " I crie
you mercy, I tooke you for a joynt
stoole."

52. *joint-stool*] joyned stool; a
low stool with three or four legs
fitted into it, made by a joiner, as
distinguished from a carpenter who
works more on the rough.

It has been suggested (*N.Q.*
23 July 1904, p. 66) that the Fool
may mean: " I took you for one of
the bench, not a prisoner." Cf.

Narcissus, 1603, " Some of them are
heires, all of good abilitye; I beseech your lordshipp with the rest of
the ioyned stooles, I would say the
bench, take my foolish iudgment,
and lett them fine for it."

53. *warp'd*] perverse, unnatural,
distorted by evil passions.

54. *store*] material, stock (Craig).
Perhaps " of evil passions " is understood. But as the word could mean
treasure, there may be an unin-
tentional echo of *Matt.* vi. 21. Perhaps it should be emended to *stuff*
(Jennens) or to *stone* (Theobald):
the latter may be supported by III. vi.
79 and v. iii. 257; and *r* for *n* is a
common misreading. Cf. collations
of IV. ii. 21.

61. *mar . . . counterfeiting*] See
Appendix, p. 253.

Be thy mouth or black or white,
Tooth that poisons if it bite;
Mastiff, greyhound, mongrel grim,
Hound or spaniel, brach or lym;
Or bobtail tike or trundle-tail;   70
Tom will make him weep and wail:
For, with throwing thus my head,
Dogs leap'd the hatch, and all are fled.
Do de, de, de. Sessa! Come, march to wakes
and fairs and market-towns. Poor Tom, thy   75
horn is dry.

Lear. Then let them anatomize Regan, see what
breeds about her heart. Is there any cause in

68-9. mongrel grim, Hound] *Rowe, subst.;* Mongrill, Grim, Hound *F;*
mungril, grim-hound *Q.*   69. lym] *Hanmer;* him *Q;* Hym *F.*   70. Or] *F;*
not in *Q.*   tike] tight *F 1, 2, 3.*   trundle-tail] *Q;* Troudle taile *F.*   71.
him] *F;* them *Q.*   73. leap'd] leapt *F;* leape *Q.*   74. Do . . . de] *F;*
loudla doodla *Q.*   Sessa!] *Malone;* sese: *F; not in Q.*

68. *grim*] Ridley suggests that the
comma before this word means that
it conceals a kind of dog, and is not
an adj. But the comma may merely
indicate that the adj. applies to all
three kinds of dog.

69. *brach*] Cf. I. iv. 118.

69. *lym*] lymmer, a species of
bloodhound, so called from the liam,
or leather thong, by which he was
led.

70. *trundle-tail*] or trindle-tail, a
dog with a long drooping tail,
which he seems to trundle along after
him (Kittredge).

72. *For . . . head*] After this line
in Edwin Booth's Prompt Book there
is a S.D. "Throws straw crown to
left." There is no warrant for this.
It may mean that Edgar jerks his
head at the imaginary dogs. In
Gielgud's 1950 production Edgar
made as though to lift his head from
his shoulders. Two other suggestions
occur to me: (i) Edgar throws his
horn at them. As 'head' means
the antlers of a deer it could be
stretched to mean the ox's horn of
Poor Tom. (ii) Edgar might put

his horn on his head, and pretend
he is an ox attacking the dogs with it.

73. *hatch*] the lower half of a
divided door. "To leap the hatch"
means to make a hurried exit.

74. *Do . . . de*] Cf. III. iv. 59.

74. *Sessa*] Cf. III. iv. 102.

74-5. *Come . . . market-towns*]
Steevens suggests this is a line from
a song in which a vagabond calls
upon a companion to accompany
him on his rounds.

75-6. *thy . . . dry*] Aubrey, *Natural
History of Wiltshire*, ed. 1847, p. 93,
mentions that "Bedlam beggars
wore about their necks a great horne
of an ox in a string or bawdrie, which,
when they came to an house for
almes they did wind, and they did put
the drink given them into this horne
whereto they did put a stopple."
This was the formula used in begging
for a drink; but Edgar also means
that he is unable to play his part any
longer (Steevens).

77-8. *what . . . heart*] as though
her heart had become as hard as
horn.

nature that make these hard hearts? [*To Edgar.*]

You, sir, I entertain for one of my hundred; only   80
I do not like the fashion of your garments: you
will say they are Persian; but let them be
chang'd.

Kent. Now, good my Lord, lie here and rest awhile.

Lear. Make no noise, make no noise; draw the   85
curtains: so, so. We'll go to supper i' th'
morning.

Fool. And I'll go to bed at noon.

Re-enter GLOUCESTER.

Glou. Come hither, friend: where is the King my master?

Kent. Here, Sir; but trouble him not, his wits are gone.   90

Glou. Good friend, I prithee, take him in thy arms;
I have o'erheard a plot of death upon him.
There is a litter ready; lay him in't,

79. make] *F;* makes *Q.*   these hard hearts?] *Rowe;* these hard-hearts. *F;*
this hardnes *Q.*   79. S.D.] *Capell not in Q, F.*   80. for] *F;* you for *Q.*   81.
garments] garment *Q 2, 3.*   you will] *F;* youle *Q.*   82. Persian] *F;* Persian
attire *Q.*   84. and rest] *Q; not in F.*   86. so, so] *F;* so, so, so *Q.*   87.
morning.] *F;* morning, so, so, so. *Q.*   88. And . . . noon] *F; not in Q.*   S.D.]
Q; after 83 F.   93. in' t] in it *Q 2, 3.*

79. *make*] subjunctive (Schmidt).
Cf. Abbott *367.

80. *entertain*] engage, take into
service. Cf. *J.C.* v. v. 60.

80. *hundred*] i.e. the hundred
knights. But one of Harsnett's
devils was a Centurion and "had
a hundred vnder his charge." Cf.
Appendix, p. 254.

82. *Persian*] Horace, *Odes,* i. 38.
Cf. note on III. iv. 147. A Persian
embassy visited England early in
James I's reign.

83. *chang'd*] Carter, *Shakespeare and
Holy Scripture,* points out that Shakespeare may have been influenced by
Dan. vi. 8: " that it be not changed,
according to the lawe of the Medes
and Persians which altereth not."

86. *curtains*] Lear imagines he is
in his own bed.

86-7. *supper . . . morning*] since
we have none to-night. Gloucester
was to provide food, but Lear needs
rest above all.

88. *And . . . noon*] Blunden, *op.
cit.* p. 336, suggests that there are
seven meanings to this sentence,
including " a pun on the people's
name for the scarlet pimpernel.
The weak-bodied Fool with his coxcomb looks like that flower. It is
the last time that the Fool speaks
during the play. He presages his
untimely death with a secondary
meaning in the word ' bed ' of
' grave.' He takes off his coxcomb for the last time to please the
audience." Other critics deny a deep
meaning in the words. There is a
proverb: " You would make me go
to bed at noon."

92. *upon*] against.

And drive toward Dover, friend, where thou shalt
    meet
Both welcome and protection.   Take up thy master: 95
If thou should'st dally half an hour, his life,
With thine, and all that offer to defend him,
Stand in assured loss.   Take up, take up;
And follow me, that will to some provision
Give thee quick conduct.

Kent.   Oppressed nature sleeps. 100
This rest might yet have balm'd thy broken sinews   *racked*
Which, if convenience will not allow,   *nerves*
Stand in hard cure.   [*To the Fool.*] Come, help to
    bear thy master;
Thou must not stay behind.

Glou.   Come, come, away.
                [*Exeunt Kent, Gloucester, and the Fool,
                                bearing off the King.*

Edg. When we our betters see bearing our woes,   105
We scarcely think our miseries our foes.
Who alone suffers, suffers most i' th' mind,
Leaving free things and happy shows behind;
But then the mind much sufferance doth o'erskip,
When grief hath mates, and bearing fellowship.   110

---

94. toward] *F;* towards *Q.*   98. take up] *F;* to keepe *Q uncorr., Q 2, 3;*
the King *Q corr.* 100-4. Oppressed . . . behind] *Q; not in F.*   100. Oppressed]
Opprest *Theobald.*   101. sinews] *Q;* senses *Theobald.*   103. S.D.]
Theobald; not in Q.   104. S.D.] *Capell; Exeunt F; Exit Q.*   105-18.]
Q; not in F.   107. suffers, suffers] suffers *Q 2, 3.*

101. *broken sinews*] racked nerves.
Schmidt cites, *V.A.* 903: " A second
fear through all her sinews spread."
Delius compares *T.N.* II. v. 83;
" We break the sinews of our plot."
Sir John Davies, *Nosce Teipsum* (ed.
Grosart, i. 70) has, in a section on
Feeling:
" Lastly, the feeling power which
    is life's root,
Through every living power
    itself doth shed
By sinews, which extend from
    head to foot,
And like a net, all o'er the body
    spread."

Theobald's emendation, *senses*, is
therefore unnecessary.

103. *Stand . . . cure*] can hardly
be cured. Cf. 98 *ante*, and *Oth.* II. i.
51.

105-18. *When . . . lurk*] Wright
thought this soliloquy was spurious.
But its style is not unlike other
passages, *Cor.* II. iii. 120-31; *Oth.* I.
iii. 210-20; *Macb.* v. iv. 16-21. It
was necessary to bring out the
parallelism between the two plots.

108. *free*] care-free.

110. *bearing*] endurance, suffering.

How light and portable my pain seems now,
When that which makes me bend makes the king
   bow;
He childed as I father'd!   Tom, away!
Mark the high noises, and thyself bewray *reveal*
When false opinion, whose wrong thoughts defile
   thee, *proof of integrity*   115
In thy just proof repeals and reconciles thee. *reinstates*
What will hap more to-night, safe 'scape the King!
Lurk, lurk.   [*Exit.*

discord among the great

115. thoughts defile] thought defiles *Theobald.* 118. S.D.] *Theobald; not in Q.*

SCENE VII.—[*A Room in Gloucester's Castle.*]

Enter CORNWALL, REGAN, GONERIL, EDMUND,
and Servants.

Corn. [*To Goneril.*] Post speedily to my Lord your
   husband; show him this letter: the army of
   France is landed.   Seek out the traitor Gloucester.
                    [*Exeunt some of the Servants.*
Reg. Hang him instantly.
Gon. Pluck out his eyes.   5
Corn. Leave him to my displeasure.   Edmund, keep
   you our sister company: the revenges we are
   bound to take upon your traitorous father are
   proposing/obliged to

Regan's idea is more practical cf p.167 Gon. is the more brutish

202

Scene VII
A . . . Castle] *Rowe, subst.; not in Q, F.*   S.D.   Regan] *not in F*
3, 4.   2. him] *Q*; hin *F 1.*   3. traitor] *F*; vilaine *Q.*   S.D.] *Capell; not in Q, F.*   7. revenges] *F*; reuenge *Q.*

111. *portable*] endurable.
113. *He . . . father'd*] He had cruel children, as I have a cruel father.
114. *Mark . . . noises*] Observe the signs of discord among the great; "attend to the great events that are approaching" (Johnson).
114. *thyself bewray*] reveal thyself, throw off thy disguise.
116. *just proof*] proof of thy integrity.
116. *repeals*] repeals the sentence

of outlawry, and recalls thee to thy proper position.
116. *reconciles thee*] i.e. to thy father.   Plural and singular words were often rhymed by Shakespeare, and there is no need to read " thought defiles " in the previous line.
117. *What*] whatever, whatsoever. Cf. Abbott, *254.

Scene VII
2. *letter*] Cf. III. v. 10.
8. *bound*] ready, prepared to, purposing to; or possibly, obliged.

not fit for your beholding. Advise the Duke,
where you are going, to a most festinate prepara-   10
tion: we are bound to the like. Our posts shall
be swift and intelligent betwixt us. Farewell,
dear sister; farewell, my Lord of Gloucester.

Enter OSWALD.

How now! where's the King?
Osw. My Lord of Gloucester hath convey'd him hence: 15
Some five or six and thirty of his knights,
Hot questrists after him, met him at gate;
Who, with some other of the Lord's dependants,
Are gone with him toward Dover, where they boast
To have well-armed friends.
Corn.   Get horses for your mistress.   20
Gon. Farewell, sweet Lord, and sister.
Corn. Edmund, farewell.
                         [*Exeunt Goneril, Edmund, and Oswald.*
                         Go seek the traitor Gloucester,
Pinion him like a thief, bring him before us.
                              [*Exeunt other Servants.*
Though well we may not pass upon his life   *death sentence*
Without the form of justice, yet our power   25
Shall do a court'sy to our wrath, which men
May blame but not control. Who's there? The
    traitor?

10. festinate] *F 2*; festiuate *F 1*; festuant *Q*.   11. posts] *F*; post *Q*.   12.
intelligent] *F*; intelligence *Q*.   13. S.D.] *Collier; Enter Steward F, at 14 Q.*
17. questrists] *F*; questrits *Q*.   19. toward] *F*; towards *Q*.   22. S.D.] *Dyce;
Exit Gon. and Bast. (after 21) Q; Exit (after 21) F.*   23. S.D.] *Capell; not in
Q, F.*   24. well] *F; not in Q.*   27. S.D.] *Capell; Enter Gloster brought
in by two or three Q; Enter Gloucester, and Servants (after comptroll) F.*

10. *festinate*] hasty, urgent. Cf.
L.L.L. III. i. 6.

10-11. *preparation*] i.e. for war.

11. *we . . . like*] we intend to do the
same.

11. *posts*] speedy messengers on
horseback.

12. *intelligent*] giving information.

17. *questrists*] seekers. Probably
a Shakespearian coinage.

24. *pass . . . life*] pass the death
sentence on him. Cf. *M.M.* II. i.
23.

26. *do a court'sy*] yield, give way.
Cf. *Hen. V.* v. ii. 293.   Other explanations: "indulge, gratify"
(Johnson); "bend to our wrath as
a courtesy is made by bending the
body" (Steevens);   to oblige
(Schmidt).

Re-enter Servants, with GLOUCESTER *prisoner.*

Reg. Ingrateful fox! 'tis he.
Corn. Bind fast his corky arms.
Glou. What means your Graces? Good my friends,
    consider   30
    You are my guests: do me no foul play, friends.
Corn. Bind him, I say.   [*Servants bind him.*
Reg.   Hard, hard. O filthy traitor!
Glou. Unmerciful lady as you are, I'm none.
Corn. To this chair bind him. Villain, thou shalt find—
                      [*Regan plucks his beard.*
Glou. By the kind Gods, 'tis most ignobly done   35
    To pluck me by the beard.
Reg. So white, and such a traitor!
Glou.   Naughty lady,
    These hairs, which thou dost ravish from my
        chin,
    Will quicken, and accuse thee: I am your host:
    With robbers' hands my hospitable favours   40
    You should not ruffle thus. What will you do?
Corn. Come, sir, what letters had you late from France?
Reg. Be simple-answer'd, for we know the truth.
Corn. And what confederacy have you with the traitors
    Late footed in the kingdom?
Reg.   To whose hands   45
    You have sent the lunatic King: speak.
Glou. I have a letter guessingly set down,
    Which came from one that's of a neutral heart,

---

30. means] *Q, F;* mean *F 4.*   32. S.D.] *Rowe; not in Q, F.*   33. I'm
none] *F;* I am true *Q.*   34. find—] *Q;* finde. *F.*   S.D.] *Johnson; not in
Q, F.* 43. simple-answer'd] *Hanmer;* simple answer'd *F;* simple answerer *Q.*
45. Late] Lately *Q 2, 3.*   46. you have sent] *Q 1, F;* have you sent *Q 2, 3.*

29. *corky*] sapless, dry and withered.
Cf. Harsnett, Appendix, p. 253.
32. *filthy*] odious. Cf. *Oth.* v. ii.
149.
33. *Unmerciful*] merciless.
37. *naughty*] wicked.
39. *quicken*] assume life.
40. *hospitable favours*] features of
your host.

41. *ruffle*] treat with such violence.
Cf. II. iv. 303.
42. *late*] lately.
43. *Be simple-answer'd*] give a
straight answer.
44. *confederacy*] conspiracy.
45. *footed*] landed. Cf. III. iii. 14.
47. *guessingly set down*] written
without certain knowledge.

> And not from one oppos'd.

Corn.   Cunning.

Reg.   And false.

Corn. Where hast thou sent the King?

Glou.   To Dover.   50

Reg. Wherefore to Dover?   Wast thou not charg'd at
  peril—

Corn. Wherefore to Dover?   Let him answer that.

Glou. I am tied to th' stake, and I must stand the
  course.

Reg. Wherefore to Dover?

Glou. Because I would not see thy cruel nails   55
  Pluck out his poor old eyes; nor thy fierce sister
  In his anointed flesh rash boarish fangs.
  The sea, with such a storm as his bare head
  In hell-black night endur'd, would have buoy'd up,

---

51. peril—] *Q;* perill. *F.*   52. answer] *F;* first answer *Q.*   54. Dover] *F;*
Douer sir *Q.*   57. anointed] *Q corr., F;* aurynted *Q uncorr., Q 2, 3.*   rash]
Q; sticke *F.*   58. as his bare] *F;* of . . . lou'd *Q uncorr., Q 2, 3;* on . . .
lowd *Q corr.*   59. hell-black night] *Pope;* Hell-blacke-night *F;* hell blacke
night *Q.*   buoy'd] *F;* layd *Q uncorr., Q 2, 3;* bod *Q corr.;* boil'd *Warburton.*

---

51. *at peril*] on peril of death.

53. *to th' stake*] like a baited bear.
Cf. *Macb.* v. vii. 2.

53. *course*] a relay of dogs set on a
baited bear.

55-60. *Because . . . fires*] Cuningham, *T.L.S.* 28 July 1927, suggests
the lines should end *see/eyes/flesh/
storm/endur'd/fires.*

57. *anointed flesh*] the flesh of the
anointed king.

57. *rash*] strike obliquely with the
tusk, as a boar does. Cf. Spenser,
Faerie Queene, iv. ii. 17.   Nares
quotes Warner, *Albion's England*,
1586, vii. 36: "Ha! cur, avant,
the boar so rashe thy hide." The
F reading 'stick' is probably an
actor's substitution, or a sophistication; but it may possibly be
a substitution on Shakespeare's

part to avoid the thrice repeated
'sh.'

59. *hell-black*] Capell suggested
that Shakespeare derived this epithet from Hakluyt, viii. 304 (Everyman ed.): "to guide the ship in
the hell-darke night, when we could
not see any shore." On p. 302
Hakluyt uses the word 'unmerciful'." Cf. 33 *ante*.

59. *buoy'd up*] risen up, as a cork
buoy when sunk in water; or, as
Schmidt suggests, used transitively.
"The sea would have lifted up the
fixed fires and extinguished them."
There is something to be said for
Warburton's emendation *boil'd* which
suggests the fury of the waves more
obviously than the F reading; but
it should nevertheless be rejected,
as *buoy'd* is so unusual a word that it
is unlikely to be a guess.

And quench'd the stelled fires; *fixed*   60
Yet, poor old heart, he holp the heavens to rain.
If wolves had at thy gate howl'd that dearn time, *dreary*
Thou should'st have said " Good porter, turn the key."

60. stelled] *F, Q corr.;* steeled *Q uncorr., Q 2, 3.*   61. holp] *F;* holpt *Q.*
rain] *F;* rage *Q.*   62. howl'd] *F;* heard *Q.*   dearn] *Q;* sterne *F.*

60. *stelled fires*] Theobald explains ' starry fires,' as if from the Latin, *stella*. But Nares, Schmidt, and Onions take it to mean ' fixed lights.' Cf. *Luc.* 1444:

" To find a face where all distress is stell'd "; and *Sonnets*, xxiv:
" Mine eye hath play'd the painter, and hath stell'd
Thy beauty's form in table of my heart."

The word, from M.E. *stellen*, O.E. *stellan*, means *fixed* in all three passages. But there is no reason why Shakespeare should not have had the secondary meaning of *starry* in mind: indeed, it is impossible to believe he did not. " Fixed stars " are stars, as opposed to " wandering stars " (planets).

61. *holp*] helped.

62. *dearn*] dreary, dread, dire. Cf. *Per.* III. Chorus, 15. The F word is comparatively weak, and doubtless a sophistication.

63-5. *Thou . . . children*] This passage has been much discussed. The problems involved are (i) Should the inverted commas be closed after *key*, or after *subscribe?* (ii) Does *Cruels* mean ' cruel acts ' or ' cruel creatures '? (iii) Are we to accept F *subscribe*, or Q *subscrib'd?*

It will be convenient to discuss them in the reverse order. As the F reading makes good sense, certainly as good as that of Q, we should accept it. *Subscribe* can be taken as a 3rd plural present indicative, or as an imperative. It can mean ' yield,' ' surrender,' ' submit,' ' assent,' ' make acknowledgement of.' It is more natural to take *cruels* to mean ' cruel creatures,' like the wolves mentioned in the context. Cf. *Sonnet* cxlix. But Verity and Perrett take it to mean ' cruel acts.' As Duthie points out, Shakespeare uses ' vulgars ' (common people. *W.T.* II. i. 94), ' potents ' (powerful people. *K.J.* II. i. 358), and ' resolutes ' (resolute people, *Ham.* I. i. 98). If we end the quotation after *subscribe*, we may paraphrase: " Good porter, unlock the door and let the wolves in. All other cruel creatures yield to compassion on occasion, on such a night as this; and so will I too." Schmidt compares *T.C.* IV. v. 105-6:

" Hector in his blaze of wrath subscribes
To tender objects."

(i.e. gives up his anger at the sight of objects of compassion). The objection to this arrangement is that Regan would be unlikely to admit her cruelty to the porter, though Duthie claims that it is quite consonant with the mood of the speech that Gloucester should attribute to Regan a cynical avowal of such self-knowledge. If, on the other hand, we take " All cruels else subscribe " to be outside the quotation, we can interpret in two ways: (*a*) " All other cruel creatures yield to feelings of compassion under strong provocation; you alone do not " (Duthie). (*b*) " Leave on one side all other cruel creatures." In the light of the *Troilus and Cressida* quotation (*a*) seems preferable.

Perret is the most persuasive of those who take *cruels* to mean ' cruel deeds.' He paraphrases: " Never mind about your other cruel deeds, . . . subscribe them, let us leave them

Yield to compassion

All cruels else subscribe: but I shall see
The winged vengeance overtake such children.   65
Corn. See 't shalt thou never.   Fellows, hold the chair.
   Upon these eyes of thine I'll set my foot.
Glou. He that will think to live till he be old,
   Give me some help!   O cruel!   O you Gods!
Reg. One side will mock another; th' other too.   70
Corn. If you see vengeance,—
First Serv.   Hold your hand, my Lord.
   I have serv'd you ever since I was a child,
   But better service have I never done you
   Than now to bid you hold.
Reg.   How now, you dog!
First Serv. If you did wear a beard upon your chin   75
   I'd shake it on this quarrel.
Reg.   What do you mean?
Corn. My villain!   *pun. serf?*   [*They draw and fight.*
First Serv. Nay then, come on, and take the chance of
      anger.
Reg. Give me thy sword.   A peasant stand up thus!
                    [*Takes a sword and runs at him behind.*

---

64. subscribe] *F;* subscrib'd *Q.*   67. these] *F;* those *Q.*   69. you] *F;*
ye *Q.*   60. th' other] *F;* tother *Q.*   71. vengeance—] *Q;* vengeance. *F.*
72. you] *not in Q 1.*   76. *Reg.*] *See note below.*   77. S.D.] *Q; not in F.*
78. Nay] *F;* Why *Q.*   79. S.D. *Q; Killes him. F.*

out of consideration—but for that
impious act of shutting out your
father in such a storm . . . I shall see
the winged vengeance overtake you
and Goneril, such children." But
I think Duthie's interpretation, given
above, is the better.

If we read ' subscrib'd,' it may be
taken as a 3rd plural past indicative
("All other cruel creatures yielded
to feelings of compassion "—Duthie).
In any case, the general meaning of
the passage is clear.   Gloucester is
telling Regan that she has been more
cruel to her father then she would
have been to wolves, and because of
this unnaturalness displayed by her
and by her sister, he will see the

swift vengeance of heaven overtake
them.

65. *winged vengeance*] divine vengeance, like a bird of prey.   But
he may be thinking of winged spirits,
or of lightning.   Cf. IV. ii. 46-7;
II. iv. 163-4; and *Ps.* cxliv. 6:
" Send forth the lyghtnyng, and
scater them, shute out thyne arowes,
and consume them."

76. *What . . . mean*] Ascribed to
Regan by Kittredge, after a suggestion
by Craig.   Furness thought the words
should be given to Cornwall.

77. *villain*] perhaps punning on
the old meaning, ' serf.'

78. *take . . . anger*] run the risk of
fighting while angry.

First Serv. O! I am slain.   My Lord, you have one eye left 80
To see some mischief on him.   Oh!   [*Dies.*

Corn. Lest it see more, prevent it.   Out, vile jelly!
Where is thy lustre now?

Glou. All dark and comfortless.   Where's my son
Edmund?
Edmund, enkindle all the sparks of nature   85
To quit this horrid act.

Reg.   Out, treacherous villain!
Thou call'st on him that hates thee; it was he
~~disclosed~~ That made the <u>overture of</u> thy treasons to us,
Who is too good to pity thee.

Glou. <u>O my follies!</u>   Then Edgar was abus'd.   90
Kind Gods, forgive me that, and prosper him!

Sadism ||*Reg.* Go thrust him out at gates, and let him smell
His way to Dover.
                    [*Exit one with Gloucester.*
How is 't, my Lord.   How look you?

Corn. I have receiv'd a hurt.   Follow me, Lady.
Turn out that eyeless villain; throw this slave   95
Upon the dunghill.   Regan, I bleed apace:
Untimely comes this hurt.   Give me your arm.
                    [*Exit Cornwall, led by Regan.*

Second Serv. I'll never care what wickedness I do
If this man come to good.

Third Serv.   If she live long,
And in the end meet the old course of death,   100
Women will all turn monsters.

---

80. *First Serv.*] *Capell; Servant Q, F.* you have] *F;* yet haue you *Q;* yet you
have *Steevens.*   81. him] them *Dyce.*   S.D.] *Q 2; not in Q 1, F.*   85.
enkindle] *F;* vnbridle *Q.* 86. treacherous] *F; not in Q.* 93. S.D.] *F; not in Q.*
97. S.D.] *Theobald; Exit Q; Exeunt F.*   98-106] *Q; not in F.*   *Second
Serv.*] *Capell; Servant Q.*   99. *Third Serv.*] *Capell; 2 Servant Q.*

---

88. *made the overture*] made the
discovery, disclosed.

90. *abus'd*] wronged, deceived.

93. *How look you?*] How do you
seem to me?   How are you feeling?

100. *old*] customary, natural.

101. *Women . . . monsters*] because
they will not fear divine vengeance,
whatever their crimes.

Second Serv. Let's follow the old Earl, and get the Bedlam
  To lead him where he would: his roguish madness
  Allows itself to any thing.
Third Serv. Go thou; I'll fetch some flax and whites of 105
    eggs
  To apply to his bleeding face.   Now, heaven help
    him!

                                        [*Exeunt severally.*

102. *Second Serv.*] *Capell; I Serv.* Q.   103. *roguish*] *Q uncorr., Q
2, 3; not in Q corr.*   105. *Third Serv.*] *Capell; 2 Ser.* Q.   106. S.D.]
Theobald; Exit Q.

  103-4. *his . . . thing*] as he is a   *Treatises concerning Diseases of the Eye,*
vagabond and a madman, he cannot   1616, p. 53, recommends for a hurt
be called to account.   eye: "Apply thereupon a plaster of
  105. *flax . . . eggs*] Bailly, *Two*   flax and the white of an egg."

ACT IV

SCENE I.—[*The Heath.*]

Enter EDGAR.

Edg. Yet better thus, and known to be contemn'd,
Than, still contemn'd and flatter'd, to be worst.
The lowest and most dejected thing of Fortune,
Stands still in esperance, lives not in fear:
The lamentable change is from the best;   5

ACT IV

Scene 1

The Heath] Capell; *An open Country Rowe; not in Q, F.*   1. and
known] unknown *Collier (conj. Johnson)*,   2. flatter'd . . . worst] . . . worst:
F; flattered to be worst, *Q;* flatter'd. To be worst *Pope;* flatter'd. To be worse
conj. Tyrwhitt. 3. dejected] deject *F 3, 4.* 4. esperance] *F;* experience *Q.*

Scene 1

1-2. *Yet . . . worst*] Perrett is one of the few critics who defends the F punctuation. He paraphrases: "Better thus, openly despised, than to be in fact worst, when flattered and yet nevertheless despised." He suggests that a dash should be inserted before 'worst' to bring out this meaning, but I cannot see any point in doing this. I would rather explain: " 'Tis better to be thus contemned and known to yourself to be contemned " (Johnson, who adds that " when a man divests himself of his real character he feels no pain from contempt, because he supposes it incurred only by a voluntary disguise which he can throw off at pleasure "); " than to be worst, that is to be equally contemned, but to be unconscious of people's scorn because it is masked by flattery." Pope's emended punctuation makes the passage easier,

though Perrett objects to making " to be worst " subject of the next sentence. This is not an insuperable objection, because Shakespeare often changes the construction in the middle of a sentence, and ' thing ' is the real subject of ' stands.' Cf. *Leir*, 2077-8:

"Why, say the worst, the worst
   can be but death,
And death is better than for to
   despaire."

3. *most . . . fortune*] a thing most dejected of Fortune. Shakespeare often transposes the adjective in this way.

3. *dejected*] abased, cast down.

3. *thing*] the word is used contemptuously.

3. *of*] at the hands of.

4. *Stands . . . esperance*] is always in a condition of hope. Cf. *T.C.* v. ii. 121.

4. *lives . . . fear*] Steevens quotes Milton, *Paradise Regain'd*, iii. 206.

146

The worst returns to laughter.   Welcome, then,
Thou unsubstantial air that I embrace:
The wretch that thou hast blown unto the worst
Owes nothing to thy blasts.   But who comes here?

Enter GLOUCESTER, *led by an old Man.*

My father, poorly led?   World, world, O world!   10
But that thy strange mutations make us hate thee,
Life would not yield to age.
Old Man.   O my good Lord!

6-9. Welcome . . . blasts] *F; not in Q.*   9. But who comes] *F;* Who's *Q.*
S.D.] *after* age, *12 Q; Enter Gloucester and an Oldman F (after* blasts, *9).*
10. poorly led?] *Q 2, F;* poorlie, leed *Q uncorr.;* parti, eyd *Q corr.;* poorly
'rayd *Conj. Muir.*   11. hate] hold *conj. A. Walker.*

6. *returns to laughter*] must inevitably change for the better.   Cf.
Macb. IV. ii. 24; Kittredge cites
Wilkins, *The Miseries of Inforst
Marriage,* 1607: "When things are
at the worst, tis hopt theyle mend."
   9. *Owes*] When a man's debts are
paid, he fears no creditors (Kittredge).
   10. *poorly led*] Greg, *Variants,* p. 169,
calls this one of the worst cruxes
of the play.   The F reading makes
sense, and it agrees substantially with
that of the Q, uncorrected; but the
corrector of Q evidently thought that
the copy has a different reading,
even though he failed to decipher
it.   As, according to Greg, the F
reading is exceedingly feeble, and
as this sheet of Q from which F
was printed was uncorrected, it is
possible that 'parti, eyd' conceals
what Shakespeare actually wrote,
which may have been corrupted by
an actor, misheard by a scribe, misread by the corrector of Q, and
perverted by the compositor.   Such
a chain of accidents would make
Shakespeare's words irrecoverable.
But the Paphlagonian King and his
kind son are first described as "an
aged man, and a young, scarcely
come to the age of a man both

poorely arrayed."   Shakespeare
may therefore have written 'poorely
'rayd.'   This   aphetic   form   of
'arrayed' makes reasonably good
sense, and might, by the accidents
mentioned above have been variously
corrupted into 'leed' and 'eyd.'
When I proposed this emendation in
T.L.S. 3 June, 1949, Miss Janet Leeper
suggested to me that if the MS. had
had 'arayed' with the initial *a*
deleted by a vertical stroke, this
might have been read as the 'l' of
'leed.'   On the other hand, Mr.
Wilson Knight points out that Edgar
would notice that his father was being
led before he noticed his clothes, and
R. Flatter (*T.L.S.* 22 July, 1949)
points out that -*ly* represents *like*
(cf. Abbott, *447), and that *poorely
led* means "led like a poor man,"
i.e. like a beggar.   Under the
circumstances, therefore, I have
retained the F reading, though one
would be happier about it if one
knew why the Q corrector had made
the change he did.
   10-12. *World . . . age*] We are only
reconciled to growing old, and to
the consequent approach of death,
by the changes and chances of this
mortal life which make us hate it.
Montaigne has a similar thought

I have been your tenant, and your father's tenant,
These fourscore years.

Glou. Away, get thee away; good friend, be gone: 15
Thy comforts can do me no good at all;
Thee they may hurt.

Old Man.   You cannot see your way.

Glou. I have no way, and therefore want no eyes;
I stumbled when I saw. Full oft 'tis seen,
Our means secure us, and our mere defects   20
Prove our commodities. Oh! dear son Edgar,
The food of thy abused father's wrath;
Might I but live to see thee in my touch,
I'd say I had eyes again.

Old Man.   How now! Who's there?

Edg. [*Aside.*] O Gods! Who is 't can say " I am at
the worst "?   25
I am worse than e'er I was.

Old Man.   'Tis poor mad Tom.

Edg. [*Aside.*] And worse I may be yet; the worst is not
So long as we can say " This is the worst."

---

14. These . . . years] *F;* this forescore—*Q.* 17. You] *F;* Alack sir, you *Q.*
20. Our . . . us] Our mean secures us *Pope;* Our needs secure us *Singer.* 21. Oh]
F; ah *Q.* 25, 27, 37, 51, 53. S.D.] *Johnson; not in Q, F.* 25. the] *not in F 2.*
28. So] *F;* As *Q.*

(tr. Florio, i. 105): " Consider we by
the ordinary mutations, and daily
declinations which we suffer, how
Nature deprives us of the sight of
our losse and empairing: what hath
an aged man left him of his youths
vigour, and of his forepast life? "

13. *tenant*] Perret points out that
this word can mean vassal.

16. *comforts*] attempts to assist me.
Cf. III. v. 20 note.

19. *I . . . saw*] Heilman, *op. cit.*
pp. 41-64, has a commentary on
these words which express one of the
central paradoxes of the play.

20. *Our . . . us*] our resources, our
prosperity, make us careless. Cf.
Oth. I. iii. 10; and Jonson, *Poems,*
ed. Herford and Simpson, viii. 113:

" Man may securely sinne, but
safely neuer."

Others take the words to mean:
" Our mean or moderate condition
makes us secure."

20-1. *our . . . commodities*] our disadvantages prove advantages.

22. *The . . . wrath*] that on which
his anger fed, the object of his anger.

22. *abused*] deceived, deluded.

25-6. *O . . . was*] Edgar is referring to his opening words in this
scene.

27-8. *the worst . . . worst*] so long
as we can comfort ourselves with
such reflections as IV. i. 1-9 we are
not without hope, and therefore not
actually at the worst.

Old Man. Fellow, where goest?
Glou.   Is it a beggar-man?
Old Man. Madman and beggar too.   30
Glou. He has some reason, else he could not beg.
　　I' th' last night's storm I such a fellow saw,
　　Which made me think a man a worm.　My son
　　Came then into my mind; and yet my mind
　　Was then scarce friends with him.　I have heard
　　　more since: 35
　　As flies to wanton boys, are we to th' Gods;
　　They kill us for their sport.
Edg. [*Aside.*]   How should this be?
　　Bad is the trade that must play the fool to sorrow,
　　Ang'ring itself and others.　[*Aloud.*] Bless thee,
　　　master!
Glou. Is that the naked fellow?
Old Man.   Ay, my Lord.   40

---

31. He] A *Q 1.*　　32. I' th'] *F;* In the *Q.*　　36. flies] *F;* flies are *Q.*
to wanton] *F 1, 2;* to th' wanton *Q, F 3, 4.* this] their *F 2.*　　37. kill] *F;* bitt
Q 1; bit *Q 2, 3;* hit *conj. Delius.*　　38. play fool to] *F;* play the foole to *Q,*
F 3, 4; play to foole *F 2.*

---

31. *He . . . reason*] He is not entirely without intelligence.

33. *worm*] Cf. *Job,* xxv. 6: " How
much more man, a worme, euen
the sonne of man, which is but a
worme? " (Geneva).

36-7. *As . . . sport*] Willian A.
Armstrong, *T.L.S.* 14 Oct. 1949,
suggests that Shakespeare transmuted
Sidney, *Arcadia,* ed. Feuillerat, III.
x. pp. 406-7: " for els to thinke
that those powers (if there be any
such) above, are moved either by
the eloquence of our prayers, or in
a chafe by the folly of our actions;
carries as much reason as if flies
should thinke, that men take great
care which of them hums sweetest,
and which of them flies nimblest."
Cf. Introduction, p. xlii and Florio,
op. cit. VI. 29: " The gods perdie
doe reckon and racket us men as
their tennis-balles."　Montaigne

was translating from Plautus.　Empson, *op. cit.* p. 196 remarks that
" Gloucester does not say it in
passing but as a summing-up of
what Lear has repeatedly implied."
But as Chambers points out, *King
Lear,* 1940, p. 30, " the gods *are*
giving Gloucester his wish, and, if
he can but be saved from despair,
he will live to know it.　Shakespeare's
irony runs deep."

37. *How . . . be?*] This may mean,
' How did he come to forgive me? '
or ' How did he lose his eyes? '
Moberly, however, thinks that
Edgar is questioning the truth of his
father's last pessimistic remark.

38. *Bad . . . trade*] Craig explains
" He treads an evil path," *trade*
being a variant of *tread.* Cf. *Rich. II.*
III. iii. 156.　But it is more likely to
mean business, occupation. Edgar
has to act as a Fool to his sorrowing
father.

Glou. Then, prithee, get thee away.   If, for my sake,
     Thou wilt o'ertake us, hence a mile or twain,
     I' th' way toward Dover, do it for ancient love;
     And bring some covering for this naked soul,
     Which I'll entreat to lead me.

Old Man.   Alack, sir! he is mad.   45
Glou. 'Tis the times' plague, when madmen lead the blind.
     Do as I bid thee, or rather do thy pleasure;
     Above the rest, be gone.

Old Man. I'll bring him the best 'parel that I have,
     Come on't what will.   [*Exit.*

Glou.   Sirrah, naked fellow,—   50
Edg. Poor Tom's a-cold.   [*Aside.*] I cannot daub it further.
Glou. Come hither, fellow.
Edg. [*Aside.*] And yet I must.   Bless thy sweet eyes,
     they bleed.
Glou. Know'st thou the way to Dover?
Edg. Both stile and gate, horse-way and foot-path.   55
     Poor Tom hath been scar'd out of his good wits:
     bless thee, good man's son, from the foul fiend!
     Five fiends have been in poor Tom at once;
     as Obidicut, of lust; Hoberdidance, prince of

41. Then, prithee] *Q; not in F.*   away] *F;* gon *Q.*   42. hence] *F;* here *Q.*
43. toward] to *Q 2, 3;* towards *Capell.*   45. Which] *F;* Who *Q.*   49.
'parel] *Rowe;* Parrell *Q, F.*   50. S.D.] *F; not in Q.*   51. a-cold] *Rowe;*
a cold *Q, F.*   daub] *F;* dance *Q.*   further] *F;* farther *Q.*   53. And . . .
must] *F; not in Q.*   56. scar'd] *F 3, 4;* scard *Q;* scarr'd *F 1, 2;* scarred
Schmidt.   57. thee . . . son] *F;* the good man *Q.*   58-63. Five . . . master]
Q; not in F.   59. as . . . lust] *Hudson (conj. S. Walker);* of lust, as
Obidicut *Q.*   Hoberdidance] Hobbididence *Q.*

46. *'Tis . . . blind*] Gloucester
uses his own situation as a symbol:
when the rulers are mad, and the
people blind.
48. *the rest*] all.
49. *'parel*] apparel. Cf. Marlowe,
The Jew of Malta, IV. iv. (1830-1).
"Here's goodly 'parrell, is there
not?"
51. *daub it further*] dissemble any
more.   Cf. *Rich. III.* III. v. 29.
The figure is taken from plastering
mortar. Cf. II. ii. 66.
55. *horse-way*] bridle-path.   Cf.
T. Heywood, *A Maydenhead Well Lost,*

(*Works,* ed. Pearson, 1874, iv. 121):
"I have one for the horse-way,
another for the foot-way, and a
third for the turning-stile."
58. *Five fiends*] Percy notes a
Harsnett parallel.   Cf. Appendix,
p. 254.
59. *as . . . lust*] I have adopted
Hudson's arrangement of these
words, following S. Walker (*Crit.
Exam.* ii. 249).
59. *Obidicut*] a corruption of
Harsnett's Hoberdicut.   See Appendix, p. 255, for this and the other
devils mentioned here.

dumbness; Mahu, of stealing; Modo, of murder; 60
Flibbertigibbet, of mopping and mowing; who
since possesses chambermaids and waiting-women.
So, bless thee, master!

Glou. Here, take this purse, thou whom the heav'ns'
plagues
Have humbled to all strokes: that I am wretched 65
Makes thee the happier: Heavens, deal so still!
Let the superfluous and lust-dieted man,
That slaves your ordinance, that will not see
Because he does not feel, feel your power quickly;

61. Flibbertigibbet] *Pope;* Stiberdegebit *Q.* mopping and mowing] *Theobald;* Mobing, & Mohing *Q;* moping and Mowing *Pope;* mobbing and mowing *Jennens.* 67. lust-dieted] lust-dieting *Capell.* 68. slaves] *F;* stands *Q.* 69. does] doth *Q 2, 3.*

61. *mopping and mowing*] Malone cited a Harsnett parallel. See Appendix, p. 256. Cf. *Temp.* IV. i. 47 and II. ii. 9 ff. The second of these passages also contains an echo from Harsnett. The phrase means " grimacing and making faces," *mow* being derived from Fr. *moue.* Huloet, *Dictionary,* 1572, defines ' mow ' or ' to make a mow ': " It seemeth a word derived of the thing, for we cannot pronounce the word mowe but we almost make a mowe."

61-2. *who . . . waiting-women*] Theobald pointed out the allusion to Sara and Friswood Williams and Anne Smith, three chambermaids in the family of Edmund Peckham who were supposed to be possessed, and whose examination is reported by Harsnett.

65. *Have . . . strokes*] have brought so low as to accept humbly the bitterest strokes of Fortune.

66-71. *Heavens . . . enough*] Cf. III. iv. 33 ff.

67. *superfluous*] pampered, having too much. Cf. II. iv. 267.

67. *lust-dieted*] whose desires are fed to the full, feeding gluttonously.

But Gloucester may be thinking specifically of his own adultery.

68. *That . . . ordinance*] " who, instead of paying the deference and submission due to your ordinance, treats it as his slave, by making it subservient to his views of pleasure and interest, and trampling on and spurning it whenever it ceases to be of service to him in either of these respects " (Heath). Steevens gives examples of ' slaves ' for ' enslaves ' from Massinger, *A New Way to Pay Old Debts,* IV. iii. &c. Wright gives others. J. Sledd, however, *M.L.N.* 1940, p. 595, ingeniously suggests that *slaves* is used in the sense of *tears away or rends* from O.E.—*slæfan.* He does not give any Elizabethan parallels. Shakespeare uses *sliver* in the next scene. IV. ii. 34, and it is just possible that he was quibbling here. Warburton suggested *braves.* Moberly refers to the parable of Dives and Lazarus, but the duty of almsgiving is not exclusively Christian.

69. *feel*] Craig takes this to mean ' suffer pain '; but it may mean rather ' feel sympathy.' The man is blind and without wisdom because he does not put himself in the place of his poor neighbours.

So distribution should undo excess,   70
And each man have enough.   Dost thou know Dover?
Edg. Ay, master.
Glou. There is a cliff, whose high and bending head
Looks fearfully in the confined deep;
Bring me but to the very brim of it,   75
And I'll repair the misery thou dost bear
With something rich about me; from that place
I shall no leading need.
Edg.   Give me thy arm:
Poor Tom shall lead thee.   [*Exeunt.*

70. undo] *F;* vnder *Q.*   74. fearfully] *F;* firmely *Q.*   in] on *Rowe.*
78. I shall] Shall I *Q 2, 3.*   leading] lending *F 2, 4, Rowe.*   79. S.D.]
F; not in Q.

SCENE II.—[*Before the Duke of Albany's Palace.*]

Enter GONERIL *and* EDMUND.

Gon. Welcome, my Lord; I marvel our mild husband
Not met us on the way.

Enter OSWALD.

                              Now, where's your master?
Osw. Madam, within; but never man so chang'd.
I told him of the army that was landed;
He smil'd at it: I told him you were coming;   5

Scene II
    Before . . . Palace] *Capell, subst.; not in Q, F.*   S.D.] *Theobald;*
Enter Goneril and Bastard Q; Enter Goneril, Bastard, and Steward F.   2. S.D.]
Theobald, subst.; not in F; Enter Steward (after master) Q.

73. *cliff*] Gloucester wants to leap off Dover Cliff partly because the exigencies of the plot demand that he should meet Lear who has gone to Dover.   But cf. Introduction, p. xlix.

73. *bending*] beetling.

74. *fearfully*] so as to inspire terror in one who looks over the edge (Kittredge).   But the cliff is personified.

74. *in*] into.   Malone suggests that Shakespeare thought of the sea as a mirror.

74. *confined*] restrained, by the cliffs. Cf. *K.J.* ii. i. 23-4. Capell suggests that Shakespeare was thinking of the narrow Straits of Dover confined on both sides by the land.

Scene II

1. *welcome*] i.e. to my palace.

2. *on the way*] i.e. from Gloucester's castle.

His answer was "The worse": of Gloucester's
     treachery,
And of the loyal service of his son,
When I inform'd him, then he call'd me sot,
And told me I had turn'd the wrong side out:
What most he should dislike seems pleasant to
     him;   10
What like, offensive.

Gon. [*To Edmund.*]   Then shall you go no further.
It is the cowish terror of his spirit
That dares not undertake; he'll not feel wrongs
Which tie him to an answer.   Our wishes on the way
May prove effects.   Back, Edmund, to my brother;   15
Hasten his musters and conduct his powers:
I must change arms at home, and give the distaff

---

10. most ... dislike] *F;* hee should most desire *Q.*   11. S.D.] *Hanmer; not in
Q, F.*   12. cowish] *Q, F;* currish *conj. Wright.*   terror] *F;* curre *Q uncorr.,*
Q 2, 3; terrer *Q corr.*   15. Edmund] Edgar *Q 1.*   17. arms] *Q;* names *F.*

---

8. *sot*] fool.

9. *turn'd . . . out*] put a wrong
complexion on the matter, since
Gloucester was not a traitor, nor
Edmund loyal. Cf. *M.A.* III. i. 68.

12. *cowish*] cowardly.   *N.E.D.*
cites Rem, *Lawless Love, Vision of
Rawe Devise,* 1579: "Amid the
crewe of cowish carped knights."
Cotgrave defines *Couard,* "a coward,
a dastard, a cow."   Wright conjectures *currish.* Cf. *M.V.* IV. i. 292.
The word is used by Armin, *op. cit.*
p. 52, and it is also to be found
in Harsnett, according to Craig.
This seems to me very possible.
The uncorrected Q reading is
'cowish curre.'   If the copy had
read 'cowish terrer,' with a marginal
correction 'curr,' the compositor
might easily have substituted 'curr'
for 'terrer' instead of for 'cow.'
The corrector, seeing that something
was wrong, might have restored
'terrer' without realising the in-
tentions of the writer. The initial
mistake of 'cowish' might be due

to a mishearing.   The F was
printed from a Q of which this sheet
was uncorrected, but though the
correction of *cowish* might have been
overlooked in preparing the copy
for F, it is safer to retain *cowish* than
to emend it.

13. *undertake*] show enterprise or
courage, or assume responsibility.

13-14. *he'll . . . answer*] he will
ignore insults which, if he noticed,
he would be obliged to resent.

13. *feel*] notice, appear to notice.

14. *answer*] retaliation. Cf. *Cym.*
v. iii. 79.

14. *our . . . way*] our hopes, as
we journeyed here, that we should
be able to consummate our love, or
get rid of my husband.

15. *may . . . effects*] may be fulfilled.

17. *change*] exchange.

17. *arms*] the insignia of our sexes,
the sword and the distaff.   Cf.
Cymb. v. iii. 32-4.   Budd, *R.E.S.,*
1935, p. 427, compares these lines

Into my husband's hands.   This trusty servant
Shall pass between us; ere long you are like to hear,
If you dare venture in your own behalf,   20
A mistress's command.   Wear this; spare speech;
                                        [*Giving a favour.*
Decline your head: this kiss, if it durst speak,
Would stretch thy spirits up into the air.
Conceive, and fare thee well.
Edm. Yours in the ranks of death.
Gon.   My most dear Gloucester!   25
                                        [*Exit Edmund.*
Oh! the difference of man and man.
To thee a woman's services are due:
My Fool usurps my body.
Osw.   Madam, here comes my Lord.
                                        [*Exit.*

Albany. — wisdom of fools

21. command] Q *corr.*, F; coward Q *uncorr.*, Q *2, 3.* S.D.] *Johnson; Gives him a ring Hanmer; Puts on a chaine Collier MS.; not in Q, F.*   24. fare thee] F; far you Q *1;* farye Q *2, 3.*   25. S.D.] *Rowe; Exit (after death) F: not in Q.*   26. O . . . man] F; *not in Q.*   difference] F; strange difference *Pope.*   27. a] *not in Q uncorr.*, Q *2, 3.*   28. My . . . body] F; My foote vsurps my body Q *uncorr.;* A foole vsurps my bed Q *corr.;* My foote vsurps my head Q *2, 3;* My fool . . . bed *Malone.*

from *The Monk's Prologue* in Chaucer's
Canterbury Tales:
   " When she comth hoom, she
      rampeth in my face,
   And cryeth, ' false coward, wreek
      thy wyf!
   By *corpus* bones! I wol have thy
      knyf,
   And thou shalt have my distaf
      and go spinne! '
   Fro day to night right thus she
      wol biginne;—
   ' Allas! ' she seith, ' that ever I
      was shape
   To wedde a milksop or a coward
      ape,
   That wol be overlad with every
      wight! ' "
   19. *like*] likely.
   21. *A . . . command*] Goneril is
quibbling on the word ' mistress.'
She is presumably going to ask
Edmund to murder Albany.

22. *Decline . . . head*] Either for
her to kiss him, or to put a chain
round his neck.
23. *Would . . . air*] Heilman,
op. cit. p. 314, suggests that this and
the following lines contain " several
kinds of sexual innuendo." Goneril
puns on *spirits* and *conceive*, and
Edmund puns on *death*, as Lear does
IV. vi. 200.
28. *My . . . body*] Greg, *Variants*,
p. 171, argues that it is more likely
that the compositor of the Q should
have misread ' bed ' as ' body,'
than that the reader should have
miscorrected ' body ' to ' bed.' On
these grounds he concludes that what
the copy actually read was ' My
foole vsurps my bed.'   Duthie,
however, thinks that the F reading
is the more forceful, and that the
Q corrector may have altered ' body '
by mistake, taking the ' o ' for an

Enter ALBANY.

Gon. I have been worth the whistle.

Alb.　　　　　　　　　　O Goneril!
　　You are not worth the dust which the rude wind　　30
　　Blows in your face.　I fear your disposition:
　　That nature, which contemns it origin,
　　Cannot be border'd certain in itself;
　　She that herself will sliver and disbranch
　　From her material sap, perforce must wither　　35
　　And come to deadly use.

Gon. No more;　the text is foolish.

Alb. Wisdom and goodness to the vile seem vile;
　　Filths savour but themselves.　What have you
　　　done?
　　Tigers, not daughters, what have you perform'd?　　40
　　A father, and a gracious aged man,
　　Whose reverence even the head-lugg'd bear would
　　　lick,

29. S.D.] *Q; not in F.*　　whistle] *F, Q uncorr., Q 2, 3;* whistling *Q corr.*
30. rude] *not in Q 2, 3.*　31-50 I . . . deep] *Q; not in F.*　32. it] *Q uncorr.,*
Q 2; ith *Q corr.;* its *Q 3.*　35. material] *Q;* maternal *Theobald.*　42.
even] *Q 1; not in Q 2, 3.*

'e' and the 'y' for a tail to the 'd.'　There is a strong case, textually, for 'bed'; but 'body' seems to me preferable on other grounds.

29. *worth . . . whistle*] The usual form of the proverb, "It is a poore dog that is not worth the whistling," led to the Q corruption.　Bransom, *The Tragedy of King Lear,* p. 140, remarks: "Once, when he was in love with her, he would have come on the road to meet her."

31. *fear*] have fears concerning.

32. *it*] its.

33. *Cannot . . . itself*] cannot be kept within fixed bounds, cannot be trusted not to break the pale.　Cf. IV. vi. 274.

34. *sliver*] tear off.　Cf. *Macb.* IV. i. 28.

34. *disbranch*] sever, cut off.

35. *material*] forming the sub-stance of a thing, nourishing, essential, necessary.

35. *perforce . . . wither*] Cf. *Oth.* v. ii. 15.　Perrett compares *Leir,* 1242-3:
　　"If so the stocke be dryed with disdayne,
　　Withered and sere the branch must needes remaine."
Cf. *also Rich. III.* II. ii. 41.

36. *come . . . use*] be used as a faggot for the burning.　See *Hebrews,* vi. 8.

37. *text*] on which you have been preaching.　Craig takes it to mean 'quotation.'

39. *Filths . . . themselves*] To the filthy all things taste filthy.　Kittredge cites: *Pravis omnia prava.*　Cf. also *Titus,* i. 15.

42. *head-lugg'd*] tugged by the head.　Wright quotes a Harsnett parallel.　See Appendix, p. 255. Cf. also *1 Hen. IV.* I. ii. 83.

Most barbarous, most degenerate! have you madded.
Could my good brother suffer you to do it?
A man, a prince, by him so benefited!   45
If that the heavens do not their visible spirits
Send quickly down to tame these vilde offences,
It will come,
Humanity must perforce prey on itself,
Like monsters of the deep.

45. benefited] *Q corr.;* beneflicted *Q uncorr., Q 2, 3.*   47. Send . . . come]
So Malone; One line in Q.   these] *Jennens (conj. Heath);* the *Q uncorr.,*
Q 2, 3; this *Q corr.*   vilde] *Q 2, 3;* vild *Q 1;* wild *Collier;* vile *Pope.*
49. Humanity] *Q corr.;* Humanly *Q uncorr., Q 2, 3.*

43. *madded*] driven mad.
46. *visible*] in visible form (Kitt-redge). Cf. *Leir*, 1651-2:
"How canst thou suffer such
    outragius acts
To be committed without iust
    reuenge?"
47. *tame . . . vilde*] The old spelling of 'vile' here preserved suggests there may be a quibble intended on *vilde* and *wild*, the opposite of tame.
47. *offences*] offenders; the abstract for the concrete.
48. *It . . . come*] This effective short line allows room for a dramatic pause before the climax of Albany's speech.
49-50. *Humanity . . . deep*] Cf. the Shakespearian addition to *Sir Thomas More* (86-7):
"men like ravenous fishes
Would feed on one another."
and *T.C.* I. iii. 123-4:
"Must make perforce an universal
    prey,
And last eat up himself."
There are many parallels in contemporary and preceding literature. F. P. Wilson, *Shakespeare Survey 3*, p. 20, refers to *Everyman*, Prologue; *Pride of Life*, 361-2; and Ponet, *Short Treatise on Politic Power*, 1556, p. 10: Ponet argues that if there were no acceptance of authority, "the rich would oppress the poor, and the poor seek the destruction of the rich, to have that he had: the

mighty would destroy the weak, and as *Theodoretus* sayeth, the great fish eat up the small, and the weak seek revenge on the mighty; and so one seeking the others destruction all at length should be undone and come to destruction." The idea goes back even beyond Theodoretus. See Hesiod, *Works and Days*, in a passage thus translated by George Chapman, i. 434-7:
"Fish, fowl, and savage beasts,
    (whose law is power)
Jove lets each other mutually
    devour,
Because they lack the equity he
    gives
To govern men, as far best for
    their lives."
The following references may be added: Bestiary in Arundel MS. 292, ed. R. Morris, 1872, 505-16; Whitney, *Emblems*, p. 52: "The mightie fishe deuowres the little frie"; Christopher Dawson, *The Making of Europe*, 1939, p. 267 (citing an example from A.D. 909); and the well-known drawing by Pieter Bruegel. But it should be noted that whereas most of these writers compare the rich to big fish and the poor to little fish, Shakespeare suggests that the violation of order would lead to actual cannibalism. The more commonplace comparison is to be found in a doubtful scene in *Pericles*, II. i. 29-34.

Gon.   Milk-liver'd man!   50
That bear'st a cheek for blows, a head for wrongs;
Who hast not in thy brows an eye discerning
Thine honour from thy suffering; that not know'st
Fools do those villains pity who are punish'd   54
Ere they have done their mischief.   Where's thy drum;
France spreads his banners in our noiseless land,
With plumed helm thy state begins to threat,

51. bear'st] *F;* bearest *Q.*   for wrongs] of wrongs *F 3, 4.*   52. eye discerning] *Rowe;* eye-discerning *F;* eye deseruing *Q.*   53-9. that . . . so] *Q;* not in *F.*   54. those] *Q 1;* these *Q 2, 3.*   56. noiseless] *Q corr.;* noystles *Q; uncorr.*   57. thy . . . threat] *Jennens;* thy slayer begin threats *Q uncorr.;* thy state begins thereat *Q corr.;* thy slaier begins threats *Q 2;* thy slayer begins his threats *Theobald;* the slayer begins threats *Hanmer;* this Lear begins threats *conj. Leo;* his state begins therat *Duthie (conj. Greg).*   58. Whil'st] *Q corr.;* Whil's *Q uncorr., Q 2, 3;* while *Capell.*   sits] *Q;* sit'st *Theobald.*   cries] *Q;* cry'st *Theobald.*

50. *Milk-liver'd]* white-livered, cowardly.
51. *a cheek for blows]* Noble compares *Matt.* v. 39.
52-3. *an . . . suffering]* an eye to distinguish between what can be honourably borne and what should be resented.
54-5. *Fools . . . mischief]* Apparently she refers to Lear, as the news of Gloucester's punishment has not yet arrived and she would not expect her husband to have heard of it. The implication is that Lear is a villain because he is in league with France. The French invasion is the *wrong* Albany is suffering meekly; and Goneril returns to the subject after referring to Lear's punishment. Malone, however, thinks that Goneril is referring not to Lear, but to the King of France; and Furness and Kittredge believe that she means that only fools will pity Albany if he is defeated or dethroned without striking a blow. This last interpretation seems to me highly unlikely, since Goneril harps on Albany's feebleness and foolishness, not on his villainy; and she regards the repelling of the invader not as mischief but as a patriotic duty.   I think

villains can scarcely apply to the King of France, since he has not been punished, though it might conceivably mean that he is about to be defeated.
56. *noiseless]* because the drum has not sounded.
57. *thy . . . threat]* This is Jennens' reading.   It makes sense, though Shakespeare is unlikely to have written it.   Greg. *Variants,* p. 174, points out that there would certainly appear to have been no ' to ' in the copy.   The letters ' reat ' are common to both uncorrected and corrected copies of *Q;* but Greg adds "what reading may be concealed in the last four letters I am at a loss to imagine."   Duthie conjectures ' road ' (i.e. inroad) but this is not very happy.   Both Greg and Duthie suggest ' his ' for ' thy,' because, in the absence of ' And,' the line requires a new subject; but we cannot assume this, and ' state ' would be awkwardly applied to the French army.   Possibly a line has dropped out.   But ' threat ' could easily be misread or miswritten as ' thereat ' and the word ' to ' may have been omitted by the scribe responsible for the copy.

Whil'st thou, a moral fool, sits still, and cries
" Alack! why does he so? "

Alb.   See thyself, devil!
Proper deformity shows not in the fiend   60
So horrid as in woman.

Gon.   O vain fool!

Alb. Thou changed and self-cover'd thing, for shame,
Be-monster not thy feature.   Were 't my fitness
To let these hands obey my blood,
They are apt enough to dislocate and tear   65
Thy flesh and bones; howe'er thou art a fiend,
A woman's shape doth shield thee.

Gon. Marry, your manhood—mew!

60. deformity] deformiry *Q 2, 3*.   shows] seemes *Q uncorr., F*.   62-9.
Thou . . . news] *Q: not in F*.   62. self-cover'd] *Q;* self-converted *Theobald;*
false-cover'd *Singer;* self-discover'd *conj. Cartwright;* self-colour'd *Moberly;* sex-
cover'd *Hudson (conj. Crosby)*.   64. hands] hands of mine *conj. Steevens*.
65. dislocate] *Q 3;* dislecate *Q 1, 2*.   68.—mew!] *Cambridge (conj. Daniel)*
mew— *Q corr.;* now— *Q uncorr., Q 2, 3*.   S.D.] *F (after 61); Enter a*
Gentleman (after 69) Q 1; after 68 Q 2, 3.

58. *moral*] moralizing.

60-1. *Proper . . . woman*] Deformity,
appropriate to the fiend, seems more
horrible in a woman, because of its
inappropriateness.   Delius explains
" deformity which conceals itself
under a pleasing, fair outside."
Cf. ' proper-false ' *T.N.* II. ii. 30.
Albany may be referring to moral
deformity, or to Goneril's face distorted by evil passions.   Cf. *Leir*,
2582, " Thou fiend in likenesse of a
humane creature."

62. *changed*] transformed.

62. *self-cover'd*] Various explanations: (i) having the real self
concealed by a woman's shape;
(ii) having assumed the appearance
of a fiend, so concealing your
woman's self; (iii) hidden from
thyself (Kinnear, who compares
A.C. II. ii. 90-1 and *Luc.* 633 ff.);
(iv) dressed in one's native semblance,
Goneril having betrayed her wickedness by changing countenance
(Schmidt).   There are also numerous
conjectural emendations (cf. colla-

tions above), none of which need
detain us.   I incline to the second
of these explanations.   Goneril
has bemonstered her appearance by
allowing the fiendish passions of her
self to show on her countenance.

63. *feature*] appearance, not merely
her face.   Cf. *Leir*, 2581:
" Nay, peace thou monster, shame
    vnto thy sexe."

63. *Were't . . . fitness*] if it were
proper for me.

64. *hands*] Steevens' conjecture is
attractive, but Abbott *508 argues
that a foot may be omitted from a
line when there is any marked pause
arising from emotion.

64. *blood*] instinct, passion.

65. *apt*] ready.

66. *howe'er*] but although.

68. *mew!*] The word is often used
as an interjection; and here Goneril,
by imitating a cat's noise, suggests
that Albany is effeminate.   Craig
adopted this reading, following a
conjecture by Daniel.   Kittredge,
Duthie, and others retain the Q

Enter a Messenger.

Alb. What news?

Mess. O! my good Lord, the Duke of Cornwall's dead;　70
　　　Slain by his servant, going to put out
　　　The other eye of Gloucester.

Alb.　　　　　　　　　　Gloucester's eyes!

Mess. A servant that he bred, thrill'd with remorse, *compassion*
　　　Oppos'd against the act, bending his sword *directing*
　　　To his great master; who, thereat enrag'd,　75
　　　Flew on him, and amongst them fell'd him dead;
　　　But not without that harmful stroke, which since
　　　Hath pluck'd him after.

Alb.　　　　　　　This shows you are above,
　　　You justicers, that these our nether crimes
　　　So speedily can venge!　But, O poor Gloucester!　80
　　　Lost he his other eye?

Mess.　　　　　　　Both, both, my Lord.
　　　This letter, Madam, craves a speedy answer;
　　　'Tis from your sister.　　　　　　[*Presents a letter.*

Gon. [*Aside.*]　　　　　　One way I like this well;
　　　But being widow, and my Gloucester with her,
　　　May all the building in my fancy pluck　85
　　　Upon my hateful life: another way,

69. news?] newes. *Q 1.*　　72. eyes!] eyes? *Q*; eyes. *F.*　　73. thrill'd]
F; thrald *Q*.　　75. thereat enrag'd] *Q*; threat-enrag'd *F.*　　79. You
justicers] *Q corr.*; your Iustices *Q uncorr.*, *Q 2, 3*; You Iustices *F.*　　83.
S.D.　*Presents a letter*] Collier *MS.*, *subst.*; not in *Q, F.*　　S.D.
Aside] Johnson; not in *Q, F.*　　85. in] *F*; on *Q*; of *Capell.*

reading. Kittredge explains: " Your
valour seems to be feeble. . . .
Shut it up in the mews awhile, as
we confine an ailing falcon that
requires diet and medicine." Ridley,
who also retains the Q reading
" your manhood mew," interprets:
" If all that is troubling you is the
difference in sex, put off your manhood (' mew ' = moult, shed) and
I shall be happy to meet you on
equal terms."

　　73. *thrill'd*] excited, moved, pierced.

73. *remorse*] compassion.

74. *bending*] directing.

75. *to*] against.

76. *fell'd*] they felled.

79. *justicers*] judges. Cf. IV. ii. 46.

79. *nether crimes*] crimes committed
here below.

85. *building . . . fancy*] castles in the
air. Cf. *Cor.* II. i. 216.

86. *hateful*] her life will be hateful
to her, because her plans for the
future have been ruined.

    The news is not so tart. [*Aloud.*] I'll read, and
        answer.   [*Exit.*
Alb. Where was his son when they did take his eyes?
Mess. Come with my Lady hither.
Alb.   He is not here.
Mess. No, my good Lord; I met him back again.   90
Alb. Knows he the wickedness?
Mess. Ay, my good Lord; 'twas he inform'd against him,
    And quit the house on purpose that their punishment
    Might have the freer course.
Alb.   Gloucester, I live
To thank thee for the love thou show'dst the king,   95
And to revenge thine eyes.   Come hither, friend:
Tell me what more thou know'st.   [*Exeunt.*

87. tart] *F;* tooke *Q.*   S.D. *Aloud*] *not in Q, F.*   S.D. *Exit*]
Q; not in F.   95. show'dst] *F;* shewdest *Q.*   96. thine] *F;* thy *Q.*
97. know'st] *F;* knowest *Q.*   S.D.] *F; Exit Q.*

SCENE III.—[*The French Camp near Dover.*]

Enter KENT *and a Gentleman.*

Kent. Why the King of France is so suddenly gone
    back know you no reason?
Gent. Something he left imperfect in the state, which
    since his coming forth is thought of; which
    imports to the kingdom so much fear and danger   5

Scene III

The . . . Dover] Steevens; *Dover* Theobald; *not in Q. F.*   1-56. Why
. . . *with me*] *Q; not in F.*   2. no] *Q 1;* the *Q 2, 3.*

90. *back*] on his way back.

Scene III

3-4. *Something . . . of*] Greg,
M.L.R., 1940, p. 445, comments:
"The public explanation was, no
doubt, on these lines, but (unless
Shakespeare is being more perfunc-
tory than we have any right to
assume) we can hardly be intended
to take it at its face value.   The real

reason . . . was that Cordelia succeeded in persuading her husband
to abandon his purpose of wresting
a portion of the kingdom for himself
and retire to his own land, thus
leaving her free to use her army in
defence of her father, should the
occasion arise."   Shakespeare had
to be wary in writing of a foreign
invasion.
    5. *imports*] portends. Cf. *Rich. III.*
III. vii. 68.

that his personal return was most requir'd and
necessary.

Kent. Who hath he left behind him general?

Gent. The Marshal of France, Monsieur La Far.

Kent. Did your letters pierce the queen to any demon-   10
stration of grief?

Gent. Ay, sir; she took them, read them in my presence;
And now and then an ample tear trill'd down
Her delicate cheek; it seem'd she was a queen
Over her passion; who, most rebel-like,   15
Sought to be king o'er her.

Kent.   O! then it mov'd her.

Gent. Not to a rage; patience and sorrow strove
Who should express her goodliest.   You have seen
Sunshine and rain at once; her smile and tears
Were like, a better way; those happy smilets   20

---

11. grief?] *Q 2;* griefe. *Q 1.*   12. sir] *Theobald;* say *Q.*   15. Over]
ore *Q 2, 3.*   17. a rage] rage *Q 3.*   strove] *Pope;* streme *Q.*   20. like,]
Duthie; like; *Hudson;* like *Q;* lik't *conj. Daniel.*   better way] wetter May
Theobald (Warburton); better day *Steevens (conj. Theobald);* better May
Malone (conj. Tollet).

---

10. *pierce*] cf. *thrill'd,* IV. ii. 73.

13. *trill'd*] trickled.

14. *delicate*] lovely.   Cf. *Oth.* II. iii.
20.

15. *passion*] emotion.

15. *rebel-like*] Perrett fancifully
suggests that Shakespeare was influenced by the rebellion of Cordelia's
nephews described in several of his
sources.

17. *patience*] self-control.

18. *express . . . goodliest*] give her the
most beautiful expression (Kittredge).

18-25. *You . . . it*] J. F. Danby
compares Sidney, *Arcadia* (ed.
Feuillerat), p. 376: " her teares
came dropping downe like raine in
Sunshine, and she not taking heede
to wipe the teares, they ranne downe
upon her cheekes, and lips, as upon
Cherries which the dropping tree
bedeweth."   On the next page
Cecropia tells Philoclea to " Take
a glasse, and see whether these
tears become your eies: although,

I must confesse, those eies are able
to make tears comely."   Here we
have the same balancing of opposites,
the same image of sunshine and rain
at once, the same reference to the
weeper's unconsciousness of her
tears, and the same suggestion that
she makes tears seem comely.   There
may even be an echo of the cherries
in the epithet 'ripe,' commonplace though it is.   Steevens quoted
part of the Sidney passage and also
Henry Wotton, *A Courtlie Contro-
versie of Cupid's Cautels,* 1578, p. 289:
" who hath viewed in the spring time,
raine and sunne-shine in one moment,
might beholde the troubled countenance of the gentlewoman, after she
had read and over-read the letters."

20. *a better way*] but after a better
fashion.   Daniel's emendation would
give the same meaning; but it is not
necessary, and the numerous other
conjectures are to be deplored.

20. *smilets*] little smiles.

[Handwritten marginalia:] Note the contrast between this language and the rest of the play. Here there are references to time & delicate emotions elsewhere where the emotions are far more earthy & bestial. There are images of jewels rather than beasts

The effect is rather naïve perhaps

cf.. W.H. Auden's Quote

That play'd on her ripe lip seem'd not to know
What guests were in her eyes; which parted thence,
As pearls from diamonds dropp'd.   In brief,
Sorrow would be a rarity most belov'd,
If all could so become it.

weak
sentimental
emotion

Kent.   Made she no verbal question?   25
Gent. Faith, once or twice she heav'd the name of "father"
Pantingly forth, as if it press'd her heart;
Cried " Sisters! sisters!   Shame of ladies! sisters!
Kent! father! sisters!   What? i' th' storm! i' th'
night?
Let pity not be believ'd! "   There she shook   30

---

21. seem'd.] *Pope;* seeme *Q.*   23. dropp'd.] dropt; *Q 2;* dropt *Q 1.*   25.
question?] *Q 2;* question. *Q 1.*   30. not] ne'er *Pope.*   pity] it *Capell.*
be believ'd] (be beleeft) *Q;* believe it *Pope, Jennens.*   There] *Q;* Then *Pope.*
32. clamour moisten'd] *Capell;* clamour moisten'd her *Q;* clamour-moisten'd
conj. S. Walker.

---

21. *seem'd*] Pope's emendation is
probably right, though Shakespeare
elsewhere drops into the historic
present.

22. *which*] i.e. the guests.

23. *pearls . . . dropp'd*] Shakespeare
often calls tears ' pearls,' and once
refers to eyes as diamonds.   Cf.
M.W. iii. iii. 58.   The implication
here is that Cordelia's eyes were
shining with tears, as well as naturally
beautiful.

25. *If . . . it*] if it could be as
becoming to others as to her.

25. *Made . . . question?*] Did she
say nothing, apart from what you
gathered from her tears?

25. *question*] speech.

26. *heav'd*] uttered with difficulty.

30. *believed*] believed to exist.
One would like to accept Jennens'
emendation.

30. *There*] Pope's emendation,
' then,' is open to the objection
that it weakens the force of the
same word two lines later.   ' There '
means ' at that point.'

30-2. *There . . . moisten'd*] The
general meaning of this passage is
that Cordelia's emotion was calmed

by a flood of tears: that seems to
be the one point on which almost all
critics are agreed.   (Walker and
Furness take " her . . . moisten'd "
to mean " her heavenly and wet-
with-wailing eyes ".)   The Q reading
is clumsy, as the ' her ' is hyper-
metrical, would involve the assumption that ' clamour ' means tears,
and not outcry, and was probably
copied by mistake from the previous
line.   We can discard ' clamour-
motion'd,'   ' clamour   soften'd,'
' clammer'd moisture ' and ' dolour
master'd ' (R. G. Brown, *T.L.S.* 23
Dec. 1944).   We are left with the
question of whether to hyphen
clamour moisten'd or not.   With the
hyphen we can take it to mean
" having her emotion calmed by a
flood of tears, as the storm is assuaged
by a shower of rain " (Craig) or
" with her cheeks wet with her
outburst of sorrow " (White).   If
the hyphen is omitted the phrase
can mean " exclamations moistened
with tears " (Heath, who takes the
phrase as an ablative absolute); or
or " moistened clamour," i.e. she
drowned her exclamations with

The holy water from her heavenly eyes,
And clamour moisten'd, then away she started
To deal with grief alone.

Kent.   It is the stars,
The stars above us, govern our conditions;
Else one self mate and make could not beget   35
Such different issues.   You spoke not with her since?

Gent. No.

Kent. Was this before the king return'd?

Gent.   No, since.

Kent. Well, sir, the poor distressed Lear's i' th' town;
Who sometime, in his better tune, remembers *moments of*   40
What we are come about, and by no means *sanity*
Will yield to see his daughter.

Gent.   Why, good sir?

Kent. A sovereign shame so elbows him: his own un-
     kindness,
That stripp'd her from his benediction, turn'd her *Lear's*
To foreign casualties, gave her dear rights *penitence*   45
fierce To his dog-hearted daughters, these things sting
His mind so venomously that burning shame
Detains him from Cordelia.

Gent.   Alack! poor gentleman.

Kent. Of Albany's and Cornwall's powers you heard not?

Gent. 'Tis so, they are afoot. *on the march*   50

35. and make] *Q 1; and mate Q 2, 3.*   49. not?] *Q 2;* not *Q 1.*

tears (Capell). The last explanation is probably the most satisfactory. I would only add that the sprinkling of the holy water seems to consecrate the clamour.   Kittredge suggests that the Gentleman is using the elegant and artificial language expected of courtiers.

34. *conditions*] characters.
35. *one self*] one and the same.
35. *make*] partner. Cf. Lyly, *Mother Bombie,* III. iv. 15; and *Sonnets,* ix. 4.
40. *sometime*] sometimes.
40. *better tune*] lucid intervals. Cf. IV. vii. 16 and *Ham.* III. i. 166.
43. *sovereign*] over-mastering.

43. *elbows him*] stands at his elbow and reminds him of the past (Wright); forcibly thrusts him back. . . . His compunction for his cruelty towards his child mastering his eagerness to approach her (Craig). The second of these interpretations is preferable: it fits in with the iterative image of the play.

44. *turn'd*] turned out.
45. *casualties*] chances.   Cf. *Per.* v. i. 94.
46. *dog-hearted*] fierce, pitiless. Cf. *Cor.* I. i. 28; *Oth.* v. ii. 361.
49. *powers*] armies.
50. *afoot*] on the march.

Kent. Well, sir, I'll bring you to our master Lear,
And leave you to attend him. Some dear cause *important reason*
Will in concealment wrap me up awhile;
When I am known aright, you shall not grieve
Lending me this acquaintance. I pray you,   55
Go along with me.   [*Exeunt.*

56. S.D.] *Pope;* Exit Q.

SCENE IV.—[*The Same.*]

Enter, with drum and colours, CORDELIA, *Doctor,*
and Soldiers.

Cor. Alack! 'tis he: why, he was met even now
As mad as the vex'd sea; singing aloud;
Crown'd with rank fumiter and furrow-weeds,
With hardocks, hemlock, nettles, cuckoo-flowers,

Scene IV

The Same] *A Camp Rowe; the Same. A Tent. Capell; not in Q, F.*
S.D.] *Enter . . . Gentlemen, and Souldiers F; Enter Cordelia, Doctor, and*
others Q.   2. mad as] *made F 3, 4.*   vex'd] *vent Q.*   3. fumiter]
Theobald; femiter Q; Fenitar F.   4. hardocks] *F 3, 4; hor-docks Q;*
Hardokes F 1, 2; burdocks Hanmer; Harlocks Steevens (conj. Farmer);
Hoar-docks Collier (conj. Steevens).

52. *dear cause*] important reason.
We are not told what.

54. *aright*] i.e. as Kent.

55. *Lending . . . acquaintance*] for
having been acquainted with me.

Scene IV

2. *vex'd*] Cf. *Temp.* I. ii. 229.

3. *rank*] luxuriant.

3. *fumiter*] fumitory. Farren,
Essays on Mania, 1833, p. 73, says
that its leaves are of a bitter taste,
and the juice was formerly employed
in cases of hypochondrism and black
jaundice. Blunden, *op. cit.* p. 335,
cites Clare, *Shepherd's Calendar;*

" fumitory too—a name
That Superstition holds to fame."

3. *furrow-weeds*] weeds that spring
up in the furrow, in ploughed land.

4. *hardocks*] the hoar or white
dock (Craig); burdock (*N.E.D.*,

Onions); corn blue-bottle (Skeat);
knapweed (Wright); harlocks
(Farmer). Drayton, *Shepherd's*
Garland, VIII. 156, mentions the
Harlocke.

4. *hemlock*] used as a poison and
as a narcotic.

4. *nettles*] " that throngs about
graves " (Blunden).

4. *cuckoo-flowers*] These have been
identified with a dozen different
plants, including *Lychnis flos-cuculi*,
Ragged Robin (Beisly); Ladies'
Smocks, *Cardamine pratensis* (Wright);
and the Bedlam Cowslip. The last
would be an apt flower for the mad
Lear; but the *Cardamine pratensis*
was used by the Greeks and Romans
for almost all affections of the head,
and according to Farren was used
as late as the last century as a remedy
for convulsions, epilepsy, and other
diseases of the brain.

    Darnel, and all the idle weeds that grow   5
In our sustaining corn. A century send forth;
Search every acre in the high-grown field,
And bring him to our eye.   [*Exit an Officer.*
                What can man's wisdom
In the restoring his bereaved sense?
He that helps him take all my outward worth.   10

Doct. There is means, Madam;
Our foster-nurse of nature is repose,
The which he lacks; that to provoke in him,
Are many <u>simples</u> operative, whose power
Will close the eye of anguish. *(physical pain)*

Cor.   All bless'd secrets,   15
All you unpublish'd virtues of the earth,
Spring with my tears! be aidant and remediate
In the good man's distress! Seek, seek for him,

herbs

---

6. sustaining] sustayning, *Q.* century] *Q, F 3, 4;* Centery *F 1, 2;* sent'ry *Johnson.*   send] *F;* is sent *Q 1, 2;* is set *Q 3.*   7. high-grown] *F;* hie growne *Q.*   8. S.D.] *Malone; not in Q, F.*   wisdom] wisdome do *Q 2, 3.*   10. helps] can help *Q.*   11. *Doct. Q; Gent. F.*   is] are *Rowe.*   17. remediate] remediant *Johnson.*   18. good man's] Goodmans *F 1, 2.*   distress] *Q;* desires *F 1, 2, 3;* desire *F 4.*

---

5. *darnel*] tares, any hurtful weed, *Lolium temulentum,* i.e. wild rye grass. Lyte, *Herbal,* 1578, says Darnell " is a vitious graine that combereth or anoyeth corne, especially Wheat." Blunden calls it " sickly and usurping." It has narcotic powers.

5. *idle*] unprofitable, worthless, opposed to ' sustaining ' corn, which is the staff of life.

6. *century*] a hundred soldiers. Perrett curiously takes it as a reference to Lear's hundred knights, now restored to him. The word is also an obsolete variant of ' sentry '; but one sentry would not be much use as a search party. Craig, who reads ' sentry,' argues that century is an anachronism since Lear lived before the Roman occupation. But cf. ' cohorts ' 1. ii. 156.

8. *What . . . wisdom*] What does man's science know.

9. *In . . . restoring*] to restore.

9. *bereaved*] robbed, impaired.

10. *helps*] cures.

10. *worth*] possessions.

11. *There . . . means*] Kellogg, *Shakespeare's Delineation of Insanity,* N.Y. 1866, p. 26 suggests that Shakespeare was wiser than the doctors of his day in his prescription.

13. *provoke*] induce.

14. *simples*] medicinal herbs.

15. *anguish*] generally used by Shakespeare of physical pain.

16. *virtues*] efficacious medicinal plants (Kittredge).

17. *aidant . . . remediate*] helpfully remedial. ' Remediate ' may be a coinage, perhaps to avoid the jingle that would be caused by ' remediant.'

Lest his ungovern'd rage dissolve the life
That wants the means to lead it.

Enter a Messenger.

Mess.   News, Madam;   20
    The British powers are marching hitherward.
Cor. 'Tis known before; our preparation stands
    In expectation of them.   O dear father!
    It is thy business that I go about;
    Therefore great France   25
    My mourning and importun'd tears hath pitied.
    No blown ambition doth our arms incite,
    But love, dear love, and our ag'd father's right.
    Soon may I hear and see him!   [*Exeunt.*

26. importun'd] *F;* important *Q;* importunate *Capell;* importune *Harrison.*
27. No] Now *F 3, 4.*   incite] *F;* insite *Q 2;* in sight *Q 1.*   28. ag'd]
aged *Q 2.*   right] Rite *F 1, 2.*   29. S.D.] *F;* Exit *Q.*

SCENE V.—[*A Room in Gloucester's Castle.*]

Enter REGAN *and* OSWALD.

Reg. But are my brother's powers set forth?
Osw.   Ay, Madam.
Reg. Himself in person there?
Osw.   Madam, with much ado:

with a lot off fuss your sister seemed bette [handwritten note]

Scene v

A . . . Castle] *Capell; not in Q, F.*   *Oswald*] Steward *Q, F.*   2.
there] *F; not in Q.*

19. *rage*] frenzy.

20. *the means*] i.e. his reason.

22. *preparation*] our troops, ready
for battle.

23-4. *father! . . . about*] Bethell,
*Shakespeare and the Popular Dramatic
Tradition,* 1946, p. 60, compares *Luke,*
ii. 49. " Knew yee not that I must
goe about my father's businesse? "

26. *importun'd*] importunate.
Shakespeare uses the passive form
with an active meaning in *1 Hen. IV.*
I. iii. 183 (where *disdain'd* means
disdainful). In the present passage
the epithet is transferred from the
King of France to Cordelia's tears.

The Q reading, ' important,' also
means importuned.   It is possible,
however, that the F reading is a
misreading of *importune* (also meaning importunate): it would be a
simple *e/d* error.

27. *blown*] puffed up, inflated
with the pride of conquest.   Cf.
1 Corinthians, xiii. 4-5: " Loue
suffereth long . . . it is not puffed
vp: . . . it seeketh not her owne
things " (Geneva).

Scene v

2. *with much ado*] after much fuss
and persuasion.   Albany was not
certain where his duty lay.

Your sister is the better soldier.

Reg. Lord Edmund spake not with your Lord at home?

Osw. No, Madam. 5

Reg. What might import my sister's letter to him? *jealousy*

Osw. I know not, Lady.

Reg. Faith, he is posted hence on serious matter.

It was great ignorance, Gloucester's eyes being out,

To let him live; where he arrives he moves 10

All hearts against us. Edmund, I think, is gone, *cold*

In pity of his misery, to dispatch *calculation*

His nighted life; moreover, to descry *cf.*

The strength o' th' enemy. *p. 138*

Osw. I must needs after him, Madam, with my letter. 15

Reg. Our troops set forth to-morrow; stay with us,

The ways are dangerous.

Osw.　　　　　　　　I may not, Madam;

My Lady charg'd my duty in this business.

Reg. Why should she write to Edmund? Might not you

Transport her purposes by word? Belike, 20

Some things—I know not what. I'll love thee much,

Let me unseal the letter.

Osw.　　　　　　　Madam, I had rather—

Reg. I know your Lady does not love her husband;

I am sure of that: and at her late being here

---

3. sister is] sister's *Q 2, 3*.   4. Lord] *F;* Lady *Q.*   6. letter] letters *Q 1.*
11. Edmund] *F;* and now *Q.*   14. o' th' enemy] *F;* at'h army *Q 1;* of the
Army *Q 2, 3.*   15. Madam] *F; not in Q.* letter] *F;* letters *Q.*   16. troops
set] *F;* troope sets *Q.* 21. Some things] *F;* Some thing *Q 1;* Something *Q 2;*
Something.—*Pope.*   22. I had] *F;* I'de *Q.*

---

5. *What . . . him?*] Regan evidently
returns to a topic discussed before
the opening of the scene.

6. *import*] bear as its purport,
express, signify.

8. *serious matter*] important business.

9. *ignorance*] folly.

12. *In . . . misery*] presumably
ironical.

13. *nighted*] darkened, because he
is blind.

18. *charg'd my duty*] earnestly enjoined me to carry out her instructions.

20. *Belike*] probably.

21. *Some things . . .*] Obviously she
suspects that Edmund and Goneril
are lovers.

amouvous looks

She gave strange œilliads and most speaking looks   25
To noble Edmund.   I know you are of her bosom.
Osw. I, Madam!
Reg. I speak in understanding; y' are, I know't:
Therefore I do advise you, take this note:
My Lord is dead; Edmund and I have talk'd   30
And more convenient is he for my hand
Than for your Lady's.   You may gather more.
If you do find him, pray you give him this,
And when your mistress hears thus much from
    you,
I pray desire her call her wisdom to her: 35
So, fare you well.
If you do chance to hear of that blind traitor,
Preferment falls on him that cuts him off.
Osw. Would I could meet him, Madam: I should show
What party I do follow.
Reg.   Fare thee well. [*Exeunt.* 40

25. œilliads] *Dyce;* aliads *Q;* Eliads *F 1;* Iliads *F 2, 3, 4;* æliads *Rowe.*
28. Y'are] *F;* for *Q.*   36. fare you well] *F;* farewell *Q.*   39. him] *Q;*
not in F.   should] would *Q 1, 2.*   40. party] *F;* Lady *Q.*   S.D.] *F;*
Exit *Q.*

25. *œilliads*] This is clearly the
word represented by the F spelling.
Cf. *M.W.* 1. iii. 68. Cotgrave defines the word as " an amorous
look, affectionate wink "; and
Steevens quotes R. Greene, *Disputation between a He and a She Cony-
Catcher,* 1592 (ed. G. B. Harrison,
p. 5) " amorous glaunces, smirking
œyliades."

25. *speaking looks*] Cf. Florio. *op.
cit.,* iii. 211.

26. *of her bosom*] in her confidence.

29. *take this note*] take note of
what I say. Delius wrongly assumes
that Regan is referring to her letter.

30. *have talk'd*] have come to an
understanding.

31. *convenient*] fitting.

32. *You . . . more*] You may deduce
more from my hints.

33. *this*] Either a token or a letter.
Only one letter, Goneril's, is found
on Oswald after his death; but as
L. Campbell, *Tragic Drama,* 1904,
p. 251, suggests, Shakespeare may
choose this way of revealing Regan's
passion, but would not wish to weaken
the scene of Oswald's death by the
complication of two letters.

34. *thus much*] what I have told
you.

SCENE VI.—[*The Country near Dover.*]

Enter GLOUCESTER *and* EDGAR *dressed like a peasant.*

Glou. When shall I come to th' top of that same hill?
Edg. You do climb up it now; look how we labour.
Glou. Methinks the ground is even.
Edg.   Horrible steep:
Hark! do you hear the sea?
Glou.   No, truly.
Edg. Why, then your other senses grow imperfect   5
By your eyes' anguish.
Glou.   So may it be, indeed.
Methinks thy voice is alter'd, and thou speak'st
In better phrase and matter than thou didst.
Edg. You're much deceiv'd; in nothing am I chang'd
But in my garments.
Glou.   Methinks you're better spoken.   10
Edg. Come on, sir; here's the place: stand still.   How
fearful
And dizzy 'tis to cast one's eyes so low!
jackdaws The crows and choughs that wing the midway air
Show scarce so gross as beetles; half way down

Scene VI

The . . . *Dover*] *Theobald;* Fields . . . *Dover Capell; The Country Rowe.*
Enter . . . *peasant*] *Theobald;* Enter Gloucester and Edgar *F;* Enter Gloster and
Edmund *Q.*   1. I] *F;* we *Q.*   2. up it now *F;* it vpnow *Q 1;* it
vp now *Q 2, 3.*   7. alter'd] *F;* altered *Q.*   speak'st] *F;* speakest *Q.*
8. In] *F;* With *Q.*   9. You're] *Rowe;* Y'are *Q 2, 3, F.*   Y'ar *Q 1;*
You are *Steevens.*   deceiv'd] *F;* deceaued *Q.*   10. you're] *Rowe;* y'are
Q 2, 3, F; y'ar *Q 1;* you are *Capell.*

Scene VI	grace. Shakespeare marks the change by making him speak in verse.

Scene VI

5-6. *your . . . anguish*] Cf. Florio,
op. cit. iv. 70: " Our senses are not
onely altered, but many times
dulled, by the passions of the mind."
But *anguish* probably means the
physical pain Gloucester is suffering,
rather than his grief at the loss of
his eyes.

10. *you're . . . spoken*] you speak
with better accent, propriety and

grace. Shakespeare marks the change
by making him speak in verse.

11-14. *How . . . headlong*] Cf.
Florio, *op. cit.* iv. 67-8, where
Montaigne discusses the effect of
dizzy heights.

13. *choughs*] jackdaws (*Corvus
monedula*); or, less likely, Cornish
choughs (*Pyrochorax graculus*) which
are sometimes to be met with on
Beachy Head, and may well then have
been common on Dover Cliff (Craig).

herb for pickling

Hangs one that gathers sampire, dreadful trade!   15
Methinks he seems no bigger than his head.
The fishermen that walk upon the beach
Appear like mice, and yond tall anchoring bark
Diminish'd to her <u>cock</u>, her <u>cock</u> a buoy   *small boat*
Almost too small for sight.   The murmuring
  surge,   20
That on th' unnumber'd idle pebble chafes,
Cannot be heard so high.   I'll look no more,
Lest my brain turn, and the deficient sight
Topple down headlong.

Glou.   Set me where you stand.

Edg. Give me your hand; you are now within a foot   25
Of th' extreme verge: for all beneath the moon
Would I not leap upright.

Glou.   Let go my hand.
Here, friend, 's another purse; in it a jewel
Well worth a poor man's taking: fairies and Gods

---

15. sampire] *Q 1, 2, F:* samphier *Q 3;* samphire *Rowe.*   17. walk] *Q;*
walk'd *F.*   beach] beake *Q 2, 3.*   18. yond] yon *Q 1, 2.*   19. a buoy]
F; a boui *Q 1;* aboue *Q 2, 3.*   21. pebble chafes] *F;* peeble chaffes *Q 1;*
peebles chafe *Q 2, 3;* pebbles chafes *Pope.*   22. so] *F;* its so *Q 1;* it is so
Q 2, 3.   26. th' extreme] the extreme *Q 2, 3.*   29. fairies] fairiegs *Q 3.*

---

15. *sampire*] samphire, *herbe de
Saint Pierre,* an aromatic plant used
for pickles.   Drayton, *Poly-Olbion,*
xviii. 763-4, as Malone points out,
associates the plant with Dover:
 "Rob   Dovers   neighbouring
  Cleeves of Sampyre, to excite
 His dull and sickly taste, and
  stirre up appetite."
Evelyn, *Accetaria,* calls a recipe for
pickling it "the Dover receipt."
 19. *cock*] cock-boat, a small ship's
boat.
 21. *unnumber'd*] innumerable,
numberless.   Cf. Drayton, *op. cit.*
i. 72: "th' unnumbered fowl."
 21. *idle*] barren (Warburton);
moved by a kind of continual and
frivolous agitation to no purpose or
effect (Eccles).
 21. *pebble*] often used as a plural,
as *pearl* is used for *pearls.*

23-4. *and . . . headlong*] and I, my
sight   failing   me,   fall   headlong
(Kittredge).   His body, to which
sight belongs, falls with the actual
organs of sight.
 23. *deficient*] Cf. *Oth.* 1. iii. 63.
 26. *extreme*] The accent is on the
first syllable.
 27. *leap upright*] because he is so
close to the edge that even if he
jumped straight up in the air he
would be in grave danger of toppling
over the cliff.
 28. *another purse*] Cf. *IV. i.* 64.
 29. *fairies*] Kittredge suggests that
this refers to the superstition that
hidden treasure is guarded by fairies,
and that they make it multiply
miraculously in the possession of
the discoverer. Cf. *W.T.* III. iii.
121 ff.

Prosper it with thee!　Go thou further off;　　　30
Bid me farewell, and let me hear thee going.
Edg.　Now fare ye well, good sir.
Glou.　　　　　　　　　With all my heart.
Edg.　[*Aside.*] Why I do trifle thus with his despair
Is done to cure it.
Glou. [*Kneeling.*]　　　　O you mighty Gods!
This world I do renounce, and in your sights　　35
Shake patiently my great affliction off;
If I could bear it longer, and not fall
To quarrel with your great opposeless wills,
My snuff and loathed part of nature should
Burn itself out.　If Edgar live, O, bless him!　　40
Now, fellow, fare thee well.
Edg.　　　　　　　　Gone, sir: farewell.
　　　　　　[*He throws himself forward and falls.*
And yet I know not how <u>conceit</u> may rob　*imagination*
The treasury of life when life itself
Yields to the theft; had he been where he thought
By this had thought been past.　Alive or dead?　　45
Ho, you sir! friend!　Hear you, sir! speak!
Thus might he pass indeed; yet he revives.
What are you, sir?
Glou.　　　　　　Away, and let me die.
Edg.　Hadst thou been aught but gossamer, feathers, air,
So many fathom down precipitating,　　　50

30. further] *F;* farther *Q.*　　32. ye] *F;* you *Q.*　　33. I do] do I *F 3, 4,*
Rowe.　　34. Is] tis *Q 2, 3, F 3, 4.*　　S.D.] *He kneeles Q; not in F.*　　39.
snuffe] *F;* snurff *Q 1.*　　40. him] *F; not in Q.*　　41. Gone] Good *F 2, 3, 4.*
S.D.] *He fals Q; not in F; He leaps and falls along. Rowe.*　　42. may] my
Q 1.　　45. had thought] thought had *Q 2, 3.*　　46. friend] *F; not in Q.*
49. gossamer] *Campbell;* goss'mer *Pope;* gosmore *Q;* Gozemore *F.*

33-4. *Why . . . cure it*] Abbott, *411,
points out that this sentence is a
confusion of two constructions " Why
I trifle is to cure " and " My trifling
is done to cure." Such a confusion
is, of course, common in colloquial
speech.

37-8. *fall To quarrel*] begin to
rebel against, and so fall into a worse
sin than suicide.

38. *opposeless*] irresistible.

39. *snuff*] the smouldering wick of
a candle.　His brief candle is nearly
burnt out.　Cf. I. iv. 226 note.

42. *conceit*] imagination, delusion.

44. *Yields*] consents.

47. *pass*] die.

50. *precipitating*] Cf. Appendix,
p. 250.

Thou'dst shiver'd like an egg; but thou dost
  breathe,
Hast heavy substance, bleed'st not, speak'st, art
  sound.
Ten masts at each make not the altitude
Which thou hast perpendicularly fell:
Thy life's a miracle. Speak yet again.   55
Glou. But have I fall'n or no?
Edg. From the dread summit of this chalky bourn.
  Look up a-height; the shrill-gorg'd lark so far
  Cannot be seen or heard: do but look up.
Glou. Alack! I have no eyes.   60
  Is wretchedness depriv'd that benefit
  To end itself by death? 'Twas yet some comfort,
  When misery could beguile the tyrant's rage,   *cheat*
  And frustrate his proud will.
Edg.   Give me your arm:
  Up: so; how is't? Feel you your legs? You
    stand.   65
Glou. Too well, too well.
Edg.   This is above all strangeness.
  Upon the crown o' th' cliff what thing was that
  Which parted from you?
Glou.   A poor unfortunate beggar.
Edg. As I stood here below methought his eyes
  Were two full moons; he had a thousand noses,   70

51. Thou'dst] *F;* Thou hadst *Q.* 52. speak'st] speakest *Q 1;* speak *F 3, 4.*
56. fall'n] falne *F;* fallen *Q.*   no?] no I *Q 1.*   57. summit] *Rowe;* Summet
F 2, 3, 4; Somnet *F 1;* sommons *Q 1;* summons *Q 2, 3.*   58. a-height]
hyphened Warburton.   shrill-gorg'd] *F;* shrill gorg'd *Q;* shrill-gor'd *F 2, 3;*
shrill gor'd *F 4, Rowe.*   63. tyrant's] tyrants *Q;* Tyranrs *F 1.*   65. is't] *F;*
not in Q.   67. o' th'] *F;* of the *Q.*   cliff what] *Q;* Cliffe. What *F.*   68.
unfortunate] unfortune *F 2.*   beggar] *F;* bagger *Q 1.*   69. methought] *Q 2;*
me thought *F;* me thoughts *Q 1.*   70. he] *F;* a *Q.*

53. *at each*] one on top of the other.
54. *fell*] fallen.
57. *bourn*] boundary of the sea,
confining it. Cf. *T.C.* II. iii. 260.
58. *a-height*] on high.
58. *shrill-gorg'd*]   shrill-throated,
shrill-voiced. Cf. *Ham.* I. i. 149-51.

63-4. *When . . . will*] See Appendix,
p. 252.
63. *beguile*] cheat.
65. *Feel you*] can you use; or,
possibly, have you any feeling in.
69-74. *As . . . thee*] Kittredge
compares *Ham.* I. iv. 69-78.

twisted　　　　　　*furrowed*

Horns whelk'd and wav'd like the enridged sea:
It　was　some　fiend;　therefore,　thou　happy
　　father,
Think　that　the　clearest　Gods,　who　make　them
　　honours
Of men's impossibilities, have preserved thee.

cf. p 149
p 210

Glou.　I do remember now; henceforth I'll bear　　　75
Affliction till it do cry out itself
　　" Enough, enough," and die.　That thing you
　　speak of
I took it for a man; often 'twould say
　　" The Fiend, the Fiend ": he led me to that
　　place.

Edg.　Bear free and patient thoughts.　But who comes
　　here?　　　　　　　　　　　　　　　　　　　　　80

ie shake off melancholia which chains
down
to one
sorrow

ie his
blindness

71. whelk'd] *Hanmer;* welk't *Q 1;* welkt *Q 2;* wealk'd *F 1, 2;* walk'd
F 3, 4. enridged] *Q;* enraged *F.* 73. make them] *F;* made their *Q.* 77.
die. That] die that *Q1.* 78. 'twould] *F;* would it *Q 1;* would be *Q 2, 3.*
80. Bear free] *F;* Bare free *Q 1;* Bare, free *Q 2, 3.* 80. S.D.] *Capell;*
Enter Lear mad (after thus 82) Q; Enter Lear (after thoughts) F.

71. *whelk'd*] twisted, convolved
(Malone).　　Cf. Golding, *Metamorphoses,* v. 416-71
" *Joves* ymage which the Lybian
　　folke by name of Hammon
　　serve,
　Is made with crooked welked
　　hornes that in ward still do
　　terve."
71. *enridged*] furrowed.　F reads
' enraged,' but Shakespeare is not
thinking of a rough sea.　Kittredge
compares *V.A.* 818-20 and *Luc.*
1436-42.
72. *father*] old man; Edgar uses
the term ambiguously, and does not
reveal his identity.
73. *clearest*] " open and righteous "
(Theobald); " the purest, the most
free from evil " (Johnson); " clear-
sighted " (Capell); " bright, pure,
glorious " (Schmidt); " who perform miracles to make themselves
clear to those who do not believe "

(Stewart, *Textual Difficulties,* 1914,
p. 113); " this word, which expresses the pure and luminous
essence of the divinity, reflects the
clear, and profound nature of the
man who utters it " (Reyher, *Essai
sur les Idées . . . de Shakespeare,* p. 500).
73-4. *who . . . impossibilities*] " who
derive to themselves honour and
reverence from man, by doing things
which he reckons impossible "
(Capell).　Furness compares *Luke*
xviii. 27: " The things which are
impossible with men are possible
with God."
76-7. *till . . . die*] This may mean
" till Affliction recognizes that I
have been afflicted enough and
itself dies "; or else " till Affliction
recognizes that I have borne enough,
and allows me to die a natural death."
80. *free*] free from sorrow, happy.
A sorrowful man is enslaved to his
grief.

Enter LEAR, *fantastically dressed with wild flowers.*

The safer sense will ne'er accommodate
His master thus.

Lear. No, they cannot touch me for coining; I am
the king himself.

Edg. O thou side-piercing sight!   85

Lear. Nature's above art in that respect. There's
your press-money. That fellow handles his bow
like a crow-keeper: draw me a clothier's yard.
Look, look! a mouse. Peace, peace! this piece
of toasted cheese will do't. There's my gauntlet;   90
I'll prove it on a giant. Bring up the brown bills.

81. ne'er] *neare Q 1;* nere *Q 2;* ne're *F.*   83. coining] *Q;* crying *F.*
85. side-piercing] *F;* side piercing *Q.*   86. Nature's] *F;* Nature is *Q.* 89-90.
piece of] *F; not in Q.*   90. do't] *F;* do it *Q.*

81-2. *The . . . thus*] The sounder
sense (i.e. a man in his right senses)
would never get himself up in this
fashion. Cf. *M.M.* I. i. 72.

83. *coining*] Lear's mad speeches
have an undertone of meaning, and
although he leaps from one subject
to another it is often possible to see
that there is a subconscious connection between them. *Coining,*
which was a royal prerogative, leads
to the thought of *press-money.* This
suggests watching recruits at target-
practice and war. War suggests
peace, which in turn suggests *piece,*
and also a challenge and brown
bills. Bills suggests *bird,* bird suggests
an arrow in flight, and its target.
See Introduction, p. xlii. It may be
mentioned that *coining* often had a
sexual significance. See *M.M.* II.
iv. 45; *Edward III.* II. i. 258; Tourneur, *The Revenger's Tragædie,* II.
ii. 60.

85. *side-piercing*] heart-rending.

86. *Nature's . . . respect*] "a born
King can never lose his natural
rights" (Schmidt). The relative importance of art and nature was
often discussed in Shakespeare's
day. See, for example, Puttenham,

The Arte of English Poesie (III. xxv.
ed. Arber, pp. 308 ff.); *W.T.* IV. iv.
87 ff.; and *A.W.* II. i. 121.

87. *press-money*] money paid to
recruits when they enlisted.

88. *crow-keeper*] a scarecrow with a
bow awkwardly tucked under its
arm; (cf. *R.J.* I. iv. 6) or, possibly,
a boy employed to scare away
rooks. Douce quotes from Ascham,
Toxophilus, ed. Arber, p. 145: "An
other coureth downe, and layeth out
his buttockes, as though he shoulde
shoote at crowes."

88. *me*] for me.

88. *clothier's yard*] The standard
English arrow was a cloth-yard in
length. Cf. *Chevy Chase,* 180:
  "An arrow of a cloth yard long
    Up to the head he drew."
Stewart, *Textual Difficulties,* p. 84,
says that "a bowman who could
draw a clothier's yard was one who,
when the butt of the shaft was at his
nose, had the strength to force the
bow out the full length of the arm."

89. *mouse*] possibly as imaginary
as the dogs in III. vi.

90. *gauntlet*] a leather glove plaited
with steel, the throwing down of
which was a challenge.

reference to arrow

O! well flown bird; i' th' clout, i' th' clout: *point of aim*
hewgh! Give the word.

Edg. Sweet marjoram.

Lear. Pass.   95

Glou. I know that voice. *mistakes Glou for her*

Lear. Ha! Goneril, with a white beard! They
flattered me like a dog, and told me I had the *hint of*
white hairs in my beard ere the black ones were *"ay" "no" suggested*
there. To say " ay " and " no " to every thing 100
that I said! "Ay" and " no " too was no *by "I know"*
good divinity. When the rain came to wet me *follows Lear*
once and the wind to make me chatter, when *mad logic*
the thunder would not peace at my bidding,
there I found 'em, there I smelt 'em out. Go 105
to, they are not men o' their words: they told

wisdom of age
flattery hypocritical
stench of evil
Goneril & Regan

92-3. i' . . . hewgh!] *F;* in the ayre, hagh *Q.*   97. Ha . . . beard!] *F;*
Ha Gonorill, ha Regan, *Q.*   98-9. the white] *F;* white *Q.*   100-1. every
thing that] *F;* euery thing *Q 1;* all *Q 2, 3.*   101. too] toe *Q 1.*   103.
the wind] wind *F 2, 3, 4.* 105. 'em . . . 'em] *F;* them . . . them *Q.* 106. o']
F; of *Q.*

91. *brown bills*] brown billmen.
A brown bill was a halberd painted
to keep off rust.

92. *well . . . bird*] The falconer's
cry when the hawk was successful;
but Lear is probably referring to the
flight of the arrow.

92. *clout*] the mark shot at. Cf.
L.L.L. IV. i. 136.

93. *hewgh*] an imitation of the
noise made by the arrow.

93. *word*] watchword, password.

94. *Sweet marjoram*] Blunden, *op.
cit.* p. 333, says that according to
Culpeper this was a remedy for
diseases of the brain.

97. *Goneril . . . beard*] This has
been interpreted in two ways:
(i) Lear takes Gloucester for Goneril
in disguise; (ii) Lear is addressing
Goneril, and asking how she could be so
cruel to her father with a white beard.

98. *like a dog*] as a dog fawns on
his master.

98-100. *the . . . there*] told me I had
the wisdom of age before I was old

enough to grow a beard. The idea
was prompted by the sight of
Gloucester's beard.

100-1. *To . . . said*] To agree with
me always, whether I was right or
wrong, like the flatterer in one of
Hall's *Satires*, vi. 1, cited by Kittredge:

" Smiles on his master for a meale
    or two;
And loues him ln his maw,
    loaths in his heart,
Yet soothes, and yeas and nays
    on eyther part."

Ay and No may have been suggested
by Gloucester's " I know."

101-2. *no . . . divinity*] not good
theology, because it went against
the biblical injunction, *James* v.
12: " But let your yea, bee yea,
and your nay, nay, lest ye fall into
condemnation." Though here and
in *Matt.* v. 37 the injunction is
against swearing, and St. Paul in
2 *Cor.* i. 18, cited by Moberly and
others, is avowing his consistency.

Lear's ego & vanity are deflated.

me I was every thing; 'tis a lie, I am not ague-
proof. — *characteristic*

Glou. The trick of that voice I do well remember:
Is't not the King?

Lear.   Ay, every inch a king: *cf L 84*   110
When I do stare, see how the subject quakes.
I pardon that man's life. What was thy cause?
Adultery? *offence*
Thou shalt not die: die for adultery! No:
The wren goes to 't, and the small gilded fly   115
Does lecher in my sight.
Let copulation thrive; for Gloucester's bastard son
Was kinder to his father than my daughters *lust*
Got 'tween the lawful sheets.   To 't, Luxury, pell-
mell! *promiscuously.*
For I lack soldiers. Behold yond simp'ring dame, 120
Whose face between her forks presages snow; *who looks frigidly chaste*

Bastards must be kinder than my cruel lawful daughters!

107-8. ague-proof] *F;* argue-proofe *Q.*   110. every] euer *Q 1.*   110-20.
Ay . . . Souldiers] *lines end* King. quakes. cause? Adultery? Fly thriue; Father,
sheets. Souldiers. *F; lines end* king: quakes, cause? Adultery? No; fly sight. son
daughters sheets. soldiers. *Johnson; prose Q.*   114. die; die;] *F;* die *Q.*
116. Does] *F;* doe *Q.*   120. lack] want *Q 2.*   yond] *F 1, 2;* yon *Q, F 3;*
you *F 4.*   120-8. Behold . . . inherit] *arranged by Johnson; prose in Q, F.*
121. presages] *F;* presageth *Q.*

109. *trick*] peculiarity, intonation.

110. *King*] The word recalls Lear
to the thought of sovereignty with
which he began (Kittredge).

110-20. *Ay . . . soldiers*] prose in Q,
mislined verse in F.

112. *cause*] charge, offence.

114. *die . . . adultery*] Noble compares *Levit.* xx. 10 and *John* vii. 5.

115. *The . . . to 't*] Florio, *op. cit.*
v. 116, translates Montaigne's quotation from Catullus:

" No pigeons hen, or paire, or
          what worse name
You list, makes with hir Snow-
          white cock such game.
With biting bill to catch when
          she is kist,
As many-minded women when
          they list."

Montaigne goes on to discuss the
worship of Priapus.

118. *kinder*] Gloucester now knows
of Edmund's ' kindness.'

119. *Luxury*] lust. Cf. *Ham.* i. v. 83.

119. *pell-mell*] promiscuously.

120-35. *Behold . . . for thee*] Q and
F both print this as prose. Johnson
printed it as verse except for the last
five lines.   Tucker Brooke thinks
the whole speech is good honest
prose.

121. *Whose . . . snow*] Who seems
to be frigidly chaste.

121. *forks*] legs; but H. C. Hart
suggests that it may mean instruments for keeping up women's hair.
Stubbes, *Anatomy of Abuses*, ed. 1877-9,
p. 67, mentions that women's hair
" is vnderpropped with forks, wyers,
and I can not tel what."

affects virtue [handwritten]

That minces virtue, and does shake the head
To hear of pleasure's name;
The fitchew nor the soiled horse goes to't
With a more riotous appetite.　　　　　　　　125
Down from the waist they are Centaurs,
Though women all above:
But to the girdle do the Gods inherit,
Beneath is all the fiend's: there's hell, there's
　　darkness,
There is the sulphurous pit—burning, scalding,　　130
Stench, consumption; fie, fie, fie! pah, pah!
Give me an ounce of civet, good apothecary,
To sweeten my imagination.
There's money for thee.

polecat [handwritten]
"prostitute" [handwritten]

They have the cunning of women and the lust of beasts [handwritten]

122. does] *F;* do *Q.*　　　123. To] *F;* not in *Q.*　　　124. The] *F;* to *Q.*
126. they are] tha're *Q 1.*　　129-31. Beneath . . . pah!] *arranged Muir; prose*
Q, F.　　　130. There is] *F;* there's *Q.*　　sulphurous] *F;* sulphury *Q.*　　131.
consumption] *F;* consumation *Q.*　　132-4. Give . . . hand] *Arranged Muir;*
lines end apothecary, thee. *Johnson.*　　132. civet,] *Q;* Ciuet: *F.*　　133. To]
Q; not in *F.*

122. *minces virtue*] affects the coy
timidity of virtue. Cotgrave translates "*faire la sadinette,*" "to mince
it, niceifie it, . . . be very squeamish,
backward, or coy."
123. *pleasure's name*] the very name
of pleasure. Florio, *op. cit.* iv. 131,
remarks: "Wee have taught Ladies
to blush, onely by hearing that
named, which they nothing feare to
doe."
124. *fitchew*] pole-cat; "a cant
term for a prostitute" (Dyce).
124. *soiled*] wanton with rich feeding in the springtime.
126. *Centaurs*] Heilman, *op. cit.*
p. 100 says "The Centaur is exactly
the right image here . . . it exhibits
man as a rational animal." Cf.
his remark on Regan and Goneril,
p. 234: "The paradox is that these
free minds, unburdened by any
conventional or traditional allegiances, become slaves to the uncontrolled animal desire, mechanisms for the attainment of irrational
objectives."

128. *But . . . inherit*] The Gods
possess only that part of the body
above the waist.
128. *inherit*] possess, hold sway.
129. *Beneath . . . fiend's*] Furness
quotes a passage by Ingleby about
an early Christian heretical sect
called the Paterniani "whose opinion
was that the upper parts of a man's
body were made, indeed, by God,
but the lower parts, from the girdle,
they held were made by the devil."
The priests who were exposed by
Harsnett tried to exorcise the devils
from the lower parts of the body.
See Appendix, p. 254.
129-35. *there's . . . for thee*] Johnson
and Jennens printed this as verse,
though most editors treat it as prose.
The present arrangement is rather
different from Johnson's. The verse
form brings out the point of having
there is instead of *ther's* (130) and the
three *fies* and the two *pahs* conveniently fill out a line.
133. *To . . . imagination*] Here I
have followed the Q reading; the

Glou.　　　　　　　　O! let me kiss that hand.

Lear. Let me wipe it first; it smells of mortality.　135

Glou. O ruin'd piece of Nature! This great world *universe*
　　　Shall so wear out to naught. Dost thou know me?

Lear. I remember thine eyes well enough. Dost thou
　　　squiny at me?
　　　No, do thy worst, blind Cupid; I'll not love.
　　　Read thou this challenge; mark but the penning
　　　of it.　140

Glou. Were all thy letters suns, I could not see.

Edg. [*Aside.*] I would not take this from report; it is,
　　　And my heart breaks at it.

Lear. Read.

Glou. What! with the *sockets* case of eyes?　145

Lear. O, ho! are you there with me? No eyes in
　　　your head, nor no money in your purse? Your

135-7. Let . . . me?] *lines end* first, Mortality. world naught. Me? *F.* 135. Let me] *F;* Here *Q.* 137. Shall] *F;* should *Q.* Dost thou] *F;* Do you *Q.* 138-40. I . . . it.] *arranged Muir; prose Q, F.* 138. thine] *F;* thy *Q.* squiny] squint *Q 3.* at] *F;* on *Q.* 140. this] *F;* that *Q.* but] *F; not in Q.* of it] *F;* oft *Q 1;* on't *Q 2, 3.* 141. thy] *F;* the *Q.* see] *F;* see one *Q. F 2, 3.* 142-3.] *Arranged by Theobald; lines end* report *and* it *F; prose Q.* 145. the] this *Rowe.* 147. nor no] nor *Q 2, 3.*

F reading, which may be explained by the accidental omission of *to* in the MS. is perfectly possible, but seems rather awkward in rhythm. Cf. Marston, *The Fawne*, II. i. (ed. Wood, p. 161) "Sweeten your imaginations, with thoughts of— ah why women are the most giddie, uncertain motions under heaven . . . onely meere chancefull appetite swayes them." This juxtaposition of satire on women with the phrase quoted suggests that Marston was imitating Shakespeare, but as *The Fawne* may have been written some time before its publication in 1606 the influence may have been the other way round.

136. *this great world*] the universe. Cf. III. i. 10.

138. *squiny*] squint. Cf. III. iv. 120.

139-40. *No . . . penning of it*] This is usually printed as, and may be, prose.

139. *blind Cupid*] the sign of a brothel. Sidney, *Arcadia*, II. xiv, contains a poem about blind Cupid, and Miso is warned not to love.

140. *challenge*] Lear's mind jumps back to his earlier speech, IV. vi. 90. Kittredge suggests the enemy is blind Cupid, but this is unlikely since he gives the challenge to Gloucester to read, and it is Gloucester he has taken for Cupid.

142. *this*] the scene he is witnessing.

145. *case*] the sockets which had once held the eyes. Cf. *Per.* III. ii. 99; *W.T.* v. ii. 14.

146. *are . . . me?*] Is that what you mean? Cf. *A.Y.L.I.* v. ii. 32.

sad plight

eyes are in a heavy case, your purse in a light:
yet you see how this world goes.

Glou. I see it feelingly.   *by feeling / keenly*   150

Lear. What! art mad? A man may see how this
world goes with no eyes.   Look with thine ears:
see how yond justice rails upon yond simple
thief.   Hark, in thine ear: change places, and,
handy-dandy, which is the justice, which is the 155
thief?   Thou hast seen a farmer's dog bark at a
beggar?

Glou. Ay, Sir.

Lear. And the creature run from the cur?   There
      thou might'st behold

The great image of Authority: 160
A dog's obey'd in office.
Thou rascal beadle, hold thy bloody hand!
Why dost thou lash that whore?   Strip thine own
      back;

---

148. a heavy] heavy *F 3, 4*.   151. this] *F;* the *Q.*   152. thine] thy *Q.*
153. yond . . . yond] *F;* yon . . . yon *Q.*   154. thine] *F;* thy *Q.*   154.
Change . . . and] *F; not in Q.*   155. handy-dandy] handy, dandy *Q1;* handy
dandy *Q 2, 3.*   justice] *F;* theefe *Q.*   156. thief] *F;* Iustice *Q.*   158.
Ay] *not in F 3, 4.*   159-61.] *Arranged Muir; prose Q, F.*   161. dog's
obey'd] *F;* dogge, so bade *Q 1;* dogge, so bad *Q 2, 3.* 162-5. Thou . . . cozener]
Arranged Pope; prose Q, F.   163. thine] *Q;* thy *F.*

---

148. *heavy case*] sad plight, with a
pun on *case*.

148. *your purse . . . light*] a quibble
on *light* which means *empty* and
merry.   Cf. *Cymb.* v. iv. 167: "purse
and brain both empty,—the brain
the heavier for being too light, the
purse too light being drawn of
heaviness."   There is a reference to
the proverb: "A heavy purse makes
a light heart."   Whiter, in an unpublished note, compares Jonson,
The New Inn, I. i. 16.

149. *how . . . goes*] Cf. Florio,
op. cit. vi. 85: "Thus goes the
world."

150. *feelingly*] another quibble:
(*a*) by my sense of feeling; (*b*)
keenly.   Lear takes him to mean (*a*).

153. *simple*] of low estate, ordinary.

155. *handy-dandy*] i.e. take your
choice.   It is a well-known children's
game.   Florio mentions it, *op. cit.* v.
259.   There are several passages in
Montaigne's essays on the guilt of
judges.   One adulterous one condemns an adulterer (*op. cit.* vi. 85);
"one same magistrate doth lay the
penalty of his change on such as
cannot do withal. . . . A horrible
image of justice" (v. 21); and
"Justice . . . is used but for a cloake
and ornament" (iii. 191).

159. *creature*] human being.

161. *A . . . office*] Montaigne
mentions "that there are Nations,
who receive and admit a Dogge to
be their King" (*op. cit.* iii. 210).

162. *beadle*] parish constable.

Thou hotly lusts to use her in that kind
For which thou whipp'st her.   The usurer hangs
    the cozener.   165
Thorough tatter'd clothes small vices do appear;
Robes and furr'd gowns hide all.   Plate sin with gold,
And the strong lance of justice hurtless breaks;
Arm it in rags, a pigmy's straw does pierce it.   169
None does offend, none, I say, none; I'll able 'em:
Take that of me, my friend, who have the power
To seal th' accuser's lips.   Get thee glass eyes;
And, like a scurvy politician, seem   *vile trickster*
To see the things thou dost not.   Now, now, now,
    now;

164. Thou] *F;* thy bloud *Q.*   166-73. Through . . . seem] *Arranged by Rowe; prose Q, F.*   166. Thorough] *F;* Through *Q.*   tatter'd clothes] *F;* tottered raggs *Q 1;* tattered ragges *Q 2, 3.*   small] *Q;* great *F.*   167. hide] *F;* hides *Q.*   167-72. Plate . . . lips] *F; not in Q.*   Plate sin] *Theobald;* Plate sins *Pope;* Place sinnes *F.*   174-5. To . . . so] *Arranged Capell; prose Q, F.*   174. Now . . . now] *F;* No now *Q.*

164. *kind*] manner.

165. *The . . . cozener*] a magistrate who has been guilty of the crime of usury passes sentence on one guilty only of petty cheating.

165. *cozener*] cheat.

166. *small*] The reading of Q. The F reading, ' great,' would mean that all vices are great when looked at through tattered clothes; but it would be difficult to convey that meaning in a theatre.   It would be easier if *great* were printed after *do.*

167. *Robes . . . all*] Lear is still thinking of judges. Cf. *Lucrece*, 93: " Hiding base sin in pleats of majesty." See also the following passage from Barclay, *The Mirrour of good Maners* (ed. 1885, p. 34):

" What difference betwene a great
    thiefe and a small,
Forsooth no more but this to
    speake I dare be bolde,
The great sitteth on benche in
    costly furres of pall,
The small thiefe at barre standeth
    trembling for colde,

The great thieues are laded with
    great chaynes of golde,
The small thiefe with yron
    chayned from all refuge,
The small thiefe is iudged, oft
    time the great is Iudge."

167. *Plate*] Theobald's emendation is certainly correct—clothe in plate-armour.

170. *None . . . offend*] Florio, *op. cit.* v. 245, has the following passage: " I say not, that none should accuse except hee bee spotlesse in himselfe: For then none might accuse." But Montaigne derived this injunction from the Gospels.

170. *able*] vouch for, warrant, authorize.

171. *that*] piece of information; or an imaginary pardon.

173. *scurvy*] vile.

173. *politician*] trickster, one who follows Machiavelli's ' policy,' not a politician in the modern sense of the word.

Pull off my boots; harder, harder; so.   175

Edg. [*Aside.*] O! matter and impertinency mix'd;
Reason in madness.

Lear. If thou wilt weep my fortunes, take my eyes;
I know thee well enough; thy name is Gloucester;
Thou must be patient; we came crying hither: 180
Thou know'st the first time that we smell the air
We wawl and cry. I will preach to thee:
mark.

Glou. Alack, alack the day!

Lear. When we are born, we cry that we are come
To this great stage of fools. This' a good block!   185
It were a delicate stratagem to shoe
A troop of horse with felt; I'll put 't in proof,

---

176. impertinency mix'd] impertinency, mixt *Q 2, 3.*   178-208. If . . . to]
verse *F; prose Q.*   178. fortunes] *F; fortune Q.*   182. wawl] *F; wayl Q.*
mark] *F; marke me Q.*   185. This'] *Singer (conj. S. Walker); This Q, F;*
'Tis *Hudson (conj. Ritson); This's Camb.*   186. shoe] *F; shoot Q.*   187.
felt] *F; fell Q.*   I'll . . . proof] *F; not in Q.*

176. *matter . . . impertinency*] sense
and nonsense. Florio uses the word
impertinency.

180. *We . . . hither*] Noble compares
Wisdom vii. 3, 5: "And when I
was borne, I receiued the common
aire, and fell vpon the earth, which
is of like nature, crying and weeping
at the first as all other doe. . . . For
there is no king that had any other
beginning of birth." Cf. Montaigne
(tr. Florio, i. 107): "So wept we,
and so much did it cost us to enter
into this life."

182. *We wawl . . . cry*] Anders
compares Holland's *Pliny*, vii, Proem
(ed. 1601, p. 152): "man alone,
poore wretch, she (Nature) hath laid
all naked vpon the bare earth, euen
on his birth-day, to cry and wraule
presently from the very first houre
that he is borne into this world."

185. *stage of fools*] See Introduction,
p. xli.

185. *This'*] this is.

185. *block*] The word was probably
suggested by *stage*, since the stage
was often called a scaffold. It is
usually assumed that Lear takes off
his hat to preach, and that his remark means "This is a good hat"
or "This hat is made in a good
fashion"; but it is unlikely that Lear
would be wearing a hat in this
scene, and it would be awkward for
him to take Edgar's or Gloucester's.
It is possible that Lear mistakes a
stone or a stump of a tree for a
mounting-block, and then quibbles
on the word. The mounting-block
would suggest horses, as the block
of a hat would suggest felt.

186. *delicate*] neat.

187. *felt*] Malone quotes a passage
from Lord Herbert of Cherbury's
Life of Henry VIII (ed. 1872, p. 147)
about a joust, in which the horses
"to prevent sliding and noise, were
shod with felt or flocks."

187. *I'll . . . proof*] I'll try the
experiment.

And when I have stol'n upon these son-in-laws,
Then, kill, kill, kill, kill, kill, kill!

No Quarter.

Enter a Gentleman, with Attendants.

Gent. O! here he is; lay hand upon him. Sir,   190
  Your most dear daughter—
Lear. No rescue? What! a prisoner? I am even
  The natural fool of Fortune. Use me well;
  You shall have ransom. Let me have surgeons;
  I am cut to th' brains.   *Imaginary wound.*
Gent.   You shall have any thing.   195
Lear. No seconds? all myself?
  Why this would make a man a <u>man of salt</u>, *tears*
  To use his eyes for garden water-pots,
  Ay, and laying autumn's dust. I will die <u>bravely</u>, *bravely / well dressed*
  Like a smug bridegroom. What! I will be jovial: 200
  Come, come; I am a king, masters, know you that?

spic & span

Gent. You are a royal one, and we obey you.

---

188. stol'n] *F;* stole *Q.*   son-in-laws] Son in Lawes *Q 1, F 1;* sons-in-law
Q 2, 3, Sonnes in Lawes *F 2, 3;* Sons-in-Laws *F 4.*   189. S.D.] *Rowe;*
Enter a Gentleman F; Enter three Gentlemen Q.   190. hand] *F;* hands *Q.*
him, Sir] *Johnson;* him, Sir *Q. F.*   Sir] Sirs *Q 2, 3.*   191. Your . . .
daughter] *F;* your most deere *Q 1; not in Q 2, 3.*   194. ransom] a ransom *Q*
2, 3.   surgeons] *F;* a surgeon *Capell;* a chirurgeon *Q 2, 3;* a churgion *Q 1.*
195. th'] the *Q 1.*   197. a man a man of] *F;* a man of *Q.*   199. Ay . . . dust]
Q; not in F; Ay, and for laying autumn's dust *Craig.*   *After this Q 2 inserts:*
Gent. Good Sir.   200. smug] *F; not in Q.*   201. masters] *F;* my maisters *Q.*
203. Come, and] *F;* nay and *Q 1;* nay if *Q 2, 3;* Nay, an *Capell.*

---

188. *son-in-laws*] This is the reading of Q and F, and is a possible
colloquial plural.   It is unwise to
blame the printer for every mistake
of grammar in Shakespeare's plays.

189. *kill, kill*] A cry of soldiers,
meaning " No quarter! " Cf. *V.A.*
652.

193. *natural . . . Fortune*] born to
be the sport of fortune. Cf. *R.J.*
II. i. 141. Empson, *op. cit.* p. 145,
seems to suggest that there is a
quibble on *natural*, which can mean
imbecile as well as *born.*

195. *cut . . . brains*] used literally
and figuratively; he is vexed to
madness, but requires a surgeon for
an imaginary wound in the head.

197. *a man of salt*] of salt tears.

199. *bravely*] two meanings: (*a*)
courageously, (*b*) in smart clothes.

200. *like . . . bridegroom*] Cf. *M.M.*
III. i. 83-5 and note on IV. ii. 23
ante.

200. *smug*] spick and span.

203. *there's . . . in 't*] the case is not
yet desperate (Johnson).

203. *and*] if.

Lear. Then there's life in't. Come and you get it,
    you shall get it by running. Sa, sa, sa, sa.
                           [Exit running. Attendants follow.

Gent. A sight most pitiful in the meanest wretch,   205
    Past speaking of in a King! Thou hast one
        daughter,
    Who redeems nature from the general curse
    Which twain have brought her to.

Edg. Hail, gentle sir!

Gent.   Sir, speed you: what's your will?

Edg. Do you hear aught, sir, of a battle toward?   210

Gent. Most sure and vulgar; every one hears that,
    Which can distinguish sound.

Edg.   But, by your favour,
    How near's the other army?

Gent. Near, and on speedy foot; the main descry
    Stands on the hourly thought.

Edg.   I thank you, sir: that's all. 215

Gent. Though that the Queen on special cause is here,
    Her army is mov'd on.

Edg.   I thank you sir. *[Exit Gentleman.*

Glou. You ever-gentle Gods, take my breath from me:
    Let not my worser spirit tempt me again
    To die before you please!

---

204. by] *F;* with *Q.*   Sa . . . sa] *F;* not in *Q.*   S.D.] *Capell, subst.*
Exit King running Q; Exit F.   206. one] *Q;* a *F.*   208.
have] *F;* hath *Q.*   210. sir] *F;* not in *Q.*   211-12. Most . . . sound] *Divided
as in Q 1; Q 2, 3 divide at* heares, *and F at* vulgar.   211. one] ones *Q 2, 3.*
hears] here's *Q 1.*   212. Which] *F;* That *Q.*   sound] *F;* sence *Q.*
214. speedy foot] *F;* speed fort *Q 1;* speed for't *Q 2, 3.* descry] *F;* descries *Q.*
215. Stands] *F;* Standst *Q 1.*   thought] *F;* thoughts *Q.*   217. Her] *F;* Hir
Q 1; His *Q 2, 3.*   S.D.] *Johnson; Exit Q; Exit F, after* on.   218.
ever-gentle] *hyphened Capell.*

204. *Sa . . . sa*] "An old hunting
cry to call a hound or to urge the
dogs forward in chase of the hare"
from Fr. *ça, ça!* It was used as a
rallying cry, or as an interjection of
challenge and defiance (Kittredge).

207. *general*] universal.

208. *twain*] Not Adam and Eve,
as Danby fancifully suggests (*op. cit.*
p. 125), but Goneril and Regan.

209. *gentle*] noble.

211. *vulgar*] in every one's mouth;
common knowledge.

214. *speedy foot*] advancing rapidly.

214-15. *the . . . thought*] we expect
to descry the main body any hour
now.

219. *worser spirit*] evil angel, evil
side of my nature.

Edg.   Well pray you, father. 220

Glou. Now, good sir, what are you? *submissive*

Edg. A most poor man, made tame to Fortune's blows;

instructed by
heartfelt Who, by the art of known and feeling sorrows,
sorrows Am pregnant to good pity.   Give me your hand, *suscept*,
experienced I'll lead you to some biding.

Glou.   Hearty thanks: 225
The bounty and the benison of Heaven
To boot, and boot!   *in addition*

Enter OSWALD.

Osw.   A proclaim'd prize!   Most happy!
That eyeless head of thine was first fram'd flesh
To raise my fortunes.   Thou old unhappy traitor,
'say your Briefly thyself remember: the sword is out   230
prayers" That must destroy thee.   *Glou desires death*

Glou.   Now let thy friendly hand
Put strength enough to 't.   [*Edgar interposes.*

Osw.   *proclaimed* Wherefore, bold peasant
Dar'st thou support a publish'd traitor?   Hence;
Lest that th' infection of his fortune take
Like hold on thee.   Let go his arm.   235

---

222. tame to] *F;* lame by *Q.*   225-7. Hearty . . . boot!] *F;* Prose *Q.*
226. bounty . . . benison] bornet and the beniz *Q uncorr.*   227. To . . . boot!] *F;*
to boot, to boot *Q corr. Q 2, 3;* to saue thee *Q uncorr.*   S.D.] *Collier; Enter*
Steward Q, F. 228. first] *not in Q uncorr.*   229. old] *F;* most *Q.*
232. S.D.] *Johnson, subst.; not in Q, F.*   233. Dar'st] durst *Q 1.*
234. that th'] *F;* the *Q.*

---

222. *tame*] submissive.

223. *by . . . sorrows*] instructed by
the heart-felt sorrows I have experienced. Cf. *W.T.* iv. ii. 8.

224. *pregnant*] disposed, susceptible.

225. *biding*] abode.

226. *benison*] blessing.

227. *To boot, and boot*] to reward
you, in addition to my thanks.
"To boot" means both "in ad-

dition" and "to enrich with an
additional gift."

227. *proclaim'd*] the accent is on
the first syllable.

230. *thyself remember*] Think of
thy sins (so as to make thy peace with
heaven).

230. *out*] of its scabbard.

231. *friendly*] because it gives him
the death he desires.

233. *publish'd*] proclaimed.

Edg. Chill not let go, zir, without vurther 'casion.

Osw. Let go, slave, or thou di'st.

Edg. Good gentleman, go your gait, and let poor
    volk pass. And 'chud ha' bin zwagger'd out of
    my life, 'twould not ha' bin zo long as 'tis by a 240
    vortnight. Nay, come not near th' old man;
    keep out, che vor' ye, or ise try whither your
    costard or my ballow be the harder. Chill be
    plain with you.

Osw. Out, dunghill!   245

Edg. Chill pick your teeth, zir. Come; no matter vor
    your foins.

        [*They fight, and Edgar knocks him down.*

Osw. Slave, thou hast slain me. Villain, take my purse.
    If ever thou wilt thrive, bury my body;

---

236. zir] *F;* sir *Q.*   vurther] *F;* not in *Q.*   'casion] *F;* cagion *Q.*
238. and] *F;* not in *Q.*   239. volk] voke *Q 1.*   ha'] *F;* haue *Q.*   zwagger'd]
zwagged *F 2, 3, 4.*   240. ha'] *F;* haue *Q.*   zo] so *Q 1.*   as 'tis] *F;*
not in *Q.*   241. vortnight] fortnight *Q uncorr.* th'] the *Q.*   242. ise] ice *F;*
ile *Q.*   whither] *F;* whether *Q.*   243. costard] coster *Q uncorr.;* costerd *Q.*
ballow] *F;* battero *Q uncorr.;* bat *Q corr.,* *Q 2, 3.*   246. Chill] Ile *Q 1.*
zir] sir *Q 1.*   vor] *F;* for *Q.*   247. S.D.] *Rowe; They fight Q; not in F.*

236-47. *Chill . . . foins*] Conventional stage dialect, "approximating to that of Somersetshire," but used for a variety of other counties. It is identical with the Devonshire dialect in *The London Prodigal* (1605), performed by Shakespeare's company. See Gill, *Logonomia Anglica,* 1621, p. 23.

236. *Chill*] I will. Cf. *The London Prodigal,* II. i. 40; and Gill, *op. cit.* p. 32.

238. *go your gait*] go your way.

239. *volk*] folk.

239. *And chud*] If I could. Cf. *The London Prodigal,* III. iii. 7, where *chud* = should.

242. *che vor' ye*] The usual explanation is "I warn you"; but the passage quoted by Capell from *The Contention between Liberality and Prodigality,* II. iii. 4 (" by gisse sir tis high time che vore ye ") and one quoted by Craig from *The London*

Prodigal, v. i. 349 (" Well, che vor ye, he is changed ") make it clear that the phrase means "I warrant you." See also *The London Prodigal,* II. iv. 80, III. iii. 43, and v. i. 355; and Gill, *op. cit.,* p. 32.

242. *ise*] I shall.

243. *costard*] literally a kind of apple (Drayton, *Poly-Olbion*), xviii. l. 684) but often used humorously for the head.

243. *ballow*] cudgel. Wright, *English Dialect Dictionary,* 1896, shows that in Nottingham a staff beaked with iron was called "a ballowe staff." Tucker Brooke, *Essays on Shakespeare,* 1948, p. 106, calls this "a possibly poetic, but quite unknown weapon, a 'ballow' instead of a plain batoon."

245. *dunghill*] dunghill born, low bred.

247. *foins*] thrusts. Cf. *2 Hen. IV.* II. i. 17.

And give the letters which thou find'st about me   250
To Edmund Earl of Gloucester; seek him out
Upon the English party: O! untimely death.
among
Death!   [*Dies.*

Edg. I know thee well: a serviceable villain;
As duteous to the vices of thy mistress   255
As badness would desire.

Glou.   What! is he dead?

Edg. Sit you down, father; rest you.
Let's see these pockets: the letters that he speaks of
May be my friends.   He's dead; I am only sorry
executioner He had no other deathsman.   Let us see: 260
Leave, gentle wax; and, manners, blame us not:
To know our enemies' minds, we rip their hearts;
Their papers is more lawful.   [*Reads.*

Let our reciprocal vows be remembered. You have
many opportunities to cut him off; if your will want 265
not, time and place will be fruitfully offer'd.   There is *plentifull*
nothing done if he return the conqueror; then am I the
prisoner, and his bed my gaol; from the loathed warmth
whereof deliver me, and supply the place for your labour.
         Your wife, so I would say—   270
                  Affectionate servant,
                           GONERIL.

limitless range   *lust*
O indistinguish'd space of woman's will!
A plot upon her virtuous husband's life,   274

252. English] *F;* British *Q.*   253. S.D.] *He dies Q; not in F.*   258. these]
F; his *Q.*   the] *F;* these *Q.*   259. sorry] sorrow *Q 1.*   262. we] *F;*
wee'd *Q.*   263. is] are *F 2, 3, 4.*   S.D.] *A Letter Q; Reads the Letter F;*
not in Q uncorr.   264. our] *F;* your *Q.*   269. for] of *F 3, 4.*   271.
Affectionate] *F;* your affectionate *Q 1;* and your affectionate *Q 2, 3.* servant]
seruant and for you her owne for *Venter, Q 1.*   273. O] Of *F 2, 3, 4.*   indistinguish'd] *Q 1, F 4;* indinguish'd *F 1, 2, 3;* vndistinguist *Q 2, 3.* space]
scope *conj. Theobald* will] *F;* wit *Q.*

248. *Villain*] serf.
252. *Upon*] among.
260. *deathsman*] executioner.
261. *Leave*] by your leave.
164. *reciprocal*] See Appendix, p. 250.
266. *fruitfully*] plentifully.

271. *servant*] lover. The nonsense
that follows in Q 1 may conceal
sense, meaning perhaps "and your
own if you dare venture for me."
Duthie suggests the words were an
actor's interpolation. Cf. IV. ii. 20.

And the exchange my brother!   Here, in the sands,
Thee I'll rake up, the post unsanctified
Of murtherous lechers; and in the mature time
With this ungracious paper strike the sight
Of the death-practis'd Duke.   For him 'tis well
That of thy death and business I can tell.   280
Glou. The King is mad: how stiff is my vile sense
That I stand up, and have ingenious feeling
Of my huge sorrows!   Better I were distract:
So should my thoughts be sever'd from my griefs,
And woes by wrong imaginations lose   285
The knowledge of themselves.   [*Drum afar off.*
Edg.   Give me your hand:
Far off, methinks, I hear the beaten drum.
Come, father, I'll bestow you with a friend.   [*Exeunt.*

---

276. the sands] *Q;* rhe sands *F 1.*   279. death-practis'd] *unhyphened Q.*
280. thy] his *Q 2, 3.*   284. sever'd] *F;* fenced *Q.*   286. S.D.] *after* griefs
284, *F;* A drum a farre off *Q.*   288. S.D.] *F; Exit Q.*

273. *O . . . will!*] O limitless
range of woman's lust!

273. *indistinguish'd*] indefinable, beyond the range of sight.

275. *sands*] Perrett points out that
only Gloucester thinks they are on the
beach.   Either Edgar is speaking
for his father's benefit, or Shakespeare
forgot.

276. *rake up*] cover up, as the
embers are covered with ashes so
that the fire will keep in.

277. *mature*] accent on the first
syllable.   When time is ripe.

278. *ungracious*] without grace,
wicked.

279. *death-practis'd*] whose death is
plotted.

281. *stiff*] obstinately unbending.

281. *vile sense*] Empson, *op. cit.*,
p. 146, explains that Gloucester's
sense is vile because it seems disloyal to outlast Lear's, but that
vile sense is commonly used for the
senses as a source of pleasure, so
that he might be regretting his past
sensualities which have coarsened
his sensibility.   This is too ingenious.
Gloucester calls his senses vile because they still allow him to be fully
conscious of his sorrows, and do not
give him the relief of insanity.

282. *ingenious*] conscious.

283. *distract*] mad.

285. *wrong imaginations*] illusions.

288. *bestow*] lodge.

288. *friend*] We are not told how
the fugitive Edgar has got in touch
with a friend.

SCENE VII.—[*A Tent in the French Camp.*]

Enter CORDELIA, KENT, *Doctor, and Gentleman.*

Cor. O thou good Kent! how shall I live and work
To match thy goodness? My life will be too short,
And every measure fail me.
Kent. To be acknowledg'd, Madam, is o'er-paid.
All my reports go with the modest truth,   5
No more nor clipp'd, but so.
Cor.   Be better suited: *clothed*
These weeds are memories [*reminders*] of those worser hours:
I prithee, put them off.
Kent.   Pardon, dear Madam;
Yet to be known shortens my made intent: *interferes with the plans I have made*
My boon I make it that you know me not   10
Till time and I think meet.
Cor. Then be't so, my good Lord. [*To the Doctor.*] How
does the King?
Doct. Madam, sleeps still.
Cor. O you kind Gods,
Cure this great breach in his abused nature!   15
Th' untuned and jarring senses, O! wind up
Of this child-changed father.

either changed by children or changed to a child

Scene VII

A . . . Camp] Capell, subst.; not in Q, F.   S.D.] Craig; Enter
Cordelia, Kent, and Gentleman F; Enter Cordelia, Kent and Doctor Q; Lear on a
bed asleep Steevens (Capell).   8. Pardon] F; Pardon me Q.
12. good] not in Q 2, 3.   S.D.] Theobald, subst.; not in Q, F.
13. Doct.] Q; Gent. F.   16. and] not in Q 3.   jarring] F; hurrying Q.
17. Doct.] Q; Gent. F.

Scene VII

3. *measure fail me*] because Kent's goodness is immeasurable. Cf. *Leir*, 2655-6:
 " Yet all I can, I, were it ne're so much
  Were not sufficient, thy true loue is such."
5. *reports*] i.e. about Lear, and his own service as Caius.
6. *clipp'd*] inaccurate through omission.
6. *so*] as I have described them.

6. *suited*] clothed.

7. *memories*] reminders.

9. *shortens . . . intent*] interferes with the plan I have made.

16. *wind up*] tune, by tightening the strings.

17. *child-changed*] " changed to a child " (Steevens); changed in mind by the cruelty of his children (Malone). Cf. *Rich. III.* III. vii. 184 ' care-crazed.' Cleanth Brooks thinks that the ambiguity is deliberate.

Doct.   So please your Majesty
That we may wake the King? he hath slept long.
Cor. Be govern'd by your knowledge, and proceed
I' th' sway of your own will.   Is he array'd?   20

Enter LEAR *in a chair carried by Servants.*

Gent. Ay, Madam, in the heaviness of sleep
We put fresh garments on him
Doct. Be by, good Madam, when we do awake him;
I doubt not of his temperance.   sanity
Cor.   ——————   Very well.   [*Music.*
Doct. Please you, draw near.   Louder the music there!   25
Cor. O my dear father!   Restoration hang
Thy medicine on my lips, and let this kiss
Repair those violent harms that my two sisters
Have in thy reverence made!
Kent.   Kind and dear Princess!
Cor. Had you not been their father, these white flakes   30
      Did challenge pity of them.   Was this a face   snowy locks
claim   To be oppos'd against the warring winds?
To stand against the deep dread-bolted thunder?
In the most terrible and nimble stroke
Of quick, cross lightning? to watch—poor *perdu!*—   35

18. That] *not in* Q *2, 3.*   20, S.D.] *F; not in* Q.   21. Gent.] *F; Doct.* Q.
of] *F;* of his Q.   23. Doct.] *Capell;* Gent. Q *1, F;* Kent Q *2, 3.*   Be . . .
Madam] *F;* Good madam be by Q. 24. not] *not in* F *1, 2.* 24-5. Very . . . there]
Q; *not in* F.   24. S.D.] *Grant White, subst.; not in* Q, F.   29.
Kind] *F;* Klnd Q *1.*   31. Did challenge] *F;* Had challenged Q.   a face]
face F *3, 4.*   32. oppos'd] *F;* exposd Q.   warring] Q; iarring F.   33-6.
To . . . helm?] Q; *not in* F.   33. dread-bolted] *hyphened Theobald.*   35.
perdu] Per du Q; perdu! *Warburton.*

24. *temperance*] sanity, normality.
25. *music*] Kittredge compares
Temp. v. i. 58-9.
30. *white flakes*] snowy locks.
31. *challenge*] claim.
32. *warring*] The F reading, 'jarring,' was a mistake, the epithet
being borrowed from l. 16 *ante.*
33. *deep*] bass.
33. *dread-bolted*] furnished with
the dread thunder-bolt.
35. *perdu*] a sentry in a perilous

position (*sentinelle perdue*].   Cf.
Tourneur, *The Atheist's Tragedy,* II.
vi. 4 (ed. Nicoll, p. 210):
      " I would you would relieue me,
            for I am
      So heauie that I shall ha' much
            adoe
      To stand out my perdu."
Moberly suggests the word means
" lost one "; and I think Shakespeare
had the derivative meaning in his
mind.

With this thin helm? Mine enemy's dog,
Though he had bit me, should have stood that
  night
Against my fire. And wast thou fain, poor father,
To hovel thee with swine and rogues forlorn,   *vagabonds*
In short and musty straw? Alack, alack!   40
'Tis wonder that thy life and wits at once
Had not concluded all. He wakes; speak to him.
Doct. Madam, do you; 'tis fittest.
Cor. How does my royal Lord? How fares your Majesty?
Lear. You do me wrong to take me out o' th' grave; 45
Thou art a soul in bliss; but I am bound
Upon a wheel of fire, that mine own tears
    as in hell Do scald like molten lead.
Cor.   Sir, do you know me?
Lear. You are a spirit, I know; where did you die?
Cor. Still, still, far wide. *his mind is astray* 50
Doct. He's scarce awake; let him alone awhile.
Lear. Where have I been? Where am I? Fair daylight?

---

36. enemy's] *F;* iniurious *Q;* injurer's *Capell.*   41. thy] my *F 3, 4.*
43. *Doct.*] *Q; Gen. F.*   45. o' th'] *F;* ath *Q.*   48. scald] *Q;* scal'd *F 1.*
do . . . me?] *F;* know me *Q 1;* know ye me? *Q 2, 3.*   49. You are] *F;* Yar
Q 1; Y'are *Q 2, 3.*   where] *Q 1, F 1, 2;* when *Q 2, 3, F 3, 4.*   51.
Doct.] *Q; Gent. F.*

---

36. *enemy's*] The Q reading ' iniurious ' may be a misreading of
iniurers, and Capell's reading may
be correct. But, as Duthie points
out *iniurious* may be a misreading
of *enemies.*

38. *Against*] before, opposite to.

39. *rogues*] vagabonds.

40. *short*] cut short for litter;
scanty, insufficient; broken up into
short lengths by constant use as
bedding (Kittredge).

42. *all*] together.

47. *wheel of fire*] Lear thinks he
is in hell. Cf. Appendix, p. 255.
H. W. Crundell has pointed out to
me that the torment of the wheel of
fire, although not scriptural, is
traditional in the medieval legends
and visions of Hell and Purgatory.

They all draw upon the New Testament Apocrypha. In *The Apocalypse
of Peter,* the *Sibylline Oracles,* and
The Acts of Thomas, the wheel of
fire is the punishment inflicted upon
the damned. Cf. M. R. James,
Apoc. N.T., pp. 390, 517, 525.
Owst, *Literature and Pulpit in Medieval England,* 1933, cites *The Pricke
of Conscience,* 6576, 7124, which
mentions scalding tears and molten
lead. Holinshed discusses the au-
thenticity of the stories of St. Patrick's
Purgatory, so we can assume that
they were known to Shakespeare's
contemporaries, though he probably
derived his information from some
intermediate source.

47. *that*] so that.

50. *wide*] astray, wandering. Cf.
M.A. IV. i. 63.

deluded

I am mightily abus'd.   I should e'en die with pity
To see another thus.   I know not what to say.
I will not swear these are my hands: let's see;   55
I feel this pin prick.   Would I were assur'd
Of my condition!

Cor.   O! look upon me, Sir,
And hold your hand in benediction o'er me.
No, Sir, you must not kneel.

Lear.   *clothing*   Pray, do not mock me:
I am a very foolish fond old man,   60
Fourscore and upward, not an hour more or less;
And, to deal plainly,
I fear I am not in my perfect mind.
Methinks I should know you and know this man;
Yet I am doubtful: for I am mainly ignorant *entirely* 65
What place this is, and all the skill I have
Remembers not these garments; nor I know not
Where I did lodge last night.   Do not laugh at me;
For, as I am a man, I think this lady
To be my child Cordelia.

Cor.   And so I am, I am.   70

Lear. Be your tears wet?   Yes, faith.   I pray, weep
    not:
If you have poison for me, I will drink it.
I know you do not love me; for your sisters
Have, as I do remember, done me wrong:
You have some cause, they have not.

Cor.   No cause, no cause.   75

Lear. Am I in France?

Kent.   In your own kingdom, Sir.

return to sanity, He recognizes cordelia for what she is.

53. e'en] even *F 3, 4.*   58. hand] *F;* hands *Q.*   59. No, sir] *Q; not in F.*
me] *not in Q 1.*   61. not . . . less] *F; not in Q.*   63. in . . . mind] perfect in
my mind *Q 2, 3.*   68. not] no *Q 2, 3.*   70. I am, I am] *F;* I am *Q.*
74. me] we *F 2.*

53. *abus'd*] deluded.   He thinks
Cordelia must be an hallucination.

53-4. *I should . . . thus*] This is not
to be taken as indulgence in self-
pity, but as an objective statement
to guide the audience in their
emotional reactions.

60. *fond*] in his dotage.

65. *mainly*] entirely.

69-70. *lady . . . child*] the contrast
between these two words indicates
Lear's return to sanity.

70. *I . . . am*] Ruskin, *Works*, ed.
1903, xiv. 17, remarks that " all
Cordelia is poured forth in that
infinite ' I am ' of fulfilled love."

deceive

Lear. Do not abuse me.

Doct. Be comforted, good Madam; the great rage, *madness*
You see, is kill'd in him: and yet it is danger
To make him even o'er the time he has lost.   80
Desire him to go in; trouble him no more
Till further settling.   *until he is calmer*

Cor. Will't please your Highness walk?   *withdraw*

Lear.   You must bear with me.
Pray you now, forget and forgive: I am old and
foolish.   [*Exeunt Lear, Cordelia, Doctor, and Attendants.*

Gent. Holds it true, sir, that the Duke of Cornwall   85
was so slain?

Kent. Most certain, sir.

Gent. Who is conductor of his people?

Kent. As 'tis said, the bastard son of Gloucester.

Gent. They say Edgar, his banish'd son, is with the   90
Earl of Kent in Germany.

Kent. Report is changeable. 'Tis time to look about;
the powers of the kingdom approach apace.

Gent. The arbitrement is like to be bloody. Fare you   94
well, sir.   [*Exit.*

Kent's attachment to Lear

Kent. My point and period will be throughly wrought,
Or well or ill, as this day's battle's fought.   [*Exit.*

78. Doct.] *Q; Gent. F.*   79. kill'd] *F;* cured *Q;* quell'd *conj. Collier*
79-80. and . . . lost] *Q; not in F.*   83. Will't] *Rowe;* Wilt *Q, F.*   83-4.
Will't . . . foolish] *as in Capell; prose in Q; three lines, ending* me; forgiue,
foolish. *F.*   84. you now] now *Q.*   S.D.] *Exeunt. Manet Kent, and
Gent. Q; Exeunt F.*   85-97.] *Q; not in F.*   85-96. Holds . . . well,
sir] *prose Q; verse Capell, lines ending* sir, sir. said, Edgar, Kent, changeable,
kingdom, arbitrement, sir. *Capell omits that (85), and* As *(89) and reads* And
the . . . most bloody *(94).*   93-6. Report . . . well, sir.] *Prose in Theobald;
three lines, ending* about, apace, sir. *Q.*   95. S.D.] *Theobald; not in Q.*
97. S.D.] *Exit Q 1; Exit Kent Theobald; not in Q 2, 3.*

77. *abuse*] deceive.

78. *rage*] frenzy, delirium.

80. *even o'er*] fill up the gap in;
to smooth over, render what had
passed unbroken in his recollection
(Wright).   Craig suggests the
metaphor is taken from the language
of accountants, *to even* means "to
make accounts even." Some take
even to be an adj. and the phrase

might then mean "precise about,"
"*au fait* with."

82. *Till´ . . . settling*] till he is
calmer. Cf. *W.T.* IV. iv. 482.

83. *walk*] withdraw.

85. *Holds it true*] is it still accepted.

88. *conductor*] leader, general.

94. *arbitrement*] decisive encounter.

96. *My . . . period*] my life's end
and object; the full-stop at the end
of my life's sentence.

ACT V

SCENE I.—[*The British Camp near Dover.*]

Enter, with drum and colours, EDMUND, REGAN, *Officers,*
Soldiers, and Others.

Edm. Know of the Duke if his last purpose hold,
    Or whether since he is advis'd by aught
    To change the course; he's full of alteration
    And self-reproving; bring his constant pleasure.
                       [*To an Officer, who goes out.*

Reg. Our sister's man is certainly miscarried.   5
Edm. 'Tis to be doubted, Madam.
Reg.   Now, sweet Lord,
    You know the goodness I intend upon you:
    Tell me, but truly, but then speak the truth,
    Do you not love my sister?
Edm.   In honour'd love.
Reg. But have you never found my brother's way   10
    To the forfended place?
Edm.   That thought abuses you.

ACT V

Scene 1

Act v *Scene* i] F; *Act* IV *Scene* viii. *conj. Spedding*
The . . . Dover] *Capell, subst.; not in Q, F; A Camp Rowe.*   S.D.]
Enter . . . Regan, Gentlemen, and Souldiers F; *Enter Edmund, Regan, and their powers*
Q.   3. he's] he is *Q 2, 3.*   alteration] abdication
Q uncorr.   4. S.D. *Capell, subst.; not in Q, F.*   8. but truly]
truly *Q 2, 3.*   9. In] F; I, *Q 1*; I *Q 2, 3.*   11-13. *Edm.* That . . .
hers] *Q; not in F.*

Scene 1

    1. *his last purpose*] i.e. to fight.
    2. *advis'd*] induced.
    3. *alteration*] vacillation.
    4. *self-reproving*] self-reproach, con-
scientious scruples.
    4. *constant pleasure*] fixed decision.
Cf. i. i. 43.
    5. *man*] Oswald.
    5. *miscarried*] come to harm.

    6. *doubted*] feared.
    7. *intend . . . you*] mean to confer
upon you.
    8. *but then*] even if the truth is
unpalatable to me.
    9. *honour'd*] honourable.
    11. *forfended*] forbidden.   *Oth.*
v. ii. 32. Goneril's bed is forbidden
by the commandment against
adultery.

Reg. I am doubtful that you have been conjunct
And bosom'd with her, as far as we call hers.

Edm. No, by mine honour, Madam.

Reg. I never shall endure her: dear my Lord,   15
Be not familiar with her.

Edm.   Fear me not.
She and the Duke her husband!

Enter, with drum and colours, ALBANY, GONERIL,
and Soldiers.

Gon. [*Aside.*] I had rather lose the battle than that sister
Should loosen him and me.

Alb. Our very loving sister, well be-met.   20
Sir, this I heard; the King is come to his daughter,
With others whom the rigour of our state
Forc'd to cry out.   Where I could not be honest,
I never yet was valiant: for this business,

12-13. I am . . . hers] *As in* Q 2, 3; *prose* Q 1.   15-16. I . . . her]
As in F; *prose in* Q 1.   16-17. Fear . . . husband!] *As in Capell; one line*
Q, F.   16. me] Q; *not in* F.   17. S.D.] F; *Enter Albany and Goneril
with Troupes* Q.   18. S.D.] *Theobald; not in* Q, F.   18-19. I . . . me]
Arranged as in Theobald; prose Q 1; *two lines, the first ending* battell Q 2, 3;
not in F.   19. loosen] cosin Q 3.   21. Sir . . . heard] F; For this I
heare Q; Sir, this I heare *Theobald.*   23-8. Where . . . nobly] Q; *not in* F.

12. *doubtful*] fearful.

12. *conjunct*] Cf. II. ii. 119.

13. *bosom'd . . . her*] embraced her, breast to breast.

13. *as . . . hers*] in the fullest sense of the word, not merely in the sense of " admitted to her confidence."

15-17. *I . . . husband*] It is possible that " I never shall endure her " should be given to Edmund (W. W. Lloyd, *N.Q.* 11 June 1892) to complete line 14, that the rest of Regan's speech should be printed as a single line, and that Edmund's next speech should likewise be printed as one line. Otherwise we must take " I never shall endure her " to mean " I could never endure her to loosen you and

me." Cf. Goneril's words ll. 18-19. *post.*

16. *Fear me not*] Don't distrust me, don't worry about me on that account. F omits the pronoun, probably by accident.

18-19. *lose . . . loosen*] The Q spelling 'loose' brings out the quibble.

20. *be-met*] met.

22. *rigour of our state*] harshness of our rule.

23-8. *Where . . . nobly*] These lines are omitted in F, perhaps because they related to the French invasion; but it seems probable that the Q text is corrupt.

23. *Where*] in a case where.

24. *for*] as for.

It touches us, as France invades our land,   25
Not bolds the King, with others, whom, I fear,
Most just and heavy causes make oppose.

Edm. Sir, you speak nobly.

Reg.   Why is this reason'd?

Gon. Combine together 'gainst the enemy;
For these domestic and particular broils   30
Are not the question here.

Alb.   Let's then determine
With th' ancient of war on our proceeding.

Edm. I shall attend you presently at your tent.

Reg. Sister, you'll go with us?

Gon. No.   35

Reg. 'Tis most convenient; pray go with us.

Gon. [*Aside.*] O, ho! I know the riddle. I will go.

25. touches] Q 1; toucheth Q 2, 3.   26. Not bolds the] Q; Not the old
conj. Mason; Not holds the Pope. 30. and . . . broils] F; dore particulars Q 1;
doore particulars Q 2, 3; dear particulars Ridley.   31. the] F; to Q.   31-2.
Let's . . . proceeding] Arranged as in Q 2, 3; prose Q 1; first line ends warre F.
32. proceeding] F; proceedings Q.   33. Edm. I . . . tent] Q; not in F.   36.
pray] F; pray you Q.   37. S.D. Aside] Capell; the whole line aside, Hanmer.
As . . . disguised] Theobald; Enter Edgar Q 1; Exit. Enter Edgar Q 2, 3;
Exeunt both the Armies; Enter Edgar F.

25. *touches*] concerns.

26-7. *Not . . . oppose*] Not because
he emboldens by supporting the
King and others who have been
induced to take up arms against us
by genuine grievances.   This is
presumably the meaning, but the
passage may be corrupt.   The
repetition " with others whom "
from l. 22 is suspicious, and l. 27
seems to be a restatement of " the
rigour . . . out." It is possible that
a line or two has dropped out before
l. 26, and that Albany said
originally: " We intend to repel
the invader, but not to treat the
King and his supporters as enemies."

26. *bolds*] emboldens, encourages,
supports. Cf. Wyatt, Poems, ed.
Muir, p. 43:
  " And therwithall bolded I seke
      the way how
    To vtter the smert that I suffre
      within."

27. *heavy causes*] weighty reasons.

28. *reason'd*] mentioned. " Why
do you want to waste time thus in
arguing with yourself about the
justice of our cause? " (Kittredge).

30. *and . . . broils*] and private
quarrels.   But this may well be
a F sophistication.   Stevens interprets the Q reading " particulars at
our very doors "; but Malone,
rightly I believe, suspects that
' dore ' is a misprint for ' dear '
(spelt ' dere ' presumably), the
phrase meaning " intimate details "
rather than " important quarrels,"
which is Malone's interpretation.

32. *th' ancient of war*] experienced
officers, ' brass-hats.'

33. *presently*] at once.

36. *convenient*] befitting.

37. *O . . . go*] This may mean
" You want to keep me under your
eye so as to observe my relations with
Edmund "; or, " You don't want

As they are going out enter EDGAR, *disguised.*

Edg. If e'er your grace had speech with man so poor,
Hear me one word.

Alb.   I'll <u>overtake</u> you. *catch you up*

[*Exeunt Edmund, Regan, Goneril, Officers,
Soldiers, and Attendants.*

Speak.

Edg. Before you fight the battle, ope this letter.   40
If you have victory, let the trumpet sound
For him that brought it: wretched though I seem,
I can produce a champion that will prove
claimed What is a<u>vouched</u> there.   If you miscarry,
Your business of the world hath so an end,   45
And machination ceases.   Fortune love you!

Alb. Stay till I have read the letter.

Edg.   I was forbid it.
When time shall serve, let but the herald cry,
And I'll appear again.

Alb.   Why, fare thee well: 49
I will o'erlook thy paper.   [*Exit Edgar.*

Re-enter EDMUND.

Edm. The enemy's in view; draw up your powers.
Here is the guess of their true strength and forces
by careful By diligent <u>discovery</u>; but your haste
recce Is now urged on you.

Alb.   We will greet the time.   [*Exit.*

38. had] did *Q 3.*   man] one *Q 2, 3.*   39. S.D.] *Theobald; see
note to 37 above.*   42. wretched] wretch *F 2, 3, 4.*   though] thoughts
Q 3.   46. And . . . ceases] *F; not in Q.*   love] *Q;* loues *F.*   49-50.
Why . . . paper] *arranged as conj. S. Walker; one line Q, F.*   50. o'erlook]
look ore *Q 2, 3.*   thy] *F;* the *Q.*   S.D.] *Dyce; Exit after* again (49)
Q, F.   52. Here] *F;* Hard *Q.*   guess] quesse *Q 1.*   54. S.D.] *not in Q 2, 3.*

me to attend the council of war,
where I shall be close to Edmund."
If Regan was herself going to attend
the council, we must assume that she
did not wish to leave Goneril behind
with Edmund even for a moment.
    44. *avouched*] maintained.
    44. *miscarry*] lose the battle, and
perish.

46. *machination*] Cf. 1. ii. 118.

50. *o'erlook*] peruse.

51. *powers*] troops.

53. *By . . . discovery*] obtained by
careful reconnoitring.

54. *greet the time*] meet the emer-
gency.

Edm. To both these sisters have I sworn my love;　　55
　　Each jealous of the other, as the stung
　　Are of the adder.　Which of them shall I take?
　　Both? one? or neither?　Neither can be enjoy'd
　　If both remain alive: to take the widow
　　Exasperates, makes mad her sister Goneril;　　60
　　And hardly shall I carry out my side,
　　Her husband being alive.　Now then, we'll use
　　His countenance for the battle; which being done,
　　Let her who would be rid of him devise
　　His speedy taking off.　As for the mercy　　65
　　Which he intends to Lear and to Cordelia,
　　The battle done, and they within our power,
　　Shall never see his pardon; for my state
　　Stands on me to defend, not to debate.　　　[*Exit.*

55. sisters] sister *Q 1.*　　56. stung] sting *Q.*　　64. who] *F;* that *Q.*
65. the] *F;* his *Q.*　　66. intends] *F;* entends *Q 1;* extends *Q 2, 3.*

SCENE II.—[*A Field between the two Camps.*]

Alarum within.　Enter, with drum and colours, LEAR,
　　CORDELIA, *and their Forces; and exeunt.*

Enter EDGAR *and* GLOUCESTER.

Edg. Here, father, take the shadow of this tree
　　For your good host; pray that the right may
　　　　thrive.

Scene II
A . . . Camps] Capell, subst.; not in *Q, F.*
F, subst.; Alarum.
Cordelia with her father in her hand Q.

56. *jealous*] suspicious.

61. *carry . . . side*] make my game,
succeed in my ambitions.　This is
the usual explanation, the image
being taken from a game of cards.
But another explanation is possible,
i.e. "fulfil my side of the bargain
with Goneril—satisfy her lust in
return for advancement."

63. *countenance*] authority, credit.

65. *taking off*] killing. Cf. *Macb.*
I. vii. 20.

68. *Shall*] they shall.

68-9. *for . . . debate*] I must take

Alarum . . . exeunt] *Enter the powers of France over the stage,*
1. tree] *F;* bush *Q.*

active steps to maintain my position,
not merely think about it.　Edmund
hopes that Goneril will kill Albany,
and kill, or be killed by, Regan, leaving him free to marry the survivor.
The survival of Lear and Cordelia
would prejudice his chances of becoming king of the united kingdom.

69. *Stands on me*] concerns me
much. Cf. *C.E.* IV. i. 68 and *Ham.*
v. ii. 63.

Scene II
Spedding, *New Shakespeare Society
Transactions,* 1877-9, p. 11, argues

(margin note: Irony Edg expects to win)

> If ever I return to you again.
> I'll bring you comfort.

Glou.   Grace go with you, sir!   [*Exit Edgar.*

Alarum; afterwards a retreat.   Re-enter EDGAR.

Edg. Away, old man! give me thy hand: away!   5
     King Lear hath lost, he and his daughter ta'en.
     Give me thy hand; come on.
Glou. No further, sir; a man may rot even here.
Edg. What! in ill thoughts again?   Men must endure
     Their going hence, even as their coming hither: 10
     Ripeness is all.   Come on.

(margin note: Q Lear, acknow his red...)

Glou.   And that's true too.   [*Exeunt.*

(margin note: Lear dies but he has achieved a maturity. He is ready for it)

4. go] be F 3, 4.   S.D. *Exit Edgar*] Pope; *Exit* F; *Exit after* comfort Q.
Re-enter Edgar] *Enter Edgar* F; not in Q 1.   8. further] F; farther Q.   9.
What . . . endure] *One line* Q; *two in* F.   11. *Glou.* And . . . too] not in Q.
S.D. *Exeunt*] F; *Exit* Q 2, 3; not in Q 1.

that as the battle is inadequately
described, Shakespeare must have
intended the fourth act to end after
l. 4 of this scene.   This would make
Act IV extremely long, and the
shortness of this scene may be rather
explained as an example of dramatic
economy, since the battle itself is
not important.   We are only interested in the result of the battle.
In *Macbeth* and *Antony and Cleopatra*
the battles are important since the
heroes of both plays are soldiers.

2. *good host*] shelterer, entertainer.

3-4. *If . . . comfort*] dramatic irony.
Cf. l. 5.

11. *Ripeness is all*] The one important thing with regard to death
is that we should be ready for it.
Steevens compares *Ham.* v. ii. 234.
The aphorism reads like a conden-
sation of Montaigne's essay, " That
to philosophize is to learne how to
die." He discusses life's " ordinary
mutations " which reconcile us to
death (*op. cit.* i. 105; cf. IV. i. 11);
he compares death with birth: " So
wept we, and so much did it cost
us to enter into this life; and so did
we spoile us of our ancient vaile

in entring into it " (*op. cit.* i. 107-8;
cf. v. ii. 9-10); and he concludes
that the actual length of our lives
is unimportant: " It consists not in
number of yeeres, but in your will,
that you have lived long enough "
(*op. cit.* p. 112).   In Elyot, *The
Gouernour*, i. xxii (Everyman ed.,
p. 98) there is a discussion of Maturity
" Maturitie is a mean betweene two
extremities, wherein nothynge lacketh
or exceedeth, and is in such astate
that it may neyther encrease nor
minysshe without losinge the de-
nomination of Maturitie . . . *Maturum*
in latyn maye be enterpretid ripe
or redy, as fruite when it is ripe,
it is at the very poynte to be gathered
and eaten . . . Therefore that word
maturitie, is translated to the actis
of man, that whan they be done with
suche moderation, that nothing in
the doing may be sene superfluous or
indigent, we may saye, that they be
maturely doone: reseruyng the
wordes rype and redy to frute and
other things separate from affaires, as
we haue nowe in usage." Cf. Edgar's
phrase, ' mature time ' (IV. vi. 277),
and *M.M.* v. i. 116 ' ripened time.'

SCENE III.—[*The British Camp near Dover.*]

Enter, in conquest, with drum and colours, EDMUND, LEAR
and CORDELIA, *prisoners; Officers, Soldiers, etc.*

Edm. Some officers take them away: good guard,
Until their greater pleasures first be known
That are to censure them.

Cor.   We are not the first
Who, with best meaning, have incurr'd the worst.
For thee, oppressed King, I am cast down;   5
Myself could else out-frown false Fortune's frown.
Shall we not see these daughters and these sisters?

Lear. No, no, no, no! Come, let's away to prison;
We two alone will sing like birds i' th' cage:
When thou dost ask me blessing, I'll kneel down,   10
And ask of thee forgiveness: so we'll live,
And pray, and sing, and tell old tales, and laugh
At gilded butterflies, and hear poor rogues

Scene III

The . . . Dover] Malone; not in Q, F. subst.; Enter . . . Souldiers, Captaine F; prisoners Q.   2. first] F; best Q. 8. No . . . no] F; no, no Q. 13. hear poor rogues] heere (poore Rogues] F 1; hear—poor rogues!—Schmidt.

Enter . . . soldiers, etc.] Capell, Enter Edmund with Lear and Cordelia 5. I am] F, Q 3; am I Q 1, 2. 12. and sing] Q 1; F; not in Q 2, 3.

Scene III

2. *greater pleasures*] wishes of the people of greater authority.

3. *censure*] judge, pass judgment on. Cf. *M.M.* I. iv. 72.

6. *Myself . . . frown*] Cf. Seneca, *Œdipus* I. i. (tr. Nevile):
"*Joc.* It is no poinct of courage stout to yeelde to fortunes frown.
Œd. Nay. Feare could never cause mee stoupe nor Fortune cast mee down."

9. *cage*] a quibble, since the word also means prison. Cf. *2 Hen. VI.* IV. ii. 56. Maxwell compares Spenser, *F.Q.* VI. vi. 4. 9.

10. *I'll . . . down*] Shakespeare was probably thinking of the scene in the source-play. See Appendix, p. 233.

12. *old tales*] improbable fictions of bygone times. Cf. *W.T.* v. ii. 66 and *A.Y.L.I.* I. ii. 128.

13. *gilded butterflies*] Craig suggests that this means "gay courtiers" as in Marston's *Antonio and Mellida*, IV. i. 49:
"Troopes of pide butterflies, that flutter still
In greatnesse summer, that confirme a prince."
But it is more likely that Lear is referring to actual butterflies, the other meaning merely suggesting the "court news" in the following line.

13. *poor rogues*] wretched creatures, presumably their fellow-prisoners or jailers. In the F this phrase is in parenthesis and must refer to Lear and Cordelia.

we will observe detachedly these things the observers of the gods

Talk of court news; and we'll talk with them too,
Who loses and who wins; who's in, who's out;   15
And take upon 's the mystery of things,
As if we were Gods' spies: and we'll wear out,
In a wall'd prison, packs and sects of great ones   *cliques*
That ebb and flow by th' moon.

Edm.   Take them away.

Lear. Upon such sacrifices, my Cordelia,   20
The Gods themselves throw incense. Have I
    caught thee?

only divine intervention can separate us.

He that parts us shall bring a brand from heaven,
And fire us hence like foxes. Wipe thine eyes;

14. talk] talkd *F 2.*   15. who's . . . who's] *F;* whose . . . whose *Q.*   19.
th' moon] *F;* the moon *Q 2, 3.*   23. eyes] eye *F 2, 3, 4.*

16. *take upon*] profess to understand
and explain.
16. *the . . . things*] the mysterious
course of worldly events, the mystery
of human life and destiny. Cf. the
use of *res* in Latin poetry; e.g.
Virgil, *Georgics,* ii. 490; Ovid,
Metamorphoses, xv. 68. G. C. Taylor
compares Florio, *op. cit.* iii. 368:
" These people . . . who know nothing themselves, and yet will take
upon them to governe the world
and know all: . . .
  What cause doth calme the Sea,
    what cleares the yeare, . . .
  What makes the Moones darke
    Orbe to wax or wane,
  What friendly fewd of things both
    will and can."
17. *Gods'*] There is no apostrophe
in F or Q, and I follow Perrett in
assuming that Shakespeare intended
the plural since he was writing of a
pagan world.
17. *spies*] This may mean " angels
commissioned to survey and report
the lives of men " (Johnson). Warburton, less plausibly, explains:
" spies placed on God Almighty to
watch his motions."
18. *packs and sects*] cliques and
parties.

20. *such sacrifices*] as their renunciation of the world (Bradley); as
those Cordelia has made for Lear's
sake (Kittredge). I think Bradley
is right; but there seems also to be
an underlying suggestion of human
sacrifice, which looks forward to
the murder of Cordelia. In an old
note-book I have found the suggestion,
perhaps based on T. Carter's *Shakespeare and Holy Scriptures,* p. 442, that
underlying Lear's speech there are
echoes of several Old Testament
stories—of Jephthah's daughter, who
was sacrificed, and of the destruction of Sodom by a brand from
heaven, of Samson and the foxes, of
Pharaoh's dream of the good and
bad years.
21. *incense*] R. W. Chambers compares *Wisdom* iii. 6.
21. *Have . . . thee?*] Cf. *M.W.* III.
iii. 45. Falstaff is quoting from the
second song in Sidney's *Astrophel
and Stella.*
22. *He . . . heaven*] We can never
be parted again by human agency.
23. *fire . . . foxes*] as foxes were
driven from their holes by fire and
smoke. Cf. the Harsnett parallel,
Appendix, p. 255.

ert beings

The good years shall devour them, flesh and fell,

we will
ot weep
ver Gon & Reg

Ere they shall make us weep: we'll see 'em starv'd
    first.   25

Come.   [*Exeunt Lear and Cordelia, guarded.*

Edm. Come hither, captain; hark.

Take thou this note;   [*Giving a paper.*
    Go follow them to prison.

One step I have advanc'd thee; if thou dost
As this instructs thee, thou dost make thy way   30
To noble fortunes; know thou this, that men
Are as the time is; to be tender-minded

ere is not
e, or it is
delicate a

Does not become a sword; thy great employment

after to
sacss

Will not bear question; either say thou'lt do 't,

24. good years] *F;* good *Q;* goodjers *Theobald;* goujeres *Hanmer.*   them]
em *Q.*   flesh] *F;* fleach *Q.*   25. 'em] *Q 3, F 3, 4;* e'm *F 1, 2;* vm *Q 1;*
em *Q 2.*   starv'd] *F;* starue *Q.*   26. Come] *not in Q 2, 3.*   S.D.] *Theobald;*
Exit F, Q 2, 3; not in Q 1.   27. S.D.] *Malone.*   29. One] *And Q uncorr.*
32. tender-minded] *Hyphened by Rowe.*   33. thy] my *Theobald.*

24. *good years*] Cf. *M.A.* I. iii. i;
2 Hen IV. II. iv. 64, 191. See also
Golding, *op. cit.* iii. 319: "And
what a goodyeare have I won by
scolding erst (she sed)." The word
goodyear "came to be used in im-
precatory phrases, as denoting some
undefined malefic power or agency"
(*N.E.D.*). It may be derived from
the Dutch phrase "wat goet iaer
is dat." Florio translates "Il mal
anno che dio ti dia" as "With a
good yeare to thee!" According
to Morwenstow (*N.Q.* v. 607, 1852)
the Goujere is the old Cornish name
of the Fiend, and this meaning was
confirmed later (*N.Q.* 11 March
1876). Croft fantastically interprets
as *gougers*, those who gouge out
people's eyes. (There is no evidence
that Lear had heard of Cornwall's
brutality to Gloucester, though he
knew Gloucester had lost his eyes.)
Nor is there any substance in
Hanmer's emendation, *goujeres* (i.e.
the pox), a word he ingeniously
but inadmissibly derived from the
Fr. *gouje* (defined by Cotgrave as
"a Souldiers Pug or Punke; a
Whore that followes the Camp").

In Pharaoh's dream (*Genesis,* xli)
the thin ears that devoured the
seven good ears symbolized seven
years of famine; and the words
'devour' (24) and 'starv'd' (25)
suggest that the story of Joseph was,
vaguely, at the back of Shakespeare's
mind. Lear may mean that Goneril
and Regan will be destroyed not by
misfortunes but by their evil prosperity, and till the day of their
ruin he and Cordelia will not deign
to weep. When Lear does weep
next Goneril and Regan are both
dead.

24. *flesh and fell*] flesh and skin,
i.e. altogether.

33. *sword*] one who wields a
sword, a soldier.

34. *Will . . . question*] will not admit
discussion; either because it must
be done promptly, or because it is
too delicate a matter to be expressed
in words. Ragan (*King Leir,* 1309-10)
when bribing a man to murder
Leir, says:
"It is a thing of right strange
    consequence,
    And well I cannot vtter it in
    words."

Or thrive by other means.

Offi.   *style yourself*   I'll do 't, my Lord.   35

Edm. About it; and write happy when th' hast done.
Mark,—I say, instantly, and carry it so
As I have set it down.

Offi. I cannot draw a cart nor eat dried oats; *I am a man*
If it be man's work I'll do 't.   *not a*   [*Exit.* 40
                                                         horse

Flourish. Enter ALBANY, GONERIL, REGAN, *Officers,
and Soldiers.*

                                                  disposition
Alb. Sir, you have show'd to-day your valiant strain,
And Fortune led you well; you have the captives
Who were the opposites of this day's strife;
I do require them of you, so to use them
As we shall find their merits and our safety   45
May equally determine.

Edm.   Sir, I thought it fit
To send the old and miserable King
To some retention and appointed guard;
Whose age had charms in it, whose title more,
To pluck the common bosom on his side,   50
And turn our impress'd lances in our eyes *conscripted*
Which do command them.   With him I sent the
          Queen;

*cf
Regan
re Glou.
p 138*

36. th'hast] *F;* thou hast *Q.*   39-40. I . . . do it] *Q; not in F.*   40. Exit]
Steevens; Exit Captaine *F; not in Q.* Flourish . . . *Officers, and Soldiers*] Flourish . . .
another Captain, Soldiers *F;* Enter Duke, the two Ladies, and others *Q.*   41.
show'd] *Q 1, F;* shewne *Q 2, 3.*   43. Who] *F;* That *Q.*
44. I] *F;* We *Q.*   require them] *F;* require then *Q.*   47. send]
saue *Q uncorr.*   48. and . . . guard] *Q corr., Q 2, 3; not in Q uncorr., F.*
49. had] *F;* has *Q.*   50. common] coren *Q uncorr.*   bosom] blossomes
Q 2, 3.   on] *F;* of *Q.*

36. *write happy*] style yourself happy.

37. *carry it so*] manage the affair
in such a way that it will appear that
Cordelia slew herself.

39. *I . . . oats*] I'm not a horse.
I don't want to be driven by necessity
after the war to become an agri-
cultural labourer.

41. *strain*] lineage, or, more probably here, disposition.

43. *opposites*] opponents, enemies.

45. *merits*] deserts.

48. *retention*] confinement.

49. *Whose*] i.e. the King's.

50. *To . . . side*] win the hearts of
the common people.

51. *impress'd lances*] conscripted
lances, i.e. soldiers.

My reason all the same; and they are ready
To-morrow, or at further space, t'appear
Where you shall hold your session.   At this time   55
We sweat and bleed; the friend hath lost his
    friend,
And the best quarrels, in the heat, are curs'd
By those that feel their sharpness;
The question of Cordelia and her father
Requires a fitter place.

Alb.   Sir, by your patience,   60
I hold you but a subject of this war,
Not as a brother.

Reg.   That's as we list to grace him;
Methinks our pleasure might have been de-
    manded,
Ere you had spoke so far.   He led our powers,
Bore the commission of my place and person;   65
The which immediacy may well stand up,
And call itself your brother.

Gon.   Not so hot;
In his own grace he doth exalt himself
More than in your addition.

Reg.   In my rights,
By me invested, he compeers the best.   70

Alb. That were the most, if he should husband you.

Reg. Jesters do oft prove prophets.

Gon.   Holla, holla!

54. at] at a *Q 2, 3.*   t'appear] *F;* to appeare *Q.*   55-60. At . . . place]
Q; not in F.   56. We] *Q corr., Q 2, 3;* mee *Q uncorr.*   58. sharpness] *Q*
corr., *Q 2, 3;* sharpes *Q uncorr.*   63. might] *F;* should *Q.*   66. imme-
diacy] *F;* imediate *Q.* 69. addition] *F;* aduancement *Q.* rights] *F;* right *Q.*
71. *Alb.*] *F;* Gon. *Q.*

57. *quarrels*] causes.
57. *in the heat*] before passion has
cooled.   Edmund implies that
Lear and Cordelia would not get
a fair trial under the circumstances.
58. *sharpness*] Greg argues that
sharpes may be the correct reading.
62. *list*] wish.
64. *spoke so far*] said so much.
66. *immediacy*] Johnson says this

means " supremacy in opposition to
subordination "; but it means more
probably, " being my immediate
representative."
69. *your addition*] the titles and
offices you have bestowed upon
him.
70. *compeers*] equals.
72. *Jesters . . . prophets*] there's
many a true word spoken in jest.

That eye that told you so look'd but a-squint.

Reg. Lady, I am not well; else I should answer
From a full-flowing stomach.   General,   ~anger~ 75
Take thou my soldiers, prisoners, patrimony;
Dispose of them, of me;   the walls are thine;   ~woman's hea as a fortress~
Witness the world, that I create thee here
My lord and master.

Gon.   ~forbidding~   Mean you to enjoy him?
Alb. The let-alone lies not in your good will.   80
Edm. Nor in thine, Lord.
Alb.   Half-blooded fellow, yes.
Reg. [*To Edmund.*] Let the drum strike, and prove my
     title thine.
Alb. Stay yet; hear reason.   Edmund, I arrest thee
On capital treason; and, in thy attaint,   ~impeachment~
This gilded serpent.   [*Pointing to Goneril.*
~superficially beautiful~   For your claim, fair sister,   85
I bar it in the interest of my wife;
'Tis she is sub-contracted to this lord,   ~Albany is wise to Edmund tricks~
And I, her husband, contradict your banes.

73. a-squint] *hyphened Rowe.*   75. full-flowing] *hyphened Theobald.*
77. Dispose . . . thine] *F; not in Q.* the . . . thine] *F; they all are thine Hanmer*
(*conj. Theobald*)   are] *F 2, 3, 4; is F 1.*   79. him] *F; him then Q.*   80.
let-alone] *hyphened Capell.*   82. Reg.] *F; Bast. Q.*   S.D.] *Malone;*
not in Q, F.   thine] *F; good Q.*   84. thy] *F; thine Q.*   attaint] *Q; arrest F.*
85. S.D.] *Johnson; not in Q, F.*   sister] *Q; Sisters F.*   86. bar] *Rowe;*
bare *Q, F.*   87. this] her *Q 2, 3.*   88. your] *F; the Q.*   Banes] *Q, F;*
bans *Malone.*

73. *That . . . a-squint*] Steevens
compares the proverb: " Love being
jealous, makes a good eye look
a-squint."

75. *From a full-flowing stomach*]
with a flood of angry words. ' Stomach ' often means ' anger.'   Cf.
T.A. iii. i. 234.

77. *the walls . . . thine*] Theobald
proposed " they all are thine."
Kinnear suggested " the whole is
thine." Wright thinks it may refer
to Regan's castle (cf. 245 *post*).
Steevens cites *Cymb.* ii. i. 68: " the
walls of thy dear honour " and
Schmidt thinks it refers to Regan's

person, which surrenders itself like
a vanquished fortress.   This is
obviously correct, and, as Kittredge
points out, a woman's heart was often
compared to a fortress, long before
Shakespeare's time.

80. *The let-alone*] the power of
saying " Thou shalt not."

81. *Half-blooded fellow*] bastard.

82. *strike*] strike up.

84. *attaint*] impeachment. The F
reading ' arrest ' was copied by
mistake from the previous line.

85. *gilded*] superficially beautiful.

88. *banes*] banns.

If you will marry, make your loves to me,
My lady is bespoke.

Gon.　　　　　　　　　　An interlude! *play*　　　　90

Alb. Thou art arm'd, Gloucester; let the trumpet
　　sound:
If none appear to prove upon thy person
Thy heinous, manifest, and many treasons,
There is my pledge;　　　　　[*Throws down a glove.*
　　　　　　　　I'll *show* make it on thy heart,
Ere I taste bread, thou art in nothing less　　95
Than I have here proclaim'd thee.

Reg.　　　　　　　　　　　Sick! O, sick!

Gon. [*Aside.*] If not, I'll ne'er trust medicine. *poison*

Edm. There's my exchange:　　[*Throws down a glove.*
　　　　　　　　What in the world he is
That names me traitor, villain-like he lies.
Call by the trumpet: he that dares approach,　　100
On him, on you, who not? I will maintain
My truth and honour firmly.

Alb.　　　　　*valour*　　A herald, ho!
Trust to thy single virtue; for thy soldiers,
All levied in my name, have in my name
Took their discharge.

Reg.　　　　　　　My sickness grows upon me.　105

Alb. She is not well; convey her to my tent.

　　　　　　　　　　　　　[*Exit Regan, led.*

---

89. loves] *F;* loue *Q.*　　90-1. *Gon.* An interlude! *Alb.*] *F; not in Q.*　　91.
let . . . sound] *F; not in Q.*　　92. person] *F;* head *Q.*　　94. S.D.] *Malone,
subst.; not in Q, F.* make] *F;* proue *Q.*　　97. S.D.] *Rowe; not in Q, F.*
medicine] *F;* poyson *Q.*　　98. S.D.] *Malone, subst.; not in Q, F.*　　he
is] *Q;* hes *F 1.*　　100. the] *F;* thy *Q.*　　102. *After this line Q inserts:*
Bast. A Herald ho, a Herald.　　103. virtue] vertues *F 3, 4.*　　105. My] *F;*
This *Q.*　　106. S.D.] *Theobald; not in Q, F.*　　S.D. *Enter a Herald*] *after*
firmly (102) *F; not in Q.*

---

90. *interlude*] play. Cf. *Cymb.* v. v.
228.

94. *pledge*] gage.

94. *make*] show or allege that
something is the case (*N.E.D.*).
Duthie suggests the Q reading may
be either a synonym-substitution or

else a memorial corruption. Cf.
92, *ante*, and 140 *post.*

97. *medicine*] a euphemism for
poison.

98. *exchange*] glove thrown down
in exchange; the technical term.

101. *maintain*] justify.

103. *virtue*] valour, Lat. *virtus.*

Enter a Herald.

Come hither, herald,—Let the trumpet sound,—
And read out this.

Offi. Sound, trumpet!   [*A trumpet sounds.*

   Her. [*Reads.*] *If any man of quality or degree within* 110
the lists of the army will maintain upon Edmund,
supposed Earl of Gloucester, that he is a manifold
traitor, let him appear by the third sound of the trumpet.
He is bold in his defence.   114

Sound!   [*First trumpet.*

Again!   [*Second trumpet.*

Again!   [*Third trumpet.*

                                [*Trumpet answers within.*

Enter EDGAR, *armed, with a trumpet before him.*

Alb. Ask him his purposes, why he appears
Upon this call o' th' trumpet.

Her.   What are you?
Your name? your quality? and why you answer   120
This present summons?

Edg.   Know, my name is lost;
By treason's tooth bare-gnawn, and canker-bit: ~~eaten by caterpilla~~
Yet am I noble as the adversary
I come to cope.~~(with)~~   ~~encounter~~

Alb. _____   Which is that adversary?

107. trumpet] Trumper *F 1*.   109. *Off.*] Capell; *Cap.* Q.   Sound,
trumpet!] Q; *not in* F.   S.D.] F; *not in* Q.   110. S.D.] F; *not in* Q.   110-11.
within the lists] F; *in the hoast* Q.   112. he is] F; he's Q.   113. by] F;
at Q.   115-17. Sound . . . Again!] *Jennens, Duthie; Bast.* Sound? Againe? Q;
Her. Againe. *Her.* Againe. *F*.   116. S.D.] *not in* Q.   117. S.D. *Third . . .*
within] F; *not in* Q.   *Enter . . . him.*] *Enter Edgar at the third sound, a*
trumpet before him Q; *Enter Edgar armed* F.   120. your] F; and Q.
121. Know] F; O know Q.   lost;] *Theobald;* lost Q.   122. tooth] *Theobald;*
tooth: F, Q 2, 3; tooth. Q 1.   123. Yet . . . as] F; yet are I mou't where is
Q 1; where is Q 2, 3.   124. cope] F; cope with all Q.   Which] What
Q 2, 3.

112. *manifold*] cf. *Temp.* v. i. 295.

115-17. *Sound . . . Again!*] It is
better to give to the Herald all these
instructions to the trumpeter, rather
than to give the first to Edmund
(as in Q). If the Herald calls for
the second and third blasts, he should

also call for the first, as Jennens
points out.

117. *S.D. with . . . him*] preceded
by a trumpeter.

122. *canker-bit*] eaten by the cater-
pillar, withered.

124. *cope*] encounter.

Edg. What's he that speaks for Edmund Earl of
　　　　Gloucester?　　　　　　　　　　　　125
Edm. Himself: what say'st thou to him?
Edg.　　　　　　　　　　　Draw thy sword,
　　That, if my speech offend a noble heart,
　　Thy arm may do thee justice; here is mine:
　　Behold, it is the privilege of mine honours, *vaunt (knighthood)*
　　My oath, and my profession: I protest, *knighthood* 130
　　Maugre thy strength, place, youth, and eminence, *with God's Reg.*
　　Despite thy victor sword and fire-new fortune, *brand new*
　　Thy valour and thy heart, thou art a traitor,
　　False to thy gods, thy brother, and thy father, *courage*
　　Conspirant 'gainst this high illustrious prince, *noun or adj* 135
　　And, from th' extremest upward of thy head
　　To the descent and dust below thy foot,
　　A most toad-spotted traitor. Say thou " No," *spotted with venom*
　　This sword, this arm, and my best spirits are bent
　　To prove upon thy heart, whereto I speak,　　140
　　Thou liest.
Edm.　　　　In wisdom I should ask thy name;

128. Thy] *F;* thine *Q.*　　129. the . . . honours] *Pope;* the priuiledge of my
tongue *Q;* my priuiledge, The priuiledge of mine Honours *F.*　130. and my] and
Q 2, 3.　　131. place, youth] *F;* youth, place *Q.*　　132. Despite] Despise *F.*
victor sword] *Capell;* victor-Sword *F;* victor, sword *Q.*　　fire-new] Hyphened
Rowe.　　fortune] *F;* fortun'd *Q.*　　134. thy gods] the gods *Q 2, 3.*　　135.
Conspirant] *F;* Conspicuate *Q.*　　137. below thy foot] *F;* beneath thy feet *Q.*
139. are] *F;* As *Q 1;* Is *Q 2, 3.*

129. *behold . . . honours*] it is the
privilege of my knighthood to draw
my sword, as this which you now
behold, for the purpose of challenging
a traitor, and it is my privilege to
have such a challenge accepted.

130. *My . . . profession*] of the oath
I swore when I was made a knight,
and of my knighthood itself.

131. *maugre*] in spite of. Cf. *T.N.*
III. i. 163.

132. *victor*] victorious.

132. *fire-new*] brand new, straight
from the forge or mint. Cf. *T.N.*
III. ii. 23.

133. *heart*] courage. Cf. *Cor.* v.
vi. 99.

135. *conspirant*] conspirator, or con-

spiring. The word is used as a
substantive by Harsnett, *op. cit.*
p. 18.

136. *upward*] top. Cf. *Temp.* I. ii.
50 (' backward ') and *Cymb.* III. iv. 6
(' inward ') for a similar use of
adjectives as substantives.

137. *descent*] the lowest part, i.e.
the sole.

138. *toad-spotted*] stained with in-
famy, as a toad is spotted and
venomous. Cf. *Rich. II.* III. ii. 134
and *A.Y.L.I.* II. i. 13. Cotgrave
defines *tache* as " spotted, stained
. . . disgraced."

141. *In wisdom*] Because he was
not bound to fight with a man of
lower rank. Cf. v. iii. 152-3 *post.*

But since thy outside looks so fair and war-like,
And that thy tongue some say of breeding breathes, *smack*
What safe and nicely I might well delay　　　　*taste*
By rule of knighthood, I disdain and spurn; *He* 145
Back do I toss these treasons to thy head, *disclaims form*
With the hell-hated lie o'erwhelm thy heart, *for such an ins-*
Since Which, for they yet glance by and scarcely bruise,
This sword of mine shall give them instant way, 149
Where they shall rest for ever.　Trumpets, speak.
　　　　　　　[*Alarums. They fight. Edmund falls.*

Alb does
not want
edm killed **Alb.** Save him! save him!
He wants **Gon.**　　　　　　This is *practice,* Gloucester: *treachery*
Edmund to By th' law of war thou wast not bound to answer *Gon*
confess to contents An unknown opposite; thou art not vanquish'd, *does n*
of the letter But cozen'd and beguil'd. *want h*
taken from **Alb.**　　　　　　　　Shut your mouth, dame, *killed so*
oswald and Or with this paper shall I stople it.　Hold, sir; 155 *she loves him*
given to Alb
by Edgar

141. should] *F; sholud Q 1.*　　143. tongue] *F; being Q.*　　144. What
. . . delay] *F; not in Q.*　145. rule] *F; right Q.*　146. Back . . . head] *not in
Q 2, 3.*　Back] *Heere Q 1.*　these] *F; those Q 1.*　147. hell-hated lie] *F;
hell hatedly Q.*　o'erwhelm] *F; oreturnd Q.*　　148. scarcely] *scarely F 1.*
150. S.D.] *Capell; Alarums. Fights. F; not in Q.*　　151. *See note below.*
practice] *F; meere practise Q.*　152. th'] *F; the Q.*　war] *F; arms Q.*
wast] *F; art Q.*　answer] *offer Q 2, 3.*　154. Shut] *F; Stop Q.*　155. stople]
Q 1; stop Q 2, 3, F.　Hold, sir] *F; not in Q.*

143. *say*] smack, taste, proof.

144. *safe and nicely*] cautiously and
punctiliously, with the letter of the
law on my side.

144. *delay*] postpone; or ' refuse '
(Schmidt).

145. *I . . . spurn*] i.e. I scorn to
insist on my legal rights under the
code of knighthood.　Edmund
changes the construction in the
middle of the sentence.

147. *hell-hated*] hated as much as
hell.

148. *Which*] these treasons.

148. *for*] since.

148. *glance*] glide.

150. *Where . . . ever*] His success
in the combat will prove that Edgar
is the traitor, and the treasons will
remain with the victim.

151. *Save him!*] " Albany desires
that Edmund's life might be spared
at present, only to obtain his confession, and to convict him openly
by his own letter " (Johnson).　Some
editors give the words to Goneril.
In some productions the words are
spoken of Edgar, when he is tem-
porarily disarmed.

151. *practice*] treachery.

155. *stople*] This is the reading of
Q 1; the F *stop* may be a sophistication, and perhaps " Hold, sir " was
added to fill out the line.

155. *Hold, sir*] Capell thought this
was addressed to Edgar, asking him
not to kill Edmund. Dyce thought
the words were spoken to Edmund,
' Hold ' being commonly used when
anyone presented anything to another

Thou worse than any name, read thine own evil:
No tearing, lady; I perceive you know it.
Gon. Say, if I do, the laws are mine, not thine:
Who can arraign me for't?
Alb.   Most monstrous!   O! 159
Know'st thou this paper?
Gon.   Ask me not what I know.   [*Exit.*
Alb. Go after her: she's desperate; govern her.
               almost hysterical   [*Exit an Officer.*
Edm. What you have charg'd me with, that have I done,
And more, much more; the time will bring it out:
'Tis past, and so am I.   But what art thou
That hast this fortune on me?   If thou'rt noble,   165
I do forgive thee.   *Edgar will kill Edm*
Edg.   Let's exchange charity.   *but in return he forgives*
I am no less in blood than thou art, Edmund;   *him.*
If more, the more th' hast wrong'd me.
My name is Edgar, and thy father's son.

---

156. name] *F;* thing *Q.*   157. No] *F;* Nay no *Q.*   159. can] *F;*
shal *Q.*   o] *F; not in Q.*   159-60. Most . . . Know'st] *F;* Monster,
know'st *Q 2, 3.*   160. *Gon.*] *Q; Bast. F.*   S.D.] *Q; after* for't (*159*) *F.*
161. S.D.] *Capell; not in Q, F.*   165. thou'rt] *F;* thou bee'st *Q.*   168. th'
hast] *F;* thou hast *Q.*

(cf. *Mac.* ii. i. 4). Kittredge takes
it to mean "Just a moment!"
Albany must attend to Goneril
before showing the paper to Edmund.
The letter was never delivered; and
we are not told whether Regan's
letter was also found on Oswald's
body. Edmund could have seen
neither, though Albany would not
know this for certain. See previous
note.

156. *Thou*] probably Goneril.
Kirschbaum thinks it is addressed
to Edmund. Bransom, *op. cit.* p. 161,
argues that the pronoun would not
have been used of Goneril by Albany.
But cf. iv. ii. 62.

157. *No tearing*] Based on an incident in the source-play. See
Introduction, p. xxxi.

159-60. *Who . . . know*] F puts
Goneril's exit after "for't" and

ascribes "Ask . . . know" to the
Bastard. Kirschbaum supports F;
but Goneril needs an hysterical, not
a defiant, exit line; Albany would
not turn to Edmund to ask his
question about the letter, and then
belatedly give instructions about his
wife; and it is difficult to reconcile
Edmund's confession (162) with his
defiance two lines earlier. Knight
and Kirschbaum argue that as
Goneril has already admitted she
knows the letter it is unnecessary
for Albany to ask again "Know'st
thou this paper?" But Goneril
has only implied that she knows the
paper in the words "Say, if I do";
Albany wants a direct admission.

166. *Let's exchange charity*] Let me
forgive you for your crimes against
me, as you have forgiven me for
killing you.

[handwritten margin notes at top: cf 149 & 173 (vice versa). Ordered universe. By revolting against nature we bring upon ourselves the plague of nature]

The Gods are just, and of our pleasant vices   170
Make instruments to plague us;
The dark and vicious place where thee he got
Cost him his eyes.

Edm.   Th' hast spoken right, 'tis true.
The wheel is come full circle; I am here.

[handwritten margin note: The same people are in authority again but their character have developed]

Alb. Methought thy very gait did prophesy   175
A royal nobleness: I must embrace thee:
Let sorrow split my heart, if ever I
Did hate thee or thy father.

Edg.   Worthy prince, I know't.

Alb. Where have you hid yourself?   179
How have you known the miseries of your father?

Edg. By nursing them, my lord. List a brief tale;
And when 'tis told, O! that my heart would burst!
The bloody proclamation to escape
That follow'd me so near,—O! our lives' sweetness,
That we the pain of death would hourly die   185
Rather than die at once!—taught me to shift
Into a madman's rags, t' assume a semblance
That very dogs disdain'd: and in this habit

170. vices] *F;* vertues *Q.*   171. plague us] *F;* scourge vs *Q.*   172. thee he]
he thee *Q 2, 3.*   173. Th' hast] *F;* Thou hast *Q.*   right] *F;* truth *Q.*
'tis true] *F; not in Q.*   174. circle] *F;* circled *Q.*   177-8. ever I Did] *F;* I did
euer *Q.*   178. know't] know it *Q 2, 3.*   184. follow'd] followeth *Q 3.*
185. we] *F;* with *Q.*   187. t'assume] *F;* To assume *Q.*

170. *The . . . just*] The dramatic
answer to Gloucester's cry, IV. i. 36.
Bishop Wordsworth compares *Wisdom* xi. 16: "That wherewith a
man sinneth, by the same also shall
he be punished." Noble also compares *Wisdom* xii. 23: "Wherefore
thou hast tormented the wicked that
haue liued a dissolute life by their
owne imaginations." "Wherefore,
whereas men haue lied dissolutely
and vnrighteously, thou hast punished
them sore with their owne abomina-
tions." Empson compares III. iv. 74.
Cf. also *Leir*, 1909:
  "The heauens are iust, and hate
    impiety."

172. *The . . . place*] the adulterous
bed, and so the act of adultery.
  172. *got*] begot.
  174. *The . . . circle*] Cf. Tourneur,
The Revenger's Tragedy, II. i. 77:
  "This wheele comes about."
Kittredge thinks that Edmund is
referring to the fact that he is back
at the bottom, where he was before
Fortune's wheel began to revolve.
  175. *gait*] Cf. *T.C.* IV. v. 14.
  177. *split my heart*] Cf. *Rich. III.* I.
iii. 300 and *W.T.* I. ii. 349.
  178. *Worthy*] noble.
  185. *That . . . die*] Cf. *Cymb.* v. i.
26-7 and *1 Cor.* xv. 31.
  186. *shift*] change. Cf. *Cymb.* I. ii. 1.

Met I my father with his bleeding rings,   *sockets without*
Their precious stones new lost; became his guide, 190   *the jewels of eyes.*
Led him, begg'd for him, sav'd him from despair;
Never—O fault!—reveal'd myself unto him,
Until some half-hour past, when I was arm'd;
Not sure, though hoping, of this good success,
I ask'd his blessing, and from first to last   195
Told him my pilgrimage: but his flaw'd heart,
Alack, too weak the conflict to support!
'Twixt two extremes of passion, joy and grief,   *of Lear's*
Burst smilingly.   *Death*
Edm.   This speech of yours hath mov'd me,   *P218.*
And shall perchance do good; but speak you on; 200
You look as you had something more to say.
Alb. If there be more, more woeful, hold it in;
For I am almost ready to dissolve,   *into tears*
Hearing of this.
Edg.   This would have seem'd a period *limit*
To such as love not sorrow; but another,   *sorrow*   205
describe To amplify too much, would make much more,
too much And top extremity. *go beyond the limmit of endurance*
detail
loud Whilst I was big in clamour came there in a man,
Who, having seen me in my worst estate,   *condition*
Shunn'd my abhorr'd society; but then, finding   210
Who 'twas that so endur'd, with his strong arms

190. Their] *F;* The *Q.*   192. fault] *F;* Father *Q.*   193. arm'd] armed
Q 2.   196. my] *Q;* our *F.*   his] this *F 4.*   202. more, more] any more more
Q 2; any more *Q 3.*   204. Hearing of this] *not in Q 2, 3.*   204-21. This
. . . slave] *Q; not in F.*   208. in] *Q; not in Theobald.*   209. worst estate]
worser state *Theobald.*

189. *rings*] sockets, without the
jewels which were his eyes.
192. *fault*] mistake. Delius suggests
it here means 'misfortune.' Cf. *Per.*
IV. ii. 79.
194. *success*] result of an action,
either good or bad.
196. *flaw'd*] cracked, damaged by
flaw. See Introduction, p. xxxviii.
203. *dissolve*] melt in tears. Cf.
A.C. v. ii. 302.
204. *period*] highest point, limit.
205. *but*] only.

205. *another*] i.e. sorrow. Some
think it means "another man,"
others that it means "another
period."
206. *To . . . much*] if I were to
describe it in detail. Shakespeare
is using the terms of rhetoric. Cf.
Baldwin, *op. cit.* ii. 228.
207. *top extremity*] go beyond the
extreme limit.
208. *big*] loud.
209. *estate*] condition.

He fasten'd on my neck, and bellow'd out
As he'd burst heaven; threw him on my father;
Told the most piteous tale of Lear and him
That ever ear receiv'd; which in recounting   215
His grief grew puissant, and the strings of life
Began to crack: twice then the trumpets sounded,
And there I left him tranc'd.

Alb.   But who was this?

Edg. Kent, sir, the banish'd Kent; who in disguise
Follow'd his enemy king, and did him service   220
Improper for a slave.

Enter a Gentleman, with a bloody knife.

Gent. Help, help!   O, help!
Edg.   What kind of help?
Alb.   Speak, man.
Edg. What means this bloody knife?
Gent.   'Tis hot, it smokes;
It came even from the heart of—O! she's dead.
Alb. Who dead? speak, man.   225
Gent. Your lady, sir, your lady: and her sister
By her is poison'd; she confesses it.
Edm. I was contracted to them both: all three
Now marry in an instant.
Edg.   Here comes Kent.

213. him] *Theobald;* me *Q.* 214. Told the most] *Q 1;* And told the *Q 2, 3.*
221. S.D.] *Camb.; Enter a Gentleman F; Enter one with a bloudie knife Q.*
222. O, help!] *F; not in Q.* Edg.] *F; Alb. Q.* 223. *Edg.] F; speech
continued to Alb. Q.* this] *F;* that *Q.* 'Tis] *F;* Its *Q.* 224. It] *not in*
F 2, 3, 4. O, she's dead!] *not in Q.* 225. Who . . . man] *F;* Who man,
speake? *Q.* 227. confesses] *F;* hath confest *Q 1;* has confest *Q 2, 3.* 229.
Here . . . Kent] *F;* Here . . . Kent sir (*after* pity 232) *Q.* S.D.] *F; after* pity
232 *Q 2, 3.*

213. *As*] as if.

216. *puissant*] powerful.

216. *the . . . life*] heartstrings.
Kent is dying.

218. *tranc'd*] senseless.

220. *enemy*] hostile. Cf. *Cor.* IV. iv.
24.

223. *smokes*] steams.

229. S.D.] F marks Kent's entrance
here, Q three lines later. He comes
slowly down the stage while Albany
is speaking.

[Handwritten margin notes:] As if · powerful · heartstrings. Kents heartstrings cracks wi grief. · Edm can join them in death

Enter KENT.

Alb. Produce the bodies, be they alive or dead;   230
                              [*Exit Gentleman.*
This judgment of the heavens, that makes us tremble,
Touches us not with pity.
                    [*To Kent.*]   O! is this he?
The time will not allow the compliment *ceremony*
Which very manners urges.

Kent.   I am come
To bid my King and master aye good night;   235
Is he not here?

Alb.   Great thing of us forgot! *Hey had forgotten that*
Speak, Edmund, where's the King? and where's *Lear & Cordelia*
    Cordelia? *sight*   *were prisoners*
Seest thou this object, Kent?
        [*The bodies of Goneril and Regan are brought in.*

Kent. Alack! why thus?

Edm.   Yet Edmund was belov'd: *Edm had felt unloved*
                                                    cf Act I sc I.

---

230. the] *F;* their *Q.*   alive] live *F 3, 4.*   S.D.] *Camb.; not in Q, F;*
Exit Gent (*after* pity) *Malone.*   231. judgment] Iustice *Q.*   232. us] *not in*
Q 2, 3.   is this] *F;* tis *Q.*   he] she *F 2, 3, 4.*   234. Which] *F;* that *Q.*
236. thing] things *Q 2, 3.*   238. S.D.] *Q; after* 230, *subst. F.*   241.
after] *not in Q 3.*

230. *dead*] According to F the
bodies are brought in here; it
seems more natural to leave a short
time, as Q does, for Albany's order
to be obeyed. Kirschbaum, who
argues for the F arrangement, says
that it is significant that Kent makes
no comment on the bodies; but he
does later (239).

233. *compliment*] ceremony.

234. *manners*] singular. Cf. *R.J.*
v. iii. 213.

236. *Great . . . forgot*] Kittredge
remarks that "this amnesia on
everybody's part is necessary for the
climax that follows." But, after all,
there is no reason why Albany
should suspect that Lear and Cordelia
were in danger; and he had had
plenty to occupy his mind during
the wasted ten minutes.

238. *object*] sight. Kirschbaum,
defending the Folio through thick
and thin, takes this to refer to Edmund, lying wounded. It is more
natural for it to refer to the bodies
of Goneril and Regan, especially
when one takes Edmund's next
speech into consideration. He is
really answering Kent's question.
The bodies are brought on the stage
so that Lear can be confronted with
his three daughters, as in the first
scene of the play.

239. *Yet . . . belov'd*] Heilman,
op. cit. p. 234, remarks that Edmund's
sole thought is of himself. But it is
a brilliant stroke to reveal here that
Edmund's career of crime was
caused by his feeling that he was not
loved.

241. *after*] afterwards.

cf Iago
sexual jealousy

The one the other poison'd for my sake,   240
And after slew herself.

Alb. Even so.   Cover their faces.

Edm. I pant for life; some good I mean to do
Despite of mine own nature.   Quickly send,
Be brief in it, to th' castle; for my writ   245
Is on the life of Lear and on Cordelia.
Nay, send in time.

Alb.   Run, run! O, run!

Edg. To who, my Lord?   Who has the office? send
Thy token of reprieve.

Edm. Well thought on: take my sword,   250
Give it the captain.

Edg.   Haste thee, for thy life.   [*Exit Officer.*

Edm. He hath commission from thy wife and me
To hang Cordelia in the prison, and
To lay the blame upon her own despair,
That she fordid herself.

Alb.   The Gods defend her!   255
Bear him hence awhile.   [*Edmund is borne off.*

Re-enter LEAR, *with* CORDELIA *dead in his arms; Officer.*

Lear. Howl, howl, howl!   O! you are men of stones: *unfeeling*
Had I your tongues and eyes, I'd use them so

244. mine] *F;* my *Q.*   245. in it to th'] *F;* int toth' *Q 1;* into the *Q 2, 3.*
castle] Chastle *F 2.*   246. Is] tis *Q 2, 3.*   248. who] whom *F 2, 3, 4.*
has] *F;* hath *Q.*   250-1. sword, Give] sword the Captaine, Giue *Q 1.*   251.
Edg.] *F;* Duke *Q 1; Alb. Q 2, 3.*   S.D.] *Exit a Captain Schmidt; Exit
Messenger Theobald; Exit Edgar Malone; Exeunt Edgar and others Capell;
not in Q, F.*   255. That . . . herself] *not in Q 2, 3.*   256. S.D. Edmund
. . . off*] Theobald; not in Q, F.*   *Re-enter*] *Dyce; Enter Q, F.*   dead]
Rowe; not in Q. F.   officer] *not in Q, F; Edgar, Officer and Others Malone.*
257. Howl, howl, howl] *F;* four times *Q.*   you] your *F 1, 2.*

251. *Haste . . . life*] This speech is
given to Albany in Q.

251. *S.D.*] Capell, Malone and
many editors assume that Edgar goes
out; but if we give the line to Edgar,
someone else has to run to the castle.

255. *fordid*] destroyed.   Cordelia
committed suicide in most of Shakespeare's sources.   See Introduction,
p. xxxvii and Appendix, p. 237.

255. *The . . . her*] They do not.

257. *men of stones*] Cf. *Rich. III.*
III. vii. 25.   Pope thought Shakespeare wrote ' stone.'   But Walker
compares *M.V.* IV. i. 31: " hearts of
flints "; and *Rich. III.* III. vii. 224:
" I am not made of stones."   Shakespeare may have been thinking of
the story of Deucalion as told by
Ovid in *Metamorphoses,* i.

That heaven's vault should crack.   She's gone for ever.
I know when one is dead, and when one lives;   260
She's dead as earth.   Lend me a looking-glass;
If that her breath will mist or stain the stone,   *mirror of polished stone or crystal.*
Why, then she lives.

Kent.   Is this the promis'd end?

Edg. Or image of that horror?   *Last Judgement*

Alb.   Fall and cease.   *Let the heavens fall & cover everything.*

Lear. This feather stirs; she lives! if it be so,   265
It is a chance which does redeem all sorrows
That ever I have felt.

Kent. [*Kneeling.*]   O my good master!

Lear. Prithee, away.

Edg.   'Tis noble Kent, your friend.

Lear. A plague upon you, murderers, traitors all!
I might have sav'd her; now she's gone for ever!   270
Cordelia, Cordelia! stay a little.   Ha!
What is't thou say'st?   Her voice was ever soft,
Gentle and low, an excellent thing in woman.
I kill'd the slave that was a-hanging thee.

Offi. 'Tis true, my lords, he did.

Lear.   Did I not, fellow?   275
I have seen the day, with my good biting falchion
I would have made them skip: I am old now,

258. I'd] *F;* I would *Q.*   259. She's] O, she is *Q 2, 3.*   262. or] and
Q 2, 3.   263. Why, then she] she then *Q 2, 3.*   266. Which] that *Q 2, 3.*
267. S.D.] *Theobald; not in Q, F.*   O] *F;* A *Q.*   269. you murderers]
F; your murderous *Q 1;* you murdrous *Q 2, 3;* you murtherers *F 2, 3, 4.* 271.
Ha!] *not in Q 2, 3.*   272. say'st] sayest *Q 1;* stay *Q 3.*   273. woman] *F;*
women *Q.*   274. a-hanging] *hyphened Dyce.*   275. *Offi.*] *Capell; Cap.*
Q; Gent. F.   276. have] ha *Q 2, 3.*   with my good] that with my *Q 2, 3.*
277. them] *Q;* him *F.*

259. *heaven's vault*] Cf. *Temp.* v. i.
43.   The term is used by Florio,
op. cit. iii. 373.

262. *stone*] a mirror of polished
stone or crystal.

263. *promis'd end*] the Last Judgment, the end of the world.   Cf.
IV. vi. 136.

264. *Fall . . . cease*] Let the heavens
fall, and everything come to an end.
Delius takes the words as sub-

stantives, in opposition to "that
horror."

276. *I . . . day*] J. M. Nosworthy,
R.E.S., 1951, pp. 259-61, compares
Porter, *The Two Angry Women of
Abingdon,* 2382; "Ha, I have seen
the day I could have danced in my
fight"; and the following Shake-
spearian passages: *R.J.* I. v. 23;
M.W. II. i. 235;   *Oth.* v. ii. 261.

276. *falchion*] a light sword, with
the point a little bent inwards.

And these same crosses spoil me.   Who are you?
Mine eyes are not o' th' best: I'll tell you straight.
Kent. If Fortune brag of two she lov'd and hated,   280
One of them we behold.
Lear. This is a dull sight.   Are you not Kent?
Kent.   The same;
Your servant Kent.   Where is your servant Caius?
Lear. He's a good fellow, I can tell you that;
He'll strike, and quickly too.   He's dead and rotten.
Kent. No, my good Lord; I am the very man,—   286
Lear. I'll see that straight.
Kent. That from your first of difference and decay,
Have follow'd your sad steps,—
Lear.   You are welcome hither.   289
Kent. Nor no man else.   All's cheerless, dark, and deadly:
Your eldest daughters have fordone themselves,

---

279. not] none *Q 2, 3.*   280. brag] bragd *Q.*   and] *F;* or *Q.*   282.
This . . . sight] *not in Q.*   This is] *F;* this' *Schmidt (conj. S. Walker).*   you
not] *F;* not you *Q.*   284. He's a] He's *F 2.*   you] *F; not in Q.*   288.
first] *F;* life *Q.*   289. Have] Hane *F 2.*   You are! *Q 2, F 2, 3, 4;* Your
are *F 1;* You'r *Q 1.*   291. fordone] *F;* foredoome *Q 1;* fore-doom'd *Q 2, 3.*

---

278. *crosses*] troubles.

278. *spoil me*] i.e. as a swordsman.

280-1. *If . . . behold*] " If Fortune
. . . should brag of two persons, one
of whom she had highly elevated,
and the other she had woefully
depressed, we now behold the
latter." (Mason.) Some think Kent
is referring to himself; others think
he is referring to Lear and himself.
In *N.Q.* 18 Oct. 1890, p. 305, the
passage is paraphrased: " If Fortune,
in the history of the world, pre-
eminently loved and then hated
two persons, here in the miserable
example of my king we have one of
them." Jennens who emended *we*
to *you* (*ye* Furness) explains that Kent
is answering Lear's question (278).
We may here have an example of a
change of thought in the middle of
a sentence, Kent meaning: " If
Fortune brag of two people, one of
whom she loved and one hated—

but no, Lear, who was thrown
down from great prosperity, can
serve as an example of both."

282. *dull sight*] melancholy spectacle; but some critics think that
Lear is referring to his own failing
eyesight.

287. *I'll . . . straight*] I'll attend
to that in a moment.

288. *first*] beginning.

288. *difference and decay*] change and
decline of fortunes.

290. *Nor . . . else*] This may mean:
" No, neither I, nor any man, is
welcome."   Or it may mean: " And
there was no one else followed you
in the days of your misfortunes "
(though the Fool was also there).
But I think it probably refers back
to " I am the very man " (286) and
that it means simply " I am really
him, and no one else."

291. *fordone*] destroyed.

from despair

And desperately are dead.

Lear.   Ay, so I think.

Alb. He knows not what he says, and vain is it
That we present us to him.

Edg.   Very bootless.   294

Enter an Officer.

Offi. Edmund is dead, my Lord.

Alb.   That's but a trifle here.
You lords and noble friends, know our intent;
What comfort to this great decay may come   *ruined piece*
Shall be appli'd: for us, we will resign,   *of nature, Lear*
During the life of this old Majesty,   *Lear dies* 299
                                                 a king
To him our absolute power: [*To Edgar and Kent.*]
                               you, to your rights,
With boot and such addition as your honours   *with such*
Have more than merited. All friends shall taste *additional*
The wages of their virtue, and all foes   *titles and*
The cup of their deservings.   O! see, see!   *rights as*
                                                you deserve

Lear. And my poor fool is hang'd!   No, no, no life!   305

darling but perhaps a quibble

+149
▸ 173
210

292. Ay . . . think] *F*; So think I too *Q 1*; So I think too *Q 2, 3.*   293.
says] *F*; sees *Q.*   is it] *F*; it is *Q.*   294. S.D.] *Capell; Enter Captaine Q;*
Enter Messenger (after him) *F.*   295. *Offi.*] *Capell; Capt. Q; Mess. F.*
297. great] *F*; *not in Q.*   300. S.D.] *Malone; To Edm. Rowe; not in Q, F.*
301. honours] *F*; honor *Q 1.*   305. No, no, no] *F*; no, no *Q.*

292. *desperately*] from despair.

297. *great decay*] the ruined piece
of nature, Lear.

298. *resign*] Lear, then, dies a
king (R. W. Chambers).

301. *With . . . addition*] with such
additional titles and rights.

301. *honours*] noble deeds.

305. *fool*] Cordelia, a term of
endearment. Sir Joshua Reynolds
thought Lear was referring to the
Fool. Brandl, Quiller-Couch and
Edith Sitwell have argued that the
two parts of Cordelia and the Fool
were taken by the same actor; but
Thaler, *T.L.S.* 13 Feb. 1930, shows
that the parts could not have been
doubled.   Perrett points out that
" when Cordelia is away her place

as the representative of utter truth-
fulness is taken by the Fool.   In this
respect the two characters are one."
And Empson, *op. cit.* p. 152, while
pointing out that the assumption
that Lear is referring to the Fool
must be wrong because in the rest
of the speech he is obviously talking
about Cordelia, remarks, following
Bradley, " that his mind has wandered
so far that he no longer distinguishes
the two. . . . Lear is now thrown
back into something like the storm
phase of his madness, the effect of
immediate shock, and the Fool seems
to him part of it.   The only affectionate dependent he had recently has
been hanged, and the only one he had
then was the Fool."

Why should a dog, a horse, a rat, have life,
And thou no breath at all?   Thou'lt come no more,
Never, never, never, never, never!
Pray you, undo this button: thank you, Sir.
Do you see this?   Look on her, look, her lips,   310
Look there, look there!   [*Dies.*
Edg.   He faints!   My Lord, my Lord!
Kent. Break, heart; I prithee, break!
Edg.   Look up, my Lord.
Kent. Vex not his ghost: O! let him pass; he hates him
That would upon the rack of this tough world
Stretch him out longer.
Edg.   He is gone, indeed.   315
Kent. The wonder is he hath endur'd so long:
He but usurp'd his life.
Alb. Bear them from hence.   Our present business
Is general woe.   [*To Kent and Edgar.*]   Friends of
        my soul, you twain
Rule in this realm, and the gor'd state sustain.   320
Kent. I have a journey, sir, shortly to go;
My master calls me, I must not say no.

306. have] of *Q 1*.   307. Thou'lt]*F;* O thou wilt *Q.*   308. Never] *five
times F; thrice Q.*   309. Pray you] pray *Q 2, 3*.   Sir] *F;* sir, O, o, o,
o(o) *Q*.   310-11. Do . . . there!] *F; not in Q.*   look, her lips,] *Johnson;*
Looke her lips *F 1;* look on her lips, *F 2, 3, 4*. 311. S.D.] *He dies F; not in Q.*
My Lord, my Lord!] my Lord. *F 4*.   312. Kent.] *F; Lear. Q.*   up] to *F 2,
3, 4*.   313. hates him] hates him much *Q 2, 3*.   314. rack] *F 4;* wracke *Q,
F 1, 2, 3*.   tough] rough *Q 3; Pope, Capell*.   315. He] *F;* O he *Q*.
319. Is] *F;* Is to *Q.*   S.D.] *Johnson; not in Q, F.*   320. realm] *F;*
kingdome *Q.*   gor'd] good *Q 2, 3*.   state] *not in Q 3*.   322. calls me] *F;*
cals, and *Q.*   (*Dyes F 2, 3, 4; not in Q, F 1*).

309. *button*] Lear feels a sense of
suffocation, and imagines it is caused
by the tightness of his clothes.   J. W.
Harvey suggests to me that Lear is
referring to one of Cordelia's buttons;
but I think this is unlikely.

310. *look*] Lear dies of joy, believing Cordelia to be alive (Bradley).

312. *Break . . . break*] Bradley
suggests that Kent may be speaking
of his own heart. Q, impossibly, gives

the words to Lear who is already beyond speech.

313. *ghost*] departing spirit.

314. *tough*] obdurate, rigid, referring perhaps to the rack as well as to
the world.   Cf. Appendix, p. 254.

315. *longer*] syllepsis (*a*) for a longer
time, (*b*) with his body extended
further by the rack.

320. *gor'd state*] See Appendix,
p. 251.

321. *journey*] to another world.

Edg. The weight of this sad time we must obey;
  Speak what we feel, not what we ought to say.
  The oldest hath borne most: we that are young
  Shall never see so much, nor live so long.   326
                          [*Exeunt, with a dead march.*

323. *Edg.*] *F; Duke. Q.*   325. hath] *F;* haue *Q.*   borne] bornue *Q 3.*
326. S.D.] *F; not in Q.*

323-6. *The . . . long*] These lines are given to Albany by *Q*; and critics have argued that the last speech should be given to the person of highest rank who survives. But Edgar has to reply to Albany's speech, and the words " We that are young " come somewhat more naturally from his mouth than from that of Albany.

FINIS.

APPENDICES

1. *The True Chronicle History of King Leir*

This play, of over 2,500 lines, is too long to print in full. But most of it has little connection with Shakespeare's play, and all the significant parallels are given in the introduction or the notes. The three scenes given here relate to the division of the kingdom and to the reconciliation of Leir and Cordella.

SCENE III

Enter Leir *and* Perillus

Leir. Perillus, go seeke my daughters,
    Will them immediately come and speak with me.
Per. I will, my gracious Lord.   [*Exit.*
Leir. Oh, what a combat feeles my panting heart,
    'Twixt childrens loue, and care of Common weale!
    How deare my daughters are vnto my soule,
    None knowes, but he, that knowes my thoghts and secret
        deeds.
    Ah, little do they know the deare regard,
    Wherein I hold their future state to come:
    When they securely sleepe on beds of downe,
    These aged eyes do watch for their behalfe:
    While they like wantons sport in youthfull toyes,
    This throbbing heart is pearst with dire annoyes.
    As doth the Sun exceed the smallest Starre;
    So much the fathers loue exceeds the childs.
    Yet my complaynts are causelesse: for the world
    Affords not children more conformable:
    And yet, me thinks, my mind presageth still
    I know not what: and yet I feare some ill.

Enter PERILLUS, *with the three daughters.*

    Well, here my daughters come: I haue found out
    A present meanes to rid me of this doubt.
Gon. Our royall Lord and father, in all duty,
    We come to know the tenour of your will,
    Why you so hastily haue sent for vs?
Leir. Deare *Gonorill*, kind *Ragan*, sweet *Cordella*,
    Ye florishing branches of a Kingly stocke,
    Sprung from a tree that once did flourish greene,
    Whose blossoms now are nipt with Winters frost,
    And pale grym death doth wayt vpon my steps,
    And summons me vnto his next Assizes.
    Therefore, deare daughters, as ye tender the safety
    Of him that was the cause of your first being,
    Resolue a doubt which much molests my mind,
    Which of you three to me would proue most kind;
    Which loues me most, and which at my request
    Will soonest yeeld vnto their fathers hest.
Gon. I hope my gracious father makes no doubt
    Of any of his daughters loue to him:
    Yet for my part, to shew my zeale to you,
    Which cannot be in windy words rehearst,
    I prize my loue to you at such a rate,
    I thinke my life inferiour to my loue.
    Should you inioyne me for to tye a milstone
    About my neck and leape into the Sea,
    At your commaund I willingly would doe it:
    Yea, for to doe you good, I would ascend
    The highest Turret in all Brittany,
    And from the top leape headlong to the ground:
    Nay, more, should you appoynt me for to marry
    The meanest vassayle in the spacious world,
    Without reply I would accomplish it:
    In briefe, commaund what euer you desire,
    And if I fayle, no fauour I require.
Leir. O, how thy words reuiue my dying soule!
Cor. O, how I doe abhorre this flattery!
Leir. But what sayth *Ragan* to her fathers will?
Rag. O, that my simple vtterance could suffice,
    To tell the true intention of my heart,
    Which burnes in zeale of duty to your grace,
    And neuer can be quench'd, but by desire
    To shew the same in outward forwardnesse.

Oh, that there were some other mayd that durst
But make a challenge of her loue with me;
Ide make her soone confesse she neuer loued
Her father halfe so well as I doe you.
I then, my deeds should proue in playner case,
How much my zeale aboundeth to your grace:
But for them all, let this one meane suffice,
To ratify my loue before your eyes:
I haue right noble Suters to my loue,
No worse then Kings, and happely I loue one:
Yet, would you haue me make my choyce anew,
Ide bridle fancy, and be rulde by you.

Leir. Did neuer *Philomel* sing so sweet a note

Cord. Did neuer flatterer tell so false a tale.

Leir. Speak now, *Cordella,* make my ioyes at full,
And drop downe Nectar from thy hony lips.

Cor. I cannot paynt my duty forth in words,
I hope my deede shall make report for me:
But looke what loue the child doth owe the father,
The same to you I beare, my gracious Lord.

Gon. Here is an answere answerlesse indeed:
Were you my daughter, I should scarcely brooke it.

Rag. Dost thou not blush, proud Peacock as thou art,
To make our father such a slight reply?

Leir. Why how now, Minion, are you growne so proud?
Doth our deare loue make you thus peremptory?
What, is your loue become so small to vs,
As that you scorne to tell vs what it is?
Do you loue vs, as euery child doth loue
Their father? True indeed, as some,
Who by disobedience short their fathers dayes,
And so would you; some are so father-sick,
That they make meanes to rid them from the world;
And so would you: some are indifferent,
Whether their aged parents liue or dye;
And so are you. But, didst thou know, proud gyrle,
What care I had to foster thee to this,
Ah, then thou wouldst say as thy sisters do:
Our life is lesse, then loue we owe to you.

Cord. Deare father, do not so mistake my words,
Nor my playne meaning be misconstrued;
My toung was neuer vsde to flattery.

Gon. You were not best say I flatter: if you do,

My deeds shall shew, I flatter not with you.
I loue my father better then thou canst.

Cor. The prayse were great, spoke from anothers mouth:
But it should seeme your neighbours dwell far off.

Rag. Nay, here is one, that will confirme as much
As she hath sayd, both for my selfe and her.
I say, thou dost not wish my fathers good.

Cord. Deare father—.

Leir. Peace, bastard Impe, no issue of King *Leir*,
I will not heare thee speake one tittle more.
Call not me father, if thou loue thy life,
Nor these thy sisters once presume to name:
Looke for no helpe henceforth from me nor mine;
Shift as thou wilt, and trust vnto thy selfe:
My Kingdome will I equally deuide
'Txist thy two sisters to their royall dowre,
And will bestow them worthy their deserts:
This done, because thou shalt not haue the hope,
To haue a childs part in the time to come,
I presently will dispossesse my selfe,
And set vp these vpon my princely throne.

Gon. I euer thought that pride would haue a fall.

Rag. Plaine dealing, sister: your beauty is so sheene,
You need no dowry, to make you be a Queene.

[*Exeunt* LEIR, GONORILL, RAGAN.

Cord. Now whither, poore forsaken shall I goe,
When mine own sisters tryumph in my woe?
But vnto him which doth protect the iust,
In him will poore *Cordella* put her trust.
These hands shall labour, for to get my spending;
And so ile liue vntill my dayes haue ending.

Per. Oh, how I grieue, to see my Lord thus fond,
To dote so much vpon vayne flattering words.
Ah, if he but with good aduice had weyghed,
The hidden tenure of her humble speech,
Reason to rage should not haue giuen place,
Nor poore *Cordella* suffer such disgrace.   [*Exit.*

SCENE VI

Enter GONORILL and RAGAN

Gon. Sister, when did you see *Cordella* last,
That pretty piece, that thinks none good ynough
To speake to her, because (sir-reuerence)
She hath a little beauty extraordinary?

Rag. Since time my father warnd her from his presence,
I neuer saw her, that I can remember.
God giue her ioy of her surpassing beauty;
I thinke, her dowry will be small ynough.

Gon. I haue incenst my father so against her,
As he will neuer be reclaymed agayne.

Rag. I was not much behind to do the like.

Gon. Faith, sister, what moues you to beare her such good will?

Rag. In truth I thinke, the same that moueth you;
Because she doth surpasse vs both in beauty.

Gon. Beshrew your fingers, how right you can gesse:
I tell you true, it cuts me to the heart.

Rag. But we will keepe her low enough, I warrant,
And clip her wings for mounting vp too hye.

Gon. Who euer hath her, shall haue a rich marriage of her.

Rag. She were right fit to make a Parsons wife:
For they, men say, do loue faire women well,
And many times doe marry them with nothing.

Gon. With nothing! marry God forbid: why, are there any such!

Rag. I meane, no money.

Gon. I cry you mercy, I mistooke you much:
And she is far too stately for the Church;
Sheele lay her husbands Benefice on her back,
Euen in one gowne, if she may haue her will.

Rag. In faith, poore soule, I pitty her a little.
Would she were lesse fayre, or more fortunate.
Well, I thinke long vntill I see my *Morgan*,
The gallant Prince of Cambria, here arriue.

Gon. And so do I, vntill the Cornwall King
Present himselfe, to consummate my ioyes.
Peace, here commeth my father.

Enter LEIR, PERILLUS and others.

Leir. Cease, good my Lords, and sue not to reuerse
Our censure, which is now irreuocable.

We haue dispatched letters of contract
Vnto the Kings of Cambria and of Cornwall;
Our hand and seale will iustify no lesse:
Then do not so dishonour me, my Lords,
As to make shipwrack of our kingly word.
I am as kind as is the Pellican,
That kils it selfe, to saue her young ones liues:
And yet as ielous as the princely Eagle,
That kils her young ones, if they do but dazell
Vpon the radiant splendor of the Sunne.
Within this two dayes I expect their comming.

Enter KINGS OF CORNWALL *and* CAMBRIA.

But in good time, they are arriu'd already.
This haste of yours, my Lords, doth testify
The feruent loue you beare vnto my daughters:
And think your selues as welcome to King *Leir,*
As euer *Pryams* children were to him.

Corn. My gracious Lord, and father too, I hope,
Pardon, for that I made no greater haste:
But were my horse as swift as was my will,
I long ere this had seene your Maiesty.

Cam. No other scuse of absence can I frame,
Then what my brother hath inform'd your Grace:
For our vndeserued welcome, we do vowe,
Perpetually to rest at your commaund.

Corn. But you, sweet Loue, illustrious *Gonorill,*
The Regent, and the Soueraigne of my soule,
Is *Cornwall* welcome to your Excellency?

Gon. As welcome, as *Leander* was to *Hero,*
Or braue *Aeneas* to the Carthage Queene:
So and more welcome is your Grace to me.

Cam. O, may my fortune proue no worse than his,
Since heauens do know, my fancy is as much.
Deare *Ragan,* say, if welcome vnto thee,
All welcomes else will little comfort me.

Rag. As gold is welcome to the couetous eye,
As sleepe is welcome to the Traueller,
As is fresh water to sea-beaten men,
Or moystned showres vnto the parched ground,
Or any thing more welcomer then this,
So and more welcome louely *Morgan* is.

Leir. What resteth then, but that we consummate,
　　The celebration of these nuptiall Rites?
　　My Kingdome I do equally deuide.
　　Princes, draw lots, and take your chaunce as falles.

Then they draw lots.

　　These I resigne as freely vnto you,
　　As earst by true succession they were mine.
　　And here I do freely dispossesse my selfe,
　　And make you two my true adopted heyres:
　　My selfe will soiorne with my sonne of Cornwall,
　　And take me to my prayers and my beades.
　　I know, my daughter *Ragan* will be sorry,
　　Because I do not spend my dayes with her:
　　Would I were able to be with both at once;
　　They are the kindest Gyrles in Christendome.

Per. I haue bin silent all this while, my Lord,
　　To see if any worthyer then my selfe,
　　Would once haue spoke in poore *Cordellaes* cause:
　　But loue or feare tyes silence to their toungs.
　　Oh, heare me speake for her, my gracious Lord,
　　Whose deeds haue not deseru'd this ruthlesse doome,
　　As thus to disinherit her of all.

Leir. Vrge this no more, and if thou loue thy life:
　　I say, she is no daughter, that doth scorne
　　To tell her father how she loueth him.
　　Who euer speaketh hereof to mee agayne,
　　I will esteeme him for my mortall foe.
　　Come, let vs in, to celebrate with ioy,
　　The happy Nuptialls of these louely payres.

Exeunt omnes, manet PERILLUS.

Per. Ah, who so blind, as they that will not see
　　The neere approch of their owne misery?
　　Poore Lady, I extremely pitty her:
　　And whilest I liue, eche drop of my heart blood,
　　Will I strayne forth, to do her any good.　　　　[*Exit.*

SCENE XXIV

Enter the GALLIAN KING *and* QUEENE, *and* MUMFORD, *with a basket,*
disguised like Countrey folke.

King. This tedious iourney all on foot, sweet Loue,
    Cannot be pleasing to your tender ioynts,
    Which ne're were vsed to these toylesome walks.
Cord. I neuer in my life tooke more delight
    In any iourney, then I do in this:
    It did me good, when as we hapt to light
    Amongst the merry crue of country folke,
    To see what industry and paynes they tooke,
    To win them commendations 'mongst their friends.
    Lord, how they labour to bestir themselues,
    And in their quirks to go beyond the Moone,
    And so take on them with such antike fits,
    That one would think they were beside their wits!
    Come away, *Roger*, with your basket.
Mum. Soft, Dame, here comes a couple of old youthes,
    I must needs make my selfe fat with iesting at them.
Cor. Nay, prithy do not, they do seeme to be
    Men much o'regone with griefe and misery.
    Let's stand aside, and harken what they say.
                [*Enter* LEIR *and* PERILLUS *very faintly.*
Leir. Ah, my *Perillus*, now I see we both
    Shall end our dayes in this vnfruitfull soyle.
    Oh, I do faint for want of sustenance:
    And thou, I know, in little better case.
    No gentle tree affords one taste of fruit,
    To comfort vs, vntill we meet with men:
    No lucky path conducts our luckless steps
    Vnto a place where any comfort dwels.
    Sweet rest betyde vnto our happy soules;
    For here I see our bodies must haue end.
Per. Ah, my deare Lord, how doth my heart lament,
    To see you brought to this extremity!
    O, if you loue me, as you do professe,
    Or euer thought well of me in my life,
                [*He strips vp his arme.*
    Feed on this flesh, whose veynes are not so dry.
    But there is vertue left to comfort you.
    O, feed on this, if this will do you good,
    Ile smile for ioy, to see you suck my bloud.

Leir. I am no Caniball, that I should delight
      To slake my hungry iawes with humane flesh:
      I am no deuill, or ten times worse then so,
      To suck the bloud of such a peerelesse friend.
      O, do not think that I respect my life
      So dearely, as I do thy loyall loue.
      Ah, Brittayne, I shall neuer see thee more,
      That hast vnkindly banished thy King:
      And yet thou dost not make me to complayne,
      But they which were more neere to me than thou.

Cor. What do I heare? this lamentable voyce,
      Me thinks, ere now I oftentimes haue heard.

Leir. Ah, *Gonorill*, was halfe my Kingdomes gift
      The cause that thou didst seeke to haue my life?
      Ah, cruell *Ragan*, did I giue thee all,
      And all could not suffice without my bloud?
      Ah, poore *Cordella*, did I giue thee nought,
      Nor neuer shall be able for to giue?
      O, let me warne all ages that insueth,
      How they trust flattery, and reiect the trueth.
      Well, vnkind Girles, I here forgiue you both,
      Yet the iust heauens will hardly do the like;
      And only craue forgiuenesse at the end
      Of good *Cordella*, and of thee, my friend;
      Of God, whose Maiesty I haue offended,
      By my transgression many thousand wayes:
      Of her, deare heart, whom I for no occasion
      Turn'd out of all, through flatterers perswasion:
      Of thee, kind friend, who but for me, I know,
      Hadst neuer come vnto this place of wo.

Cor. Alack, that euer I should liue to see
      My noble father in this misery.

King. Sweet Loue, reueale not what thou art as yet,
      Vntill we know the ground of all this ill.

Cor. O, but some meat, some meat: do you not see,
      How neere they are to death for want of food?

Per. Lord, which didst help thy seruants at their need.
      Or now or neuer send vs helpe with speed.
      Oh comfort, comfort! yonder is a banquet,
      And men and women, my Lord: be of good cheare;
      For I see comfort comming very neere.
      O my Lord, a banquet, and men and women!

Leir. O, let kind pity mollify their hearts,
That they may helpe vs in our great extreames.
Per. God saue you, friends; & if this blessed banquet
Affordeth any food or sustenance,
Euen for his sake that saued vs all from death,
Vouchsafe to saue vs from the gripe of famine.
[She bringeth him to the table.

Cor. Here father, sit and eat, here sit and drink:
And would it were far better for your sakes.

PERILLUS *takes* LEIR *by the hand to the table.*

Per. Ile giue you thanks anon: my friend doth faynt,
And needeth present comfort.   *[Leir drinks.*
Mum. I warrant, he ne're stayes to say grace:
O, theres no sauce to a good stomake.
Per. The blessed God of heauen hath thought vpon vs.
Leir. The thanks be his, and these kind courteous folke,
By whose humanity we are preserued.

They eat hungerly, Leir drinkes.

Cor. And may that draught be vnto him, as was
That which old *Eson* dranke, which did renue
His withered age, and made him young againe.
And may that meat be vnto him, as was
That which *Elias* ate, in strength whereof
He walked fourty dayes, and neuer faynted.
Shall I conceale me longer from my father?
Or shall I manifest my selfe to him?
King. Forbeare a while, vntill his strength returne,
Lest being ouer ioyed with seeing thee,
His poore weak sences should forsake their office,
And so our cause of ioy be turnd to sorrow.
Per. What chere, my Lord? how do you feele your selfe?
Leir. Me thinks, I neuer ate such sauory meat:
It is as pleasant as the blessed Manna,
That raynd from heauen amongst the Israelities:
It hath recall'd my spirits home agayne,
And made me fresh, as earst I was before.
But how shall we congratulate their kindnesse?
Per. Infayth, I know not how sufficiently;
But the best meane that I can think on, is this:
Ile offer them my dublet in requitall;
For we haue nothing else to spare.
Leir. Nay, stay, *Perillus*, for they shall haue mine.

Per. Pardon, my Lord, I sweare they shall haue mine.
> *Perillus proffers his dublet: they will not take it.*

Leir. Ah, who would think such kindnes should remayne
Among such strange and vnacquainted men:
And that such hate should harbour in the brest
Of those, which haue occasion to be best?

Cor. Ah, good old father, tell to me thy griefe,
Ile sorrow with thee, if not adde reliefe.

Leir. Ah, good young daughter, I may call thee so;
For thou art like a daughter I did owe.

Cor. Do you not owe her still? what, is she dead?

Leir. No, God forbid: but all my interest's gone,
By shewing my selfe too much vnnaturall:
So haue I lost the title of a father,
And may be call'd a stranger to her rather.

Cor. Your title's good still; for tis alwayes knowne,
A man may do as him list with his owne.
But haue you but one daughter then in all?

Leir. Yes, I haue more by two, then would I had.

Cor. O, say not so, but rather see the end:
They that are bad, may haue the grace to mend:
But how haue they offended you so much?

Leir. If from the first I should relate the cause,
Twould make a heart of Adamant to weepe;
And thou, poore soule, kind-hearted as thou art,
Dost weepe already, ere I do begin.

Cor. For Gods loue tell it, and when you haue done,
Ile tell the reason why I weepe so soone.

Leir. Then know this first, I am a Brittayne borne,
And had three daughters by one louing wife;
And though I say it, of beauty they were sped;
Especially the youngest of the three,
For her perfections hardly matcht could be:
On these I doted with a ielous loue,
And thought to try which of them lou'd me best,
By asking them, which would do most for me?
The first and second flattred me with words,
And vow'd they lou'd me better then their liues:
The youngest sayd, she loued me as a child
Might do: her answere I esteem'd most vild,
And presently in an outragious mood,
I turned her from me to go sinke or swym:
And all I had, euen to the very clothes,

I gaue in dowry with the other two:
And she that best deseru'd the greatest share,
I gaue her nothing, but disgrace and care.
Now mark the sequell: When I had done thus,
I soiournd in my eldest daughters house,
Where for a time I was intreated well,
And liu'd in state sufficing my content:
But euery day her kindnesse did grow cold,
Which I with patience put vp well ynough,
And seemed not to see the things I saw:
But at the last she grew so far incenst
With moody fury, and with causelesse hate,
That in most vild and contumelious termes,
She bade me pack, and harbour somewhere else.
Then was I fayne for refuge to repayre
Vnto my other daughter for reliefe,
Who gaue me pleasing and most courteous words;
But in her actions shewed her selfe so sore,
As neuer any daughter did before:
She prayd me in a morning out betime,
To go to a thicket two miles from the Court,
Poynting that there she would come talke with me:
There she had set a shaghayrd murdring wretch,
To massacre my honest friend and me.
Then iudge your selfe, although my tale be briefe,
If euer man had greater cause of griefe.

King. Nor neuer like impiety was done,
Since the creation of the world begun.

Leir. And now I am constraind to seeke reliefe
Of her, to whom I haue bin so vnkind;
Whose censure, if it do award me death,
I must confesse she payes me but my due:
But if she shew a louing daughters part,
It comes of God and her, not my desert.

Cor. No doubt she will, I dare be sworne she will.

Leir. How know you that, not knowing what she is?

Cor. My selfe a father haue a great way hence,
Vsde me as ill as euer you did her;
Yet, that his reuerend age I once might see,
Ide creepe along, to meet him on my knee.

Leir. O, no mens children are vnkind but mine.

Cor. Condemne not all, because of others crime:

But looke, deare father, looke, behold and see
Thy louing daughter speaketh vnto thee.

              [She kneeles.

Leir. O, stand thou vp, it is my part to kneele,
 And aske forgiuenesse for my former faults.   *[he kneeles.*
Cor. O, if you wish I should inioy my breath,
 Deare father rise, or I receiue my death.   *[he riseth.*
Leir. Then I will rise, to satisfy your mind,
 But kneele againe, til pardon be resigned.   *[he kneeles.*
Cor. I pardon you: the word beseemes not me:
 But I do say so, for to ease your knee.
 You gaue me life, you were the cause that I
 Am what I am, who else had neuer bin.
Leir. But you gaue life to me and to my friend,
 Whose dayes had else, had an vntimely end.
Cor. You brought me vp, when as I was but young,
 And far vnable for to helpe my selfe.
Leir. I cast thee forth, when as thou wast but young,
 And far vnable for to helpe thy selfe.
Cor. God, world and nature say I do you wrong,
 That can indure to see you kneele so long.
King. Let me breake off this louing controuersy,
 Which doth reioyce my very soule to see.
 Good father, rise, she is your louing daughter, *[He riseth.*
 And honours you with as respectiue duty.
 As if you were the Monarch of the world.
Cor. But I will neuer rise from off my knee,
 Vntill I haue your blessing, and your pardon
 Of all my faults committed any way,
 From my first birth vnto this present day.
Leir. The blessing, which the God of *Abraham* gaue
 Vnto the trybe of *Iuda*, light on thee,
 And multiply thy dayes, that thou mayst see
 Thy childrens children prosper after thee.
 Thy faults, which are iust none that I do know,
 God pardon on high, and I forgiue below.   *[she riseth.*
Cor. Now is my heart at quiet, and doth leape
 Within my brest, for ioy of this good hap:
 And now (deare father) welcome to our Court,
 And welcome (kind *Perillus*) vnto me,
 Myrrour of vertue and true honesty.
Leir. O, he hath bin the kindest friend to me,
 That euer man had in aduersity.

Per. My toung doth faile, to say what heart doth think,
    I am so rauisht with exceeding ioy.
King. All you haue spoke: now let me speak my mind,
    And in few words much matter here conclude: [*he kneeles.*
    If ere my heart do harbour any ioy,
    Or true content repose within my brest,
    Till I haue rooted out this viperous sect,
    And repossest my father of his Crowne,
    Let me be counted for the periurdst man,
    That euer spake word since the world began.   [*rise.*
Mum. Let me pray too, that neuer pray'd before;
                    [*Mumford kneeles.*

    If ere I resalute the Brittish earth,
    (As (ere't be long) I do presume I shall)
    And do returne from thence without my wench,
    Let me be gelded for my recompence.   [*rise.*
King. Come, let's to armes for to redresse this wrong:
    Till I am there, me thinks, the time seemes long. [*Exeunt.*

2. HOLINSHED

Leir the sonne of Baldud was admitted ruler ouer the Britaines
in the yeare of the world 3105, at what time Joas reigned in
Juda. This Leir was a prince of right noble demeanor, gouerning
his land and subiects in great wealth. He made the towne of
Caerleir now called Leicester, which standeth vpon the riuer
of Sore. It is written that he had by his wife three daughters
without other issue, whose names were Gonorilla, Regan, and
Cordeilla, which daughters he greatly loued, but specially
Cordeilla the yoongest farre aboue the two elder. When this
Leir therefore was come to great yeres, & began to waxe vn-
weldie through age, he thought to vnderstand the affections of
his daughters towards him, and preferre hir whome he best
loued, to the succession ouer the kingdome. Whervpon he
first asked Gonorilla the eldest, how well she loued him: who
calling hir gods to record, protested that she loued him more
than hir owne life, which by right reason should be most deere
vnto hir. With which answer the father being well pleased,
turned to the second, and demanded of hir how well she loued
him: who answered (confirming hir saiengs with great othes)
that she loued him more than toong could expresse, and farre
aboue all other creatures of the world.

Then called he his yoongest daughter Cordeilla before him,

and asked of hir what account she made of him, vnto whome she made this answer as followeth: " Knowing the great loue and fatherlie zeale that you haue alwaies borne towards me (for the which I maie not answere you otherwise than I thinke, and as my conscience leadeth me) I protest vnto you, that I haue loued you euer, and will continuallie (while I liue) loue you as my naturall father. And if you would more vnderstand of the loue that I beare you, assertaine your selfe, that so much as you haue, so much you are worth, and so much I loue you, and no more." The father being nothing content with this answer, married his two eldest daughters, the one vnto Henninus the duke of Cornewall, and the other vnto Maglanus the duke of Albania, betwixt whome he willed and ordeined that his land should be diuided after his death, and the one halfe thereof immediatlie should be assigned to them in hand: but for the third daughter Cordeilla he reserued nothing.

Neuertheless it fortuned that one of the princes of Gallia (which now is called France) whose name was Aganippus, hearing of the beautie, womanhood, and good conditions of the said Cordeilla, desired to haue hir in mariage, and sent ouer to hir father, requiring that he might haue hir to wife; to whome answer was made, that he might haue his daughter, but as for anie dower he could haue none, for all was promised and assured to hir other sisters alreadie. Aganippus notwithstanding this answer of deniall to receiue anie thing by way of dower with Cordeilla, tooke hir to wife, onlie moued thereto (I saie) for respect of hir person and amiable vertues. This Aganippus was one of the twelue kings that ruled Gallia in those daies, as in the British historie it is recorded. But to proceed.

After that Leir was fallen into age, the two dukes that had married his two eldest daughters, thinking it long yer the gouernment of the land did come to their hands, arose against him in armour, and reft from him the gouernance of the land, vpon conditions to be continued for terme of life: by the which he was put to his portion, that is, to liue after a rate assigned to him for the maintenance of his estate, which in processe of time was diminished as well by Maglanus as by Henninus. But the greatest griefe that Leir tooke, was to see the vnkindnesse of his daughters, which seemed to thinke that all was too much which their father had, the same being neuer so little: in so much that going from the one to the other, he was brought to that miserie, that scarslie they would allow him one seruant to wait vpon him.

In the end, such was the vnkindnesse, or (as I maie saie) the vnnaturalnesse which he found in his two daughters, notwithstanding their faire and pleasant words vttered in time past, that being constreined of necessitie, he fled the land, & sailed into Gallia, there to seeke some comfort of his yongest daughter Cordeilla, whom before time he hated. The ladie Cordeilla hearing that he was arrived in poore estate, she first sent to him priuilie a certeine summe of monie to apparell himselfe withall, and to reteine a certeine number of seruants that might attend vpon him in honorable wise, as apperteined to the estate which he had borne: and then so accompanied, she appointed him to come to the court, which he did, and was so ioifullie, honorablie, and louinglie receiued, both by his sonne in law Aganippus, and also by his daughter Cordeilla, that his hart was greatlie comforted: for he was no lesse honored, than if he had beene king of the whole countrie himselfe.

Now when he had informed his sonne in law and his daughter in what sort he had been vsed by his other daughters, Aganippus caused a mightie armie to be put in a readinesse, and likewise a great nauie of ships to be rigged, to passe ouer into Britaine with Leir his father in law, to see him againe restored to his kingdome. It was accorded, that Cordeilla should also go with him to take possession of the land, the which he promised to leaue vnto hir, as the rightfull inheritour after his decesse, notwithstanding any former grant made to hir sisters or to their husbands in anie maner of wise.

Herevpon, when this armie and nauie of ships were readie, Leir and his daughter Cordeilla with hir husband tooke the sea, and arriuing in Britaine, fought with their enimies, and discomfited them in battell, in the which Maglanus and Henninus were slaine; and then was Leir restored to his kingdome, which he ruled after this by the space of two yeeres, and then died, fortie yeeres after he first began to reigne. His bodie was buried at Leicester in a vaut vnder the chanell of the riuer of Sore beneath the towne.

Cordeilla the yoongest daughter of Leir was admitted Q. and supreme gouernesse of Britaine, in the yeere of the world 3155, before the bylding of Rome 54, Vzia was then reigning in Juda, and Jeroboam ouer Israell. This Cordeilla after hir father's deceasse ruled the land of Britaine right worthilie during the space of fiue yeeres, in which meane time hir husband died, and then about the end of those fiue yeeres, hir two nephewes Margan and Cunedag, sonnes to hir aforesaid sisters, disdaining to be vnder the gouernment of a woman, leuied warre against hir, and destroied a great part of the land, and finallie tooke hir prisoner, and laid hir fast in ward, wherewith she tooke suche griefe, being a woman of a manlie courage, and despairing to recouer libertie, there she slue hirselfe.

3. EDMUND SPENSER

The Faerie Queene, Book Two, Canto X.

27

Next him king *Leyr* in happie peace long raind,
   But had no issue male him to succeed,
   But three faire daughters, which were well vptraind,
   In all that seemed fit for kingly seed:
   Mongst whom his realme he equally decreed
   To haue diuided Tho when feeble age
   Nigh to his vtmost date he saw proceed,
   He cald his daughters; and with speeches sage
Inquyrd, which of them most did loue her parentage.

28

The eldest *Gonorill* gan to protest,
   That she much more then her owne life him lou'd:
   And *Regan* greater loue to him profest,
   Then all the world, when euer it were proou'd;
   But *Cordeill* said she lou'd him, as behoou'd:
   Whose simple answere, wanting colours faire
   To paint it forth, him to displeasance moou'd,
   That in his crowne he counted her no haire,
But twixt the other twaine his kingdome whole did shaire.

29

So wedded th'one to *Maglan* king of Scots,
   And th'other to the king of *Cambria*,
   And twixt them shayrd his realme by equall lots:
   But without dowre the wise *Cordelia*
   Was sent to *Aganip* of *Celtica*.
   Their aged Syre, thus eased of his crowne,
   A priuate life led in *Albania*,
   With *Gonorill*, long had in great renowne,
That nought him grieu'd to bene from rule deposed downe.

30

But true it is, that when the oyle is spent,
   The light goes out, and weeke is throwne away;
So when he had resigned his regiment,
   His daughter gan despise his drouping day,
   And wearie waxe of his continuall stay.
Tho to his daughter *Regan* he repayrd,
   Who him at first well vsed euery way;
But when of his departure she despayrd,
Her bountie she abated, and his cheare empayrd.

31

The wretched man gan then auise too late,
   That loue is not, where most it is profest,
Too truely tryde in his extreamest state;
   At last resolu'd likewise to proue the rest,
   He to *Cordelia* him selfe addrest,
Who with entire affection him receau'd,
   As for her Syre and king she seemed best;
And after all an army strong she leau'd,
To war on those, which him had of his realme bereau'd.

32

So to his crowne she him restor'd againe,
   In which he dyde, made ripe for death by eld,
And after wild, it should to her remaine:
   Who peaceably the same long time did weld:
   And all mens harts in dew obedience held:
Till that her sisters children, woxen strong
   Through proud ambition, against her rebeld,
And ouercommen kept in prison long,
Till wearie of that wretched life, her selfe she hong.

4. JOHN HIGGINS

Cordila shewes how by despaire when she was in prison she slue herselfe.
the yeare before Christe. 800.

My grandsyre *Bladud* hight that found the Bathes by skill, [36
A fethered king that practisde for to flye and soare:
Whereby he felt the fall God wot against his will,
And neuer went, roode, raignde nor spake, nor flew no more.

Who dead his sonne my father *Leire* therefore,
Was chosen kinge, by right apparent heyre,
Which after built the towne of *Leircestere.*

He had three daughters, first and eldest hight *Gonerell:*
Next after hir, my sister *Ragan* was begote:
The thirde and last was, I the yongest namde *Cordell,*
And of vs all, our father *Leire* in age did dote.
So minding hir that loude him best to note,
Because he had no sonne t'enioye his lande:
He thought to giue, where fauoure most he fande.

What though I yongest were, yet men me iudgde more wise
Then either *Gonorell,* or *Ragan* had more age,
And fayrer farre: wherefore my sisters did despise
My grace, and giftes, and sought my praise t'swage:
But yet though vice gainst vertue die with rage,
It cannot keepe her vnderneth to drowne,
But still she flittes aboue, and reapes renowne.

Yet nathelesse, my father did me not mislike:
But age so simple is, and easye to subdue:
As childhode weake, thats voide of wit and reason quite:
They thincke thers nought, you flater fainde, but all is true:
Once olde and twice a childe, tis said with you,
Which I affirme by proofe, that was definde:
In age my father had a childishe minde.   [63

He thought to wed vs vnto nobles three, or Peres:
And vnto them and theirs, deuide and part the lande:
For both my sisters first he sent as first their yeares
Requirde their mindes, and loue, and fauour t'understand.
(Quod he) all doubtes of duty to abande,
I must assaye and eke your friendships proue:
Now tell me eche how much you do me loue.

Which when they aunswered, they loude him wel and more
Then they themselues did loue, or any wordly wight:
He praised them and said he would againe therefore,
They louing kindnes they deserude in fine requite:
So found my sisters fauour in his sight,
By flatery fayre they won their fathers hart:
Which after turned, him and mee to smart.

But not content with this he minded me to proue,
For why he wonted was to loue me wonders well:
How much dost thou (quoth he) *Cordile* thy father loue?   [80
    I will (said I) at once my loue declare and tell:
I loude you euer as my father well,
No otherwise, if more to know you craue:
We loue you chiefly for the goodes you haue.

    Thus much I said, the more their flattery to detect,
But he me answerd thereunto again with Ire,
Because thou dost thy fathers aged yeares neglect,
That loude the more of late then thy desertes require,
Thou neuer shalt, to any part aspire
Of this my realme, emong thy sisters twayne,
But euer shalt vndotid ay remayne.

    Then to the king of *Albany* for wife he gaue
My sister *Gonerell*, the eldest of vs all:
And eke my sister *Ragan* for *Hinnine* to haue,
Which then was Prince of *Camber* and *Cornwall:*
These after him should haue his kingdome all
Betwene them both, he gaue it franke and free:
But nought at all, he gaue of dowry mee.

    At last it chaunst the king of *Fraunce* to here my fame,
My beutie braue, was blazed all abrode eche where:
And eke my vertues praisde me to my fathers blame
Did for my sisters flattery me less fauoure beare.
Which when this worthy king my wrongs did heare,
He sent ambassage likte me more then life,
T'intreate he might me haue to be his wife.

    My father was content withall his harte, and sayde,
He gladly should obtaine his whole request at will
Concerning me, if nothing I herein denayde:
But yet he kept by their intisment hatred still,
(quoth he) your prince his pleasure to fulfill,
I graunt and giue my daughter as you craue:
But nought of me for dowry can she haue.

    King *Aganippus* well agreed to take me so,
He deemde that vertue was of dowries all the best:
And I contentid was to *Fraunce* my father fro
For to depart, & hoapte t'enioye some greater rest.

I maried was, and then my ioyes encreaste,
I gate more fauoure in this prince his sight,
Then euer princesse of a princely wight.

But while that I these ioyes enioyd, at home in *Fraunce*
My father *Leire* in *Britayne* waxed aged olde,
My sisters yet them selues the more aloft t'aduance,
Thought well they might, be by his leaue, or sans so bolde:
To take the realme & rule it as they wold.
They rose as rebels voyde of reason quite,
Ans they depriude him of his crowne and right.   [125

Then they agreed, it should be into partes equall
Deuided: and my father threscore knightes & squires
Should alwayes haue, attending on him still at cal.
But in six monthes so much increasid hateful Ires,
That *Gonerell* denyde all his desires,
So halfe his garde she and her husband refte:
And scarce alowde the other halfe they lefte.

Eke as in *Scotlande* thus he lay lamenting fates,
When as his daughter so, sought all his vtter spoyle:
The meaner vpstarte gentiles, thought themselues his mates
And betters eke, see here an aged prince his foyle.
Then was he faine for succoure his, to toyle.
With all his knightes, to *Cornewall* there to lye:
In greatest nede, his *Raganes* loue to trye.

And when he came to *Cornwall*, *Ragan* then with ioye,
Receiued him and eke hir husbande did the lyke:
There he abode a yeare and liude without a noy,
But then they tooke, all his retinue from him quite
Saue only ten, and shewde him dayly spite,
Which he bewailde complayning durst not striue,
Though in disdayne they laste alowde but fiue.

On this he deemde him, selfe was far that tyme vnwyse,
When from his doughter *Gonerell* to *Ragan* hee:
Departed erste yet eache did him poore king despise,   [150
Wherfore to *Scotlande* once againe with hir to bee
And bide he went: but beastly cruell shee,
Bereaude him of his seruantes all saue one,
Bad him content him selfe with that or none.

Eke at what time he askte of eache to haue his garde,
To garde his grace where so he walkte or wente:
They calde him doting foole and all his hestes debarde,
Demaunded if with life he could not be contente.
Then he to late his rigour did repente,
Gainst me and sayde, *Cordila* now adieu:
I finde the wordes thou toldste mee to to true.

And to be short, to *Fraunce* he came alone to mee,
And tolde me how my sisters him our father vsde:
Then I besought my king with teares vpon my knee,
That he would aide my father thus by them misusde
Who nought at all my humble heste refusde:
But sent to euery coste of Fraunce for ayde,
Wherwith my father home might be conueide.

The soldiers gathered from eche quarter of the land,
Came at the length to know the king his mind & will: [170
Who did commit them to my fathers aged hand,
And I likewise of loue and reuerent mere goodwill
Desirde my king, he would not take it ill,
If I departed for a space withall:
To take a parte, or ease my fathers thrall.

This had: I parted with my father from my fere,
We came to *Britayne* with our royall campe to fight:
And manly fought so long our enmies vanquisht were
By martiall feates, and force by subiectes sword and might.
The Britishe kinges were fayne to yelde our right,
And so my father well this realme did guide,
Three yeares in peace and after that he dide.   [182
        (Cordila reigns as queen of Britain for five years, and then
        on the death of her husband she is dethroned and im-
        prisoned by her nephews, Morgan and Conidagus.)

Was euer lady in such wofull wreckfull wo:
Depriude of princely powre, berefte of libertie,
Depriud in all these wordly pompes, hir pleasures fro,
And brought from welthe, to nede, distresse, and misery?
From palace proude, in prison poore to lye:
From kingdomes twayne, to dungion one no more:
From Ladies wayting, vnto vermine store.

From light to darke, from holsom ayre to lothsom smell:
From odewr swete, to sweate: from ease, to grieuous payne:
From sight of princely wights, to place where theues do dwell:
From deinty beddes of downe, to be of strawe full fayne:
From bowres of heauenly hewe, to dennes of dayne:
From greatest haps, that worldly wightes atchieue:
To more distresse then any wretche aliue.

(Despair appears to her in prison and offers her various
means of suicide, including the knife with which Dido
slew herself.   Cordila prays for vengeance on her nephews,
and stabs herself, or is stabbed by Despair.)

5. SIR PHILIP SIDNEY

Arcadia, ii. 10

The pitifull state, and storie of the Paphlagonian *vnkinde King, and
his kind sonne, first related by the son, then by the blind father.*

It was in the kingdome of *Galacia*, the season being (as in
the depth of winter) very cold, and as then sodainely growne to
so extreame and foule a storme, that neuer any winter (I thinke)
brought foorth a fowler child: so that the Princes were euen
compelled by the haile, that the pride of the winde blew into
their faces, to seeke some shrowding place within a certaine
hollow rocke offering it vnto them, they made it their shield
against the tempests furie.   And so staying there, till the violence
thereof was passed, they heard the speach of a couple, who not
perceiuing them (being hidde within that rude canapy) helde a
straunge and pitifull disputation which made them steppe out;
yet in such sort, as they might see vnseene.   There they per-
ceaued an aged man, and a young, scarcely come to the age of
a man, both poorely arayed, extreamely weather-beaten; the
olde man blinde, the young man leading him: and yet through
all those miseries, in both these seemed to appeare a kind of
noblenesse, not sutable to that affliction.   But the first words
they heard, were these of the old man.   Well *Leonatus* (said he)
since I cannot perswade thee to lead me to that which should
end my griefe, & thy trouble, let me now entreat thee to leaue
me: feare not, my miserie cannot be greater then it is, & nothing
doth become me but miserie; feare not the danger of my blind
steps, I cannot fall worse then I am.   And doo not I pray thee,
doo not obstinately continue to infect thee with my wretchednes.
But flie, flie from this region, onely worthy of me.   Deare father

(answered he) doo not take away from me the onely remnant of my happinesse: while I haue power to doo you seruice, I am not wholly miserable. Ah my sonne (said he, and with that he groned, as if sorrow straue to breake his harte,) how euill fits it me to haue such a sonne, and how much doth thy kindnesse vpbraide my wickednesse? These doleful speeches, and some others to like purpose (well shewing they had not bene borne to the fortune they were in,) moued the Princes to goe out vnto them, and aske the younger what they were? Sirs (answered he, with a good grace, and made the more agreeable by a certaine noble kinde of pitiousness) I see well you are straungers, that know not our miserie so well here knowne, that no man dare know, but that we must be miserable. In deede our state is such, as though nothing is so needfull vnto vs as pittie, yet nothing is more daungerous vnto vs, then to make our selues so knowne as may stirre pittie. But your presence promiseth, that cruelty shall not ouer-runne hate. And if it did, in truth our state is soncke below the degree of feare.

This old man (whom I leade) was lately rightfull Prince of this countrie of *Paphlagonia*, by the hard-harted vngratefulnes of a sonne of his, depriued, not onely of his kingdome (whereof no forraine forces were euer able to spoyle him) but of his sight, the riches which Nature graunts to the poorest creatures. Whereby, & by other his vnnaturall dealings, he hath bin driuen to such griefe, as euen now he would haue had me to haue led him to the toppe of this rocke, thence to cast himselfe headlong to death: and so would haue made me (who receiued my life of him) to be the worker of his destruction. But noble Gentlemen (said he) if either of you haue a father, and feele what duetifull affection is engraffed in a sonnes hart, let me intreate you to conuey this afflicted Prince to some place of rest & securitie. Amongst your worthie actes it shall be none of the least, that a King, of such might and fame, and so vniustly oppressed, is in any sort by you relieued.

But before they could make him answere, his father began to speake, Ah my sonne (said he) how euill an Historian are you, that leaue out the chiefe knotte of all the discourse? my wickednes, my wickednes. And if thou doest it to spare my eares, (the onely sense nowe left me proper for knowledge) assure thy selfe thou dost mistake me. And I take witnesse of that Sunne which you see (with that he cast vp his blinde eyes, as if he would hunt for light,) and wish my selfe in worse case then I do wish my selfe, which is as euill as may be, if I speake vntruely; that nothing is so welcome to my thoughts, as the publishing of my shame. Therefore know you Gentlemen (to whom from my harte I wish that it may not proue ominous foretoken of misfortune to haue mette with such a miser as I am) that whatsouer my sonne (ô God, that trueth binds me to reproch him with the name of my sonne) hath said, is true. But besides those truthes this also is true, that hauing had in lawful mariage, of a mother fitte to beare royall children, this sonne (such one as partly you see, and better shall knowe by my shorte declaration) and so enioyed the expectations in the world of him, till he was growen to iustifie their expectations (so as I needed enuie no father for the chiefe comfort of mortalitie, to leaue an other ones-selfe after me) I was caried by a bastarde sonne of mine (if at least I be bounde to beleeue the words of that base woman my concubine, his mother) first to mislike, then to hate, lastly to destroy, to doo my best to destroy, this sonne (I thinke you thinke) vndeseruing destruction. What waies he used to bring me to it, if I should tell you, I should tediously trouble you with as much poysonous hypocrisie, desperate fraude, smoothe malice, hidden ambition, & smiling enuie, as in any liuing person could be harbored. But I list it not, no remembrance, (no, of naughtines) delights me, but mine own; & me thinks the accusing his traines might in some manner excuse my fault, which certainly I loth to doo. But the conclusion is, that I, gaue order to some seruants of mine, whom I thought as apte for such charities as my selfe, to leade him out into a forrest, & there to kill him.

But those theeues (better natured to my sonne then my selfe) spared his life, letting him goe, to learne to liue poorely: which he did, giuing himselfe to be a priuate souldier, in a countrie here by. But as he was redy to be greatly aduanced for some noble peeces of seruice which he did, he hearde newes of me: who (dronke in my affection to that vnlawfull and vnnaturall sonne of mine) suffered my self so to be gouerned by him, that all fauours and punishments passed by him, all offices, and places of importance, distributed to his fauourites; so that ere I was aware, I had left my self nothing but the name of a King: which he shortly wearie of too, with many indignities (if any thing may be called an indignity, which was laid vpon me) threw me out of my seat, and put out my eies; and then (proud in his tyrannie) let me goe, nether imprisoning, nor killing me: but rather delighting to make me feele my miserie; miserie indeed, if euer there were any; full of wretchednes, fuller of disgrace, and fullest of guiltines. And as he came to the crowne by so vniust meanes, as vniustlie he kept it, by force of stranger souldiers in *Cittadels*, the nestes of tyranny, & murderers of libertie; disarming all his own countrimen, that no man durst shew himself a wel-willer of mine: to say the trueth (I think) few of them being so (considering my cruell follie to my good sonne, and foolish kindness to my vnkinde bastard:) but if there were any who fell to pitie of so great a fall, and had yet any sparkes of vnstained duety lefte in them towardes me, yet durst they not shewe it, scarcely with giuing me almes at their doores; which yet was the onelie sustenaunce of my distressed life, no bodie daring to shewe so much charitie, as to lende me a hande to guide my darke steppes: Till this sonne of mine (God knowes, woorthie of a more vertuous, and more fortunate father) forgetting my abhominable wrongs, not recking danger, & neglecting the present good way he was in doing himselfe good, came hether to doo this kind office you see him performe towards me, to my vnspeakable griefe; not onely because his kindness is a glasse even to my blind eyes, of my naughtines, but that above all griefes, it greeues me he should desperatly aduenture the losse of his soul-deseruing life for mine, that yet owe more to fortune for my deserts, as if he would cary mudde in a chest of christall. For well I know, he that now raigneth, how much soeuer (and with good reason) he despiseth me, of all men despised; yet he will not let slippe any advantage to make away him, whose iust title (ennobled by courage and goodnes) may one day shake the seate of a neuer secure tyrannie. And for this cause I craued of him to leade me to the toppe of this rocke, indeede I must confesse, with meaning to free him from so Serpentine a companion as I am. But he finding what I purposed onely therein since he was borne, shewed himselfe disobedient vnto me. And now Gentlemen, you haue the true storie, which I pray you publish to the world, that my mischieuous proceedinges may be the glorie of his filiall pietie, the onely reward now left for so great a merite. And if it may be, let me obtaine that of you, which my sonne denies me: for neuer was there more pity in sauing any, then in ending me; both because therein my agonies shall ende, and so shall you preserue this excellent young man, who els wilfully folowes his owne ruine.

The matter in it self lamentable, lamentably expressed by the old Prince (which needed not take to himselfe the gestures of pitie, since his face could not put of the markes thereof) greatly moued the two Princes to compassion, which could not stay in such harts as theirs without seeking remedie. But by and by the occasion was presented: for *Plexirtus* (so was the bastard called) came thether with fortie horse, onely of purpose to murder this brother; of whose comming he had soone aduertisement, and thought no eyes of sufficient credite in such a matter, but his owne; and therefore came him selfe to be actor, and spectator. And as soone as he came, not regarding the weake (as he thought) garde of but two men, commaunded some of his followers to set their handes to his, in the killing of *Leonatus*. But the young Prince (though not otherwise armed but with a sworde) how falsely soeuer he was dealt with by others, would not betray him selfe: but brauely drawing it out, made the death of the first that assaulted him, warne his fellowes to come more warily after him. But then *Pyrocles* and *Musidorus* were quickly become parties (so iust a defence deseruing as much as old friendship) and so did behaue them among that companie (more iniurious, then valiant) that many of them lost their liues for their wicked maister.

Yet perhaps had the number of them at last preuailed, if the King of *Pontus* (lately by them made so) had not come vnlooked for to their succour. Who (hauing had a dreame which had fixt his imagination vehemently vpon some great daunger, presently to follow those two Princes whom he most deerely loued) was come in all hast, following as well as he could their tracke with a hundreth horses in that countrie, which he thought (considering who then raigned) a fit place inough to make the stage of any Tragedie.

But then the match had ben so ill made for *Plexirtus*, that his ill-led life, & worse gotten honour should haue tumbled together to destruction; had there not come in *Tydeus & Telenor*, with fortie or fiftie in their suit, to the defence of *Plexirtus*. These two were brothers, of the noblest house of that country, brought vp from their infancie with *Plexirtus:* men of such prowesse, as not to know feare in themselues, and yet to teach it others that should deale with them: for they had often made their liues triumph ouer most terrible daungers; neuer dismayed and euer fortunate; and truely no more setled in their valure, then disposed to goodnesse and iustice, if either they had lighted on a better friend, or could haue learned to make friendship a child, and not the father of Vertue. But bringing vp (rather then choise) hauing first knit their minds vnto him, (indeed craftie inough, eyther to hide his faultes, or neuer to shew them,

but when they might pay home) they willingly held out the
course, rather to satisfie him, then al the world; and rather to
be good friendes, then good men: so as though they did not like
the euill he did, yet they liked him that did the euill; and though
not councellors of the offence, yet protectors of the offender.
Now they hauing heard of this sodaine going out, with so small
a company, in a country full of euill-wishing minds toward him
(though they knew not the cause) followed him; till they found
him in such case as they were to venture their liues, or else he
to loose his: which they did with such force of minde and
bodie, that truly I may iustly say, *Pyrocles & Musidorus* had
neuer till then found any, that could make them so well repeate
their hardest lesson in the feates of armes.   And briefly so they
did, that if they ouercame not; yet were they not ouercome,
but caried away that vngratefull maister of theirs to a place of
securitie; howsoeuer the Princes laboured to the contrary.
But this matter being thus far begun, it became not the con-
stancie of the Princes so to leaue it; but in all hast making forces
both in *Pontus* and *Phrygia*, they had in fewe dayes, lefte him
but only that one strong place where he was.   For feare hauing
bene the onely knot that had fastned his people vnto him, that
once vntied by a greater force, they all scattered from him;
like so many birdes, whose cage had bene broken.

In which season the blind King (hauing in the chief cittie
of his Realme, set the crowne vpon his sonne *Leonatus* head)
with many teares (both of ioy and sorrow) setting forth to the
whole people, his owne fault & his sonnes vertue, after he had
kist him, and forst his sonne to accept honour of him (as of his
newe-become subiect) euen in a moment died, as it should seeme:
his hart broken with vnkindnes & affliction, stretched so farre
beyond his limits with this excesse of comfort, as it was able no
longer to keep safe his roial spirits.   But the new King (hauing
no lesse louingly performed all duties to him dead, then aliue)
pursued on the siege of his vnnatural brother, asmuch for the
reuenge of his father, as for the establishing of his owne quiet.
In which siege truly I cannot but acknowledge the prowesse
of those two brothers, then whom the Princes neuer found in
all their trauell two men of greater habilitie to performe, nor
of habler skill for conduct.

But *Plexirtus* finding, that if nothing els, famin would at last
bring him to destruction, thought better by humblenes to creepe,
where by pride he could not march.   For certainely so had
nature formed him, & the exercise of craft conformed him to

all turnings of sleights, that though no man had lesse goodnes
in his soule then he, no man could better find the places whence
arguments might grow of goodnesse to another: though no
man felt lesse pitie, no man could tel better how to stir pitie:
no man more impudent to deny, where proofes were not manifest; no man more ready to confesse with a repenting manner
of aggravating his owne euil, where denial would but make the
fault fowler.   Now he tooke this way, that hauing gotten a
pasport for one (that pretended he would put *Plexirtus* aliue
into his hands) to speak with the King his brother, he him
selfe (though much against the minds of the valiant brothers,
who rather wished to die in braue defence) with a rope about
his necke, barefooted, came to offer himselfe to the discretion
of *Leonatus*.   Where what submission he vsed, how cunningly
in making greater the faulte he made the faultines the lesse,
how artificially he could set out the torments of his owne conscience, with the burdensome comber he had found of his
ambitious desires, how finely seeming to desire nothing but
death, as ashamed to liue, he begd life, in the refusing it, I am
not cunning inough to be able to expresse: but so fell out of it,
that though at first sight *Leonatus* saw him with no other eie,
then as the murderer of his father; & anger already began to
paint reuenge in many colours, ere long he had not only gotten
pitie, but pardon, and if not an excuse of the fault past, yet an
opinion of future amendment: while the poore villaines (chiefe
ministers of his wickedness, now betraied by the author thereof,)
were deliuered to many cruell sorts of death; he so handling it,
that it rather seemed, he had rather come into the defence of
an vnremediable mischiefe already committed, then that they
had done it at first by his consent.

6. FLORIO AND *KING LEAR*

There have been numerous books and articles dealing with
the influence of Florio's translation of Montaigne on Shakespeare,
including J. M. Robertson's *Montaigne and Shakespeare* (1897),
Elizabeth Robins Hooker's article (*P.M.L.A.* 1902), and A. H.
Upham's *The French Influence in English Literature* (1911).   The
best treatment of the subject is that by George Coffin Taylor
in *Shakespeare's Debt to Montaigne* (1925), and there is a later
essay, dealing only with *King Lear*, by W. B. Drayton Henderson
(*S.A.B.* Oct. 1939, Jan. 1940).

According to Taylor, there are 23 Montaigne passages

echoed in *King Lear*, and 116 words used by Shakespeare in that play, and not used by him before 1603, which are to be found in Florio's translation. I have not been able to trace all these words, but the following list, which includes words used in a different sense before 1603, will give an idea of the extent of Florio's influence on the vocabulary of the play.

Affectionate	Exist	Mongrel
Allowance	Exposed	Mutation
Amplify		
Assaulted	Fitly	Numbed
Auricular	Flawed	
Avouched	Flay	Parricide
	Ford	Pilferings
Bastardizing	Frustrate	Plaited
Bellyful		Planetary
Brim	Goatish	Ponder
	Gored	Portable
	Gratitude	Precipitating
Catastrophe		
Changed	Handy-dandy	Rake up
Clap	Hafted	Rarity
Cock	Hereditary	Reciprocal
Compeer	Heretofore	Ripeness
Contentious		Roguish
Creaking		Roughness
Curiosity	Imperfect	Rumble
	Impertinency	
Depositaries	Impetuous	Sectary
Debauched	Improper	Sharpness
Depraved	Incestuous	Smilingly
Deride	Intelligent	Soliciting
Derogate	Interessed	Sophisticated
Descent		Sprigs
Disaster	Jovial	Sterility
Discommend	Justicer	Sumpter
Dislocate	Justification	Syllable
Disnatured		
Dissipation	Lowness	Trilled
Distribution		
Divisions	Marble-hearted	Unquietly
	Marjoram	
Eminence	Menaces	Visible
Enormous	Milky	
Epicurism	Monopoly	Waywardness
Evasion	Mortar	Windowed

This list should be received with caution. Taylor gives 125 words that Shakespeare used in *Hamlet*, and not before; yet it is probable that that play was on the stage a year or two before the publication of Florio's translation. He may, of

course, have read it in MS. Then one has to reckon with the
fact that every play of Shakespeare's contains a number of words
he does not use elsewhere; and many of the words in the above
list he could have seen in other books, or heard in conversation.
Yet as there is no doubt that he did read Florio's translation,
it is reasonable to assume that he enlarged his vocabulary by
a study of it, especially as some of these words seem to be Florio's
coinages.

Taylor also gives a list of phrases used by Florio and in
King Lear. Some of these are too commonplace to be significant
—" essay of virtue " (Temple ed. ii. 131), " heaven's vault "
(iii. 373), " felled him dead " (i. 11) and " furred gown "
(iii. 22). Another, " court holy water " (ii. 140), is to be found
in John Eliot. More interesting are those parallels in which
the words juxtaposed are significant only from their juxtaposition.
" Depositary and guardian " (vi. 40) may be compared with
" my guardians, my depositaries "; " Necessitie must first pinch
you by the throat " (ii. 143) may have suggested " Necessity's
sharp pinch "; " Frustrate the Tyrants cruelty " (ii. 65) may
have suggested the lines—

> When misery could beguile the tyrant's rage
> And frustrate his proud will;

" The breath of a Lawyer " (iii. 86) resembles " the breath of
an unfee'd lawyer "; and " Mangled estate," closely followed
by " Gored " (iii. 5-6) may be compared with " gor'd state."
A few longer passages are quoted in the notes. These include
Edgar's alleged views on fathers (i. ii. 47 ff.), Lear's remarks
on " unaccommodated man " (iii. iv. 109), and some passages
on justice in iv. vi.

Several critics have argued that Shakespeare was also influenced by Montaigne's philosophy, and Henderson claims
that Shakespeare, in writing *King Lear*, made particular use of
the *Apology for Raymond Sebonde*. Montaigne mentions that once
" some articles of their religion be made doubtfull and question-
able," people will " immediately reject (as a tyrannicall yoke)
all impressions they had in former times received by the authori-
tie of Lawes, or reverence of ancient custome "—as Edmund
repudiates custom (iii. 185. Cf. i. ii. 3). Montaigne wishes to
trample human pride under foot

to make them feele the emptinesse, vacuitie, and no worth of man; and
violently to pull out of their hands the silly weapons of their reason (iii. 201);

and in many passages he exposes the weakness of unaccommodated man,

man alone without other help, armed but with his owne weapons, and unprovided of the grace and knowledge of God (iii. 203.   Cf. pp. 215, 250, 268,
309).

He considers " the power and domination " of the stars,

not onely upon our lives, and condition of our fortune . . . but also over our
dispositions and inclinations, our discourses and wils, which they rule (iii.
205.   Cf. IV. iii. 33, I. ii. 124 ff.)

It is the stars that make

> sonnes kill fathers, fathers sonnes destroy,
> Brothers for mutuall wounds their armes do beare (iii. 207).

Montaigne mentions that " there are Nations, who receive and
admit a Dogge to be their King" (iii. 210.   Cf. IV. vi. 161).
He refers to the speaking looks of lovers (iii. 211), the habits of
ants (iii. 217.   Cf. II. iv. 67) and to the fact that

we must be besotted ere we can become wise, and dazled before we can be
led (iii. 284).

The weaknesse of our judgement helps us more than our strength to compasse
the same, and our blindnesse more than our cleare-sighted eyes (iii. 298).

Our wisedome is lesse wise, then our folly (iv. 19).

These three passages link up with the theme of " reason in
madness " discussed in the Introduction (p. lvii).   Montaigne
mentions that the Stoics supposed the soul to be situated " within
and about the heart " (iii. 377.   Cf. III. vi. 78).   He discusses
the effect of dizzy heights in a passage which may have contributed something to the description of Dover Cliff, and he says
that

if but a tree, a shrub, or any out-butting crag of a Rock presented it selfe unto
our eyes, upon those steepie and high Alpes, somewhat to uphold the sight,
and divide the same, it doth somewhat ease and assure us from feare (iv. 68).

Shortly afterwards, he declares that " our senses are . . . many
times dulled by the passions of the mind " (iv. 70)—an idea that
occurs twice in the play (III. iv. 8, IV. vi. 6).

There are also several parallels with other essays.   Montaigne
declares that

one same magistrate doth lay the penalty of his change on such as cannot
do withal . . . and the guide striketh the blinde man he leadeth.   A horrible
image of justice (v. 21.   Cf. IV. vi. 160).

He mentions that we are all sinners:

I say not, that none should accuse, except hee bee spotlesse in himselfe: For
then none might accuse (v. 245).

A judge who condemns an adulterer will write a love-letter to
his fellow-judge's wife—" Thus goes the world, and so goe men "

(vi. 85. Cf. iv. vi. 149). He quotes Catullus to the effect that women are as lustful as pigeons (v. 116). He declares that ladies " blush, onely by hearing that named, which they nothing feare to doe " (iv. 131); and that

> the same woman from whom you came lately . . . will soone after even in your presence, raile and scold more bitterly against the same fault in her neighbour, than ever Portia or Lucrece could (vi. 85. Cf. iv. vi. 115 ff.).

Some of these ideas, perhaps all of them, Shakespeare might have derived from other sources or invented on his own; but it seems to me that it would be unreasonable to deny that Montaigne had a substantial influence on the thought of *King Lear*. On the other hand, it is difficult to go all the way with Henderson, some of whose views are rather fanciful.

7. SAMUEL HARSNETT AND *KING LEAR*

I have discussed elsewhere Shakespeare's use of *A Declaration of Egregious Popishe Impostures* (*R.E.S.* 1951, pp. 11-21). Here it will be sufficient to print the relevant extracts with line references to the corresponding passages in the play.

Sig. A 3. These lighter superfluities, whom they disgorge amongst you . . . in the fashion of great Potentates, vntill Gods reuengefull arme doth vncase them to the view of the world, and then they suffer the mild stroke of iustice with a glorious ostentation (iii. iv. 28 ff.).

p. 1. The names of the Actors in this holy Comedie were these, *Edmunds* . . .

p. 12. the harbinger . . . the steward, the vauntcourrier, . . . and the Pandar (iii. ii. 5).

p. 18. so violent, boystrous, and bigge, as that he will ruffle, rage, and hurle in the ayre . . . and blow downe steeples, trees, may-poles (iii. ii. 1).

p. 19. with all conspirants in any badde practice (v. iii. 135).
marred the play (iii. vi. 60-1).

p. 22. spoyle the play (iii. vi. 60-1).

p. 23. an old corkie woman (iii. vii. 31).

p. 24. *Marwood* . . . being pinched with penurie (ii. vi. 213)
and hunger, did lie but a night, or two, abroad in the fieldes, and beeing a melancholicke person, was scared with lightning, and thunder, that happened in the night, & loe, an euident signe that the man was possessed . . . this pittifull creature . . . (iii. iv.).

p. 25. Ma: *Maynie* had a spice of the *Hysterica passio*, as seems from his youth, hee himselfe termes it the Moother (ii. iv. 56-8).

p. 38. to frame themselues iumpe and fit vnto the Priests humors, to mop, mow, iest, raile, raue, (iv. i. 61)
roare, commend, & discommend, and as the (ii. ii. 110)
priests would haue them, vpon fitting occasions . . . in all things to play the deuils accordinglie . . .

p. 41. brimstone (iv. vi. 130).

p. 41. mortified patience (iii. ii. 37; ii. iii. 15).

p. 42. there were two needles thrust into her legge . . . and she wist it not (ii. iii. 15-16).

p. 43. she attempted to runne from the house, and to wade through a brooke (iii. iv. 52).

p. 45. our *stygian* Imposters goe farre beyond that *stygian* lake (iii. vi. 7).

p. 46. Captaine *Maho, Saras* deuil, Captaine *Modu, Maynies* deuil . . . (iii. iv. 147).

p. 47. and therefore like a melancholick *Priuado*, he affects *Marwood* to lie in the fields, and to gape at the Moone, and so of a *Cæsars* humor, he raignes in *Marwood* alone (iii. vi. 6).

        Trayfords deuill, was a Centurion . . . and had a hundred vnder his charge (iii. vi. 80).   *Smolkin* (iii. iv. 144).

        Hiaclito, a Prince, & Monarch of the world . . . he said that hee had no fellowes, but two men, and an vrchin boy.   It was little beseeming his state (I wis) beeing so mighty a Monarch, to come into our coasts so skuruily attended, except hee came to see fashions in England (iii. iv. 146-7; iii. vi. 81).

p. 48. hell was cleere, and had not a deuill to cast at a mad dogge (iii. vi. 64).

p. 49. fiddle . . . (iii. vi. 6).

        except he allow theyr Commision that tenders him his oath: . . . (iii. vi. 39).

        Frateretto, Fliberdigibbet, Hoberdidance . . . (iii. vi. 6, iii. iv. 118, iii. vi. 31) And least you should conceiue, that the deuils had no musicke in hell, especially that they would goe a maying without theyr musicke, the Fidler comes in with his Taber, & Pipe, and a whole Morice after hime, with motly visards for theyr better grace (iii. vi. 6).

p. 50. now the many, rascality, or black-guard of (ii. iv. 35)

        hell, were God knows how many in her: for all were there tag, and ragge, cut and long-tayle (iii. vi. 68 ff.).

        . . . *Puffe*, and *Purre*, the two fat deuils, . . . (iii. vi. 46).

        These were all in poore *Sara* at a chop . . . shee poore wench had all hell in her belly (iv. i. 58).

p. 52. a shelter against what wind or weather so euer (iii. ii. 62).

        . . . Sara Williams was furnished with all the devils in hell, at a clap (i. iv. 303).

p. 54. *Maynie* . . . comes mute vpon the stage, with his haire curled vp. *Loe heere . . . comes vp the spirit* (iii. iv. 86) *of* pride . . . auarice . . . Enuie . . . Sloth . . . the seauen deadly sinnes . . . (iii. iv. 94; iv. i. 58 ff.).

p. 55. hee slinkes closely away, like a dogge at the sight of a whip . . . (iii. vi. 65).

p. 58. couch them as a curre at the sound of his Maisters whippe . . . (i. iv. 120).

p. 59. his lodge in a homely place (iii. ii. 61).

p. 61. the bottomlesse pit of hell . . . (iii. vi. 7)

        to play bo-peepe (i. iv. 184).

p. 62. a pad in the straw (iii. iv. 43).

        vnsauorie smels . . . in a peculiar part or the body, but onely in the wenches (iv. vi. 131).

p. 63. lodging the deuil . . . in the inferiour parts (iv. vi. 131).

p. 66. afflicted, and tormented . . . tough weatherbeaten spirit (v. iii. 314-6).

p. 68. scalded (IV. vi. 130).

p. 73. launces, swords, and kniues dash through me . . . lightning from heauen denoure mee, . . . rent with a thousand nayles . . . (II. iii. 16). *Prometheus* with his Vulture . . . *Ixion* with his wheele (II. IV. 136; IV. vii. 47).

How doost thou vexe, how dost thou wring me? (III. iv. 61).

p. 74. thou art neuer but plaguing me with torment and fire: . . . so cunningly to act, & feigne the passions, and agonies of the deuil, that the whole companie of spectators shal by his false illusions be brought into such commiserations, and compassion, as they shall all weepe, crie, and exclaime, as loud as the counterfet deuil . . . (III. vi. 60).

p. 76. your dogges being curres (III. vi. 65).

p. 77. pue-fellow (III. vi. 38).

p. 80. sparrow-blasting, or sprite-blasting (III. iv. 59).

p. 89. In a wel sorted cry of hounds, the dogs are not all of a qualitie, and sise: some be great, some of a midle, some of a low pitch: some good at a hot chase, some at a cold sent: some swift, and shalow, some slow and sure: some deepe and hollow-mounted, some very pleasant, and merrie at traile . . . (III. vi. 66 ff.).

p. 93. and how would he winch, skip, and curuet, hauing so many fiery needles in his skin at once? (II. iii. 6 ff.).

p. 94. thicke smoake, & vapour of hell; the swords, darts, and speares of fire, pointed with grisly death . . . the Furies, and tormentors of hell, with black vgly visages, grisly with smoake, with whips of blood, and fire in theyr hands, theyr armes gored with blood: and a huge bunch of a thousand snakes crawling down theyr haire . . . (III. vi. 15-16).

p. 95. streamers of scorching smoke . . . breathing out fire, and brimstone . . . burning (IV. vi. 130).

p. 97. fire him out of his hold, as men smoke out a Foxe out of his burrow: . . . (v. iii. 23) certaine deuils in the likenes of dogges (III. vi. 68).

p. 100. neather-stockes (II. iv. 11).

p. 101. in the likenes of a Toade . . . (III. vi. 32).

p. 106. as men leade Beares by the nose, or Iack an Apes (II. iv. 8) in a string . . . deuil-blasting . . . (III. iv. 59).

p. 108. in steede of thunder, and lightning to bring (III. ii. 49) *Iupiter* vpon the stage . . . thundring, clapping, and flashing out . . . hearing the huge thunder cracke of adiuration . . .

p. 109. Brimstone . . . vgly blacknes, smoake, scorching, broyling, and heate . . . (IV. vi. 130).

p. 113. hunger-bitten (v. iii. 122).

p. 114. foule-mouthed fiend (III. iv. 61).

p. 115. vice-bitten (v. iii. 122).

p. 116. Bedlam . . . hunger-bitten . . . whips, scourges, serpents, scorpions, brimstone, coales, flames . . . bottomlesse burning pit . . . (II. iii. 14; v. iii. 122; IV. vi. 130).

p. 119. The Prince of hel . . . Hoberdicut . . . (III. iv. 147) the poore deuil chattered his teeth (IV. i. 59; IV. vi. 103).

p. 120. on the racke (v. iii. 314).

p. 128. To disguise, difforme, and monster-like to mishape the nature (IV. ii. 60).

p. 136. against hayle, thunder, lightning, (III. ii) biting of mad dogges . . . (III. vi. 65).
sparrow-blasting . . . (III. iv. 59).

and she haue a little help of the Mother, Epilepsie, or *Cramp*, to teach her role her eyes, wrie her mouth, gnash her teeth, startle with her body, hold her armes and hands stiffe, make antick faces, girne, mow, and mop like an Ape, tumble like a Hedgehogge (IV. i. 61).

p. 137. Owle-blasted (III. iv. 59).

p. 139. a dog of two colours . . . a Spaniell (III. vi. 66, 69).

p. 140. a whirlewind (III. iv. 59). *Smolkin* . . . whom *Sara* espied . . . to goe out at *Trayfords* right eare in the forme of a *Mouse* (III. iv 144).

p. 141. his deuils went out in the forme of those creatures, that haue neerest resemblance vnto those sinnes: as for example: the spirit of *Pride* went out in the forme of a *Peacocke* (forsooth): the spirit of *Sloth* in the likeness of an *Asse;* the spirit of *Enuy* in the similitude of a *Dog;* the spirit of *Gluttony* in the forme of a *Woolfe* . . . *Luxury* (III. iv. 94 ff.).

p. 146. pined (I. iv. 78).

p. 159. that all the sensible accidents should be made pendulous in the ayre, like Archimedes *doue* . . . (III. iv. 67).

p. 166. a Sisternity of mimpes, mops, and idle holy women, that shal grace *Modu* the deuil, with their idle holy presence and be as ready to cry out, at the mowing of an apish wench . . . (I. iv. 176).

p. 168. Prince of darkness (III. iv. 147).

p. 195. if they heard any croaking in her belly, (a thing whereunto many women are subiect, especially when they are fasting) then they would make a wonderful matter of that. One time shee remembreth, that shee hauing the said croaking in her belly, or making of herselfe some such noyse in her bed, they said it was the deuill that was about the bedde, that spake with the voyce of a Toade (III. vi. 34).

p. 214. did thrust a pinne into her shoulder (II. iii. 16).

p. 219. one *Alexander* . . . hauing brought with him . . . a new halter, and two blades of kniues, did leaue the same vpon the gallerie floare in her Maisters house (III. iv. 50 ff.).

p. 225. Nightingale (III. vil 31).

p. 228. to drowne or kill themselues (III. iv. 50. ff.).

It should be added that the following words and phrases are used in *King Lear* and also by Harsnett: carpe (A3), intelligences (6), pestilent, pernicious (8), auricular (9), fashioned (24), frame (38), asquint (96), currish (98), allay (121), gaster (135), propinquitie (143), at a clap (164), what a good year (165), fellow Iustice (223), counterfeit Demoniack (252). Waltham Forest is mentioned on p. 166 (cf. note on III. iv. 56-7). See also K. Muir, *N.Q.* (1952), pp. 555-6.

ADDITIONAL NOTES

p. xv.　A. S. Cairncross, *R.E.S.* (1955), pp. 252-8, has neatly demonstrated that the compositor of F 1 used a copy of Q 2 as well as one of Q 1. This means that on certain pages some errors of Q2 were probably carried over into the Folio text.

p. xxiv.　Professor Leo Kirschbaum has called my attention to another link between *King Lear* and *Sejanus*. Shakespeare, who acted in Jonson's play, remembered a description of two flatterers in the first scene:

> There be two,
> Know more, then honest councells: whose close brests
> Were they rip'd up to light, it would be found
> A poore, and idle sinne, to which their trunkes
> Had not been made fit organs. These can lye,
> Flatter, and sweare, forsweare, deprave, informe,
> Smile, and betray; make guilty men; then beg
> The forfeit lives, to get the livings; cut
> Mens throats with whisperings; sell to gaping sutors
> The emptie smoake, that flies about the Palace;
> Laugh, when their patron laughes; sweat, when he sweates;
> Be hot, and cold with him; change every moode,
> Habit, and garbe, as often as he varies;
> Observe him, as his watch observes his clock;
> And true as turkise in the dear lords ring,
> Looke well, or ill with him . . .

There can be little doubt that these lines contributed to Kent's attack on Oswald (II. ii. 76 ff.) and possibly to other lines in the same scene (98, 104) and to Kent's account of himself (I. iv. 34 " honest counsel "). Lear later uses the word " deprav'd " of Goneril's conduct (II. iv. 138).

p. xxxvi.　S. Musgrove, *R.E.S.* (1956), pp. 294-8, suggests that Shakespeare took the names of some of his characters from Camden's *Remaines*. Camden mentions that Oswald means " House-ruler or Steward "; that Eadgar is derived from " *Eadig-ar, Happy,* or *blessed honor,* or *power* "; and that Edmund is derived from " *Eadmund,* Happy, or blessed, peace". Musgrove suggests that Shakespeare's eye may have been caught by the next sentence and that this would explain why Edmund does not live up to his name: "Our Lawyers yet doe acknowledge *Mund* for *Peace* in their word *Mundbrech,* for breach of *Peace.*" Musgrove shows too that Hakluyt in his early pages refers to Edgar as " Pacificus ", and as one who conceived the idea " ' of the whole and onely one mysticall citie universall ' under the protection of British peace and justice " (p. 6). There are references to two Edmunds, another Edgar, and an Oswald on neighbouring pages (pp. 8-9). The names of various earls of Kent and Gloucester are to be found in the early pages of Hakluyt and in Camden. Camden mentions Caius with the words on his monument, FVI CAIVS (cf. v. iii. 281-90). In the section on Impresas Camden quotes " Ex nihilo nihil " (cf. I. i. 90, I. iv. 138).

p. xlii.   I have shown, *Shakespeare's Sources* (1957), that the episode of Dover Cliff and Edgar's description of the imaginary fiend were suggested by the account of Corineus's fight with Gogmagog, told by Holinshed two pages before the story of Lear.

p. 13.   I. i. 149.   *Reuerse thy doome* Q] Cf. *T.A.* III. i. 24.

p. 14.   I. i. 164.   *Revoke thy gift*] Cf. with Q reading *3 Hen. VI*, II. vi. 46.

p. 46.   I. iv. 197. *frontlet*] Cf. ' frontier ', *I. Hen. IV*, I. iii. 19 (Wright).

p. 68.   II. ii. 8.   *Lipsbury pinfold*] Possibly a quibble on the two senses of *lip*, ' to kiss ' and ' to shear (a sheep) ' (Hilda M. Hulme).

p. 69.   II. ii. 15.   *knave*] Possibly a pun on *knave* which could mean ' a contrivance in which a spool or spindle revolves ' (Hulme citing *N.E.D.*).

p. 74.   II. ii. 84.   *Sarum plain*] Hulme cites Udall's translation of Erasmus' *Apophthegemes* where " his malaparte tongue ' is linked with " Thom Trouthe, or plain Sarisburie."

p. 85.   II. iv. 46.   *wild-geese*] Cf. Lady Wildgoose (Introduction, p. xliii).

pp. 89-90.   II. iv. 122-7.   " Lear's heart has been as foolishly tender towards his daughters, but it is too late now to cry ' down ' to it and play the stern father " (New Camb.).

p. 91.   II. iv. 134.   Kent's exit here was suggested by Ringler, *S.Q.* (1960), 311-17. So in S.D. l. 288 *Gentlemen* is substituted for *Kent.*

pp. 96-7.   II. iv. 223-7.   *But . . . blood.*] Clifford Leech compares the following passage from Elyot's *The Gouernour*, II. iv. ' for the bloode in our bodies beinge in youthe warme, pure, and lustie, it is the occasion of beautie, whiche is euery where commended and loued; but if in age it be putrified, it leseth his praise. And the goutes, carbuncles, lepries, and other lyke sores and sickenesses, whiche do procede of bloode corrupted, be to all men detestable.' Leech suggests that Lear may be seeing Goneril, as she is now behaving, as a disease incident to his age.

p. 98.   II. iv. 268.   *nature . . nature*] The first nature is " human nature ", the second " animal nature " (G. K. Hunter).

pp. 98-9.   II. iv. 270-2.   *If . . . need*] Even the little clothing worn by a lady is superfluous to the needs of man the animal; but the needs of man the spiritual being—they are quite different (G. K. Hunter).

p. 115.   II. iv. 37.   *Fathom and half*] Edgar " pretends to be one of the freshwater mariners of whipjacks who ' run about the country with a counterfeit licence . . . feigning either shipwreck or spoiled by pirates ' ", as described in Harman's *Caveat* (New Camb.).

p. 117.   III. iv. 58.   *Bless . . . a-cold*] F. P. Wilson, *Sh. Sur. 13*, p. 107, quotes from Orlando Gibbons' ' The London Cry ': " Poor naked Bedlam, Tom's a cold, a small cut of thy bacon or a piece of thy sow's side, good Bess, God Almighty bless thy wits ".

pp. 119-20.   III. iv. 85-9.   Davenoirtm *N.Q.* (1953, p. 21, compares Donne, *Elegies*, IV. 46 ff.

p. 131.   III. vi. 9-14.   Davenport, *op. cit.*, compares J. Hall, *Virgidemiae*, 1-2, 77-80.

p. 136.   III. vi. 88.   *And . . . noon*] Hulme cites from John Heywood a wife's complaint of her young husband's infidelity " It semeth ye wolde make me go to bed at noone "; and she suggests that Shakespeare intended the Fool's last words " to indicate Lear's decision—conscious or half-conscious—to withdraw from the actual world into the world of hallucination ".

p. 147. IV. i. 10. *poorly led*] In support of my conjecture, it may be mentioned that Tottel has " poorly rayd " (ed. Arber, p. 108) (J. C. Maxwell).

p. 158. IV. ii. 60. *proper*] one's own (J. C. Maxwell).

p. 173. IV. vi. 73. *clearest Gods*] Possibly, as G. K. Hunter suggests, an anglicisation of *candidissimi dei*.

p. 174. IV. vi. 81-2. *The . . . thus*] Hulme argues, not very convincingly, that Edgar is referring not to Lear but to his father: " Gloucester's newly-recovered and precarious mental balance—his resolution to endure affliction until death—will never be able to maintain itself against the shock and horror of encountering Lear as he now is."

p. 179. IV. vi. 155. *handy-dandy*] In Langland (B. iv. 75) this is a term for bribery (G. K. Hunter).

p. 181. IV. vi. 185 *block*] Empson, *T.L.S.*, 19 Dec. 1952, suggested that this means a boot-block. Muir, *T.L.S.*, 30 Jan. 1953, supported the suggestion by reference to the first scene of *J.C.* where the sequence of ideas (*cobbler, surgeon, shoes, blocks, shout, weep*) probably suggested the sequence here. Perhaps the scaffold suggested the executioner's block, and thence the boot block, the mounting block, and the hat block, the last three suggesting ll. 186-7.

p. 202. v. iii. 39. *I . . . oats*] G. K. Hunter suggests that the contrast is between man as a moral being and a horse as amoral.

p. 216. v. iii. 280-1. *If . . . behold*] " The two objects of *fortune's love* and her *hate* are—himself and his master " (Capell, cited New Camb.).

p. 218. v. iii. 309. *button*] Cf. correspondence in *T.L.S.*, 14 Nov. 1952 *et seq.*

THE DUTHIE-WILSON TEXT

The following are among the readings accepted in the New (Cambridge) Shakespeare *King Lear*, edited by G. I. Duthie and J. Dover Wilson (1960). The reading of the present edition is followed by the Duthie-Wilson reading and its source. Those marked with an asterisk are, I think, improvements.

I. i. 74. *square*] *spirit* (Hanmer)*

I. i. 149. *falls*] *stoops* (Q)

I. i. 163. *thy fee*] *the fee* (Q)

I. i. 168. *vows*] *vow* (Q)*

I. i. 195. *less*] *less?* (Q, F)

I. i. 206. *in*] *on* (Q)

I. i. 237. *intends to do*] *intends* (A. Walker)

I. i. 281. *covers*] *covert* (Mason conj.)

I. ii. 67. *his?*] *his* (F)*

I. iv. 118. *Lady*] *Lady's* (Letherland conj.)*

I. iv. 240-3. *I . . . daughters*] verse, ending at *marks, reason,* daughters. But the first two of these lines are unmetrical. Alice Walker proposes for the middle of these lines ' Of sovereignty, of knowledge, and of reason '.

I. iv. 266. *Sir*] omitted, on the grounds that the metre would be better without it, and that the two sirs in 266-7 are ill-suited to Lear's anger.

I. iv. 281. S.D. ' Knights and Kent go '.*

I. v. l. *Gloucester*] *Cornwall* (Granville-Barker, Greg conj.)

II. ii. 78. *Being*] *Bring* (Q)*

II. ii. 83. *Smoile*] *Smile* (F4)*

II. iv. 20. *Yes*] *Yes, yes.* (J. C. Maxwell conj.)*

II. iv. 55. *for*] *from* (Singer)

II. iv. 76. *have . . . follow*] *ha' . . . use* (J. C. Maxwell conj.)

II. iv.102. *commands, tends*] *commands her* (Q corr.) (I prefer ' *commands their* '
(Alexander, Gould conj.))

II. iv. 171. *mood is on*] *mood—* (Q)* (*O the blest Gods*! completes l. 169)

II. iv. 188. *fickle*] *sickly* (F3)

III. i. 48. *that*] *your* (Q)

III. ii. 85-94. Duthie, largely following Warburton, rearranges in the following
order 91-2, 85-90, 93-4.

III. iv. 46. *winds*] *cold winds* (J.D.W.)*

III. iv. 81. *word's justice*] *word justly* (Pope)*

III. iv. 101. *no*] *nonny* (J.D.W.)

III. vi. 54. *store*] *stone* Theobald conj.)

III. vii. 3. S.D.] omit, as Cornwall is " laying his plans ".

III. vii. 58. *bare*] *loved* (Q uncorr.)

IV. i. 10. *led?*] *eyed*! (Q corr.)

IV. i. 60. *dumbness*] *darkness* (J.D.W.)

IV. i. 61. *mopping*] *mocking* (G.I.D.)

IV. ii. 28. *My . . . body*] *A . . . bed* (Q corr.)*

IV. ii. 29. *whistle*] *whistling* (Q corr.)

IV. iii. 30. *not be believ'd*] *ne'er believe it* (Pope)*

IV. iii. 32. *And*] *That* (J.D.W.)*

IV. vi. 166. *small*] *great* (F)

IV. vi. 252. *English*] *British* (Q)*

IV. vii. 49. *where*] *when* (Q2)

V. i. 21. *heard*] *hear* (Q)*

V. iii. 184. *lives'*] *life's* (J. C. Maxwell)

V. iii. 196. *my*] *our* (F)

V. iii. 250. Edg.] Alb. (Q)

V. iii. 250. S.D. Exit Officer] Edgar hurries forth (J.D.W.)

V. iii. 300. *you, to*] *to you* (Pope)

RECENT CRITICISM (1962)

There are nine articles on *King Lear* in *Shakespeare Survey 13* (1960).   Barbara
Heliodora Carneiro de Mendonça argues that Shakespeare was influenced by
Gorboduc; Leo Kirschbaum writes on the character of Albany; J. K. Walton
and J. Stampfer comment on Lear's last speech; Winifred M. T. Nowottny
discusses the style of the play; and in an article on " Madness in *King Lear* ",
I point out that between Act I and Act IV Scene vii Lear makes no reference to
Cordelia.

Barbara Everett in " The New King Lear " (*Critical Quarterly*, II, 1960,
pp. 325-39) complains that modern critics have tried to turn the play into a
partial, or a total, Christian allegory, and she claims that the play is grimmer
than they pretend. There were replies by William Empson, John F. Danby and
Kenneth Muir (III, 1961, pp. 67-72).

John Holloway devotes a chapter of *The Story of the Night* (1961) to the play.
He stresses a number of parallels with the book of Job and discusses Lear as a
scapegoat.

Russell A. Fraser in *Shakespeare's Poetics in Relation to King Lear* (1962)
discusses the iconology of the play and the way Shakespeare deals with Elizabethan commonplaces on providence, order, fortune, anarchy, reason and will.
His evidence is drawn partly from books, but mainly from pictures.